Endgame

Endgame

A New Commentary on the Book of Daniel

JERRY A. GLADSON

Foreword by Heather G. Hunnicutt

WIPF & STOCK · Eugene, Oregon

ENDGAME
A New Commentary on the Book of Daniel

Copyright © 2021 Jerry A. Gladson. All rights reserved. Except for brief quotations in critical publications or reviews, no part of this book may be reproduced in any manner without prior written permission from the publisher. Write: Permissions, Wipf and Stock Publishers, 199 W. 8th Ave., Suite 3, Eugene, OR 97401.

Wipf & Stock
An Imprint of Wipf and Stock Publishers
199 W. 8th Ave., Suite 3
Eugene, OR 97401

www.wipfandstock.com

PAPERBACK ISBN: 978-1-6667-0411-2
HARDCOVER ISBN: 978-1-6667-0412-9
EBOOK ISBN: 978-1-6667-0413-6

Scripture quotations from biblical books other than Daniel, unless otherwise noted, are from the *New Revised Standard Version* Bible, copyright © 1989 National Council of Churches of Christ in the United States of America. Used by permission. All rights reserved worldwide.

Scripture references to the *Common English Bible* (CEB), copyright © 2011, all rights reserved, are used by permission.

Scripture references to the *New American Standard Bible* (NASB), © Copyright The Lockman Foundation 1995, are used by permission.

Scripture taken from *The Holy Bible: New International Version*® (NIV), copyright © 1984 by International Bible Society. Used by permission of Zondervan. All rights reserved.

Scripture quotations from the *New Jerusalem Bible* (NJB), copyright © 1985 by Darton, Longman & Todd Limited and Doubleday, are used by permission.

Scripture quotations from *The Jewish Bible: Torah, Nevi'im, Kethuvim* [TANAKH or TNK], copyright © 1985 by The Jewish Publication Society, are used by permission.

08/26/21

In Memoriam
Howard and Laura Gladson
Victor Wilson and Pansy Hayes
Raymond and Billie Hollis
Michael Gladson
Jonathan Hayes
Stephen Hayes

Hope, like the gleaming taper's light, adorns and cheers our way;
And still, as darker grows the night, emits a lighter ray.
—Oliver Goldsmith

Contents

Foreword by Heather G. Hunnicutt — ix
Preface — xi
Abbreviations — xvii

PART I: INTRODUCTION

Introducing Daniel — 3

PART II: COMMENTARY

Conflict at the Royal Court — 45
DANIEL 1 — 45

The March of Nations — 57
DANIEL 2 — 57

The God of Gold — 80
DANIEL 3 — 80

The Mad King — 93
DANIEL 4 — 93

Handwriting on the Wall — 112
DANIEL 5 — 112

The Plot against Daniel — 127
DANIEL 6 — 127

A Vision of Four Beasts — 141
DANIEL 7 — 141

The Abomination of Desolation — 161
DANIEL 8 — 161

The Seventy Weeks	177
DANIEL 9	177
Prelude to a Final Vision	199
DANIEL 10	199
Finale	209
DANIEL 11	209
Time of the End	235
DANIEL 12	235

PART III: THE ADDITIONS TO DANIEL

The Prayer of Azariah	249
DANIEL 3:24–45	249
The Song of the Three Young Men	258
DANIEL 3:46–90	258
Susanna	266
DANIEL 13	266
Bel	279
DANIEL 14:1–22	279
The Dragon	287
DANIEL 14:23–42	287
Bibliography	295

Foreword

I have had the great gift of calling Jerry Gladson friend and mentor for some eight years. We met in preparation for co-teaching a trauma conference abroad some years ago, where I became fast friends with him and his wife, Laura. We began attending the same church while I was studying to become a licensed professional counselor. After I decided to go on to seminary, Jerry began to teach me first biblical Hebrew, then Koine Greek in his spare time. (This, between teaching classes in both a graduate university and a seminary, assisting in pastoral duties at our church, and, of course, writing his books!) He mentored me through the process of ordination in the Christian Church (Disciples of Christ) and supported me when I decided to go on for my doctorate in theology, much as he would have liked for me to follow in his footsteps and study the Hebrew Bible. These last two years, he has cheered me on in both my counseling practice and my pastoral work. It is a rare thing for a young theologian to have a mentor so deeply devoted to her intellectual and pastoral formation, and my gratitude knows no bounds.

If this text represents your first exposure to Gladson's work, you are in for a treat. What you will read in these pages is a deft combination of analyses, guided by a lifelong devotion to the biblical text, and decades of experience in the arts of translation and exegesis. In this text, Gladson weaves together the best of the academy with the great depth of his pastoral heart. As he is ever a thinker, ever a pastor, academics and parish clergy alike will find value in what is, by all accounts, a strange book of the Bible.

While I was reading Gladson's very fine text on Daniel, Rainer Maria Rilke's quote in *Letters to a Young Poet* sprang to mind: "Have patience with everything that is unsolved in your heart, like closed rooms and like books written in a very strange tongue." Daniel is, of course, a book written in a very strange tongue, full of very strange images. It is shrouded in mystery, yet grounded in hope. Daniel contains some of my favorite childhood biblical stories, the ones I learned at my grandmother's knee as she placed paper figures on the flannel graph in our Sunday School class: the fiery furnace into which Shadrach, Meshach, and Abednego were cast (Dan 3); the handwriting on the wall (Dan 5); and of course Daniel in the lion's den (Dan 6).

Daniel also contains many apocalyptic visions which were most definitely *not* Sunday school fodder, including the four beasts (Dan 7), the two goats (Dan 8), and the seventy weeks (Dan 9). Apocalypse means to uncover or disclose, and Gladson's commentary does just that with respect to those chapters. Thanks to Jerry's use of a hermeneutic of retrieval, these stories become more accessible to contemporary readers and therefore more applicable to our milieu. In part 1 of the text, Gladson offers a thoroughgoing historical-critical grounding for the book of Daniel, followed by his verse by verse commentary, and ending with the additions to the Daniel text. All parts are needful and useful for coming to understand this strange book of the Bible.

If you do not have the pleasure of calling Jerry friend, I hope you will find in these pages something of a kinship with our author. Even more deeply, I hope you will come to a fresh understanding of the Holy One in your reading of this ancient text. Ultimately, Daniel is about the certainty that, through all our trials and travails, God will indeed prevail. Gladson writes of the book of Daniel, "Its inspiring tales of faithfulness under duress and deliverance from mortal trouble strengthen the resolve of the faithful by God's grace to live faithfully and generously in a world created and finally redeemed by the Lord God Almighty." This is a most timely message indeed. Within the pages of *Endgame*, I believe you will find not only critical information about the book of Daniel, but also a vision of holy apocalypse—the revelation of the world we wish to embody. For casting that vision, and for a call to bring it to bear, we owe Gladson a debt of gratitude.

THE REV. HEATHER G. HUNNICUTT, LPC
Salem United Church of Christ
Pocono Pines, Pennsylvania
March 2021

Preface

While in high school, I became captivated by the book of Daniel. Having just become a Christian, in that first warm spiritual glow, I often spent my weekday evenings, after I had finished my homework, reading Uriah Smith's *Prophecies of Daniel and the Revelation*, a widely circulated, classic nineteenth-century work on the topic. This book had been published in 1873 but had gone through numerous editions, until in 1944 it appeared in the red, clothbound edition I held in my hands. I knew nothing then of the currents of modern biblical scholarship regarding apocalyptic literature but found Smith highly readable and engaging to a history buff, which I admit I was.

The denomination to which I belonged had made Daniel and the New Testament book of Revelation the cornerstone of its theology, so as a matter of course I listened to many sermons on Daniel. I enthusiastically pursued this interest in Daniel while in college, where a semester-long course in the book was offered, and then into my subsequent career in parish ministry. With something akin to apocalyptic fervor, I wrote and preached sermons from Daniel, all aimed at persuading congregants of the urgency of its cryptic message. All Daniel's prophecies, I believed, were rapidly converging on the present. The end of the world Daniel envisioned—as a huge stone crushing, pulverizing the nations of the world—was fast approaching. I had to prepare for the end of all things and the second advent of Jesus, soon to break suddenly upon the world. Daniel and Revelation virtually became my Bible within the Bible or canon within the canon.

As I studied the book of Daniel more carefully, however, I gradually began to realize that Daniel, like any other book in the Bible, has to be read in terms of its literary and historical setting. It has to be read against the times in which it was written, just as we do any other text, sacred or secular.

All human writings are inextricably linked to the setting in which they are composed. My doctoral studies in Hebrew Scripture at Vanderbilt University only intensified this awareness. Subsequent reading and study since have reinforced this conviction.

In this book, after a career divided equally between pastoral ministry and teaching in college, seminary, and university, and after having published full-length commentaries on Ruth, Ecclesiastes, and Job, I return once more to my earlier, youthful interest in Daniel and attempt in this study to shed light on its meaning and relevance for our times. When I set out to write this study, my goal was to write in two hundred pages or less a midrange commentary accessible to lay persons, clergy, and scholars alike. Alas, the result is a work almost double that number! Perhaps a more effective writer than I could have accomplished this goal with greater brevity. I wanted to speak to all the major issues in Daniel, and it has taken me these many pages to accomplish it. My goal in writing has been to interpret Daniel historically in the light of modern scholarship, building upon the impressive gains modern historical and religious scholarship has provided for the study of biblical and apocalyptic literature.

What I attempt here is known as a hermeneutic of retrieval. My aim is to recover as nearly as possible the original meaning of the text of Daniel—how it was understood by its first readers—free as possible from the complex overlay the book has received over the centuries. Such a goal is daunting, however. There is "no innocent interpretation, no unambiguous tradition, no history-less, subject-less interpreter, no abstract, general situation, no method to guarantee certainty" in such interpretation.[1] We postmoderns can never fully enter the minds of Daniel's author or its first readers. Having only the text to guide us, along with the contemporary socio-historical data at our disposal, we can only approximate the original meaning. With such a cryptic text as Daniel, even after all our exegetical effort, much remains vague and uncertain. Still, we will have grasped something of the truth of the text, even if only partially.

Although biblical scholarship has presently shifted its focus to the text itself—with less interest in its development or prehistory—and to the reader of the text, it may rightly be claimed the overall tendency in modern biblical scholarship since at least the nineteenth century has been the recovery of the original meaning of biblical texts. Interest in the original meaning of biblical texts is a legacy of the Protestant Reformation, which broke with the allegorical approaches so popular at the time (sixteenth century CE). The present study is very much in keeping with this historical inclination.

---

1. Tracy, "Theological Method," 36.

My aim is to recover so far as possible the meaning intended by the author in light of the contemporary setting and available data. Every application or use of the text—historically or theologically—is or should be founded upon this original meaning. "It is not the province of the scholar to go beyond the meaning of the text and the presumed intention of the author," the noted scholar David Noel Freedman once advised. "The most careful attention to linguistic detail, to grammatical form, and to lexical nuance will be well rewarded by a better understanding of what the passage meant when it was uttered. To accomplish this is to fulfill our obligation" as biblical scholars.[2]

Klein is even more insistent: "We are convinced that the goal of hermeneutics is to enable interpreters to arrive at *the meaning of the text that the biblical writers or editors intended their readers to understand*."[3]

This goal is not easily realized because every interpreter arrives at the text with certain presuppositions, aware of some, unaware of others. Pure objectivity eludes. As interpreters, we do our best to limit these assumptions and try to keep them from unduly influencing the interpretation of the text.

To anyone familiar with contemporary hermeneutical theory, however, such an approach sounds overly simplistic. There are numerous challenges facing any interpreter set on recovering the original meaning of a biblical passage. Besides the interpreter biases just mentioned, there is the problem of the intricate textual transmission of the biblical book, including the various stages through which the manuscript may have passed before reaching its final form. The linguistic vagaries and uncertainties of the Hebrew and Aramaic often interfere. Then, too, there is often the absence of critical archaeological, historical, anthropological, and sociological data from the environment of the text necessary to clarify its meaning. All these problems and more descend like an avalanche upon one attempting to understand so puzzling a text as Daniel. So problematic can be the goal of arriving at the original meaning, scholars often disparage this approach as falling into the intentional fallacy. Not only do contemporary readers lack access to the objectives of author or original readers, but they do not have realistic access to the circumstances surrounding a document long separated from them in time and place.

While these challenges seem formidable, still there remains the valid prospect of approximating the original meaning of a biblical passage. Many uncertainties persist, of course, especially with a book like Daniel. These will be acknowledged as our study unfolds. While the history or reception of Daniel—the ways it has been interpreted or misinterpreted—is

2. Freedman, "On Method in Biblical Studies," 157.
3. Klein et al., *Biblical Interpretation*, 153. Italics added.

colorful and fascinating, this commentary will focus primarily on the original meaning(s) of Daniel, leaving the reader to make what application or use of the meaning(s) she or he deems appropriate.

Our emphasis will naturally be the final literary form of the book of Daniel, the form of Daniel now represented in the Masoretic Text (MT) of the Hebrew Bible (HB) preserved in the great Codex Leningradensis (1008 CE) and reappearing in the critical printed edition known as the *Biblia Hebraica Stuttgartensia* (1977). Most modern English (and other language) translations are based on *Biblia Hebraica Stuttgartensia* (*BHS*). This commentary presents the author's new formal English translation of Daniel based on this Hebrew and Aramaic text. For the translation of the Additions to Daniel found in the Greek Septuagint (LXX), I have used the standard seventh edition of the *Septuaginta*, edited by Alfred Rahlfs (1935).

This work is arranged in the following manner. Part 1 contains an introduction dealing with authorship, setting, historical background, provenance, canonicity, literary genres, and text, issues necessary for an intelligent reading of the book against its original environment. This is followed in part 2 by the commentary itself, arranged in the order of the chapters in Daniel, and in part 3 by a commentary on the additions made to Daniel in the Greek LXX tradition. Each chapter in the commentary contains a brief introduction, followed by an English translation of the text and then a close reading of the text. Special issues relevant to the text are treated within the commentary rather than in separate addenda. Technical matters are often relegated to the footnotes, where are also found additional resources for further study.

A study of this nature would never see the light of day without the assistance of many people. To the many scholars who appear in the footnotes and bibliography I owe a huge debt. Their careful work on the text of Daniel has made this commentary possible. My wife, Laura, the love of my life, has endured many long and lonely hours as I hunched over the computer in my study or out on the deck in the warm summer sunshine working on this manuscript. My two daughters, JoAnna and Paula, have provided continuing encouragement, not only for this project, but for many more. I salute our four fine grandsons—and one great-grandson—Spencer, Josh, Aidan, Jasper, and Salem. Dare I hope someday one of them will take up the task and joy of interpreting Holy Scripture? My sister, Deena (D. J.) Pett, read almost the entire manuscript, at various stages, even when it still proved incoherent and fragmented, and offered many helpful suggestions.

This manuscript would never have gotten to completion without the superb editorial and exegetical skills of Jaclyn Myers, who patiently read and critiqued each page of the manuscript and offered many recommendations for improvement in both content and form. She flagged my obsessive love of commas and patiently helped me eliminate many of the unnecessary ones.

Always in the background of my publications are colleagues past and present: James Crenshaw, my doctoral mentor at Vanderbilt University, a true scholars' scholar; Mel Campbell, who skillfully taught teachers the best methods of teaching science in their classrooms; Douglas Clark, who, when not pouring over the Hebrew text, could be found sifting through the ruins of ancient cities; Edwin Zackrison, lifelong friend and faculty ally, pastor and professor of theology; Heather Goff Honeycutt, pastor, licensed professional counselor, and ThD candidate, who patiently listened to my numerous ruminations about Daniel while studying Hebrew with me, and graciously consented to write the foreword; and William Doverspike, professor of psychology at Richmont Graduate University, who helped me unpack the psychopathology exhibited by Nebuchadnezzar in Daniel 4. Any errors that remain in this commentary are the responsibility of the author.

The time has come for me to release this study to the public where, I sincerely hope, it will stimulate a deeper study of the book of Daniel. May this study lead to a renewal of faith in the God of history, even in these chaotic times.

JERRY A. GLADSON, PHD
Kennesaw, Georgia
March 2021

Abbreviations

1 En	The pseudepigraphic book of 1 Enoch, an Ethiopic apocalypse
1QM	The War Scroll found in Cave 1 at Qumran
4QPrNabar	The Prayer of Nabonidus, from Cave 4 at Qumran.
11Q13	Fragmentary text of eschatological midrash of Melchizedek from Cave 11 at Qumran
AB	Anchor Bible
ABD	*Anchor Bible Dictionary*. Edited by David Noel Friedman. 6 vols. New York: Doubleday, 1992.
ABRL	Anchor Bible Reference Library
ACCS	*Ancient Christian Commentary on Scripture*. Edited by Thomas C. Oden. 29 vols. Downers Grove, IL: Intervarsity, 2008.
Ag. Ap.	Josephus, *Contra Apionem* (*Against Apion*)
'Ag. Ber.	*'Aggadat Bereshit* (a rabbinical text)
Ant.	Josephus, *Antiquitates judaicae* (*Jewish Antiquities*)
ANEP	*The Ancient Near East in Pictures Relating to the Old Testament*. Edited by James B. Pritchard. 2nd ed. Princeton: Princeton University Press, 1969.
ANET	*Ancient Near Eastern Texts Relating to the Old Testament*. Edited by James B. Pritchard. 2nd ed. Princeton: Princeton University Press, 1969.

ANF	*The Ante-Nicene Fathers.* Edited by Alexander Roberts and James Donaldson. 10 vols. 1885–1887; Reprint, Peabody, MA: Hendrickson, 1994.
APOT	*The Apocrypha and Pseudepigrapha of the Old Testament.* Edited by R. H. Charles. 2 vols. Oxford: Clarendon, 1913.
As. Mos.	Assumption of Moses (Old Testament Pseudepigrapha)
AT	The author's translation (of a biblical text or other document)
AUSS	*Andrews University Seminary Studies*
b. B. Bat.	Tractate Baba Batra of the Babylonian Talmud
b. B. Meṣ.	Tractate Baba Meṣiʿa of the Babylonian Talmud
b. Nid.	Tractate Niddah of the Babylonian Talmud
b. Pesah.	Tractate Pesahim of the Babylonian Talmud
b. Sanh.	Tractate Sanhedrin of the Babylonian Talmud
BA	*Biblical Archaeologist*
BASOR	*Bulletin of the American Schools of Oriental Research*
BCOTWP	Baker Commentary on the Old Testament Wisdom and Psalms
BDB	Brown, Francis, S. R. Driver, and Charles A. Briggs. *A Hebrew and English Lexicon of the Old Testament.* Oxford: Oxford University Press, 1907.
BDAG	Danker, Frederick W., Walter Bauer, William F. Arndt, and F. Wilbur Gingrich. *Greek-English Lexicon of the New Testament and Other Early Christian Literature.* 2nd ed. Chicago: University of Chicago Press, 1979.
BHS	*Biblia Hebraica Stuttgartensia.* Edited by Karl Elliger and Wilhelm Rudolph. 5th ed. Stuttgart, Germ.: Deutsche Bibelgesellschaft, 1977.
Bib	*Biblica*
BJRL	*Bulletin of the John Rylands University Library of Manchester*
BTB	*Biblical Theology Bulletin*
BSt	*Biblische Studien*
BZAW	Beiheft zur Zeitschrift für die alttestamentliche Wissenschaft
CBQMS	Catholic Biblical Quarterly Monograph Series

ChrTod	*Christianity Today*
COS	*The Context of Scripture.* Edited by W. W. Hallo. 3 vols. Leiden, Neth.: Brill, 1997–2002.
Cyr.	Xenophon, *Cyropaedia*
Deut. Rab.	Deuteronomy Rabbah (a Jewish midrashic text)
DBTEL	*A Dictionary of Biblical Tradition in English Literature.* Edited by David Lyle Jeffrey. Grand Rapids: Eerdmans, 1992.
DSB	The Daily Study Bible Series
DTIB	*Dictionary for Theological Interpretation of the Bible.* Edited by K. J. Vanhoozer. Grand Rapids: Baker Academic, 2005.
EncJud	*Encyclopedia Judaica.* Edited by Fred Skolnik and Michael Berenbaum. 2nd ed. 22 vols. New York: Thomson Gale, 2007.
FOTL	Forms of Old Testament Literature
Gen. Rab.	Genesis Rabbah (a Jewish midrashic text)
HAT	Handbuch zum Alten Testament
HBC	*HarperCollins Bible Commentary.* Edited by J. L. Mays et al. Rev. ed. San Francisco: HarperCollins, 2000.
HDR	Harvard Dissertations in Religion
HTR	*Harvard Theological Review*
HTS	Harvard Theological Studies
IB	*Interpreter's Bible.* Edited by G. A. Buttrick et al. 12 vols. Nashville: Abingdon, 1951–1957.
ICC	International Critical Commentary
IDBSup	*The Interpreter's Dictionary of the Bible: Supplementary Volume.* Edited by Keith Crim. Nashville: Abingdon, 1976.
IFE	*The Illustrated Family Encyclopedia of the Living Bible.* Edited by Charles F. Kraft et al. 14 vols. Chicago: San Francisco Productions, 1967.
IRT	Issues in Religion and Theology
JAOS	*Journal of the American Oriental Society*
JNES	*Journal of Near Eastern Studies*
JSOT	*Journal for the Study of the Old Testament*
JSPSup	Journal for the Study of the Pseudepigrapha Supplement Series

Jub	Jubilees (a book in the Old Testament Pseudepigrapha)
J.W.	Josephus, *Bellum judaicum* (*Jewish War*)
KAT	Kommentar zum Alten Testament
KBL	Koehler, Ludwig, and Walter Baumgartner. *Lexicon in Veteris Testamenti libros.* 2nd ed. Leiden, Neth.: Brill, 1958.
KHC	Kurzer Hand-Commentar zum Alten Testament
KTU	*Die keilalphabetischen Texte aus Ugarit.* Edited by Manfried Dietrich et al. Münster, Germ.: Ugarit, 2013.
LSJ	Liddell, Henry George, Robert Scott, Henry Stuart Jones. *A Greek-English Lexicon.* 9th ed. with revised supplement. Oxford: Clarendon, 1996.
LXX	Ancient Greek translation of the Hebrew Bible, known as the Septuagint
m. Sanh.	Tractate *Sanhedrin* of the Mishnah
NCE	The *New Catholic Encyclopedia.* Edited by Berard L. Marthaler. 2nd ed. New York: Thomson Gale, 2002.
NIB	*The New Interpreter's Bible.* Edited by Leander Keck. 12 vols. Nashville: Abingdon, 1994–2004.
NICOT	New International Commentary on the Old Testament.
NIDB	*New Interpreter's Dictionary of the Bible.* Edited by Katharine Doob Sakenfeld. 5 vols. Nashville: Abingdon, 2006–2009.
NISB	*New Interpreter's Study Bible: New Revised Standard Version with the Apocrypha.* Edited by W. J. Harrelson. Nashville: Abingdon, 2003.
NJB	The New Jerusalem Bible translation
NJBC	*The New Jerome Biblical Commentary.* Edited by R. E. Brown et al. Englewood Cliffs, NJ: Prentice Hall, 1990.
Num. Rab.	The Rabbah of the book of Numbers
Op.	Hesiod, *Opera et dies* (*Works and Days*)
OTL	Old Testament Library
OTM	Old Testament Message
OTP	*Old Testament Pseudepigrapha.* Edited by James H. Charlesworth. 2 vols. New York: Doubleday, 1983–1985.

PL	*Patrologia Latina*. Edited by Jacques-Paul Migne. 217 vols. Paris: n.p., 1844–1864.
RevExp	*Review and Expositor*
SBL	The Society of Biblical Literature
SBLDS	Society of Biblical Literature Dissertation Series
SBLSBS	Society of Biblical Literature Sources for Biblical Study
SBLWAW	Society of Biblical Literature Writings from the Ancient World Series
SBS	Stuttgarter Bibelstudien
StudBib	*Studia Biblica*
Syb. Or.	The Sibylline Oracles
T. 12 Patr.	Testaments of the Twelve Patriarchs (a book in the Old Testament Pseudepigrapha)
T. Ab.	Testament of Abraham (a book in the Old Testament Pseudepigrapha)
T. Naph.	Testament of Naphtali (a portion of the Testaments of the Twelve Patriarchs)
TBC	Torch Bible Commentaries
TBl	*Theologische Blätter*
TCS	Texts from cuneiform sources
TDOT	*Theological Dictionary of the Old Testament*. Edited by G. Johannes Botterweck et al. Translated by J. T. Willis et al. 16 vols. Grand Rapids: Eerdmans, 1974–2018.
TOTC	Tyndale Old Testament Commentaries
UCOP	University of Cambridge Oriental Publications
VT	*Vetus Testamentum*
VTSup	Supplements to *Vetus Testamentum*
WBC	Word Biblical Commentary. Edited by David A. Hubbard et al. 52 vols. Nashville: Thomas Nelson, 1982—2012.
WTJ	*Westminster Theological Journal*
WUNT	Wissenschaftliche Untersuchungen zum Neuen Testament
ZAW	*Zeitschrift für die alttestamentliche Wissenschaft*
ZTK	*Zeitschrift für Theologie und Kirche*

PART I

Introduction

Introducing Daniel

Each situation—nay, each moment—is of infinite worth;

for each represents a whole eternity.

—Johann Wolfgang von Goethe

The book of Daniel was written with great expectation. Beginning with the destruction of Jerusalem in the sixth century BCE, it ends with a prophecy about the coming of the kingdom of God upon earth. Along the way between these epochal events, the book explores through narrative and apocalyptic the meaning of history under the sovereignty of God. Beyond the chaotic rise and fall of nations, the endless wars, the greed, and the lust for power that inevitably shapes the social and political conditions under which all peoples live, Daniel offers a fresh perspective that rises to the cosmic, transcendent level. The reader grasps something of the faithfulness of God, who raises up kings and deposes them according to the inscrutable divine will, while presiding over the course of history, ultimately sustaining those faithful to God. The characters in the narratives of the book model persons who live faithfully in alien lands amid the upheaval of history and the whims of governing despots. Wherever persons today find themselves oppressed and overwhelmed by the crushing tide of evil, the stalwart people on the pages of Daniel offer inspiration and courage. The visions in the book nurture hope.

Despite emphasis on these great themes, perhaps more than any other book in the Bible, with the notable exception of Revelation, the book of

Daniel has been trivialized. Apocalyptic enthusiasts have repeatedly mined the book to apply its visions to contemporary political and religious events. The Protestant Reformers found in Daniel's bizarre imagery the Roman papacy out to destroy the faithful Protestants. Fundamentalists read the same texts for traces of the end-time antichrist believed about to draw the entire world into a dangerous, pernicious alliance. Some Christian sects have even found in Daniel the precise date on which the world will end, only to have their hopes dashed by time's relentless assault.

Daniel deserves better. Behind its bizarre imagery, the colorful stories of Jews in conflict with gentile powers, lies a vital faith in the Lord of creation and of history. The book is a "powerful testimony to faithful conduct in the midst of almost unbearable persecution."[1]

Daniel is one of the most remarkable books in the Bible, worthy of our careful study. How it got to be such a stellar contribution to the biblical canon is the story about to unfold.

THE TEXTURE OF THE BOOK OF DANIEL

Daniel 1–12 falls into two distinct, yet linked, sections. Daniel 1–6 comprises a series of court tales, set against the backdrop of the sixth-century BCE Babylonian and Persian (Achaemenid) royal courts.[2] Daniel is the hero in all but one of these stories. Written in narrative style, the stories then introduce the apocalyptic visions in Dan 7–12.

The narratives in Dan 1–6 tell of four Hebrew captives taken into the service of the royal courts of Babylon and Persia. The first chapter serves as an introduction to the book. The Babylonians, having captured some of the Hebrews during a siege of Jerusalem, select Daniel and his companions—Hananiah, Mishael, and Azariah—for royal administrative service. Curiously, Daniel and these three, given the Babylonian names by which we know them—Shadrach, Meshach, and Abednego—after Dan 2 never appear together in any other tale. In the opening story, apparently for purity reasons, they refuse to eat royal rations of food and wine (Dan 1:12–16). Divine assistance enables them to excel in their training. Daniel surpasses the others in all visions and dreams (1:17), a skill evident in the next story (ch. 2) about Nebuchadnezzar's dream of a metallic statue representing the great empires, which Daniel interprets. Daniel's interpretation of the great

---

1. Crenshaw, *Story and Faith*, 372–73.

2. The Persian Empire is often referred to as the Achaemenid Empire, a designation derived from a legendary ancestor (Hakhamanis) of Persian royalty from the mountainous region in southwestern modern Iran.

metallic image foreshadows the later visions about the march of empires in Dan 7–12.

Shadrach, Meshach, and Abednego are next condemned to die when they refuse to honor Nebuchadnezzar's golden statue (ch. 3). Thrown into a blazing kiln, they are miraculously rescued by a heavenly mediator with the appearance of a god (Dan 3:25). Daniel is inexplicably absent from this story.

Then comes Nebuchadnezzar's strange descent into madness (ch. 4). For a time, cast out from the royal court, he must live like an animal in the field. Upon regaining sanity, he honors Daniel's God. This court tale is followed by a great festival in Babylon. Strange writing appears on the plastered wall of the royal hall, illumined by a blazing lampstand, catching Belshazzar, the acting regent, brashly desecrating the sacred vessels plundered from the Jerusalem temple (ch. 5). Daniel's interpretation of the mysterious writing signals Babylon's doom. "God has numbered [the days of] your kingdom and finished it" (Dan 5:26). Babylon falls to the Persians that very night.

Daniel now transitions into the royal service of the conquering Achaemenid empire (ch. 6). Out of political envy, his enemies secure an edict condemning Daniel for worshiping a deity other than the king. Upon violating the edict, he is thrown into a lions' pit to await death. During the night, an angel prevents the lions from devouring or harming him.

There are intriguing parallels between these stories. When the Babylonians take the sacred vessels from the emple in Jerusalem along with the Hebrew captives (Dan 1:1–2), they inadvertently prepare for Belshazzar's callous desecration of these vessels during the great feast in chapter 5. Daniel 3 and 6 concern a test of faith. In chapter 3, Shadrach, Meshach, and Abednego refuse to honor the king's gold-plated image and are miraculously delivered from the furnace. In chapter 6, Daniel refuses to abandon the worship of his God and is consigned to the pit of lions, where God rescues him by restraining the ferocity of the lions.

Forming the center of the narratives are chapters 4–5. Both deal with divine judgment upon a monarch. In chapter 4, having lost his sanity, Nebuchadnezzar is driven from society until he acknowledges the Most High God. In chapter 5, when reminded of Nebuchadnezzar's insanity, Belshazzar sacrilegiously defiles the sacred vessels impounded from the Jerusalem temple and suddenly faces judgment. In the aftermath of Belshazzar's arrogance, Babylon falls to the Persians.

With these stories as the literary frame, apocalyptic visions begin the second section (Dan 7–12). Symbolized by monstrous, grotesque animals, four terrifying empires arise, then fall in chapter 7, under divine judgment. In chapter 8, a ram and goat do battle: the ram, representing the kings of

Media and Persia; the goat, Alexander the Great. At the breakup of Alexander's empire, an unidentified evil king emerges, symbolized as a little horn. Then he "shall be broken, and not by human hands" (Dan 8:25). After a heartfelt prayer for Israel's long-delayed deliverance (ch. 9), Daniel receives a new interpretation of the prophecy of Jeremiah (Jer 25:11; 29:10) of the seventy years promised as the length for Israel's exile. The seventy years are now recalculated as 490 years, ending with the bringing in of everlasting righteousness (Dan 9:24).

The course of history from the Persian Cyrus II to the breakup of Alexander's empire unfolds in the longest vision (chs. 10–12), climaxing in the profanation of the second temple[3] and the death of the evil king. After this decisive event, deliverance comes through a resurrection of the faithful and final retribution for the wicked. The book then closes with several temporal estimates as to when this promised deliverance—from the perspective of the author—will arrive (ch. 12).

Whoever combined these court tales about Daniel and his friends with the apocalyptic visions has done so with a fine sense of literary balance. The author has brought the various materials together in a skillful literary unity. Daniel is "far from an arbitrary patchwork."[4] True, here or there, the text has experienced editorial or textual alteration, but overall, it presents a remarkable unity.[5] The entire book, in its present form, "shows unmistakable signs of a theological and religious purposefulness," considers Anderson. "The compiler, in good Hebraic fashion, has not removed all the 'rough places,' but has dexterously woven his material to serve his main aim."[6]

The Greek edition of Daniel, preserved in the Septuagint (LXX), has made four interesting additions.

THE ADDITIONS

The ancient Greek translations, both the LXX and Theodotion,[7] contain these Additions: the Prayer of Azariah (Dan 3:24–45); the Song of the Three

---

3. The second temple was constructed after the Jewish people returned to Judah from the Babylonian exile and was completed in 515 BCE (see Ezra 6:13–15).

4. Carey, *Ultimate Things*, 44.

5. See Talmon, "Daniel," 343–56.

6. Anderson, *Signs and Wonders*, 46.

7. The Septuagint, abbreviated LXX, is the earliest ancient translation of the Hebrew text into another language, begun in the third century BCE but not completed until probably the first century CE. This translation contains the apocryphal or deuterocanonical books such as 1–2 Maccabees, Tobit, Judith, and the Additions to Daniel. For additional clarity in Daniel (as well as other books), scholars try to recover the earliest

Young Men (Dan 3:52–90); Susanna (ch. 13); and Bel and the Dragon (ch. 14).[8] Daniel is not the only book in the HB to which additions have been made. The LXX contains a Greek version of the book of Esther with six additions interspersed throughout.[9] The Additions to Daniel, as well as in Esther, are considered Scripture in the Roman Catholic and Orthodox communities, but not by Protestants. Protestants, however, value them for their literary and religious significance. This study of Daniel would not be complete were we not to take into consideration the Additions.

The Prayer of Azariah is inserted between Dan 3:23 and 24 in the story of the three Hebrews cast into the furnace for refusing to honor the king's golden idol. It contains a prayer of penitence and petition for deliverance from Azariah (a.k.a. Abednego), one of Daniel's companions. Following the prayer comes a prose interlude (3:46-51) describing the lethal effects of the furnace, and then the Song of the Three Young Men praising and thanking the Lord for deliverance from the power of death (3:52-90). These Additions supply what dramatically seems missing from the Aramaic text of Dan 3:23-24.[10] Apparently omitted are the method of deliverance and how they may have reacted. By supplying these elements, the prayer and song liturgically emphasize the intimate relationship between God and God's people, as well as the worship of the God of Israel.[11]

In Susanna (Dan 13:1-63), a youthful Daniel intervenes to rescue the Jewish maiden Susanna, who has been falsely accused of adultery and faces

---

renderings into Greek that preceded the LXX. Where recoverable, these are identified as the Old Greek translation (OG). The Theodotion translation comes from c. 190 CE and represents a new or revised translation from the Hebrew into Greek, and in Daniel, made partly from the Hebrew/Aramaic original and partly from the OG text.

8. The Additions have come down in two slightly differing Greek versions: the Septuagint (LXX), from a single ninth-century cursive manuscript known as Codex Chrisianus 88, and Theodotion's revision of the LXX based on the HB. The Kölner Papyrus 967, from c. 150 CE, contains Dan 5-12, Susanna, and Bel and the Dragon, but not the Prayer of Azariah and the Song of the Three Young Men. Theodotion replaced the LXX in the church by 250 CE. The translation of the Additions in this commentary is based on Theodotion.

9. Additions A (11:1—12:6), B (13:1-7), C (13:8-18), D (15:1-16), E (16:1-24), F (10:4—11:1). I have discussed the problem of the textual history of the additions to Esther elsewhere (Gladson, *Five Exotic Scrolls*, 338-44).

10. The Prayer of Azariah and the Song of the Three contain four (or three) separate, independent units: (1) Prayer of Azariah (Dan 3:24-45); (2) a prose narrative (vv. 46-51); (3) the ode (vv. 52-56); and (4) the psalm or hymn (vv. 57-90).

11. The liturgical use of the prayer and the song may be experienced today when the prayer is read in the Church of England as an example of instruction in manners. In the rubric of the first prayer book of Edward VI (1549), the song was to be read during Lent as a response to the Old Testament lesson at morning prayer.

death. With clever cunning in cross examination of her accusers, like Perry Mason, Daniel convinces the court of the accusers' perfidy and wins acquittal. The Greek tradition offers slightly differing versions of this story, one in Theodotion, the other in the older LXX. Theodotion also places this story before chapter 1; the LXX, following the main text as chapter 13.

In Bel and the Dragon, two separate stories in one chapter, Bel is the story of a statue of Bel (Dan 14:1–22).[12] The king worships Bel as the living god. The king also believes Bel eats the sacrificial food normally set before him by the priests. Daniel exposes the fraud—the priests themselves eat the food—and so the king has Daniel destroy the fraudulent image.

Like the story of Bel, the tale of the Dragon (Dan 14:23–42) mocks idolatrous religion. Daniel slays the dragon (a snakelike creature) without weapons. He makes cakes of bitumen, fat, and hair, and feeds them to the dragon. Ingested, these swell up and burst, killing the snake. Immediately, the populace condemns Daniel, and he is thrown into the lions' pit. During his six-day confinement, he remains unharmed. The prophet Habakkuk, miraculously transported to Babylon, supplies food to Daniel. When the king comes to see what has happened, he finds Daniel alive and well. With the addition of these stories, the Greek versions of Daniel constitute a "small Danielic library."[13]

With the Additions as the main difference between Daniel in the HB and in the LXX, we have before us two versions of the book of Daniel. Our study deals with both. In the light of these stories, the question arises: did Daniel really exist, or was he a fictional character?

QUEST FOR THE HISTORICAL DANIEL

It may well be the book of Daniel originally received its title from a tag attached to the scroll to distinguish it from other scrolls stacked on a shelf or placed in a clay jar like the ancient scrolls found at the Dead Sea.[14] Daniel is clearly the principal character in the book.

---

12. Bel, from the Akkadian *bēlu* (Lord), is an exalted title for Marduk, the god of Babylon and supreme ruler of Mesopotamia. Bel is here used as Marduk's proper name (Abusch, "Marduk," 543).

13. Newsom, "Daniel and Additions," 163. See Steussy, *Garden in Babylon*.

14. In 1947, Bedouin shepherds came across several biblical scrolls hidden in clay jars in a cave near the northern end of the Dead Sea at a place called Qumran. This was the initial discovery of what later became known as the Dead Sea Scrolls, the most important manuscript find of modern times.

INTRODUCING DANIEL 9

The historical nature of our study makes us ask, did the Daniel reported in the book exist? Was Daniel a real, historical character, whose name might someday pop up in an ancient Babylonian cuneiform clay tablet?

The name Daniel (דָּנִיֵּאל, *Daniyyel*) means "*El* (God) is my judge," "my judge is *El* (God)," or even "*El* (God) is the defender of my right," all highly appropriate, given what we read about him. The name Daniel also appears elsewhere in the HB, indicating it must have been common in the fifth century BCE or earlier.[15] With one exception, the Daniel in the book, unfortunately, cannot be identified with any other person bearing this name in the HB.

The exception may be found in Ezekiel. "Even if Noah, Daniel, and Job, these three, were in it," the prophet writes, "they would save only their own lives by their righteousness" (Ezek 14:14, 20). "You are indeed wiser than Daniel; no secret is hidden from you" (28:3). Daniel is hailed in Ezekiel for his superior righteousness and wisdom, attributes he possesses in the book of Daniel.[16] Is this the same person as the Daniel of the book?

This seems unlikely. For one thing, Ezekiel mentions this Daniel alongside Noah and Job, both of whom lived centuries before Ezekiel, indicating Ezekiel has in mind persons from remote antiquity. Ezekiel was active in the sixth century, probably in the Babylonian area. He was thus an older contemporary of the Daniel in the book. It seems highly unlikely Daniel would have already gained such prominent reputation for piety and wisdom were he but a younger contemporary of Ezekiel.

Centuries earlier than Ezekiel, in a fourteenth-century BCE Ugaritic text, the *Tale of Aqhat*, there also appears a legendary Canaanite king by the name of *dnil* (pronounced *danilu*), famed for wisdom and benevolence and revered as an ancestral hero.[17] The spelling of this name in Ugaritic (*dnil*) is essentially the same as the unvocalized Hebrew of Ezekiel (דנאל, *dnl*). Is this *dnil* from the ancient city of Ugarit the legendary figure mentioned by Ezekiel? If so, Ezekiel may have drawn upon a popular tradition about this Ugaritic hero *dnil* and included him in this oracle. The two figures may well have coalesced in the tradition, Frost suggests. The legendary figure of *dnil* in the *Tale of Aqhat* may have shifted over time, as tales are wont to

---

15. See Ezra 8:2; Neh 8:4; 10:2, 6, 23; 1 Chr 3:1; 1 Enoch 6:7; 69:2; Jubilees 4:20.

16. See Dan 1:17; 2:47–48; 5:11–12; 6:16; 12:3.

17. "Now Daniel, man of Rapiu, / the hero ... takes care of the case of the widow, / defends the need of the orphan" (2 Aqhat 5, 4–7) (Parker, "Aqhat," *Ugaritic Narrative Poetry*, 58). See also del Olmo Lete and Sanmartin, "dnil," *Dictionary of Ugaritic Language*, 1:276. The Ugaritic texts come from cuneiform clay tablets found at Ugarit (Ras Shamra) on the Syrian coast in 1930–31. They date to the fourteenth century BCE and are written in a Northwest Semitic language (Ugaritic) related to Hebrew.

do, into the Daniel of the Israelite exile, much as Arthur and the Knights of the Round Table shifted in the British cycle of King Arthur.[18] Thus, Daniel's legendary wisdom and righteousness may have blended with his unshakable faith in God and courage in the face of persecution.

Since Daniel in Ezekiel appears in company with the esteemed ancient figures of Job and Noah, however, it is unlikely Ezekiel would have introduced a legendary Canaanite king into the honored company of Job and Noah. Ezekiel's reference is therefore probably not to the Canaanite *dnil*. Who, then, is the Daniel in Ezekiel's oracle?

The question is still unresolved. It is entirely possible, in my opinion, that a real historical person by this name lived among the Judean exiles in Babylon, and there, while in the service of a foreign state, exemplified uncommon wisdom, character, and fortitude. Although the stories about him may have been embellished—such stories generally are—during their oral transmission, they may rest upon a core of empirical fact. Unfortunately, we have no way of historically confirming this.[19]

Considered from a broader religious perspective, however, we do not need a historically verified Daniel to be inspired by the character Daniel in the stories. Daniel is presented as a youthful exile brought to Babylon by Nebuchadnezzar II (Dan 1:2). He is initially active as a diviner in Nebuchadnezzar's court and then into the reign of the Persian Cyrus II, seventy years later (1:21). Not surprisingly, like many of the biblical heroes, several legends have grown up around Daniel in Jewish, Christian, and Muslim folklore. According to tradition, his burial site is either in a synagogue in Susa, the ancient Persian capital, or in the royal vault in Babylon, west of the acropolis.[20]

THE COMPOSITION OF DANIEL

If we know who wrote a biblical book and under what circumstances, we are in a better position to understand it. This is especially true with a book like Daniel, largely written in an obscure, apocalyptic style, strange to our eyes. It is axiomatic that every writing—ancient or modern—is inextricably

---

18. Frost, "Daniel," 761–62. "Any attempt to derive historical information from these stories [in Daniel]," Collins cautions, "encounters insuperable problems" (J. Collins, *Introduction to Hebrew Bible*, 566).

19. "There is therefore no evidence [of Daniel] outside the book that could be used in solving the dilemma" (Pfeiffer, *Introduction to Old Testament*, 754).

20. Slotki, *Daniel*, xi.

related to the historical and sociological setting in which it was produced.[21] Who, then, wrote Daniel? Who composed the six tales of life at the royal court in the Babylonian exile and the four apocalyptic visions of the march of nations and the malignant growth of evil on the international stage, culminating in the divine judgment and the deliverance of the people of God? Furthermore, who wrote the Additions in the Greek versions of Daniel?

With Daniel, the answer is not simple. Because there has been so much heated, bitter debate over this issue, we need to spend a little time unpacking the origin of Daniel and the Additions.

Prior to the modern era, Jewish and Christian scholars took for granted that Daniel, a Jewish exile living in Babylon in the latter part of the sixth century BCE, composed the book, although not necessarily the Additions. On the surface, at least, this assumption appears to be accurate. All apocalyptic visions in chapters 7–12 are attributed to Daniel, who receives, describes, and acknowledges the visions. They are related in the first person and interpreted by an angel mediator. "Daniel said, 'I saw in the visions in the night'" (Dan 7:2). "A vision appeared to me, I, Daniel" (8:1). "In the first year of his reign, I, Daniel, discerned in the books" (9:2). "In those days, I, Daniel, had been mourning three full weeks" (10:2). Finally, Daniel is to seal the book and hide it away (12:4): "Then I, Daniel, looked, and two others were standing" (v. 5).

From these references, it has been inferred the court tales in chapters 1–6 were likewise written by Daniel. This claim, however, is not found anywhere in chapters 1–6, nor in the Additions. The court tales, written in the third person, contain no indication of who composed them. In this respect, they are anonymous. While third person point of view does not preclude Danielic authorship, because Daniel is given heroic status in the stories, it seems unlikely he personally wrote them. They were written about him, not by him. Indeed, this is suggested at the end of the collection: "This Daniel prospered in the reign of Darius and in the reign of Cyrus the Persian" (Dan 6:28). That is, these stories are about Daniel, who appears as a heroic character. Such comment is editorial, possibly made by an editor, who is someone other than Daniel. The text of Dan 1–12, at the very least, gives a mixed message regarding its authorship.

Edward Young, a leading modern defender of the traditional view of Daniel's authorship, admits there are "difficulties in the traditional view of the authorship of Daniel. Not to acknowledge this would be to close one's

---

21. Scholars refer to this in a German phrase as the *Sitz im Leben* of a document. *Sitz im Leben* (situation in life or life situation) refers to the setting within the life of Israel or the early church (with the NT) in which certain written or oral forms took shape.

eyes to the facts."[22] Also recognizing the problem, Joyce Baldwin suggests the book may have been written by an anonymous person in the late sixth or early fifth century.[23] Several other conservative commentators, however, continue to claim Daniel as the author.[24]

Danielic authorship was not questioned until the third century CE. The first to challenge was evidently the Neoplatonist Porphyry (c. 233–304 CE). Porphyry studied under the Roman philosopher Plotinus and the Greek philosopher Longinus. Although his birth name was Malchus, after his father, Longinus renamed him Porphyry ("purple"). While living in Sicily, at age forty, Porphyry wrote his magnus opus of fifteen volumes, *Against the Christians*. Most of this work has been lost, but fragments of the fourth volume have been preserved in Jerome's (c. 342–420 CE) *Commentary on Daniel*. Porphyry's intent, as you can tell from the title, was to discredit Christianity. On philosophical grounds, he claimed there is no such thing as predictive prophecy. It is impossible for finite, timebound human beings, he argued, who cannot see the future, to predict it accurately. Moreover, predictions of the future—far distant from them—would have been of little relevance to Daniel's original readers. The visions in Daniel, for Porphyry, were not prophecy in the strict sense. They were retrospectively written after the events had already transpired and thus made to appear as predictions.[25] Scholars call this retrospection *vaticinium ex eventu*, a prophecy from an outcome, namely, history written as though it were predicted. Consequently, Porphyry situated Daniel in the time of the Seleucid king Antiochus IV Epiphanes (175–164 BCE), the period when Daniel's visions appear to reach fulfillment, rather than in the sixth century BCE, as in the traditional view.

Porphyry's views were adopted thirteen hundred years later by the Jewish scholar Uriel da Costa (1590–1647), who claimed the book had been

---

22. Young, *Prophecy of Daniel*, 24.

23. Baldwin, *Daniel*, 46.

24. "Daniel wrote the book substantially as it exists today," Stephen Miller insists. "The prophecy is historically reliable, and . . . its predictions are supernatural and accurate." He concedes the book may have experienced "some modernization of the language," or that another contemporary of Daniel may have recorded the book (S. Miller, *Daniel*, 23–24). Gleason Archer Jr. remains unequivocal: "The clear testimony of the book itself is that Daniel was the author" (Archer, "Daniel," 4). John C. Whitcomb argues the book "was clearly written by one author," whom he thinks was Daniel (Whitcomb, *Daniel*, 11–13).

25. The Church Father Jerome quotes Porphyry on this point: The book was "composed by someone who lived in Judea in the reign of Antiochus who was surnamed Epiphanes, and he did not predict coming events but narrated past ones" (cited in Ginsberg, "Daniel, Book of," 422). See the discussion of Porphyry in Young, *Prophecy of Daniel*, 317–20.

composed by some of the Pharisees in support of the doctrine of the resurrection of the body.[26] Shortly after da Costa, the English deist Anthony Collins, drawing again on Porphyry, disputed the prophecies in the book.[27] By the late eighteenth and early nineteenth centuries, biblical scholars, who by then had begun a thorough investigation into the origin of biblical documents, no longer accepted at face value the traditional claim of Daniel's authorship. It fell to the German scholar Leonard Bertholdt to offer the first modern historical view of the matter in 1808.[28] From this point on, the latter part of Daniel (chs. 7–12), at least, was generally located in the time of Antiochus IV Epiphanes, where its content seemed best to fit.[29] During the nineteenth century, when the struggle between traditional and modern historical-critical scholarship seemed to reach its zenith,[30] the book of Daniel became "one of the flashpoints" of the struggle.[31]

The shift from the traditional view of Danielic authorship, even though originally prompted by Porphyry's rationalist notion of the impossibility of prophecy, is today no longer the primary reason for the shift.[32] Instead, it rests upon substantive evidence derived from the book of Daniel and from detailed literary comparison with other Jewish and Christian apocalypses.[33] Since Hermann Gunkel (1862–1932), biblical scholars have learned to read biblical texts in the light of comparable documents from the ancient Near East and Greco-Roman world.[34] Among these documents, most of which

26. da Costa, *Sobre a mortalidade da alma*. See Dan 12:1–3.

27. Anthony Collins, *Scheme of Literal Prophecy* (1727).

28. Bertholdt, *Daniel* (1806–1808).

29. Porphyry's "main results are now accepted by the vast majority of Christians who are aware of the evidence" (Casey, "Porphyry and Daniel," 33).

30. In brief, historical criticism is an approach that understands an ancient text, such as the Bible, in the light of its historical origins, time and place of writing, sources, literary development, events, dates, persons, places, things, cultural customs, and so on, mentioned or implied in the text. Historical criticism and related disciplines are credited with most of the gains that have been made in the study of the Bible in modern times. See Richard and R. Kendall Soulen, *Handbook of Biblical Criticism*, 79–80. Contrary to some conservative scholars, historical criticism is not the enemy of Scripture. It is not "an attack upon the entire Scriptures," as John Walvoord wrongly claims (*Daniel*, 17). At its best, it is an attempt to understand the Scriptures in their original environment. This may lead to conclusions that disconfirm traditional views, of course, but such revisions are the consequences of historical research.

31. Newsom, *Daniel*, 7.

32. J. Collins, *Daniel* (Hermeneia), 26.

33. We are reminded of the dictum of Thomas Hobbes (1588–1679) that the time and origin of a biblical book should be determined from the book itself, irrespective of the tradition (Hobbes, *Leviathan* 3.33, as cited in Bentzen, *Daniel*, 10).

34. I refer here to the development of form criticism, the analysis of typical oral and

have come to light in modern times, are included Jewish and Christian apocalypses from c. 200 BCE to 100 CE. These texts are written in an apocalyptic style much like Daniel. Such apocalyptic writing sheds considerable light on how books like Daniel were written, why they used an apocalyptic style, and of course, the intrinsic meaning of such writing. Below, we will examine more closely the apocalyptic style and its significance.

When it comes to authorship, these extra-biblical apocalypses generally utilized a widespread ancient literary strategy of writing under an assumed name or a pen name, usually that of a renowned individual. This practice, known as pseudonymity, is not to be considered false, as Pusey mistakenly claimed,[35] but merely as following a popular literary custom of the day. Most ancient apocalyptic writings consist of visionary material under the name of an ancient worthy.[36] "All the apocalypses," Toni Craven explains, "are retrospective prophecies that present past historical events as if they are still to happen."[37]

The book of 1 Enoch, a composite work, the earliest part of which (the Astronomical Book [chs. 72–82]) dates to the. third or perhaps the fourth century BCE,[38] illustrates what Craven points out. First Enoch is composed under the name of Enoch, the same primeval Enoch who "walked with God; then he was no more, because God took him" (Gen 5:24). "The angel Uriel responded and said to me, 'Behold I have shown you everything, Enoch, and I have revealed everything to you . . . . So I [Enoch] looked at the tablets of heaven, read all the writing (on them), and came to understand everything" (80:1; 81:2, *OTP*). Scholars are uncertain, but 1 Enoch may well be the first of the apocalypses—even before Daniel—to use pseudonymity. Afterward, the style became pervasive among Jewish and Christian apocalyptic writings.

A clear example—later than Daniel—is the notable apocalypse of 2 Esdras (also known as 4 Ezra). A composite text with portions of both Jewish and Christian origin from the late first century CE, the middle of the second century, and the early third century, the book is attributed to Ezra,

---

literary forms in which human existence is linguistically expressed.

35. "The book of Daniel is especially fitted to be a battle-ground between faith and unbelief," he wrote. "It admits no half-way measures. It is either Divine or an imposture . . . . The writer, were he not Daniel, must have lied on a most frightful scale" (Pusey, *Daniel the Prophet*, 1).

36. See Bickerman, *Four Strange Books*, 51–138.

37. Craven, "Daniel and Its Additions," 192.

38. The book of 1 Enoch is composite. Chapters 1–36 probably comes from c. 175 BCE; chs. 83–90 from c. 164–160; chs. 72–82 from the third or fourth centuries BCE. If these dates are accurate, then 1 Enoch historically precedes Daniel.

the priest who disseminated the Torah (or a major part of it) among the Judeans after the Babylonian exile in the fifth century BCE, hundreds of years earlier than 2 Esdras. "In the thirtieth year after the destruction of the city [of Jerusalem], I was in Babylon—I, Salathiel, who am also called Ezra. I was troubled as I lay on my bed, and my thoughts welled up in my heart, because I saw the desolation of Zion and the wealth of those who lived in Babylon" (2 Esdras 3:1–2). The opening sentence in 2 Esdras claims this is "the book of the prophet Ezra" (1:1). Various visions within the book are also attributed directly to Ezra, even though the book of 2 Esdras comes from five hundred years or more later.

Pseudonymity was as common in the Greco-Roman world as in the Jewish, particularly in Hellenistic times, where Daniel is now generally located. In addition to the apocalypses just mentioned, we know of the Apocalypse of Zephaniah; 2 Baruch; 3 Baruch; the Apocalypse of Adam; the Apocalypse of Elijah; the Sibylline Oracles; and so on.[39] Pseudonymous literature also may be found in the deuterocanonicals (Apocrypha): Wisdom of Solomon, Baruch, and the Epistle of Jeremiah. In the HB itself, it is in Ecclesiastes, the Song of Solomon, and, as we now realize, no doubt Daniel.[40]

Careful study of these pseudonymous apocalyptic and other writings has convinced scholars that the same practice was at work in the composition of Daniel. Today, most scholars have concluded Daniel is a pseudonymous apocalyptic text completed in the second century BCE.

When looked at from a modern perspective, with our legal standards of intellectual propriety, pseudonymity may seem "morally tendentious, but this needn't have been the case for the ancients."[41] It was rather a conventional way of composing apocalyptic (and other) literature. "That pseudonymity is a rarer literary device in our culture, especially in religious contexts," points out Goldingay, "should not allow us to infer that God could not use it in another culture." Daniel's initial readers, who were acquainted with the

---

39. For the text of all these and many other apocalypses, see Charlesworth, *OTP*, vol. 1. A tabular list of all forty-seven apocalyptic texts may be found in Soulen and Soulen, *Handbook of Biblical Criticism*, 148–49.

40. In the NT, the Gospel of John, 2–3 John, 2 Thess, 1–2 Tim, 1–2 Pet, Jas, and Jude are suspected pseudonyms. "Pseudonymity in these instances is probably not to be thought of from a modern (cynical) point of view as a means of gaining authority and wide circulations for a work but rather as a product of the sincere conviction that truly inspired scripture was not of one's own doing but God's, or the Holy Spirit's, and must therefore be attributed to an acknowledged instrument of revelation" (Soulen and Soulen, *Handbook of Biblical Criticism*, 149).

41. Sparks, *Ancient Texts*, 250.

apocalyptic style, would have recognized pseudonymity and known how to read it.⁴² Frost puts it decisively:

> We forget that our standards of judgment in matters of authorship, plagiarism, pseudonymity, and interpolation are not those of the ancient world, but are largely the creation of the printing press, which fixes a text unalterably, and the necessary economics of the publishing trade, which can be carried on only if copyright is respected; our standards on these matters are not absolute ethical criteria. Our author played fair by the standards of his day, for he did not create his message, but received it from the tradition of the apocalyptic movement.⁴³

We are probably safe, then, in assuming the origin of Daniel is to be found in a process by which the parts of the book were composed, transmitted, adapted, and edited into the book as we now know it. The composition in two languages (Hebrew and Aramaic), the two (or three) versions of the book, the supplementary Additions (Prayer of Azariah, Song of the Three Youths, Susanna, and Bel and the Dragon) strongly suggest such development. Moreover, scholars notice all the apocalyptic visions (chs. 2, 7–12) depicting the rise and fall of ancient Near Eastern empires begin with symbolic depictions of the empires as metals, grotesque animals, or as literal kings and rulers in deadly conflict. Details are sketchy and partially inaccurate. With the final (fourth) empire, however, the visions suddenly become increasingly detailed.⁴⁴ Considerably more space is allocated to the fourth empire and its various iterations. Predictions about the fourth empire, now recognized as the Greek Seleucid empire under Antiochus IV, become amazingly accurate. In the fourth and longest vision, the author takes forty-one verses to describe the Hellenistic era wherein Antiochus IV flourished (Dan 11:5–46), with the last twenty-six verses devoted to Antiochus himself. Such consummate detail has led to the conclusion that the author of this vision,

---

42. Goldingay, *Daniel*, xi. "It is not essential to or distinctive of apocalypses to be pseudonymous or quasi-prophetic," states Goldingay. "Both features are missing from Revelation and present in works of other genres. But ancient Near Eastern parallels to visions such as these—there being no OT parallels—are all pseudonymous quasi-prophecies, not actual prophecies of known authorship. This also suggests that there is no reason to assume that the authors would necessarily have intended—or hoped—to deceive hearers regarding the visions' origin; the latter would have known how to hear them" (Goldingay, *Daniel*, 321).

43. Frost, "Daniel," 768.

44. See Dan 2:40–46; 7:8, 19–27; 8:9–14, 22–26; 9:27; 11:21–46. See W. Schmidt, *Old Testament Introduction*, 288.

if not the others, was probably active in the time of Antiochus IV (175–164 BCE) or slightly later.

Antiochus's death occurred in 164. Our author, for some reason, misconstrues the circumstances of his death. Although he is familiar with Antiochus's life leading up to this, he seems unaware of the circumstances of his death.[45] The final demise of Antiochus IV depicted in Daniel does not coincide with the actual course of events. The apocalyptic seer erroneously predicts the wrong location of Antiochus's fate. The passage begins with an eschatological phrase, "at the time of the end," then predicts a military campaign by Antiochus against Egypt, and finally forecasts Antiochus will meet his doom "between the sea and the beautiful holy mountain," a reference to the region between the Mediterranean and Jerusalem (Dan 11:40–45). Antiochus instead died a miserable death, not in Palestine or the vicinity of Jerusalem, but hundreds of miles away in Persia. "He will come to his end and there will be no help for him" (v. 45). It follows then that the vision in Dan 10–12 was apparently written shortly before 164 and the untimely death of Antiochus. Since the apocalyptic visions in Dan 7–12 end with the demise of Antiochus, it is likely the author wrote between 168 and 164, but before the death of Antiochus near the end of 164.[46] This is as close as scholars come to the time of the writing of Dan 7–12.

As for the court tales in Dan 1–6, the final author was probably not responsible for these, but instead adapted well-known traditions of faithful Jewish exiles that had originated during the Babylonian and Persian empires or shortly thereafter. In other words, Daniel bears evidence of a collaborative origin: it is drawn from various sources, not necessarily written by the same person. Both Baruch Spinoza (1632–1677) and Isaac Newton (1642–1727), careful students of Daniel, noticed this as early as the seventeenth and eighteenth centuries.[47] "The biblical book of Daniel is not the unified work of a single author," confirms Paul Schäfer, "but a collected work in which materials of diverse sorts and from different historical periods have been reworked."[48] These traditional stories had no doubt been handed down orally in popular culture. The same may be true of the Additions. They appear to have been added to the book in its Greek edition after the Hebrew/Aramaic text was essentially complete.

45. Soggin, *Introduction to Old Testament*, 477.
46. Wright, *Biblical Archaeology*, 215n23; Crenshaw, *Story and Faith*, 365.
47. Note Newton: "The book of Daniel is a collection of papers written at several times. The six last chapters contain Prophecies written at several times by Daniel himself; the six first are a collection of historical papers written by others" (Newton, *Observations upon Prophecies*, 145).
48. Schäfer, "Hellenistic and Maccabean Periods," 540.

The final author/editor adapted the stories in chapters 1–6 for the period of Seleucid rule in Palestine in the second century BCE and used them as a setting for the apocalyptic visions in chapters 7–12.[49] The link may even be closer. It is possible the visions may have been composed with the stories in mind.[50] Thus the real historical setting of the author—the *Sitz im Leben* (life setting)—is the Seleucid period of the mid-second century BCE, while the literary or fictive setting is the Neo-Babylonian and Achaemenid periods of the sixth century. This may seem confusing. If we compare it with a modern historical novel, we may better grasp the distinction. Let us say a novelist writing in the twenty-first century sets her imaginary story in the seventeenth century (this would be the historical setting of the story) but actually composes the story in the twenty-first century (the literary setting of authorship).[51]

This analysis of Danielic authorship, of course remains conjectural. The book of Daniel simply does not tell us its origin or who may have put it in final order. Nonetheless, it seems likely that in the second century (168–164 BCE), at the time of the Maccabean revolt against the Syrian Seleucids, then ruled by Antiochus IV Epiphanes, an unknown Jewish apocalyptic writer (or writers) in Palestine compiled and composed the Hebrew and Aramaic text of Daniel, including the apocalyptic visions (chs. 7–12).[52] For these stories, the author(s) drew upon older materials (chs. 1–6). The Additions represent a later supplement to this Hebrew/Aramaic text.

---

49. Hartman and Di Lella offer a more complicated analysis. The vision in Dan 7 seems to have been written during the reign of Antiochus IV Epiphanes (175–164 BCE), but before Antiochus began his persecution of the Jewish people (c. 168 BCE). Dan 8 stems from after the time of Antiochus's desecration of the temple (Dec. 167), while chs. 10–12 appear to precede an anticipated campaign of Antiochus against Egypt (165). Dan 9, which contains an interpolated prayer (vv. 4–20), may come from after the victory of Antiochus over Artaxias of Armenia in the autumn of 165. Smaller glosses in all the visionary reports in chs. 7–12 give evidence of further editorial work (Hartman and Di Lella, *Book of Daniel*, 13–14). For instances of suspected editorial glosses, see Eissfeldt, *Old Testament*, 526–27.

50. Goldingay, *Daniel*, 327.

51. In this case, by means of the style of writing and linguistic clues, such as anachronisms, if we did not know the authorship of a novel, we could figure out the author was writing in a different era than the one in which the story takes place. Similarly, we can distinguish between the historical setting of the writing of Daniel and the literary setting of its storyline.

52. "We have before us," writes Joseph Klausner, "not a prophet of the time of the Babylonian exile, but an apocalyptist of the time of Antiochus Epiphanes, who composed his book near the year 164 BCE" (Klausner, *Messianic Idea in Israel*, 225–26). For a contrary view, see Hasel, "Book of Daniel," 37–49, 211–25; Talbot, *Prophecies of Daniel*, 10–11.

THE LANGUAGES AND TEXT OF DANIEL

The book of Daniel, including the Additions, has come down to us in essentially two ancient versions. The first is the Hebrew/Aramaic version found in the HB, consisting of twelve chapters (Dan 1-12), with parts in Hebrew and Aramaic.[53] A second version, probably originally translated from Hebrew/Aramaic, is found in the Greek Septuagint (LXX). This version contains four supplements not found in the Hebrew/Aramaic, two inserted into the text of Dan 3 and two in additional chapters (Dan 13-14).

Daniel in the HB is curiously written in two languages. The book starts at Dan 1:1 in Hebrew, switches to Aramaic in the middle of a sentence at 2:4b, then back to Hebrew for 8:1—12:13. The Additions appearing in the LXX and Theodotion versions of Daniel are in Greek, which adds a third language, although their original language was probably Hebrew or Aramaic.

The Hebrew of Daniel resembles Late Biblical Hebrew, similar to the Hebrew in 1-2 Chronicles and the Dead Sea Scrolls.[54] The Aramaic is Imperial, Official (German: *Reichsaramäisch*), or Standard Literary Aramaic, a language widely used by the Achaemenid empire as the *lingua franca* of diplomacy and communication.[55] The ancient Persians and others employed it for official correspondence, judicial records, and inscriptions. Various dialects of Aramaic were in widespread use throughout the Near East from roughly 700 to 200 BCE.[56] Interestingly, several other HB passages besides Daniel are also written in Imperial Aramaic.[57] The Aramaic of Daniel also contains a few Akkadian and Persian loan words, with three taken from Greek.

No one really knows why the book appears in two languages. Was it originally intended as a bilingual composition? Was the original text composed in Aramaic, then portions subsequently translated into Hebrew?[58] Conversely, was the book initially written in Hebrew, then an Aramaic

---

53. Several small portions of the HB, including parts of Daniel (2:4b—7:28), are in Aramaic, a Northwest Semitic language related to Hebrew; Dan 1 and 8-12 are in Hebrew.

54. Late Biblical Hebrew (LBH) comes from the fifth century BCE or later. See S. R. Driver, *Introduction to the Literature*, 506-8; Hackett, "Hebrew (Biblical and Epigraphic)," 140-41.

55. Greenspahn, "Aramaic," 94-95. See also Gzella, "Introduction," xxxviii-xliii.

56. See S. R. Driver, "Aramaic of Daniel," 110-19.

57. Ezra 4:8-6:18; 7:12-16; Jer 10:11; Gen 31:47 (two words).

58. The Hebrew of the book, it should be noted, appears to have been written by someone more at home in Aramaic (Goldingay, *Daniel*, xxv).

translation prepared for those who could not read Hebrew? Did the author write in Aramaic when addressing matters pertaining to the Babylonian and Persian empires, but in Hebrew when concerned with Jewish issues, such as the temple and the future of Israel?[59] Or when putting the book together, did the author incorporate older, pre-existing Aramaic material into a work originally composed in Hebrew?[60]

The two languages may represent an ABA literary pattern like in the book of Job, which begins with prose (A), turns to poetry (B), then climaxes with prose (A'). Here the author begins with (A) Hebrew (Dan 1:1—2:4a), then takes up (B) Aramaic (2:4b—7:28) and reverts to (A') Hebrew (8:1—12:13).[61] As intriguing as various theories may be, nonetheless, no one really knows why the book now appears in two languages, with abrupt changes in the middle of a sentence at 2:4b and 8:1 at the beginning of a chapter.

Some point to the languages as indicators of the origin of Daniel. However, to rely on the Hebrew or Aramaic style in the book as a marker of the date of composition is too imprecise to be of help.[62] When we consider normal evolutionary changes occurring in any language, we realize the Aramaic and Hebrew of Daniel could have been written at any time between the late sixth and second centuries BCE. They are thus of minimal help in establishing a precise date for the book.

The fragments of the Hebrew and Aramaic text of Daniel discovered among the Dead Sea Scrolls at Qumran at the northern end of the Dead Sea confirm the essential integrity of the Masoretic text (MT).[63] The transition from Hebrew to Aramaic, which occurs at Dan 2:4b, is attested in one of these fragments (*1QDaniel*[a] [1Q71]).[64] As these Qumran fragments (c. 100

59. For this explanation, see Archer, "Daniel," 6; Zimmerman, "Aramaic Origin," 255–72; Baumgartner, "Das Aramäische," 81–133.

60. For a discussion of all the theories, see J. Collins, *Daniel* (Hermeneia), 12–25.

61. Gordon and Rendsburg, *Bible and Ancient Near East*, 78–79.

62. See Kitchen, *Notes on Some Problems*, 31–79.

63. These are *1QDaniel*[a] [1Q71] (1:10–17; 2:2–6); *1QDaniel*[b] [1Q72] (3:22–30); *4QDaniel*[a] [4Q112] (1:16–20; 2:9–11, 19–49; 3:1–2; 4:29–30; 5:5–7, 12–14, 16–19; 7:5–7, 25–28; 8:1–5; 10:16–20; 11:13–16); *4QDaniel*[b] [4Q113] (5:10–12, 14–16, 19–22; 6:8–22, 27–29; 7:1–6, 11(?), 26–28; 8:1–8, 13–16); *4QDaniel*[c] [4Q114] (10:5–9, 11–16, 21; 1:1–2, 13–17, 25–29); *4QDaniel*[d] [4Q115] (3:8–10?, 23–25; 4:5–9, 12–16; 7:15–23); *4QDaniel*[e] [4Q116] (9:12–17); *pap6QDaniel* [6Q7] (8:16–17?, 20–21(?), 10:8–16; 11:33–36, 38). Additionally, *4QFlorilegium* [4Q174] contains a citation of Dan 11:32 and 12:10.

64. This designation simply means this is one of the fragments ([a]) of Daniel found in the first cave (1) at Qumran (Q). An alternative designation for these texts is listed in accompanying brackets. Abegg, Flint, and Ulrich translate Dan 2:4 from this fragment: "Then [the Chaldeans] said [to the king in Aramaic], "O king, li[ve] forever! [Tell your servants the dream], and we will reveal its meaning" (Abegg et al., *Dead Sea Scrolls*

BCE–50 CE) show, the bilingual text goes back at least to the first or second century BCE.

The Additions have been preserved in the LXX Greek text, but it is not clear whether their original language was Greek, or more likely, Hebrew or Aramaic. The LXX translation was probably begun in Alexandria at the beginning of the third century BCE, but not completed until at least the second century CE.[65] This translation, however, was replaced in Christian circles by a new Greek translation of Theodotion, completed near the end of the second century CE.[66] These two Greek translations differ in details, particularly in Dan 4–6, leading to the suspicion that behind them may lie two distinct editions of Daniel.[67] The Additions are preserved in the LXX and Theodotion. Here our focus is on Dan 1–12 in the MT text, with occasional references to the LXX and Theodotion. In the Additions, the translation will be from Theodotion.

It is worth lingering a moment to admire the literary architecture of Daniel. The opening and conclusion of the book—in Hebrew (Dan 1:1—2:4a and 8—12)—frame an Aramaic portion (2:4b—7:28). In the Aramaic section, the book uses a concentric arrangement.[68] Chapters 2 and 7 form the outer extremities, each presenting the four kingdoms. The narratives in chapters 3 and 6 demonstrate God's power to deliver, while the middle chapters 4–5 pronounce divine judgment on haughty rulers. The six stories contain six instances of human opposition to God. God always triumphs in the stories, while the characters either recognize and celebrate the divine or are humiliated by failure to acknowledge God. There are parallels between the four empires represented by the various metals in the great metallic statue in Dan 2 and the four beastly empires in Dan 7–8. Daniel

---

Bible, 486). The fragments *4QDaniel*[a-b] [4Q112–113] attest the shift from Aramaic to Hebrew at 8:1.

65. The development of the LXX translation is more complicated than this statement implies. Text critics, those who study the textual development of the Bible, think the LXX was based on earlier Greek translations collectively known as the Old Greek (OG). The critical LXX text used in this commentary is the *Septuaginta*, ed. Alfred Rahlfs, which contains both the LXX and Theodotion versions of Daniel.

66. Of this, Jerome (c. 342–420 CE) writes: "The Septuagint [LXX] version of Daniel the prophet is not read by the Churches of our Lord and Saviour. They use Theodotion's version, but how this came to pass I cannot tell" (Jerome, *Principal Works*, 492). Some scholars question whether this recension (translation) was done by Theodotion, a proselyte from Asia Minor. Theodotion's translation may well be, at least in part, a revision of an earlier one. Theodotion will serve as the basis of our translation and interpretation of the Additions in the Greek text in this commentary. See Würthwein, *Text of the Old Testament*, 108–9.

67. For a discussion of these differences, see Tov, *Textual Criticism*, 318–19.

68. This follows Lenglet, "Structure Littéraire," 169–90.

7–12 takes lessons illustrated by the stories and projects them onto an international stage. "The book of Daniel is a sophisticated literary unit," James Sims attests, "bound together in a final shape that is aesthetically satisfying, thematically clear, and yet, finally, open-ended and mysterious."[69]

DANIEL'S PLACE IN THE BIBLICAL CANON

Unlike some other books in the Writings, the third division of the HB,[70] namely, Ecclesiastes, Esther, and Song of Solomon, there apparently was never any dispute over whether Daniel should be included in the biblical canon. It is well represented among the Dead Sea Scrolls, where it seems to have been held in high esteem. A citation is included in a list of passages from the Hebrew prophets found at the Dead Sea, indicating it was then considered a part of the canonical literature.[71]

Within the HB, however, Daniel is found, not in the Prophets (*Neviim*) but surprisingly in the *Ketuvim* or the Writings, the third division of the HB, where it comes after Esther and before Ezra-Nehemiah. Placement in the Writings, which contains an assortment of poetry, narrative, wisdom, and history, rather than in the Prophets, seems somewhat odd, since Daniel is so obviously portrayed as a seer or prophet of great ability, although he is never specifically called a prophet (נָבִיא, *nabi*).[72] This classification suggests

69. Sims, "Daniel," 330. Sims offers an analysis of the literary unity of Daniel (330–34).

70. The HB consists of three major divisions: (1) Torah [the Pentateuch]; (2) Prophets [Joshua—2 Kings, Isaiah—Malachi]; (3) Writings [Psalms, Proverbs, Job, Song of Solomon, Ruth, Lamentations, Ecclesiastes, Esther, *Daniel*, Ezra-Nehemiah, 1–2 Chronicles]. While the Torah was probably complete by the fifth century BCE and the Prophets by the beginning of the second, the Writings may not have been finalized until the late first century CE. Ben Sira's grandson, writing c. 132 BCE, mentions the Law, the Prophets, and the incomplete rest of the books—the rudiments of the threefold canonical divisions (prologue to Sirach). Jesus refers to this threefold arrangement in Luke 24:44.

71. This list is known as 4Q174Flor(ilegium). See Beckwith, *Old Testament Canon*, 78.

72. See Dan 1:17. This objection may press matters too literally. Daniel obviously exhibits experiences usually credited to the Prophets (Matt 24:15). Wood claims Daniel was originally considered among the Prophets. In the Talmud, b. B. Bat. 15a includes it among the Prophets. So do Josephus and Melito, bishop of Sardis (CE 170). Origen (c. CE 254) lists Daniel before Ezekiel and the twelve minor prophets. Daniel was not included among the Prophets in the Hebrew canon, Wood thinks, because he served in a foreign court and did not prophesy directly to Israel (Wood, *Commentary on Daniel*, 15–16n11). Archer insists the final placement among the Writings took place under the Masoretes, the Jewish scribes entrusted with the preservation of the HB, during the period 500–900 CE. Before that, he argues, Daniel was included with the prophetic writings (Archer, "Daniel," 7–8). Nevertheless, the Jewish scribes finally rejected Daniel's place among the Prophets: "They [Haggai, Zechariah, and Malachi] are prophets,

Daniel was completed after the prophetic section was closed to additional entries (c. 200 BCE),[73] or the mixed narrative and apocalyptic genres of Daniel—stylistically distinct from Hebrew prophecy—was deemed out of place among the prophetic books. Moreover, the book begins with stories about the diaspora (the Babylonian exile) like Esther, which immediately precedes it. It may have been for this reason that the book was placed among the Writings following Esther.[74]

Modern English Christian translations—indeed most other modern language translations—place Daniel immediately after Ezekiel and before Hosea, thus making it in effect the last of the Major Prophets. This arrangement goes back at least to the LXX and the Latin Vulgate. The LXX and the Vulgate also offer versions of Daniel, including the Additions, that are considerably longer than the text in the HB. To the Greek text of Dan 3, as mentioned earlier, there was added the Prayer of Azariah (3:24-45) and the Hymn of the Three Young Men (3:46-90). In varying places in different manuscripts, but usually added to the end of Daniel, are three additional tales, the story of Susanna (13:1-64), Bel (14:1-22), and the Dragon, revered by the Babylonians (14:23-42).

We naturally wonder about the source of these Additions. Why were they added to the text of Daniel? Do they represent an even larger cycle of stories about Daniel? Are the Additions evidence of this? It would seem so. At the Dead Sea, among the many ancient scrolls and fragments found, archaeologists have recovered the Prayer of Nabonidus (4QPrNab[ar]), which may be a variant version of the story of the mad king now appearing in Dan 4 (see the commentary on Dan 4). So far, however, no Hebrew or Aramaic manuscript containing the Additions is known. Seven of the Daniel scrolls found at the Dead Sea, as we have seen, indicate by the time of Qumran (c. 125 BCE-50 CE), Daniel contained only the Hebrew and Aramaic text of Daniel, without the Additions.[75]

---

while he [Daniel] is not a prophet" (b. Sanh. 93b-94a).

73. This would explain why even though he knows of both the Torah and prophetic sections of the canon, ben Sira (c. 190 BCE) omits Daniel from his eulogy of Israel's heroes of faith, although he includes many of the prophets (Sir 44-50).

74. Its placement among the Writings, Goldingay suggests, would have indicated a "more pedagogical reading of the book" than a purely apocalyptic or prophetic reading (Goldingay, *Daniel*, xxx).

75 Abegg et al., *Dead Sea Scrolls Bible*, 482-83. Although some scholars suggest the Additions may have been present in the Hebrew and Aramaic *Vorlage* (original source document) of Daniel used by the LXX and Theodotion Greek translators, it is more likely the translators of the LXX themselves were responsible for inserting the Additions into the book.

DANIEL AS AN APOCALYPSE

One of the advances in biblical scholarship in the past century or so has been the reading of biblical texts in the light of distinctive ancient literary genres. A genre is a type or style of literature, for example, poems, narratives, prayers, novels, etc. In our culture, because we intuitively recognize common genres, we seldom give the genre of what we read a second thought. We know a novel, for instance, is a work of fiction; we do not read it as literally true in every detail. A newspaper article is one thing, an opinion editorial (op ed) another. A personal letter differs greatly from an encyclopedia article, and so on. There are oral genres, too, not just literary ones, especially in a primarily oral culture such as the biblical world. Over the past two hundred years, archaeologists have unearthed hundreds of written texts from the ancient world, written in genres once common in antiquity.[76] One of the genres emerging from the study of the ancient world is known as an apocalypse.

The book of Daniel belongs to this category. It is, in fact, the only full-blown apocalypse in the HB. It may well be the first Jewish apocalyptic text. Strictly speaking, however, only chapters 7–12 are apocalyptic; chapters 1–6 are narratives.

The book of Revelation supplies the term apocalypse or apocalyptic. Early Christians entitled this book: Ἀποκάλυψις Ἰησοῦ Χριστοῦ, *Apokalupsis Iesou Christou*, the Apocalypse of Jesus Christ (Rev 1:1). The word apocalyptic, drawn from the Greek ἀποκάλυψις (*apokalypsis*) means revelation, unveiling, or disclosure. The book of Revelation, containing many allusions to Daniel and other apocalyptic writings, may be regarded as the prime example of an apocalypse.[77]

Modern scholars have rediscovered a whole cluster of ancient Jewish and Christian apocalypses, mostly produced between c. 200 BCE and 100 CE. These include writings comparable to Daniel and Revelation, such as 1 Enoch, 2 Enoch, 2 Esdras, 2 Baruch, 3 Baruch, the Apocalypse of Zechariah, the Testament of Abraham, and the Apocalypse of Abraham.[78] An additional collection of even more ancient texts from Mesopotamia, Egypt, Persia,

---

76. See the annotated inventory of these in Sparks, *Ancient Texts*.

77. One of the leading scholars of apocalyptic, Paul Hanson, considers Revelation the benchmark—the model—of the apocalyptic genre. His approach, while acknowledging the wide diversity in this literature, is "to sketch the typical features of the work originally designated 'apocalypse' in antiquity, the book of Revelation, and then to consider which other compositions of the same era show sufficient similarity to justify extension of the term to them as well" (Hanson, "Apocalypse, Genre," 27).

78. The texts mentioned here may all be found with analysis in Charlesworth, *OTP*, 1:3–770.

and Greece, some of them precursors to apocalyptic, also shed important light on the Jewish apocalypses.[79] This important cache of ancient literature has greatly aided our understanding, not only of Daniel, but of various other apocalyptic writings.

Scholars now identify two basic types of apocalypses. The first, represented by 1 Enoch 1–36, 2 Enoch, and 3 Baruch present heavenly journeys, where the writer ascends through heavenly realms and happens upon all kinds of wonderful, other-worldly sights. Other apocalypses, like Daniel, where the emphasis is on history and its termination, are called historical apocalypses.

Apocalyptic is an unusually difficult genre. Within an apocalypse often occur many other sub-genres: visions, prayers, narratives, hymns, etc. Apocalyptic may be compared to a vacuum cleaner: it picks up imagery, symbols, and literary expressions from here, there, and everywhere and combines them into a variegated, complex mixture. We see this already in Daniel. While the overall genre of the book is an apocalypse, it contains a series of court tales (chs. 1–6), one of which has an apocalyptic dream within it (ch. 2), followed by a series of labyrinthine apocalyptic visions (chs. 7–12). One of these apocalyptic visions contains a long prayer of confession (Dan 9:3–19) instead of a vision. The Greek version of Daniel also inserts a prayer and a hymn (ch. 3), plus two additional stories of Daniel's exploits (chs. 13–14). So, while Daniel is clearly an apocalypse, it is an extraordinarily complex one.

What then distinguishes apocalyptic? We need some idea of the characteristics of apocalyptic—how it functions and communicates—before we attempt to read Daniel.

Drawing from an analysis of all ancient apocalyptic texts, the Society of Biblical Literature Genres Project proposes the following definition of the apocalyptic genre:

> An apocalypse is a genre of revelatory literature with a narrative framework, in which a revelation is mediated by an otherworldly being to a human recipient, disclosing a transcendent reality which is both temporal, in so far as it envisages eschatological salvation, and spatial insofar as it involves another, supernatural world.[80]

---

79. Sparks, *Ancient Texts*, 240–51.

80. *Semeia* 14 (1979) 9, as cited in Sparks, *Ancient Texts*, 240. According to John Gammie, apocalyptic literature may be identified when it contains (1) some form of revelation, whether of future events or the heavenly realm; (2) a cluster of sub-genres or component genres; and (3) a cluster of ideational elements common to works already agreed to belong to the apocalyptic literature (Gammie, "Classification," 192–93).

Characteristic of apocalyptic, then, is a clear-cut distinction (known as dualism) between the present world and the world to come. There is often an exact reckoning of time, couched in comprehensive, fantastic visions, replete with animal and mythic imagery, displaying a universal cosmic history leading to the time of the end. Written in cryptic coded language, in other words, comes a vivid depiction of angels and the otherworldly life to come. These writings, as we have seen, are also usually pseudonymous.[81]

Most apocalyptists believe they are living in the final epoch of human history. The end of all things is almost upon them. Apocalyptic arises in and speaks to societal existential crises. That is why apocalyptic literature enjoys unusual popularity among the religious in times of existential despair.[82] Historical events have plunged the people of God into abject despair. Things seem hopeless. Society has been almost completely given over to evil. Yet, the Eternal stands poised, ready to break in upon the world. The end of days has come. "In the days of these kings," Daniel envisions, "the God of heaven will set up a kingdom that will be forever . . . . It will shatter and put an end to all these kingdoms, and it will stand forever" (Dan 2:44). Deliverance comes not from human sources but catastrophically and ultimately through divine intervention. Judgment is meted out for all, righteous and wicked alike. The wicked are condemned to destruction, the righteous granted everlasting life (12:1–3).

Since this impending kingdom is supranatural—it comes from the transcendent realm—only supranatural, mythic language is capable of expressing it. The rise and fall of nations in Daniel are thus depicted in the form of grotesque beasts, the last sprouting a little horn, uttering blasphemy (Dan 7:25). In apocalyptic, there is a turning from the proximate historical situation, now considered hopeless and given over to the grip of evil, to a new heavenly order not of this world but soon to break in upon it.

In its symbolism, apocalyptic writing may be compared to cartooning, especially political cartooning. In political cartoon art, anthropized animal imagery is often used to caricature political leaders and nations. Some physical feature of a political leader, such as Jimmy Carter's teeth, Barack

---

81. Walter Baumgartner, "Ein Vierteljahrhundert Danielforschung," 136, cited in von Rad, *Old Testament Theology*, 2:302n2.

82. There no doubt existed religious communities, characterized by an apocalyptic vision, who may have inspired the writing and study of such apocalyptic documents. We know little about such ancient apocalyptic communities, however, and must infer their existence from the writings left behind. It is uncertain whether the book of Daniel stems from such a community. Throughout history, however, there have been religious communities emphasizing apocalypticism and drawing their primary inspiration from the biblical apocalypses. Modern examples of such religious communities are the Jehovah's Witnesses and the Seventh-Day Adventists.

Obama's ears, or Donald Trump's hair, is exaggerated as an iconic symbol for that leader. Once while teaching a college class in apocalyptic literature, I introduced a political cartoon from a major news magazine depicting a presidential primary. A large elephant faced off against a smaller, angry-looking donkey with bared teeth and glowering red eyes. Astride the elephant and donkey were several unspecified riders, each with exaggerated physical features, allowing the reader to identify the riders as the various presidential candidates. Because the class was familiar with the contemporary political scene, they could readily understand the symbols. The Democrats (symbolized by the donkey) and the Republicans (the elephant) each had several candidates vying for the American presidency.

Political cartooning, like apocalyptic, is coded language. The meaning of the apocalyptic text is encoded in the symbols. For this same class, I introduced another political cartoon from an American presidential election of the 1840s. I asked what the cartoon depicted. No one—not even the history majors in the class—could clearly identify the symbols. They came from a social and political setting long since forgotten. The cartoon's coded symbols were lost on the class.

Readers of ancient apocalyptic, contemporaries of the original writers and familiar with the social, political, and religious events of the day, would probably have been able to identify most, if not all, the entities symbolized in the text. They would have been able to decode them. With the passage of time, however, this once vivid awareness tended to fade and recede into the past. Once the code was largely forgotten, later readers tended to reinterpret the imagery and apply it to persons or events in their own era, often far removed from the original setting. Apocalyptic is thus left open to multiple readings and reinterpretation. Already, by the first century CE, we have an example: the haughty king who considers himself "greater than any god" (Dan 11:36) originally referred to Antiochus IV, who desecrated the temple by the installation of an idol, the Olympian Zeus. The NT reapplies this to a mysterious first-century figure who "opposes and exalts himself above every god or object of worship, so that he takes his seat in the temple of God, declaring himself to be God" (2 Thess 2:4). Some think this NT reference is to the Roman emperor Caligula (37–41 CE), who attempted to install an image of himself in the Jerusalem temple.[83]

While this commentary focuses primarily on reading Daniel in its original social and historical setting, we will not entirely ignore this tendency for diverse reinterpretation. It is important for a full understanding of the

---

83. A. Smith, "Second Thessalonians," 759. Smith alludes to but does not advocate this view.

book to consider how Daniel has been received and understood throughout history. This is the design of a recent commentary by Carol Newsom and Brennan Breed.[84] Maintaining a dual focus—Daniel as originally understood and Daniel as reinterpreted during history—Newsom and Breed have given us a full, balanced treatment of Daniel. Since almost all reinterpretation of Daniel is ultimately based on the original significance of its text, this commentary will concentrate primarily on the original stage, the interpretation of the final form of Daniel as we have it.[85] In our study, we also include the Additions, which are regarded as canonical by Catholic and Orthodox Christianity. As nearly as possible, then, we will try to read Daniel much as its original readers would have read and understood it.

In its present form, the stories (chs. 1–6) provide the narrative frame into which the Daniel apocalypse (chs. 7–12) has been fitted. But the stories are more than a narrative frame. They are court tales with a moralistic and theological emphasis, intended to encourage a life of faithfulness, resistance, and trust for those living through difficult times.[86] They introduce Daniel, the central character, whose visionary perception and fidelity inspires and whose reception of heavenly visions unveils the work of God among the nations. The stories challenge pagan idolatry while they speak of a God sovereign over heaven and earth. God will deliver the faithful triumphant in the end.[87]

Considered as a whole, then, Daniel is an apocalyptic text. Since it concerns the march of history, it may be considered a historical apocalypse, in that it contains both historical and cosmic eschatology.[88] It is an apocalypse nestled in a narrative frame consisting of six court stories plus several additions.

---

84. Newsom, *Daniel*. Given that in its literary development Daniel may have passed through several editions and interpretations, reinterpretation may have already been happening. Breed indicates, "It is quite likely that these various groups who together wrote and rewrote the book of Daniel . . . did not understand the text in exactly the same way" (Newsom, *Daniel*, 29).

85. For scholars, identifying this final form of any book in the HB has proven elusive. By the first century CE, there were extant perhaps as many as five different text types of the HB. The MT eventually prevailed over all the other text types and became the standard edition of the HB. It is this text type (MT) that is taken here as theoretically representing the final form or present form as we have it.

86. J. Collins, *Daniel* (Hermeneia), 33, 38.

87. Goldingay, *Daniel*, 320–21.

88. This leads Sims to posit a dual genre: "On balance, the best generic classification of the book is apocalyptic prophecy" (Sims, "Daniel," 326).

INTERPRETING DANIEL

Given the challenges so evident in apocalyptic, we agree with Di Lella: "The Book of Daniel is one of the most fascinating portions of the Bible, and *one of the most difficult* as well."[89] The book of Daniel has been a perennial enigma to all interpreters. Perhaps no other book of the Bible (other than Revelation) has been more abused by well-intentioned interpreters and applied to more different historical situations than Daniel.[90] "People wreak all kinds of havoc in the interpretation of the books of Daniel and Revelation," warns Michael Gorman, "when they do not realize that these writings are *apocalyptic* writings that freely use lavish symbolism and need to be read more like poetry, or even a series of political cartoons, than historical narrative or video footage of the future."[91] Bizarre imagery, savage beasts with heads of lions, human bodily parts, sprouting horns that speak blasphemy from atop animal heads, the skies opening and celestial beings descending from above, obscure time calculations, writings secreted until the end of all things, have led readers to come up with fantastic interpretations ranging from the sublime to the ridiculous. How are we to understand Daniel? How are we to read this strange, mysterious book? What principles are there to guide us?

The apocalyptic visions in Dan 7–12 obviously pose most of the problems; hence we will focus on them here. While the narratives (Dan 1–6, 13, 14) present challenges of their own, we will leave the interpretation of the court tales and the Additions to the commentary.

To start, it is advantageous to get in mind some of the ways, broadly speaking, the book has been interpreted. The terminology I use here for these interpretive trends is a bit outdated, but still offers a convenient way of distinguishing the different approaches.

Interpreters have tried at least four main approaches. One school of thought—known as *futurism*—finds in the apocalyptic of Daniel (chs. 7–12) and most of Revelation (chs. 4–22) a forecast or prediction of the distant future. The popular success of the *Left Behind* series,[92] with its vision of

---

89. Hartman and Di Lella, *Daniel*, vi; italics added. "Opinions are divided on almost every issue" in the book, notes Baldwin (Baldwin, *Daniel*, 17).

90. It is "even more necessary than with other books of the Bible," Soggin warns, "to be particularly careful in reading it and to avoid making the text say things it cannot say" (Soggin, *Introduction to Old Testament*, 478).

91. Gorman, *Elements of Biblical Exegesis*, 86; italics in original.

92. The *Left Behind* series consists of sixteen books, written by Jerry Jenkins and Tim LaHaye in the late 1990s and early 2000s, published by Tyndale House. In novelistic style, this series sets forth the futurist vision of the end times. The series inspired several Hollywood movies.

a world torn apart by the harsh, oppressive rule of the antichrist, dramatizes how prevalent futurism is today as an interpretive approach. In futurism, for instance, the little horn symbol in Dan 7:8, 20, 25 becomes the last-day antichrist who dominates the world at the end of human history (the future in futurism). The seventieth week of Dan 9:24–27 is extricated and transposed to the end of history, the great tribulation when the antichrist is to dominate the world.[93] Futurism is the accepted method of interpreting Daniel and Revelation in dispensationalist theology.[94] This way of reading apocalyptic is certainly alive and well, but it dubiously wrenches many predictions in Daniel from their original contexts and assigns them to events far removed from the original writer. In effect, the futurist interpretation renders these texts irrelevant, or at least completely obscure, to their original audience.[95]

A second approach, known as *historicism*, popular in the eighteenth and nineteenth centuries, has roots stretching back at least to Jerome (c. 342–420 CE). Historicism posits a gradual, continuous unfolding or historical fulfillment of the prophecies of Daniel during Middle Eastern and Western history, rather than fulfillments mainly clustered at the end of time as in futurism. According to Leroy Froom, historicism sets forth "the progressive and continuous fulfillment of prophecy in unbroken sequence from Daniel's day and the time of John [Revelation], on down to the second advent and the end of the age."[96] Thus, for historicists, Daniel predicts the rise and fall of the great empires of antiquity—Babylon, Persia, Greece, Rome—the breakup of Rome, the rise of the Roman Catholic Church, and final events leading to the great judgment and second advent of Jesus. There is in Daniel (and Revelation) a gradual unfolding of predicted historical events from the time of Daniel to the end of the world. To many, this approach appears to make a great deal of sense. It accepts Daniel as genuine prophecy. It measures Daniel's visions against the actual march of recorded history.[97]

The problem with historicism, however, is twofold. Upon the sketchiest of information found in the text, historicists readily identify the symbols in Daniel with highly specific historical empires and political entities.

---

93. Ice, "Seventy Weeks of Daniel," 337–42.

94. Dispensational theology sees history divided into various dispensations or stages, each with its own divine revelation and method of salvation and human accountability. Scripture is taken to reveal three to seven dispensations, depending on the interpreter. Walvoord's exegesis and interpretation of Daniel is a contemporary example of the futurist approach (Walvoord, *Daniel*, 25–27).

95. See Grabbe, "Fundamentalism and Scholarship," 133–52.

96. Froom, *Prophetic Faith*, 1:22–23.

97. The *Adventist Bible Commentary* (4:818–81) offers a historicist interpretation of Dan 7–12 (Nichol, *Seventh-Day Adventist Bible Commentary*).

Secondly, these identifications are often made with the interpreter's own era, whether the nineteenth, twentieth, or twenty-first centuries. For this reason alone, such subjective, intuitive application is suspicious. The interpreter using the historicist approach tends often to find the fulfillment of an apocalyptic vision in her or his own present or proximate future, centuries removed from the historical horizon of Daniel. A historicist reads Daniel with the Bible in one hand and the newspaper in the other, to paraphrase Karl Barth, constantly looking to contemporary events for some fulfillment of an apocalyptic prediction. There is often a basic ignoring of the original literary and historical situation of Daniel.

On the opposite side of the spectrum from futurism and historicism lies an approach known as *preterism* (from Latin *praeter*, beyond or in the past). Preterism takes seriously the historical past circumstances under which Daniel was written. Daniel's apocalyptic visions, in other words, have primarily to do with a second century BCE Palestinian setting, not some far-off future events in the twentieth or twenty-first centuries, as in futurism, nor in the gradual unfolding of history extending through ancient, medieval, and modern times far beyond the times of Daniel, as in historicism.[98] Apocalyptic is a literary style whose primary concern was to the era in which it was written. Preterism, however, is usually criticized for its indebtedness to Porphyry's skeptical idea that predictive prophecy is simply impossible. It seems to rule out that Daniel could make credible predictions about future events.

Briefly, let me mention a fourth approach. This approach, generally known as *idealism*, takes the obscure literary images in the text as almost entirely symbolic.[99] They are allegorical or metaphorical and thus atemporal. The images are more like modern science fiction than history or prophecy. They merely speak metaphorically and offer spiritual encouragement and existential hope against the evil encountered in life. This approach, in effect, reads apocalyptic texts more as poetry than as prose.

These hermeneutical modes—historicism, futurism, idealism, preterism—are all well-intentioned methods of reading Daniel. None of them, however, is without difficulties. The interpretation of Daniel has always been enigmatic and, in extreme cases, excessive, fanatical, and even downright embarrassing. "No other genre of the Bible has been so fervently read with such depressing results as apocalyptic," emphasizes Randolph Tate.[100]

---

98. A representative of the preterist view is Chilton, *Paradise Restored*.

99. "The book of Revelation [as well as Daniel for Judaism] is not merely futurology but also a redemptive-historical and theological psychology for the church's thinking" (Beale, *Book of Revelation*, 177).

100. Tate, *Biblical Interpretation*, 173. See Pate, *Interpreting Revelation*.

Biblical scholars have gradually learned the best way to understand a biblical book is through careful attention to the historical and social situation out of which it arose. They have learned to read a biblical book for what it is, not what they think or suppose it should be. This principle is the legacy of the historical-critical method. Every human composition is related to a specific historical and literary situation, to its setting in life. Every writing—ancient or modern—is inextricably connected to its life setting. Biblical books, despite their religious perspective, are no different.

We refer to this as the context of a writing. Context has many permutations. There is the historical context, its place in time and amid the events in history. Its social context comprises the human community and authors who gave rise to it. Then there are theological and philosophical contexts that call attention to the currents of thought in which the author was a participant. Literary contexts have to do with the literary form of the writing (genre) and its place within them. Reader contexts address how a text is interpreted from specific social locations.

Due to the vagaries in apocalyptic imagery, some of which are probably intentional—it is, after all, coded literature—even the most careful interpretation leaves many unanswered questions. No matter how closely we read the texts in the light of their socio-historical and literary contexts, we are still left with mixed results. These ambiguities leave Daniel open to a variety of interpretations, not only about the primary significance, but also about future implications.

Apocalyptic readily lends itself to these multiple interpretations. Revelation takes the imagery of the four kingdoms in Dan 7 and applies it to the Roman emperor. Thus, the beast rising out of the sea has the characteristics of a leopard, bear, and lion, with ten horns and seven heads, upon which were blasphemous names. This beast speaks "haughty and blasphemous words" against God (Rev 13:1–6).[101] The symbolism of the four kingdoms in Daniel is now blended and applied to the Roman rule, contemporary with the writer of Revelation.[102]

In such reinterpretation, the NT writers found an approach for dealing with the problem of how the HB can be integrated into the gospel and into the writings of the early Christian community (NT). It offered a way to handle the continuity and discontinuity between the OT and NT. In turn, since reinterpretation is found throughout Scripture, it suggests the canonical text—including Daniel—may be open to fresh interpretation in new

---

101. For these same images, see Dan 7:2–8, 19–25; 8:9–14.

102. "The imagery suggests the Roman Empire," notes Eugene Boring, "especially Emperor Nero, who had killed himself but was widely believed to still be alive" (Boring, "Revelation of St. John," 2230).

circumstances. The scriptural writings show an "ever-renewed reflexion upon the meaning of historical events, reflexion which of course always appears only in the guise of *ad hoc* interpretations." These represent a "'boundless quest' for the meaning of her history."[103]

All of this raises the question whether these later reapplications, even within Scripture, are to be regarded as fulfillments of Daniel or simply as reinterpretations, that is, reimaging of the original symbolism in response to a new social and historical context.[104] The lines between fulfilment and reinterpretation too often seem to blur, even in the biblical text.[105]

We will not pretend here to resolve all the enigmas of Daniel or any other apocalypse. However, we try to approach the book with an awareness of its literary, social, and historical context, insofar as this can be determined, and with appreciation for the apocalyptic and narrative nature of its style.

This approach involves taking the book for what it is: a pseudonymous apocalypse that integrates historical events into several apocalyptic visions. The sweep of the history of ancient nations, all interacting with Israel in some fashion, is written imaginatively in an apocalyptic mode. Apocalypses "contain prophecy of the future in the form of 'revelations,' 'visions,' and 'appearances' filled with enigmatic figures of speech, which are actually a review of what is past, but purport to be *a look into the future*, a glimpse of things to come."[106] Pseudonymity, we have noted, was a conventional, ancient literary technique used when writing an apocalypse (or other writing). Almost all Jewish and Christian apocalypses—some dated shortly after Daniel or later—are written in this style.[107] In order to read Daniel in its own literary context, then, we should not allow preconceived notions of

---

103. von Rad, *Old Testament Theology*, 1:117.

104. Desmond Ford calls this the "apotelesmatic principle," the multiple fulfillments of apocalyptic prophecy (Ford, *Daniel*, 49). These double or threefold fulfillments are not fulfillments, that is, intentional predictions of the original author, however, but reinterpretations of the original symbols for a new context. They are not necessarily inherent in the original texts.

105. Note J. Barton Payne: "The purposes of apostolic citations of the OT may range from that of affirming the fulfilment of detailed prophecies down to mere allusions about similar happenings or to the reuse of familiar phrases" (Payne, *Encyclopedia of Prophecy*, 76). Particularly with Daniel, the notion of plenary (fuller) interpretation is often invoked. The primary passage has been infused with a fuller sense than is obvious in a plain reading of it. This fuller sense may be detected by later readers.

106. Klausner, *Messianic Idea in Israel*, 227–28; italics in original.

107. The book of Revelation seems to be about the only exception. It is attributed to "his [Christ's] servant John," who traditionally has been identified with the author of the Gospel and the Johannine Epistles (1–3 John). This may not be the case, however. The John mentioned in 1:1 may be a pseudonymous attribution to a person already well-known in early Christianity.

the nature of biblical writings to cause us to misread the apocalyptic genre. We remind our conservative readers, in the words of John Goldingay, that because "pseudonymity is a rarer literary device in our culture, especially in religious contexts, [that] should not allow us to infer that God could not use it in another culture."[108]

We should aim at understanding as much of the meaning as possible, without insisting on understanding everything. Moving beyond the details in the text to the overall meaning of a passage greatly assists. What is the text about as a whole? What does it say about the nations and monarchs and the victims of their rapacity? The symbols and numbers we take seriously but not literally. Numbers are often used in apocalyptic as symbols, not as precise delineations of chronology. Other symbols, such as animals of one hideous kind or another, are often meant to communicate sentiments of horror, rage, or even passionate relief. The emotional connotation of such symbols conveys human helplessness and intensifies the yearning for divine deliverance. The symbols themselves are drawn graphically from ancient artistic and mythic imagery. Finally, we should compare the apocalyptic discourse in Daniel with the New Testament, other biblical passages, and additional, extra-biblical apocalypses. Such comparison sheds much light on Daniel.

This commentary aims to interpret Daniel in the light of these principles. If we want to know what Daniel signifies for us, we must first seek what its author sought to convey to the original audience(s). Rather than see the book as primarily speaking to generations far removed from its own time, we should read the book of Daniel against the backdrop of its original contexts, then from these discover its broader resonance for future generations. The original historical context is the fundamental basis upon which all other interpretation rests. "The exegete's first responsibility," F. F. Bruce puts it, "is to establish the primary historical reference of the author and his original readers, and then to decide how far visions or oracles whose primary sense is thus ascertained can be related, by implication or in principle, to later situations."[109]

---

108. Goldingay, *Daniel*, xi.

109. Bruce, *Canon of Scripture*, 320. "Whereas the Chronicler's outlook is altogether retrospective, and the compiler of Ezra-Nehemiah records contemporaneous events, the author of Daniel professes to be concerned with 'prospective' history. It is presumably this visionary perspective that made the motifs, imagery, and episodes of Daniel a source of inspiration to writers and artists of much later generations. The apocalyptic utopian—that is, nonhistorical—character of the visions facilitates their use as prototypes. By applying, in essence, the same technique so well known from the Qumran pesher writings, the ad hoc interpretation of prophetic pronouncements which the author of Daniel had himself practiced, later readers could discern their own situation prefigured in the ancient tales and visions of Daniel" (Talmon, "Daniel," 355).

With these hermeneutical principles in mind, let us now turn to the original cultural and historical context of Daniel.

THE CULTURAL AND HISTORICAL SETTING OF DANIEL

If the final writing and redaction of Daniel took place in Palestine in the middle of the second century (168-164 BCE), it is to this era we are to look for Daniel's historical and cultural setting.[110]

The story of this era really begins when Nebuchadnezzar II (605-562), famed ruler of Babylon and a main character in Daniel, deported Daniel and his colleagues from Jerusalem to Babylon (Dan 1:1-2).[111] In 587, after a period of resistance, the city of Jerusalem along with the Judean nation, of which it was the capital, finally succumbed to Nebuchadnezzar and was destroyed. Deportation then took place and again in a second raid in 582.[112] There in the environs of Babylon, the ill-fated Hebrew exiles found a home until after c. 538—following the fall of Babylon—when the Achaemenid king Cyrus II (c. 550-531) as a part of his policy of political amnesty toward refugees in his realm permitted them to return to their homeland (see Ezra 1:1-4). Slowly but surely over the next century, many Judeans did return from Mesopotamia under their Persian and later Hellenistic rulers, where they for the most part enjoyed religious freedom but limited political autonomy. The messianic hopes of a magnificent, renewed nation these returnees cherished unfortunately never materialized, setting up desperate social and religious conditions conducive for apocalyptic texts like Daniel.[113]

When the Hellenistic empire under Alexander the Great (356-323) fell apart following his untimely death, the Palestinian region, originally subdued by Alexander in 332, found itself caught precariously between two hostile, warring empires, the Ptolemies in Egypt, and the Seleucids in Syria. For the better part of two centuries, these two kingdoms vied for the control of Coele-Syria.[114] After a century under Ptolemaic rule (301-198), the Seleucid

---

110. There is space here only for a general portrayal of this period. For a fuller description, see Schäfer, "Hellenistic and Maccabean Periods," 576-96; Pfeiffer, *History of New Testament*, 5-24; Kaiser, *History of Israel*, 459-75.

111. This event is incorrectly dated in Daniel to the third year of Jehoiakim (606/5 BCE). See the commentary on Dan 1:1-2 for a discussion of this problem.

112. See 2 Kgs 24-25; Jer 52:12-20, 28-30.

113. Hanson, "Old Testament Apocalyptic Reexamined," 48-51.

114. Daniel 11:2-45 vividly depicts the conflict between the Ptolemies and the Seleucids.

armies led by Antiochus III the Great (223–187) finally defeated the Ptolemies at the battle of Paneion (198), near the site of Caesarea Philippi. Under Antiochus III, however, the Palestinian populace continued to enjoy certain privileges, including the right to live according to their ancestral law (Torah).

Antiochus III, who aspired to be a second Alexander the Great, however, had ambitions of greater territorial conquest. The Romans, a new, ambitious power from the west, destined to rule the entire Mediterranean world, however, stopped his aggressive quest at the battle of Magnesia (190), forcing Antiochus to redirect his ambitions in the opposite direction, toward Mesopotamia and the lands farther east. At Magnesia, he had to surrender his war elephants, his navy, and even his younger son Antiochus, who, after spending twelve years as a captive in Rome learning Roman ways, would assume the Seleucid throne as Antiochus IV.[115] Antiochus III was subsequently killed while unscrupulously plundering the temple of Bel in Susa (Persia) to shore up the empire's crumbling finances (see Dan 11:18–19). Succeeding the ineffective Seleucus IV Philopator (187–175), who reigned for a little more than a decade, Antiochus IV Epiphanes (175–164), the brother of Seleucus, ascended the Seleucid throne. This king becomes notorious in the apocalyptic visions of Daniel.

Meanwhile, Jerusalem was caught up in bitter internecine social and political strife. Political alliances divided between the pro-Ptolemaic and pro-Seleucid or Hellenistic parties. Hellenism—Greek cultural innovation—since the time of Alexander the Great had been popular with the upper classes in Jerusalem, who mainly identified politically and religiously with the Hellenists. They favored the adoption of Hellenistic culture and mores. Pottery remains, together with lamps, utensils, and jewelry, used by archaeologists to assess the culture of this period, show widespread adoption of Hellenistic fashion styles and culture in Palestine.[116] Siding with the Hellenistic party, Antiochus IV, himself a passionate advocate of Hellenization, approved the attempt to turn Jerusalem into a new city renamed Antiochia and to dispense with the Torah as the city's revered constitution. In the eyes of the Jews loyal to the Torah, many of whom were pro-Ptolemaic, this indiscriminate adoption of Hellenistic culture was morally and theologically reprehensible, as the writer of 1 Maccabees indicates. "In those days certain renegades came out from Israel and misled many, saying, 'Let us go and make a covenant with Gentiles around us'" (1 Macc 1:11–15).[117]

115. Kaiser, *History of Israel*, 464.

116. Wright, *Biblical Archaeology*, 213.

117. First and Second Maccabees, in the deuterocanonical writings (Apocrypha), are considered primary historical references for this period.

Accepting a bribe from Jason for the office of the high priesthood, Antiochus ousted Onias III, who had held the priestly office up until that time. Later, also through a bribe, he would in turn install Menelaus as high priest. The act of selling the high priesthood to the highest bidder, as we would expect, worsened the resistance already building among the Jewish leaders. Antiochus sent an army under Apollonius to Jerusalem to put down the uprising. Apollonius attacked the city on the Sabbath, and finding the Jews idle from work, "rushed into the city with his armed warriors and killed great numbers of people" (2 Macc 5:26). Antiochus ordered parts of the city's wall torn down, while he constructed the fortress of Akra, in which he installed a garrison of soldiers to keep order in the city. The Akra, like the flag of the victor, stood for at least two decades as a symbol of Seleucid power over the Jews.[118] For added measure, Antiochus placed onerous sanctions on the city aimed at compelling the adoption of Hellenism. The Jews were required to abandon their ancestral faith and adopt Hellenistic customs, such as the eating of pork.[119] First Maccabees describes the tension:

> The king wrote to his whole kingdom that all should be one people, and that all should give up their particular customs. All the Gentiles accepted the command of the king. Many even from Israel gladly adopted his religion; they sacrificed to idols and profaned the sabbath. And the king sent letters by messengers to Jerusalem and the towns of Judah; he directed them to follow customs strange to the land, to forbid burnt offerings and sacrifices and drink offerings in the sanctuary, to profane sabbaths and festivals, to defile the sanctuary and the priests, to build altars and sacred precincts and shrines for idols, to sacrifice swine and other unclean animals, and to leave their sons uncircumcised. They were to make themselves abominable by everything unclean and profane, so that they would forget the law and change all the ordinances. (1 Macc 1:41-49)

When Antiochus IV then violated the Jerusalem temple,[120] placing a small altar to the god Zeus on or near the altar of burnt offerings, armed resistance broke out in 167 near Modein, seventeen miles northwest of Jerusalem, with Judas Maccabeus leading the insurgency. Daniel calls this desecration of the temple the "abomination that makes desolate."[121] The story is

---

118. Cline, *Jerusalem Besieged*, 78-79.
119. 1 Macc 1:62-63; 2 Macc 6:18; Lev 11:7-8.
120. See 2 Macc 6:1-2; Dan 8:9-14; 11:29-31.
121. Dan 11:31; 9:27; 12:11. Maccabees understands this literally: "The temple was filled with debauchery and reveling by the Gentiles, who dallied with prostitutes and

vividly told in 1–2 Maccabees, written in this period (see 1 Macc 1:54–61). Judas's guerrilla fighters, angered by such repression and desecration, recaptured the temple a few years later. They purified and rededicated it in the winter of 164, and a royal amnesty was declared. The statue of the god Zeus they ground into dust and then erected a new altar to Yahweh.[122] The Maccabees subsequently fortified the area around the Temple Mount, but had to leave the Seleucids, garrisoned in the Akra, in control of the rest of the city. This arrangement would continue until Judea became an independent state in 142–141, twenty-five years after the rebellion had first begun.[123]

This Maccabean period, concerned with the Antiochene oppression, is the general era when the book of Daniel must have taken the form we now know.[124] Its apocalyptic visions are situated during the stormy period of Antiochus IV's vicious suppression of the Jews. This conflict forms the climax in Daniel's four apocalyptic visions (Dan 7–12). The visions then move beyond Antiochus, who died in 164, to the establishment of God's eternal kingdom, which was expected to take place shortly after Antiochus's death. The visions in Daniel should thus be read against the backdrop of the Antiochene crisis, and the book (without the Additions, which come later) dated a short time before the death of Antiochus IV and the rededication of the temple in December 164 BCE.

Less so the court tales, whose background is more diffuse. The tales appear to have originated during the Babylonian exile in the latter days of the Babylonian and Persian rule and were probably orally transmitted. In their present written form, they may come from the late fourth or early third century BCE.[125] Jennie Grillo perceptively suggests the writer(s) of these tales may have used the story of the Babylonian envoys coming to Hezekiah (Isa 39:1–7; 2 Kgs 20:12–18) as a literary model for a dramatic, fictional Babylonian court as the background for the narratives about Daniel and his companions. The opening scene in Daniel (Dan 1:1–7), with its reference to the confiscated vessels from the temple and the captive Israelites serving at the court, surely alludes to Isa 39. In the postexilic era, the period known as Second Temple Judaism, many Jewish writers borrowed earlier

---

had intercourse with women within the sacred precincts, and besides brought in things for sacrifice that were unfit" (2 Macc 6:4).

122. 1 Macc 4:36–59; 2 Macc 10:1–8; Kaiser, *History of Israel*, 472.

123. Cline, *Jerusalem Besieged*, 82–85.

124. See Gese, "Bedeutung der Krise," 373–88. For an alternative view, see Ferch, "Book of Daniel," 129–41.

125. Eissfeldt, *Old Testament*, 522. Collins suggests a late third century BCE diasporic composition (J. Collins, *Introduction to Hebrew Bible*, 574).

scriptural texts for use as a backdrop for depicting Israel's contemporary experiences.[126]

The court tales' value, at least in part, lies in their preservation of inspirational stories of Jewish exiles in service to and in conflict with foreign royalty and faced with the temptation to compromise or abandon their identity, in much the same way the Jewish people were called upon to do in the days of Antiochus IV Epiphanes. The Additions, which are similar, come from later but may have diasporic (exilic) origins as well.

THE MESSAGE OF DANIEL

The book of Daniel is about people living under foreign domination and oppression. Its faithful characters no longer have the luxury of political independence or the freedom of religious and cultural expression. They are being challenged to conform to the dominant religious culture. The book of Daniel encourages the Jewish people living in a hostile foreign environment. The stories (chs. 1–6), although they concern characters at the heart of the government, are about courage and faithfulness to God in an alien culture, in this case, the diaspora, or the scattering of the Jewish people among the gentile nations of the ancient Near East. In the apocalyptic section (chs. 7–12)—in apocalyptic symbolism—the theme of good versus evil in the oppression and persecution of God's people is played out on an international stage. Such an epic book contains many themes. Here we emphasize two important ones: the faithfulness of God and the corresponding faithfulness of God's people.

Human fidelity is the complement of God's faithfulness in preserving and delivering the Jewish people. God is faithful to those who are faithful. "Those who honor me I will honor" (1 Sam 2:30). In the stories, individuals stand resolute in their dedication to God, despite the royal threat of punishment and death (Dan 3:13–23). The kings in the narratives, whose tendency is to assume godlike qualities, are humbled and compelled to acknowledge the sovereignty of Israel's God (4:36–37). The stories provide models for dealing with similar threats from the dominant, oppressive powers in other times and places. The faithful may survive extreme tests, such as the blazing furnace and the lions' pit, by depending upon the help of the faithful God. The Additions, especially the Prayer of Azariah and the Song of the Three Young Men (3:24–90) and Bel and the Dragon (ch. 14) continue the narrative of how faithfulness triumphs over deadly fires and the slavish devotion to other gods. In Susanna (ch. 13), a wise Daniel liberates a Jewish woman

---

126. Grillo, "From a Far Country," 363–80.

from unjust accusation, leading the people to exclaim, God "saves those who hope in him" (v. 60).

The apocalyptic visions (chs. 7–12) react to hostile powers who have now become especially suppressive. In the visions, Israel is on the verge of being absorbed into the alien gentile world. The battle is joined between Israel and the empires of the day. There is spirited concern over the future of the nations with which Israel must interact. The sovereign God, who determines the fate of the nations and of God's people, is poised, ready to intervene in the fray. This intervention will not come from human resources but is more like a stone "cut from the mountain not by hands" that smashes earthly empires (Dan 2:45 NRSV). It is the vivid hope of divine intervention to bring about a redemptive, just conclusion to the chaos of history. "God is faithful to his people and . . . his purposes will triumph."[127] The ruling powers of earth will decisively acknowledge the God of heaven. "With trust in God," Shemaryahu Talmon puts it, "and obedience to his commandments, the Jewish people will overcome all setbacks in the present age, as in the past, and pave the way for the ultimate triumph of God and Israel in history."[128]

The visions especially emphasize God's faithfulness in the ongoing struggle of history. They reveal a transcendent dimension above and beyond the mundane order, interacting with and determining the twists and turns of human history. The heavenly/earthly dualism, present in all the visions, is specifically obvious in the angelic discourse in Dan 10:13—11:1. Heavenly emissaries, whose stunning glory overpowers Daniel, are engaged in a titanic struggle with the rulers of Greece and Persia to alter the course of history. In the visions, Daniel and his angelic emissaries mediate between the transcendent heavenly realm and the earthly. Daniel thus presupposes a metanarrative (overarching framework) of salvation history. Human history, Daniel indicates, is not lived in isolation from the transcendent celestial realm. God will ultimately achieve the divine salvific purpose in a world temporarily given over to evil human machinations.

While ironically preserving human freedom, the transcendent God "deposes kings and sets up kings" (Dan 2:21). God judges the powers of earth, permitting temporal sovereignty even to bestial, evil kingdoms. Human rulers, depicted as ferocious, rapacious animals, wreak havoc upon the earth. The opening lines of the book (1:1–2), however, signal that human governments rule only under the sovereignty of God. God gives or hands over the Israelite king Jehoiakim—and the sacred temple vessels—into the keeping of the Babylonian Nebuchadnezzar. In the final divine judgment,

---

127. Lucas, "Daniel, Book of," 158.
128. Talmon, "Daniel," 344.

however, God gives dominion over to "one like a human . . . coming" upon the clouds of heaven (7:13). Thus, God's purpose in creation will be achieved, even though God's people experience severe suffering before the kingdom is finally given over to them (7:21-22). "There will be a time of distress such has never been since the nations until that time" (12:1). Because they live in an evil world under control by human rulers, God's people must endure suffering. Sometimes this means martyrdom. Ultimately, however, the faithful people of God will experience the triumph of God's redemptive purpose, which is yet in the future.

Eschatology is thus a major motif in the book.[129] Someday God will institute a new order; the faithful will be rewarded and God honored. When the kingdom of God breaks into history, evil will come to an end, and the people of God will inherit dominion, honor, and authority,

> that peoples, nations, and languages
>> should serve him.
> His dominion is an everlasting dominion
>> that will never pass away,
>> and his kingly authority
>> will never be destroyed. (Dan 7:14)

Daniel's response to the perennial problem of theodicy—why God allows evil to flourish in God's good creation—is essentially this: God's purpose, along with God's people, will eventually prevail over all evil! This is the enduring message of Daniel. God's sovereignty over all the world, over even the processes of history, brings comfort to God's faithful people, who patiently await deliverance.

With such a vital, existential message, both the court tales and the apocalypse found deep spiritual resonance for the Jewish people living under the oppression of hostile rulers—and for all generations of the faithful since.

OUTLINE OF THE BOOK OF DANIEL

The commentary follows this outline of Daniel.

1. The court tales (1:1—6:28)

---

129. The doctrine of eschatology is concerned with the last or final events, such as death, judgment, heaven, and hell.

a. Daniel and his three friends introduced in Nebuchadnezzar's court (1:1–21)
   b. The king's dream of the composite metal statue (2:1–49)
   c. The three Hebrews in the blazing furnace (3:1–30)
   d. Nebuchadnezzar's madness (4:1–37)
   e. Belshazzar's feast and the handwriting on the wall (5:1–31)
   f. Daniel in the lion's pit (6:1–28)

2. The apocalyptic visions (7:1—12:13)

   a. The four beasts and the son of man (7:1–28)
   b. The ram, the male goat, and the desecration of the sanctuary (8:1–27)
   c. The seventy weeks and Jeremiah's prophecy of exile (9:1–27)
   d. The final revelation of the rise and fall of nations and advent of God's kingdom (10:1—12:13)

3. The Additions (in the LXX)

   a. The Prayer of Azariah, with an interlude (3:24b–50)
   b. The Song of the Three Hebrews (3:51–90)
   c. Susanna (13:1–64)
   d. The story of Bel (14:1–22)
   e. The story of the Dragon (14:23–42)

PART II

Commentary

Conflict at the Royal Court

Daniel 1

Religious faith is not a storm cellar to which men and women can flee for refuge from the storms of life. It is, instead, an inner spiritual strength which enables them to face those storms with hope and serenity.

—SAM J. ERVIN

A conflict over food opens the book of Daniel. A seemingly inconsequential dietary contest prepares the reader for all other conflicts that exiles in an alien culture must painfully confront. As in the following court tales (chs. 1–6), a crisis of faith looms. As a part of their assimilation into high Babylonian culture, it is assumed the four Judean youths, pressed into the service of the Babylonian king, would meekly accept the royal rations (Dan 1:8). The price of being set apart from all other Judean exiles to receive a royal education would require—so the Babylonians expected—almost complete assimilation to Babylonian religious, political, and cultural realities. Since the royal rations included foods that, from their religious perspective, would ritually defile them, the youths in good conscience cannot partake. On such a seemingly small matter, the conflict is enjoined.

The first chapter thus serves as an introduction to some of the tensions the book explores. It also succinctly prepares the reader for the apocalyptic section (chs. 7–12): "As for these four youths, God gave them knowledge and understanding in all literature and wisdom; Daniel also had insight into all *visions and dreams*" (Dan 1:17; italics added). This same Daniel, we are told, continued until the first year of Cyrus the king (1:21; 10:1), well into the vision cycle.

It is worth noting the artful design of the first six chapters containing the court tales. Each story in Dan 1–6, with the notable exception of chapters 4–5, fits a basic literary pattern:[1] In each, the Jewish heroes face external pressure from the regnant culture to abandon their religious values and conform to a new, more alien reality. They adamantly refuse to submit to external pressure and abandon their faith. God then intervenes to deliver the faithful.

INTRODUCTION (1:1–2)

> In the third year of the reign of Jehoiakim, king of Judah, Nebuchadnezzar, king of Babylon, came to Jerusalem and laid siege to it. ² The Lord gave Jehoiakim king of Judah into his hand, so he took the vessels of the house of God and brought them to the land of Shinar, the house of his gods. The vessels he put into the treasury of his gods.

The author sets this court tale at the beginning of the Babylonian exile, after Judah had been invaded by the Babylonians and some of the population taken into exile to Mesopotamia. This siege of Jerusalem (v. 1) is said to have occurred in the third year of king Jehoiakim of Judah (609–598 BCE). After the siege, Nebuchadnezzar plundered the sacred vessels of the temple as sacred booty (v. 2).[2] These he placed in the Babylonian temple treasury, a typical practice in antiquity when one nation conquered another.

The date given for this siege, however, is problematic. There are two related problems here. One is chronological, the other, historical. The third year of Jehoiakim would be 606 BCE. The date 606, however, conflicts with the date given in Jeremiah, who equates the fourth year of Jehoiakim with the "the first year of King Nebuchadnezzar" (Jer 25:1), i.e., 605.[3] If the third year of Jehoiakim (606) is meant in Daniel, Nebuchadnezzar would not yet have assumed the title king of Babylon. In 605, Nebuchadnezzar II (605–562), whose Akkadian name was *Nabu-kudurri-utsur* ("O Nabu, protect my heir"), more properly transliterated into Hebrew with an *r* sound as *Nebuchadrezzar*, was then campaigning in northern Syria. Following his victory over the Egyptians at the famous battle of Carchemish (605), word came of

---

1. Carey, *Ultimate Things*, 43.

2. A description of this confiscated loot is given in Jer 52:17–23.

3. Jeremiah also places the battle of Carchemish, mentioned below, in the fourth year of Jehoiakim (Jer 46:2).

his father's (Nabopolasser) death. He then hurried to Babylon to receive the crown, lest a usurper claim it.

There is thus a discrepancy in the date between Daniel and Jeremiah. This chronological inconsistency is usually explained by the differences between the way the Hebrews reckoned the reigns of kings and the way the Babylonians did. In Judah, the year in which a king ascended to the throne was considered his first year. This is known as the non-accession year method. In Babylon, by contrast, an accession year method was used. Only the first full year of a monarch's reign was counted as the first year. When the accession year was not a complete year, as in this case, the part of the year in which the king ascended the throne would not be counted. It may therefore be the case that the Danielic author used the Babylonian or accession year method, while Jeremiah followed the Judean non-accession year. This would plausibly account for the chronological difference between the two passages.[4]

If we accept 605 as the date for Nebuchadnezzar's siege mentioned in Dan 1:1, there is still the historical problem of the siege itself. There is no reference in the Bible or in extant contemporary ancient Near Eastern records to a siege of Jerusalem before the battle of Carchemish in 605. Chronicles does mention that Nebuchadnezzar took Jehoiakim captive and brought him to Babylon, along with some of the vessels of the Temple (2 Chr 36:5-9), but no date is assigned, nor is there any reference to a siege, such as mentioned in Daniel. The record in Kings is slightly different. Nebuchadnezzar made Jehoiakim "his servant for three years" (2 Kgs 24:1), but again this is not dated, nor is there reference to a siege. The earliest mention in the Bible (outside Daniel) to such a siege is the seventh year of Nebuchadnezzar (598/597). It is not clear how we are to fit the siege in Dan 1:1 into a chronological reconstruction of the stormy political relationship between Babylon and Judah in the latter part of the seventh and early sixth centuries BCE.

A group of cuneiform texts now in the British Museum, known as the Babylonian Chronicles, sheds some light on the problem. These texts were evidently written to inform the Achaemenid kings of the earlier history of Babylon before the Persians conquered it in 539. The cuneiform texts span the time from the reign of Sargon of Akkad (c. 2350 BCE) down to the rule of the Persians over Babylon in the sixth century, an almost two-thousand-year period.

Although there are chronological gaps in the Babylonian Chronicles, particularly for the years 622-617, 594-557, and 556-555, there is also no

---

4. Archer, "Daniel," 13-14; Baldwin, *Daniel*, 20-21.

reference to a siege of Jerusalem around the year 605. While following the battle of Carchemish, Nebuchadnezzar did give chase to the defeated Egyptians, subduing much of northern Syria in the process, these texts contain no record of Nebuchadnezzar laying siege to Jerusalem in the crucial few months between Carchemish and his urgent coronation in Babylon in September of 605.[5] According to 2 Kings, it was in 598/97—not 605—that Nebuchadnezzar besieged Jerusalem, "carried off all the treasures of the house of the Lord," and put them in the palace in Babylon.[6] He finally subdued the city on March 15/16, 597. "Some of your own sons who are born to you shall be taken away," Isaiah's earlier prediction had indicated. "They shall be eunuchs in the palace of the king of Babylon" (Isa 39:7; 2 Kgs. 20:18).

This omission in the contemporary biblical and archaeological record has never been satisfactorily resolved. Nebuchadnezzar II's siege of Jerusalem in the third/fourth year of Jehoiakim (606/5) thus cannot be corroborated from ancient extra-biblical records. This must not, however, be taken as an indication it never happened. "Absence of evidence is not evidence of absence," historians sometimes say. It only means we have no extra-biblical confirmation of the event. The problem may be due, somewhat ironically, to the missing records themselves.[7]

Scholars have advanced various explanations. Some suggest the writer of Daniel was not really concerned about the technical accuracy of such dates. To put it differently, he was merely recounting an older tradition without concern for chronological precision.[8] Still others propose that by dating the Babylonian siege of Jerusalem to 606/5 instead of 597, the writer was able to accommodate more easily the seventy years of captivity in Babylon predicted by Jeremiah. This reckoning would then extend approximately 606–538.[9] This view has merit because the seventy-year period would later be at issue in Daniel (Dan 9:1–2). In 539/38, the Persian king Cyrus II (c. 559–531) officially released the Judean captives, permitting them to return to their homeland. Goldingay suggests the writer's literary interests may have required a conflating of accounts of the subjugation of Jerusalem

---

5. The *Chronicles of Chaldean Kings* record that in 598/97 Nebuchadnezzar "laid siege to the city of Judah (*Ia-a-hu-du*) and the king took the city on the second day of month Addaru. He appointed in it a (new) king of his liking, took heavy booty from it and brought it into Babylon" ("Conquest of Jerusalem," translated by A. Leo Oppenheim [*ANET*, 564a]). See Freedman's discussion of this text (classified as British Museum 21946) in "Babylonian Chronicle," 34–35.

6. 2 Kgs 24:10–17; cf. 2 Chron 36:5–10.

7. Baldwin, *Daniel*, 19–20.

8. Hartman and Di Lella, *Daniel*, 128–29.

9. Lacocque, *Book of Daniel*, 25. See Jer 25:11–14; 29:10.

rather than historical exactness, at least not according to modern notions of historical reconstruction.[10]

In antiquity, it was widely assumed that when one kingdom conquered another, it meant the gods of the conquering people had subdued the gods and people of the vanquished. When the conqueror plundered the sacred temple of the vanquished and carried away the idols and other sacred icons, this validated the victory. (We may compare this to taking down the flag of a conquered nation and replacing it with the victor's flag.) The sacred objects were generally whisked away and deposited in the temples of the victor. When the Philistines defeated Israel at Shiloh in the eleventh century BCE, they "captured the ark of God" and "brought it into the house of Dagon and placed it beside Dagon" (1 Sam 5:1-2). The Philistines, part of the so-called Sea Peoples, embraced Dagon, a Syro-Palestinian god, after their arrival in Palestine in the thirteenth century. Nebuchadnezzar's absconding with the vessels of the house of God in Jerusalem, the closest things to physical representations of the aniconic (imageless) Hebrew deity, indicated that Nebuchadnezzar's reign and his gods were more powerful than Judah's. Judah was now under his sole domination.

Astonishingly, Daniel claims all this happened at the bidding of God. God, in other words, allowed it. The Lord gave the king and these vessels into Nebuchadnezzar's hands. God handed over or placed in Nebuchadnezzar's hands Jerusalem, the king, the people, and the sacred vessels of the temple. This terrible, devastating event did not happen solely because of the might of Nebuchadnezzar's army against an inferior one. Nebuchadnezzar was only the instrument.[11] It happened because the Lord enabled it. God wills that Judah suffer this humiliation on account of Israel's national sin, as Daniel later mentions in his prayer (Dan 9:7-10). In the book of Daniel, nothing on this national scale happens unless the Lord permits. With the mysterious writing of doom on the palace wall, Daniel grimly reminds Belshazzar, "The Most High God gave your father Nebuchadnezzar kingship, greatness, glory, and majesty," so "he did whatever he wanted, whenever he wanted: killing or sparing, exalting or humbling" (5:18-19 CEB) He

---

10. Goldingay, *Daniel*, 14. See Young for an extensive review of other solutions to this problem and a defense of the event as described in Daniel (Young, *Prophecy of Daniel*, 267-70). Kaiser proposes that as Nebuchadnezzar made the mad dash back to Babylon following his victory at Carchemish, he took Daniel, his three colleagues, and other captives with him (Kaiser, *History of Israel*, 391). He gives no documentary support for this, however.

11. Cf. Assyria as an instrument of God's wrath in the eighth century: "Ah, Assyria, the rod of my anger—the club in their hands is my fury! Against a godless nation I send him" (Isa 10:5-6 NRSV).

reminds Belshazzar that even the rapacious Babylonian empire is under the sovereignty of the Lord.

Despite the perennial rise of egocentric, corrupt tyrants whose genocidal rages doom millions to poverty and death, it is reassuring to know history is under the control of a benevolent, loving God who will see justice finally done. Even as we try to make sense of the chaos of history, we are assured the world—even in all its confusion—remains under God's ultimate sovereignty.

SELECTION OF THE JEWISH YOUTH (1:3–7)

> ³ The king then instructed Ashpenaz, chief of his eunuchs, to bring in from the sons of Israel, from the royalty, and from the nobles, ⁴ youths who have no defect and desirable in appearance, perceptive in all wisdom, who care about knowledge, and are astute in learning, who are competent to serve in the palace of the king, to teach them the literature and language of the Chaldeans. ⁵ The king appointed them a portion of the king's fine food day by day, and from his own wine, thus to educate them for three years. At the end of a certain time they would serve before the king. ⁶ Now among them from the sons of Judah were Daniel, Hananiah, Mishael, and Azariah. ⁷ The chief of the eunuchs gave them names; thus, he designated Daniel, Belteshazzar; Hananiah, Shadrach; Mishael, Meshach; and Azariah, Abednego.

Nebuchadnezzar instructs Ashpenaz, one of his trusted royal officials in charge of eunuchs,[12] to select representatives from the captive Jewish exiles for specialized training in the Babylonian language, literature, and culture. These persons were considered superlative candidates for such training. They had no defect and were desirable in appearance. Youths without obvious physical defects and fine-looking were thought to have superior intellectual ability. Since they came from the royalty and nobles (v. 3)—from Jewish leadership—this would make them even more suitable for potential Babylonian governmental service, perhaps for dealing with specific Jewish issues that might arise. Generally, the Babylonians showed respect to the higher classes among exiles while, as we would suspect, subjecting the lower classes to harsher treatment. The selection of Daniel and his friends for state

---

12. The term eunuch (סָרִיס, *saris*) generally refers to a castrated individual who attends female rulers (2 Kgs 9:30–32) or royal harems (Esth 4:4–5), but the term can also designate a married royal official (Gen 39:1).

service shows the extent the Babylonians were willing to go to encourage foreign talent to serve the interests of the empire.[13] As indicated earlier, this opening scene—as well as the court tales that follow—may have drawn upon Isaiah's depiction of the state visit of Babylonian envoys to King Hezekiah. "Some of your own sons who are born to you shall be taken away; they shall be eunuchs in the palace of the king of Babylon" (Isa 39:7 NRSV). The Isaianic passage may have provided a backdrop for the narrative creation of an idealistic Babylonian court that Daniel and his three companions inhabit.[14]

They are assigned a rigorous three-year course of study, provided rations of royal food and wine, and set to their studies (v. 5). The period of three years of study concurs with a similar time in the Persian Zoroastrian sacred text, the *Avesta*,[15] but seems much too short for anyone without acquaintance with Akkadian (the language of ancient Babylon) literature. This was not Aramaic literature, written in the square script later popularized in Hebrew, but Akkadian, called here the literature and language of the Chaldeans,[16] probably the professional literature of the Babylonian omen texts, written in wedge-shaped cuneiform characters.

It would be fascinating to know the core curriculum of Daniel's training. The book represents him frequently in the role of interpreter of dreams as well as more famously a recipient of visions. "Daniel also had insight into all visions and dreams" (Dan 1:17; 2:18, 27–30; 4:5–9). He is a member of the king's wise men (חַכִּים, *hakim*), the counselors and advisers of the court (2:18). From the Babylonian perspective, he would probably have been regarded as a diviner (*baru*), counselor (*ummanu emqu*), or even exorcist (*ashipu*),[17] The wise in these professions had to master voluminous, difficult omen texts, and were typically trained as apprentices under the learned experts in such secret lore, from which they customarily gave special counsel to the court. Exorcists were masters of various apotropaic rituals (rituals to ward off evil). Specialized skill sets were usual for all these professional Babylonian courtiers.

13. Harrison, *Old Testament Times*, 261.

14. Grillo, "From a Far Country," 367–70. See Isa 39:1–7 = 2 Kgs 20:12–18.

15. "How long a time of a year's length shall a student go to a master of spiritual learning? For a period of three springtides he shall gird himself with the holy education" (*Zendo-Avesta*, 311, cited in J. Collins, *Daniel* [Hermeneia], 140).

16. Originally, the name Chaldean designated the people of southern Babylonia, but in Daniel it appears as a designation for a class of astrologers (see Baldwin, *Daniel*, 28–29).

17. Sweet, "Sage in Akkadian Literature," 45–65. Since there are in Akkadian several terms designating these and other offices, these titles are only representative (Sweet, "Sage in Akkadian Literature," 47–51).

To prepare them for training in these skills, the four carefully chosen youths are given new Babylonian names, a symbol of their dependent status (v. 6). Daniel is renamed *Belteshazzar*, "protect the prince's life"; Azariah, *Abednego*, perhaps a distortion meaning "servant of Nabu"; Hananiah, *Shadrach*, a word of uncertain etymology, but may mean "shining"; and Mishael, *Meshach*, the first element of which may be taken from the Persian religious name *Misa*, a variant of the name of the god Mithra (v. 7).[18] Although these names were imposed, it is common practice even today for emigrants to adopt new names upon entering a new culture. Renaming often begins the process of cultural assimilation. The allusion to the Babylonian gods in the names, however, does not become an issue in the book. The Babylonians were aware of the propagandistic value of putting captives under the nominal symbol of the imperial gods. Taking the vessels from the temple in Jerusalem was a corollary of this policy.[19]

The three friends later take center stage in Dan 3, the only story principally focused on them, and make a cameo appearance in Dan 2. They also appear in the Song of the Three in one of the Additions. These youths stand for the faithful in Israel. Now in the custody of a foreign hostile nation, it would seem they could expect only the rancor and humiliation usually reserved for a subjugated people. Despite the fact the book of Daniel begins with a catastrophe, however, already in this story a redemptive theme emerges in the person of Daniel and his friends.[20]

RESISTANCE TO THE KING'S FOOD (1:8–17)

> [8] But Daniel resolved in his mind that he would not defile himself with the king's food or with the wine which he drank; so he asked the chief of the eunuchs that he not defile himself. [9] God gave Daniel favor and compassion in the presence of the chief of the eunuchs. [10] The chief of the eunuchs said to Daniel, "I fear my Lord the king since he has appointed your food and drink; for why should he notice your appearance is more pitiful than the youths who are of your age, and you lay blame on my head with the king?"
> [11] Then Daniel asked the overseer whom the chief of the eunuchs had appointed over Daniel, Hananiah, Mishael, and Azariah, [12] "Please test your servants for ten days, and let us be

---

18. J. Collins, *Daniel* (Hermeneia), 141.
19. Smith-Christopher, "Book of Daniel," 38.
20. Lacocque, *Book of Daniel*, 25–26.

given vegetables and let us eat, water, and let us drink. ¹³ Then let our appearance and the appearance of the youths who eat the food of the king be observed before you. Then whatever you see, take care of with your servants." ¹⁴ So he listened to them regarding this matter. Then he tested them for ten days.

¹⁵ At the end of the ten days their appearance was seen to be good and stouter than all the youths who had been eating the food of the king. ¹⁶ So the overseer continued to withhold their food and wine they were to drink and gave them vegetables.

¹⁷ As for these four youths, God gave them knowledge and understanding in all literature and wisdom; Daniel also had insight into all visions and dreams.

The royal food and drink become a problem (v. 8). Daniel takes the initiative in confronting his supervisor about the matter, thus assuming the hero role he retains throughout the stories (v. 9). Why he becomes the spokesman for the group, we are not told. Daniel "set in his heart" (literal translation), so that he would not defile himself with the royal rations, the government-supplied diet.

Why does Daniel want to abstain from the royal rations? The exiled Judean king Jehoiachin appears to have accepted similar provisions, and this is taken as a sign of honor and of the approaching liberation of Judah (2 Kgs 25:29-30). During and after the Babylonian exile, ritual defilement from unclean food assumes a great deal of importance. Judith refuses the Assyrian Holofernes's delicacies and wine when she is invited to dine with him. "I cannot partake of them," she says, "or it will become an offense" (Jdt 12:1-2). Antiochus IV tries to compel the seven Jewish brothers and their mother to "partake of unlawful swine's flesh" by torturing and later mercilessly killing them (2 Macc 7:1-41). Ancient Hebrew purity laws received strong emphasis in the postexilic Jewish community.²¹ As Mary Douglas has shown, concerns over the purity of the body were representative of concern for the integrity of the community. Such purity laws, as here, act as barriers to social assimilation,²² a real danger for people who cherish their national and religious identity while having to live in foreign cultures.

Nevertheless, there are no regulations prohibiting such royal food and drink in the Torah. Nor is wine forbidden, except to those who have taken a Nazarite vow (Num 6:1-4). The purity restrictions of unclean foods in the Priestly Code were probably only sporadically engaged before the end

---

21. See Isa 65:2-7; Tob 1:10-11; Add Esth 14:17; 1 Macc 1:62-63; 2 Macc 5:27; 6:8-10, 18-31; 7:1-2.

22. Douglas, *Purity and Danger*.

of the fifth century.²³ In this instance, Daniel's concern is that he not defile himself. The Hebrew verb גאל (*gaal*, defile or become impure) has ritual connotations. Daniel is concerned about becoming ritually defiled and thus ineligible for the ritual practice of his faith (see Hos 9:3–4). But there is more to this episode than ritual defilement. Throughout biblical history, control of food is symbolic of power.²⁴ As the famine worsened in Egypt during Joseph's tenure, for instance, the Egyptian people surrendered first their wealth, then their livestock, their lands, and finally themselves, becoming slaves to Pharaoh. The food they were given in exchange indicated Pharaoh's control over their lives (Gen 47:13–21). The dispensing of royal food to Daniel and his three friends is an indication of Babylonian hegemony.

The purity laws, because they distinguished Jew from Greek, became an issue during Antiochus IV Epiphanes's persecution of the Jews. The story of Daniel's ritual faithfulness thus provided a model for the Jews during Maccabean times when, as we have seen, the book of Daniel was being edited into its final form.²⁵ Here Daniel asks for and is given special dispensation—unlike under Antiochus IV—for his ritual dietary needs.

To lessen the overseer's trepidation about all this, Daniel proposes a test (v. 11). He requests for ten days that he and his friends be given vegetables and water (v. 12), and at the end of this time be subjected to an examination (v. 13). Vegetables literally indicates seeds (זֵרֹעִים, *zeronim*), but the diet probably consisted of more than dry peas or beans. The *zeronim* are evidently thought to be a purer or more kosher diet than the royal fare. The proposed period of testing—ten days—is a stereotypical period but seems much too short to make a difference in the physical fitness of the youths.

Not because it was vegetarian does the diet make a difference. God's blessing resting upon the four faithful Hebrew youths makes the critical distinction. In Young's words, this is the "first triumph of grace in Babylonia."²⁶ We are reminded that God often works in and through human activity. In fact, this seems to be God's preferred method of operation. It is not a question of either human effort or divine grace, but rather of God's grace assisting and supporting human endeavor.

At the end of the ten days, they appear good and stouter than all the youths who had been eating the food of the king (v. 15). Their exemplary progress greatly contrasts with the other anonymous young men presumably

---

23. See Lev 11:1–47; Deut 14:1–21. While in exile, the priests concentrated on the codification of the Levitical purity laws. However, see Judg 13:7.

24. Smith-Christopher, "Book of Daniel," 40–41.

25. See Dan 11:32–33; 12:3, 8–13.

26. Young, *Prophecy of Daniel*, 44.

in the same educational program. As a result, the diet can continue (v. 16). This same divine assistance enables them in their mastery of literature and wisdom, the complex Akkadian omen texts (v. 17). Daniel's abilities even exceed this: he is seen to possess God-given psychic powers in visions and dreams, divinatory skills soon on display in Dan 2.

TRIUMPH OF RESISTANCE (1:18–21)

> [18] At the end of the days which the king had designated for their presentation, the chief of the eunuchs brought them before Nebuchadnezzar. [19] Then the king conversed with them but could not find any among them all like Daniel, Hananiah, Mishael, and Azariah. Thus, they were stationed in the presence of the king. [20] In every matter of wisdom and understanding that the king sought he even found them ten times better than all the magicians and conjurers who were in the entire kingdom.
>
> [21] Thus, Daniel continued until the first year of Cyrus the king.

At the end of three years, here indicated by the metonym days, comes the final examination before Nebuchadnezzar (v. 18). Appearing before the king provides a literary frame for the chapter. At the beginning, they stand before the king when they are introduced (v. 3). Now at the end, they again stand before the king. Nebuchadnezzar's interrogation shows them to be at the top of their class. That they began to attend the king indicates they had not only graduated—with high honors—but taken up royal service (v. 19). Their abilities are ten times better than all the magicians and conjurers in the realm. This means, of course, that they appear superior to other professional dream interpreters. As a result, the king approves them for royal service. Daniel, at least, would enjoy a long career in royal service, until the first year of Cyrus the king, which would be 539/538 BCE (v. 21). A later reference (Dan 10:1) at the beginning of the fourth vision mentions the third year of Cyrus, although the LXX has first year in this same text. According to the chronology adopted by the book (1:1–2), this would be almost seventy years. If Daniel was in his late teens or early twenties at the time of his capture, then he would have been almost ninety by the first year of the Persia king Cyrus.

This chapter sets the stage for the following stories and apocalyptic visions. Here we learn Daniel was gifted with prophetic discernment, skilled in Babylonian omen literature and ritual, yet faithful to his God. All this will be tested in the stories and visions to follow. Here we discover also "God rescues and advances his servants in wonderful ways."[27] Such a story would have found meaning among Jewish people who lived in the diaspora (exile) and who faced difficult choices demanded by assimilation to a foreign culture. In this first story, Daniel is drafted into the service of a foreign king and subjected to the pressures of professional training in the divinatory, cultic rites of the Babylonians. Up until this time, Daniel's identity had been shaped by the devotion of his community. His loyalty to God had become definitive of his identity. Now a new identity, alien to his faith, was being imposed upon him. Yet he—and his three companions—stand firm in their loyalty to God by refusing defilement at the king's table. Not only the Jewish exiles in the Babylonian diaspora, but also the Jewish victims of Antiochus IV's persecution, would have drawn courage and inspiration from such a story. When we, too, are tempted to sublimate or abandon our convictions because of the subtle lure of political or religious power or influence, we do well to remember Daniel and his friends who said, "No!"

According to Jeremiah, the Jewish people in Babylonian exile were to live in peace with the foreign nation. "Seek the welfare of the city where I have sent you into exile," the prophet advises, "and pray to the Lord on their behalf" (Jer 29:7). In this story, Daniel and his friends comply with this advice. At the same time, when put to the test, they stand resolutely for their God.

While Western culture provides a much more congenial atmosphere for religious faith, there are nonetheless times when the faithful must firmly resist secularism, violence, injustice, and tyranny. In resistance, they may take courage from the example of Daniel and his three companions.

---

27. J. Collins, *Daniel* (FOTL 22), 46.

The March of Nations

Daniel 2

It is so impossible for the world to exist without God that if God should forget it, it would immediately cease to be.

—Søren Kierkegaard

Having heard about Daniel's insight into all visions and dreams (Dan 1:17), now we see a stellar display of his skills. The editor may have placed this story here, following Daniel's introduction to the Babylonian court, to display these abilities.

Although we consider chapters 7–12 to be the apocalyptic portion of the book, in chapter 2 occurs the first apocalyptic vision. It comes in the form of a dream (*halom*, חֲלוֹם) revealed to Nebuchadnezzar rather than Daniel. The dream report is nestled within the narrative rather than the other way around. Although the dream originates with Nebuchadnezzar, the interpretation comes in a vision (חֵזוּ, *hezu*) to Daniel. Daniel unravels Nebuchadnezzar's dream about a huge, metallic statue. "Your god is God of gods and Lord of kings," Nebuchadnezzar finally exclaims, underscoring the point of the whole episode, "He reveals secrets" (Dan 2:47).

Despite the apocalyptic vision/dream at its heart, this chapter must be considered a court legend like others in the book.[1] Humphreys calls it a "Tale of Court Contest,"[2] while Goldingay points to features of legend, aretalogy

---

1. J. Collins, *Daniel* (FOTL 22), 49. In this commentary, I have generally followed the form-critical judgment of Collins, although I often refer to the tales in Daniel as stories, a less technical term.

2. Humphreys, "Life-Style for the Diaspora," 217.

(miracle story), and midrash (imaginative commentary on Scripture) found in the story.[3] The story demonstrates the superiority of Israel's wisdom, divinely revealed through Daniel, over that of the Babylonian sages.

There are parallels between this story and the court tales of Joseph's interpretation of Pharaoh's dreams in Egypt. The story, in fact, may appropriately be considered a midrash on the Joseph story.[4] In both stories, a foreign ruler has a dream any professional diviner cannot decipher. The magicians and soothsayers are powerless to comprehend the secret things of God. Instead, a Hebrew exile steps forward and through divine assistance interprets the dream. The ruler then rewards the Hebrew captive. He is given major responsibilities in the realm. This story is what Talmon calls the type-plot of the "Successful Exile."[5] Although there are differences,[6] the Danielic author may have known of the Joseph story yet refrained from slavishly following it. In Daniel, to cite one difference, God is in control, not only of mundane events, as in the Joseph story, but of the nations as well.

This story, with the dream report at its core, looks forward to the apocalyptic vision of Dan 7. These chapters (2 and 7) significantly begin and end the Aramaic portion of Daniel and thus connect the two main sections of the book (chs. 1-6; 7-12). Both present four empires, symbolized by the composite metallic statue and the four hideous beasts, respectively. The four empires are represented by two sets of symbols. Both end in the destruction of the dominant powers and the setting up of God's kingdom.

Many motifs in this chapter also parallel those in subsequent stories. Lists of diviners occur repeatedly (Dan 4:7; 5:7; 6:7). Frequently also appears the requirement to interpret dreams (4:9-10; 5:7). When the diviners or courtiers are unable to respond to the king's demands, there comes the cruel threat of dismemberment and destruction of personal property (3:29; 6:24). The king lashes out in rage, furious at the obtuseness of his courtiers (3:19). The kingdom of God, unlike the earthly kingdoms represented by the non-Israelite monarch, lasts forever (4:3; 6:26). These and other motifs bind the series of stories together.[7]

The plot, like other stories in Dan 1-6, is rather simple, the characters few. The king has a disturbing dream. His diviners are unable to interpret it. Becoming angry, he finally takes counsel from Daniel (Dan 2:1-16). Daniel

3. Goldingay, *Daniel*, 36.

4. See Gen 40-41, esp. 41:1-43; Goldingay, *Daniel*, 37.

5. This type-plot contains the tale of a "destitute (fatherless) young Judean or Israelite exile who rises to an unprecedented height at a foreign court" (Talmon, "Daniel," 350).

6. Russell, *Daniel*, 37.

7. For a complete list of parallels, including those to other parts of the HB, see Goldingay, *Daniel*, 37-39.

not only successfully recounts the forgotten dream, but also interprets it. It is a dream about the four empires finally giving way to the kingdom of God (vv. 17–45). At the end, the king acknowledges the superiority of Daniel's God, whom he calls the God of gods, and rewards Daniel (vv. 46–49).

NEBUCHADNEZZAR'S DREAM (2:1–11)

In the second year of the reign of Nebuchadnezzar, Nebuchadnezzar dreamed dreams. His spirit was troubled, and his sleep deserted him. ² So the king commanded to call the magicians, the conjurers, the sorcerers, and the Chaldeans to tell the king his dreams. They came and stood before the king. ³ The king said to them, "I have dreamed a dream and my spirit is troubled to understand the dream."

⁴ The Chaldeans spoke to the king (in Aramaic), "O king, live forever! Relate the dream to your servants and the interpretation we will reveal."

⁵ The king replied to the Chaldeans, "The matter is certain on my part: If you do not make known to me the dream and its interpretation, you will be dismembered, and your houses made a dung heap. ⁶ But if you tell the dream and its interpretation, from me you will receive gifts, a reward, and great honor. Therefore, tell me the dream and its interpretation."

⁷ They answered a second time, "Let the king tell his servants the dream and we will make known the interpretation."
⁸ The king replied, "With certainty I know that you seek to buy time because you see that the matter has been fully determined by me. ⁹ For if you do not make known to me the dream, one is your verdict, and the matter is false and corrupt. You have agreed among yourselves to speak to me until the time is changed. Therefore, tell me the dream and I will know that you can make known to me its interpretation."

¹⁰ The Chaldeans answered before the king, "There is no man upon earth who is able to make known the matter, because no great king or ruler has asked anything like this with respect to any magician, conjurer, or Chaldean. ¹¹ The thing the king has asked is difficult; there is no one who can make it known before the king except the gods whose dwelling is not with humankind."

In the previous story (ch. 1), Daniel and his companions were assigned professional training (Dan 1:3–5). This happened in the first year of Nebuchadnezzar. They were committed to three years of training. Now, in the second year (603 BCE) of Nebuchadnezzar (v. 1)—before Daniel has completed this training—he is called before the king to interpret a mysterious dream. It is difficult to miss this chronological discrepancy. Daniel has not yet completed his three-year training—begun in Nebuchadnezzar's first year—for the role he plays in this story in Nebuchadnezzar's second year. The span of three years thus may refer to fractions of three years, not to three entire years, that is, a part for the whole.[8] The problem may be imaginary rather than real, since the two stories may have circulated independently before incorporation in the book. The editor took them as he found them, and without trying to impose chronological consistency upon them, placed the stories side by side with no chronological adjustment.[9]

Be this as it may, Nebuchadnezzar has a terrifying dream.[10] This is no mere personal dream, such as we all experience, but one Nebuchadnezzar acutely recognizes to have political as well as existential significance.[11] The ancients, particularly those in leadership, superstitiously took such dreams as omens with the utmost gravity.[12] In the Bible, as well as in the ancient Near East, dreams and omens were often regarded as modes of divine communication. Nabonidus (555–539 BCE) reports a dream where he saw an apparition of Nebuchadnezzar, his predecessor.[13] Dreams were believed to be harbingers of good or evil. Even today, a terrifying, visceral dream may affect us for days afterward. In ancient monarchies, the threat of revolt, attack, or assassination by internal or external enemies loomed threateningly, especially in hereditary monarchies like Babylon.

Plagued by anxiety, guilt, and sleeplessness, the king sends for the magicians, the conjurers, the sorcerers, and the Chaldeans to interpret the dream (vv. 2–3). This is the professional class with which Daniel is now associated, all advisory to the king. Four technical terms (all plurals) of uncertain meaning describe the work of these individuals.[14] The magicians

---

8. Young, *Prophecy of Daniel*, 55–56.

9. Smith-Christopher, "Book of Daniel," 49. See also Porteous, *Daniel*, 39.

10. The text speaks of *dreams* (חֲלֹמוֹת, *halomoth*). Whether this is one of a series of dreams, or whether the plural is used to refer to the entire experience, is not clear.

11. Goldingay, *Daniel*, 45.

12. See Oppenheim, "Dreams," 179–373. See Gen 41:14–25; 2 Macc 5:1–4.

13. In a text found etched on a basalt stela now in Istanbul containing the inscription of Nabonidus, we read: "In the same dream . . . my royal predecessor Nebuchadnezzar and one attendant (appeared to me) standing on a chariot" ("Neo-Babylonian Empire and Its Successors," translated by A. Leo Oppenheim [*ANET*, 310a]).

14. Of the concentration of all these mantic titles, "old and new words for magicians and diviners are simply heaped up to suggest a totality," P.-E. Dion writes, "to the greater credit of the one man of God, whose genuine inspiration was able to put to shame this whole roster of evil know-how" (Dion, "Medical Personnel," 213–16).

(חַרְטֻמִּים, *hartummim*, probably a term of Egyptian origin) generally refers to priests and magicians who dealt with the occult, proficient in interpretation of dreams and omens. The conjurers (אַשָּׁפִים, *ashaphim*) were those skilled in conjuring or necromancy (conferring with the dead), while the sorcerers (מְכַשְּׁפִים, *mekashephim*) emphasized incantations and magic. The Chaldeans (כַּשְׂדִּים, *kasedim*) originally referred to an ethnic community in lower Mesopotamia, but in the book of Daniel designates the entire category of court diviners,[15] as does the term *wise* (חַכִּים, *hakkim*), which appears in verse 24. The wise in this context are distinguished from the wise of whom the Hebrew wisdom books speak.[16] Here, wise refers to experts in esoteric divinatory wisdom and visionary arts, sometimes called mantic wisdom. Daniel's gift of wisdom, too, differs from traditional Hebrew wisdom. It was more in keeping with mantic wisdom, as evidenced by his ability to interpret dreams and other mysteries.[17] The Babylonians were deeply interested in the occult, astrological phenomena, magical incantations, demonology, angelology, and the resulting eschatological predictions.

When the Chaldeans address the king, the author shifts to *Aramaic* (v. 4b) and continues in this language through Dan 7:28. The abrupt appearance of Aramaic represents an editorial gloss signaling the beginning of the Aramaic in the book. Here is the puzzle of the dual languages of the book (see "The Languages and Text of Daniel" in the introduction). This Aramaic is Imperial or Official Aramaic, used formally by the empires of this period as the *lingua franca* of diplomacy and communication.

"O king, live forever" is a standard reverential way in the Near East of addressing a royal monarch. The courtiers request the king tell them what his dream was about; they will then be able to explain its meaning. The recounting of the dream, they evidently believed, much like modern therapeutic disclosure, was a way of neutralizing its influence upon the dreamer.[18]

Annoyed at their caution, the king threatens. If you do not make both the dream and its meaning clear, he says, your bodies will be dismembered, your homes turned into piles of dung (v. 5). Both punishments were cruel penalties that totalitarian states all over the world have used. The Romans were fond of crucifying prisoners on crosses to maximize pain and humiliation (as with Jesus). The royal demand, however, is a catch-22. The courtiers are directed to relate the dream—unaware of its content—then interpret the

---

15. See Dan 1:20; 2:10, 27; 4:7; 5:7, 11, 15. For a similar list of such persons, see Isa 44:24–26; Sibylline Oracles 3:225.

16. See Prov 1:1–7. Hebrew wisdom, however, many have included elements of this divinatory skill (Prov 16:33).

17. J. Collins, *Introduction to Hebrew Bible*, 574.

18. J. Collins, *Daniel* (Hermeneia), 156–57.

meaning of the dream. This calls for insight they clearly lack; and as they admit, so does everyone else (v. 10). It is hinted that the king has forgotten all or at least parts of the dream and so unreasonably expects the courtiers to recall it for him. Thus, the king holds out a threatening stick. The carrot he promises (v. 6), should they interpret a dream the contents of which they have yet to learn, is that they will be given great honor and presumably career advancement. Probably Nebuchadnezzar has not forgotten the dream or at least little of it. How much of our personal dreams do we remember when we awake? He may be using this impossible gambit to test the reliability of the soothsayers' interpretation (v. 9).

That this is the king's ruse now becomes apparent. When the courtiers ask the king to relate the dream for them to interpret (v. 7), he accuses them of needless delay (v. 8). Perhaps the king will change his mind (v. 9), they may have calculated, perhaps forget all about the matter. The king, however, forcefully reiterates his demand.

Impossible! the Chaldeans rejoin. No great king (note the irony) has asked anything like this with respect to any magician, conjurer, or Chaldean (v. 10). It is extremely difficult, impossible, really. No one can read the king's mind except the gods, whose dwelling is not with humankind (v. 11). This reply sets the stage for a divine intervention, so important in Daniel—and in other apocalyptic writings—when the veil separating heaven and earth is momentarily pulled aside, and impinging heavenly realities come into focus.

DANIEL AND HIS FRIENDS ENDANGERED (2:12-23)

> ¹² Because of this the king became furiously enraged, so he ordered to destroy all the wise men of Babylon! ¹³ So the decree went forth that the wise men were to be executed. Thus, they sought Daniel and his companions to be executed.
> ¹⁴ Then Daniel responded with prudence and discretion to Arioch, the king's chief executioner, who had gone out to execute the wise men of Babylon. ¹⁵ He asked Arioch, the officer of the king, "Why is the decree so harsh from the king?" Then Arioch explained the matter to Daniel. ¹⁶ Daniel went in and requested from the king that he give him time to make known to the king the interpretation.

For Nebuchadnezzar, such a feckless admission is unacceptable. He flies into a rage and orders the immediate elimination of all the wise men of Babylon (vv. 12-13), which tragically includes Daniel and his companions.

A desperate, frightened Daniel urgently seeks help from Arioch, the king's executioner (v. 14), as though Arioch might be able to mitigate the king's harsh edict. By the postexilic era, the term טַבָּח (*tabbah*, executioner) had taken on the sense of bodyguard or even high court official. In this verse, however, Arioch receives orders to execute the wise men. Why is the death decree so cruel (v. 15)? Daniel asks. Perhaps rumor has already reached him of the king's impossible demand, and thus he questions both its severity and impulsiveness. Daniel successfully gains an audience with the irate king (v. 16) and requests time out—something denied the other courtiers—to consult his Jewish colleagues. Daniel's preferential treatment, while his professional peers remain under a death sentence, says something about the king's favorable disposition toward him. According to verse 25, however, the king seems not even to have been aware of Daniel, in contrast to chapter 1, where he considers Daniel "ten times better" than all the other courtiers (Dan 1:18-20). Has Nebuchadnezzar simply forgotten?

Hartman and Di Lella explain Nebuchadnezzar's memory lapse by suggesting Dan 2:13-23, the exchange between Daniel and Arioch, is a later insertion into the narrative.[19] This makes sense. If verses 13-23 are removed, the narrative reads smoothly from verse 12 to verse 24. While Hebrew narrators often inserted prayers, hymns, and other supplementary material into contexts where it was deemed aesthetically or thematically appropriate,[20] no textual evidence from the ancient manuscripts has come to light confirming this supposition.[21]

> [17] Then Daniel went to his house and made known the matter to Hananiah, Mishael, and Azariah, his companions, [18] and requested they seek mercies from the God of the heavens about this secret so that Daniel and his companions might not perish with the rest of the wise men of Babylon. [19] Then the secret was revealed to Daniel in a vision of the night. Subsequently, Daniel blessed the God of the heavens.
>
> [20] Daniel said:
>
> "May the name of God be blessed from boundless age to age,
>
>   for wisdom and might are his.
>
> [21] He changes times and seasons,

---

19. Hartman and Di Lella, "Daniel," *NJBC* 411; Anderson, *Signs and Wonders*, 14.

20. For example, compare 1 Sam 2:1-10 (the Song of Hannah); 2 Sam 22:2-51; 23:2-7 (songs of David, taken from the psalter and inserted into Samuel). Daniel also contains such an insertion in the long prayer in Dan 9:4-19.

21. Among the Daniel fragments discovered at Qumran, *4QDaniel*ᵃ [4Q112] has Dan 2:17-23 in the text. If 2:12-23 is supplementary, it would have been inserted into the Aramaic text before the Daniel fragments from Qumran were circulating (c. 125-50 BCE).

deposes kings and sets up kings;
he gives wisdom to the wise
    and knowledge to those who have understanding.
²² He reveals the deep and hidden things;
    he knows what is in the darkness,
    and the light abides with him.
²³ To you, O God of my ancestors,
    I give thanks and praise,
because you give wisdom and might to me.
    and now you have made known what we have asked of you,
    for you have made known to us the matter of the king."

The narrative draws a sharp contrast between Daniel's prayer and Babylonian divinatory practices, a contrast featured prominently in this story. For aid, Daniel turns to his three friends, who appear for the second time in the book (v. 17). He asks them to join him in seeking favor from God about the king's impossible mandate. Within himself, within his own God-given intelligence, even within the training he has now received, Daniel does not have any way of figuring out the content of the dream—or its significance (v. 18) If he does not get some insight from God, he and his three friends, mentioned here by their Hebrew names, will perish with the rest of the wise men of Babylon. At first, his motivation seems purely for self-preservation, until we learn in verse 24 that Daniel also intervenes to save the rest of the Babylonian diviners. Daniel and his friends still harbor an entirely normal fear of the capricious, autocratic king. Their faith needs reinforcing through some type of divine response. When the secret is revealed to Daniel in a night vision, this reinforcement comes (v. 19).

Two important expressions in the book appear in this passage: God of the heavens (v. 18) and the God who reveals secrets (v. 22). God of the heavens (אֱלָהּ שְׁמַיָּא, *elah shemayya*) appears in Gen 24:7 in its Hebrew equivalent (אֱלֹהֵי הַשָּׁמַיִם, *elohei hashamayim*), where the title is ascribed to Yahweh. It is a favorite designation for God in Daniel and occurs (in Aramaic) three times in this chapter alone (vv. 18, 37, 44). Used often in biblical texts from the Persian period, it is found even on the lips of various Persian kings.[22] It is the equivalent of the Canaanite expression *Baal Shamen* (Baal [Lord] of the heavens), which in turn loosely corresponds to the Greek title *Zeus Olympios*, the name of the god Antiochus IV Epiphanes installed at the altar

---

22. Ezra 1:2; 5:11–12; 6:10; 7:12, 21, 23; Neh 1:4; 2:5, 20; Jonah 1:9; Dan 2:18; 5:23; Tob 10:12; Jdt 5:8; 6:19; 11:17.

in the JerusalemtTemple courtyard.[23] This name may have been selected here due to Persian influence. Among the Persians, the reformer Zoroaster (c. 660 BCE) elevated the god Ahura-Mazda to become the supreme deity and thus the god of the heavens. In Daniel, the God of the heavens, of course, is a reference to Yahweh.

We also learn the God of the heavens is the One who reveals secrets (רז, *raz*, secret or mystery). The secret here has to do with the inscrutable way God governs history (vv. 21–22). From a human perspective, the course of history, the rise and fall of nations, appears quite random, often turning on loosely or even disconnected events, impervious to human awareness. We rely on historians after the fact to sort it all out and make sense of it. Sometimes we can discern certain patterns in events, but usually only in hindsight, seldom beforehand. Deeper still is the mystery of how God works out the divine purpose on the stage of human history. "The constant parallel established by Daniel between the celestial God and the mysterious character of history," remarks Lacocque, "is remarkable."[24]

For the first time in the book, the author explicitly brings up divine providence. God did not set up the world and the universe to run like clockwork, as in deism, and then go off to retire from the scene. God is a constant—although unseen—Factor in the world, directing, guiding, sustaining, upholding, and above all, showing goodwill. In all that transpires, the providence of God is active, operative, and determinative: this is the message of Daniel. As Paul put it, there is "one God and Father of all, who is above all and through all and in all" (Eph 4:5). In the apocalyptic vision of the world, the God who is above all, through all, and in all guides the nations to their destiny. In the court tales of Daniel, God is also active in individual lives, not just national.

Upon receiving the much-needed answer to his prayer—in a vision rather than a dream—Daniel breaks out in a hymn (vv. 20–23), which owes its style to the Hebrew psalter and other Hebrew prayers,[25] praising God for wisdom and might, God's governance of nations, and God's revelation of deep and hidden mysteries,[26] such as the dream of Nebuchadnezzar. There is little apparent difference in this book, we notice here, between a vision and a dream. The prayer, an expression of Daniel's personal piety, celebrates God's sovereignty over human history and the gift of wisdom God bestows

---

23. See Dan 8:13–14; 9:25–27; 11:31; Russell, *Daniel*, 43–44.
24. Lacocque, *Book of Daniel*, 43.
25. See Ps 41:13; Job 12:12–25; Neh 9:5.
26. "He uncovers the deeps out of darkness, and brings deep darkness to light" (Job 12:22).

upon the wise. Particularly important is how God changes times and seasons, deposes kings and sets up kings (v. 21). This clause represents the keynote, not only for Nebuchadnezzar's dream, but of the entire book. Out of the mystery of the sovereign God, the rise and fall of nations materializes. The apocalyptist bids us think of the rise and fall of empires in the same mysterious light. Although the relationship between God and the nations is complex, even inexplicable, ultimately, political leaders are accountable to God. They may appear to be autocratic, but in the final analysis, they really are not. Nebuchadnezzar's dream of the metallic statue dramatically illustrates this very point.

DANIEL INTERPRETS THE DREAM (2:24-45)

> [24] Therefore Daniel went to Arioch because he had gone forth from the king to execute the wise men of Babylon. Thus, he said to him, "Do not execute the wise men of Babylon. Take me before the king and I will make known the interpretation to the king."
> [25] Then Arioch hastily brought Daniel before the king, and thus spoke to him, "I have found a man among the exiles of Judah who can make the interpretation known to the king."
> [26] The king asked Daniel, whose name was Belteshazzar, "Are you able to make known to me the dream that I have seen and its interpretation?"
> [27] Daniel answered the king, "The secret that the king has requested no wise men, conjurers, magicians, diviners, are able to make known to the king. [28] Nevertheless, there is a God in the heavens who reveals secrets and makes known to king Nebuchadnezzar what will be at the end of days. This was your dream and the visions of your head upon your bed:
> [29] "You, O king, your thoughts upon your bed came up as to what will be after this. The revealer of secrets has made known to you what will be. [30] But as for me, not by wisdom which is in me more than any living persons, this secret was revealed to me. Therefore, the interpretation should be made known to the king so that you may know the thoughts of your mind."

Eager to announce the news, Daniel goes to Arioch, the king's official, and urges him to stay the executions of the wise men because Daniel now has in mind the king's dream and its interpretation (v. 24). This passage assumes Daniel is unknown to the king (v. 25)—he is a man found among the exiles of Judah—but this may be merely a deferential way of introducing Daniel.

By all this back-and-forth between the king, his courtiers and agents, and Daniel and his three companions, the author successfully delays the climax of the narrative. This is a literary device—delaying the climax—important to good storytelling.

Daniel carefully explains where he obtained the interpretation of the mysterious dream. It does not come from the wise men, conjurers, magicians, or diviners (vv. 26–27), from the usual divinatory resources widely employed in the ancient Near East. It comes from the God of the heavens, the great Revealer of secrets (גְּלֵא רָזִין, *gale razin*) (v. 28). Verse 29 repeats this in reverse word order.

The dream concerns the end of days, namely, the climax of history when God will usher in the divine kingdom. It deals with what lies beyond the contemporary horizon. The Aramaic expression אַחֲרִית יוֹמַיָּא (*aharit yomayya*, end of the days) or its Hebrew equivalent appears fourteen times in the Bible.[27] In several cases, the texts are not concerned with the terminal point of human history. These texts merely point to indefinite, decisive future change, a radical shift in human events,[28] but not the termination of all human affairs. In Daniel, the phrase seems to acquire the strict eschatological meaning of the end of history, namely, the indefinite future when God's kingdom will be established.

In his explanation, Daniel follows the conventional way such dreams were interpreted in the ancient Near East. First, the entire dream is recounted, as in verses 31–35. Then, individual aspects are singled out and identified.[29]

> [31] "You, O king, were watching, and lo! a great statue. This statue was huge and its splendor extraordinary; it stood before you, and its appearance was frightening. [32] The head of this statue was of fine gold, its chest and loins of silver, its belly and thighs of bronze, [33] its lower legs of iron, its feet part of iron and part

---

27. Gen 49:1; Num 24:14; Deut 4:30; 31:29; Isa 2:2; Mic 4:1; Jer 23:20; 30:24; 48:47; 49:39; Ezek 38:16; Dan 10:14; Hos 3:5. Lacocque notes this expression already occurs with eschatological significance in Akkadian texts, viz., *ina ahrat ume* (Lacocque, *Book of Daniel*, 45). Note the comparable Hebrew expression in Genesis: "Then Jacob called his sons, and said, 'Gather around, that I may tell you what will happen to you in days to come [אַחֲרִית הַיָּמִים, *aharit hayyamim*]'" (Gen 49:1).

28. George Buchanan rightly warns: "Modern Bible students should not be misled by the word *eschaton* in this expression and should not read eschatological meanings into contexts which do not anticipate any kind of an end, but only future time" (Buchanan, "Eschatology," 188–93).

29. Collins suggests the dream and its interpretation (Dan 2:31–45) were not originally composed for this context but have been inserted here (J. Collins, *Daniel* [Hermeneia], 169).

of clay. ³⁴ You were watching until a stone was cut out without hands, and it struck the statue upon its feet of iron and clay and broke them in pieces. ³⁵ Then like one the iron, the clay, the bronze, the silver, and the gold shattered into pieces and became like chaff from the summer threshing floors, and the wind carried them away and no place was found for them. But the stone that struck the statue became a great mountain and filled the entire earth."

The dream focuses on a great statue of impressive, yet indeterminate size (v. 31). Anthropoid in form, its head of pure gold, chest and arms of silver, waist and thighs of bronze or copper, and legs of iron, its feet are a curious mixture of iron and clay (vv. 32–33). While the statue stands towering and majestic, a huge, airborne stone, cut out of a quarry without human aid, strikes the statue on its feet of iron and clay and breaks them in pieces (v. 34). The entire statue collapses, its broken shards blow away into oblivion like chaff from the summer threshing floors (v. 35), while the stone becomes a great mountain and fills the entire earth.

The pattern of the dream is that of many ancient dreams and visions. They are often populated by huge, anthropomorphic figures. The thirteenth-century Egyptian pharaoh Merneptah, whose victory stela discovered at Thebes is the first inscription outside the Bible to mention Israel,[30] in a dream saw a giant statue of the Egyptian god Ptah, the main deity at Memphis, the Egyptian capital and royal residence. His name, Merneptah, contains this divine designation: *Mer-ne-ptah* (beloved by Ptah). Herodotus, the Greek historian (b. 484 BCE), mentions a huge statue in the temple of Bel in Babylon, "a figure of a man, twelve cubits high, entirely of solid gold."[31] In Dan 2, the statue does not represent a deity, but rather the nations as they would have been known in the ancient Near East. The nations have been subsumed under a colossal anthropomorphic figure.

The image is composed of various metals. These are significant. Symbolism of metals representing the ages of history was common in antiquity. Hesiod, the epic Greek poet from the time of Homer (c. 751–650 BCE), describes the course of history as regressively worsening—going from bad to worse, we would say. Each of the five epochs or periods of history, except one, is symbolized by a metal. The golden generation begins the cycle. Next comes a second of silver, followed by an age of bronze, then a fourth not

---

30. The Hymn of Victory of Mer-ne-Ptah (also known as the Israel Stela) mentions "Israel is laid waste, his seed is not" (translated by John A. Wilson [*ANET*, 378a]).

31. Herodotus, *Hist.* 1:183.

specified by a metal, and finally, the fifth, an age of iron.[32] The declining values of the metals, as the poem makes clear, symbolize the decline of human civilization.

In a Persian text, the deity Ahura Mazda shows Zoroaster the trunk of a tree, on which were four branches, "one of gold, one of silver, one of steel, and one of mixed iron." These were the "four periods which will come" in the millennium of Zoroaster, founder of the Zoroastrian religion.[33] In this parallel, the four metals represent kingdoms, just as they do here. While Daniel may have been influenced by such parallels, the imagery is more likely a common motif. The notion of four empires followed by a fifth, according to Swain, was known in Rome "several years before the rise of Judas Maccabaeus and the composition of the Book of Daniel."[34] This is the first example in the book of Daniel of how an apocalyptist borrows symbols—in this case, metals and a statue—to depict nations and events.

The most vulnerable part of the statue is its feet, composed of a mixture of iron and clay. The Aramaic term for clay (חֲסַף, *hasaph*, pottery clay) suggests the clay was externally attached to the image, perhaps like inlaid terra-cotta tile.[35] Since the feet supported the entire statue, crushing them would cause the statue itself to collapse and shatter into pieces. The stone that strikes the image then grows to become a great mountain and fills the entire earth.

> [36] "This was the dream, and its interpretation we will tell before the king. [37] You, O king, the king of kings, to whom the God of the heavens has given you the kingdom, power, might, and honor, [38] so that wherever human beings dwell, the beasts of the field and the birds of the heaven he has given into your hand, and he has made you sovereign over them all—you are the head of gold!
>
> [39] "After you will arise another kingdom of earth inferior to you; then another, a third kingdom of bronze, shall rule over all the earth. [40] Then the fourth kingdom will be strong as iron; just as iron breaks and shatters everything, so like iron that crushes all these, it will smash and crush. [41] Then you saw the feet and toes partly of potter's clay, so the kingdom will be divided, part of the strength of iron will be in it; hence you saw the iron mixed

---

32. Hesiod, *Op.* 109–201. Hesiod inserts an Age of Heroes between the Bronze and Iron Ages, thus having five ages between time of humanity's innocence and his own day: gold, silver, bronze, heroes, iron.

33. *Bahman Yasht*, ch. 1, cited in J. Collins, *Daniel* (Hermeneia), 163.

34. Swain, "Theory of Four Monarchies," 9.

35. Hartman and Di Lella, *Daniel*, 141.

with clay. ⁴² As the toes of the feet were partly of iron and partly of clay, part of the kingdom will be strong, part of it brittle. ⁴³ As you saw the iron mixed with the clay, they will be mixed with human seed, but they will not cling one to another, even as iron is not mixed with clay.

⁴⁴ "In the days of those kings the God of the heavens will set up an unending kingdom that will never be destroyed, and the kingdom will not be left to another people. It will crush and put an end to all these kingdoms, and it will stand in perpetuity. ⁴⁵ Because you saw a stone cut out from the mountain—without hands—and it shattered the iron, bronze, clay, silver, and gold, the great God has made known to the king what will be after this. The dream is certain and its interpretation trustworthy."

Nebuchadnezzar is the head of gold. Daniel prefaces the first item in the interpretation by acknowledging the near-universal sovereignty of the Babylonian monarch over the ancient Near East and even the beasts of the field and the birds of the heaven, with the important caveat authority has been given him by the God of the heavens (vv. 37–38). As far as the statue goes, then, Nebuchadnezzar is the head of gold. Jeremiah's comment about his contemporary Nebuchadnezzar is fitting: "All the nations shall serve him and his son and his grandson, until the time of his own land comes; then many nations and great kings shall make him their slave" (Jer 27:7). Nebuchadnezzar ruled from 605 to 562 BCE, but his empire did not endure much more than two decades after him. Evil-Merodach (Amel-Marduk), his son, ruled from 561 to 560; then Meriglissar (or Nergal-shar-usur), 559 to 556; and Labashi-Marduk, 556. Nabonidus led a coup d'état in 555 and reigned until the Persian takeover in 539.

There would follow Nebuchadnezzar another kingdom, usually understood to be inferior to Babylon (v. 39). Although most translations render the compound Aramaic preposition מִנָּךְ (*minnak*) as inferior or less than, it can also mean different from or even more than.³⁶ It is comparative here, contrasting this second kingdom with Nebuchadnezzar, either as inferior or at least different. This kingdom corresponds to the silver metallic chest and arms of the statue. A third kingdom of bronze follows, then an iron kingdom that crushes all the previous kingdoms (v. 40). The iron strength fades with the next development, feet mixed of potter's clay and iron. Part of the kingdom will be strong, part of it brittle (vv. 41–42), possibly a reference to intermarriage of the ruling classes.

Who are the four kingdoms symbolized by the metallic statue?

---

36. *Minnak* is a compound, joining the preposition *min* (מִן, from) with the objective pronoun (ךְ-, you).

The enigma of the identity of the four kingdoms in Dan 2 has been a matter of perennial debate. With a single exception, Dan 2 does not identify which four kingdoms are represented by the different metals. Only the first empire is indicated. "You are the head of gold," Daniel says to Nebuchadnezzar, identifying him—or his reign—and the Neo-Babylonian empire as the first of four successive empires (v. 38). The others are not specified, but they appear to come on the scene in sequence. Another kingdom inferior to Babylon, then a third kingdom, and a fourth kingdom, as though Daniel is checking off the dominant empires of antiquity like bullet points on a list. The four empires, succeeded by a fifth in the form of a great stone, have accordingly been variously identified.[37] Traditionally, at least since the first-century CE, students of Daniel have recognized the following sequence:[38]

- Babylon
- Persia (Medo-Persia)
- Greece
- Rome

The sequence ending with Rome as the fourth kingdom first appears in Josephus, the first-century CE Jewish historian.[39] Although Josephus is frequently cited in this connection, his description of the great metallic image does not specifically identify Rome as the fourth empire. He only implies it. By the time of 2 Esdras (late first or early second century CE), the original four kingdoms of Daniel have been re-shuffled and the fourth has now become the Roman empire. Says the angel mediator to Ezra, "It [the fourth kingdom in Daniel] was not explained to him as I now explain to you or have explained it" (2 Esd 12:10–12).[40]

This proposed sequence, however, has dominated the interpretation of Daniel down to modern times.[41] The apocalypses of 2 Esdras and 2

---

37. Even in antiquity, there was debate over the exact sequence of empires. Jerome (c. 347–420 CE) identified the fourth empire with Rome (*Jerome's Commentary on Daniel*, 32), as did the third-century Roman presbyter Hippolytus (*ANF* 5:209–10), while Ephrem the Syrian (c. 306–373 CE) pointed to the Greeks under Alexander, with the toes of the image representing the ten Hellenistic kings from Alexander's old empire (Ephrem the Syrian, "In Danielem," 2:207).

38. See Archer, "Daniel," 46–48; Young, *Prophecy of Daniel*, 74–76; Talbot, *Prophecies of Daniel*, 44–49; Gaebelein, *Daniel*, 28–29.

39. Josephus, *Ant.* 10.10.4.

40. On this, see Gammie, "Classification," 203–4.

41. Eissfeldt, *Old Testament*, 520; Whitcomb, *Daniel*, 94–96. See Hippolytus, *Commentary on Daniel* 7:7, as cited in Stevenson, "Daniel," in Stevenson and Glerup, *Ezekiel, Daniel*, 225. Our aim in this commentary is to recover the *original* understanding of

Baruch, as noted above, echo this interpretation. The Jewish Talmud also follows this arrangement. It may further be found in such medieval Jewish interpreters as R. Saadiah Gaon (882–942), one of the prominent leaders of Babylonian Judaism, R. Moshe ben Maimon, and R. Moshe ben Nachman. The sixteenth-century Protestant Reformers in their dispute with the Roman Catholic hierarchy also identified the fourth kingdom with Rome. A half century later, English Puritans gladly found Daniel conducive for theological and political criticism of the established Anglican church. They understood themselves as the "holy ones of the Most High" (Dan 7:27). In seventeenth-century Cromwellian England, a non-conformist Puritan sect calling themselves the Fifth Monarchists took the fourth kingdom in this vision as the Roman pope (and as the antichrist). The great stone signified the second coming of Christ, which would inaugurate a millennial reign upon earth (Rev 20:1–15). They identified themselves as the saints who would inherit the earth when Christ returned, hence their name Fifth Monarchists, taken from the fifth (stone) kingdom in Dan 2. The Fifth Monarchists saw themselves divinely charged to overthrow the secular government and abolish all remnants of worldly rule in England, a goal they hoped to attain by the year 1666.[42] Although the Fifth Monarchists played a significant role in the civil and military affairs at the time, they were finally suppressed in 1661. On a more sober note, utilizing Daniel's visions of empires, Sir Isaac Newton wrote *Observations upon the Prophecies of Daniel and the Apocalypse of St. John* (1733), in which he tried to unravel a world chronology. Much present-day conservative scholarship also sees the regimes as Babylon, Persia, Greece, and Rome.[43]

Most contemporary biblical scholars, however, propose an alternative sequence which most likely goes back to the original Danielic order:

- Babylon
- Media
- Persia

---

these visions rather than focus on later reinterpretation.

42. Moynahan, *Faith*, 473. For a discussion of this sect and its interpretation of Daniel, see Froom, *Prophetic Faith*, 2:566–79.

43. Archer, "Daniel," 25, 85–87. In the nineteenth century, E. B. Pusey was the foremost defender of the traditional view (Pusey, *Daniel the Prophet*). Young also adopts this view: "The fourth monarchy represents not only the historical Roman empire, but a *revived* Roman empire" (Young, *Prophecy of Daniel*, 75; italics in original). See also Young, *Daniel*, 143–47; 275–94; Talbot, *Prophecies of Daniel*, 47–49; U. Smith, *Prophecies of Daniel*, 41–55; Haskell, *Story of Daniel*, 35; VanGemeren, "Daniel," 593; Ford, *Daniel*, 95. Nichol, *Seventh-Day Adventist Bible Commentary*, takes a similar position (4:771–75).,

- Greece

Some evidence suggests this order originated in Persia, where it initially was Assyria, Media, then Persia; but Daniel has substituted Babylon for Assyria, probably because Babylon, successor to the Assyrians, was obviously more relevant for Jewish history of the time.[44] This same sequence may be found in the Sibylline Oracles, which adds a fifth kingdom (Rome).[45]

The main problem with this order—Babylon, Media, Persia, and Greece—is that Media never attained a status comparable to any of the other great empires. It also did not follow the Neo-Babylonian empire but existed conterminously with it.[46] The Neo-Babylonian empire passed directly to the Persians under Cyrus the Great in 539, so Persia was Babylon's successor, not Media. Media in this sequence, however, may have drawn inspiration from the prophecy in Isaiah:[47]

> See, I am stirring up the Medes against them,
>> who have no regard for silver
>> and do not delight in gold.
> Their bows will slaughter the young men . . .
> And Babylon, the glory of kingdoms,
>> the splendor and pride of the Chaldeans,
> will be like Sodom and Gomorrah
> when God overthrew them. (Isa 13:17–19)

Some assistance in resolving the identity of these empires occurs in three other visions in Daniel. There we find a comparable sequence of empires ending with Greece—not Rome—and the evil king who arises from the Greek empire.

In Dan 7, there is an order consisting of a lion, bear, leopard, and a terrible, horrific creature representing four kings that arise out of the earth (v. 17). Again, as in Dan 2, the identity of these animal images is not specified.

---

44. Sybylline Oracles 4:49–54; Testament of Naphtali 5:8; see J. Collins, *Daniel* (Hermeneia), 163–64.

45. Sybylline Oracles 4:49–129; see also Herodotus, *Hist.* 1.95, 130; Tob 14:3–4, 15.

46. Porteous is even more specific, calling Media an apocryphal kingdom, "the existence of which, between the Babylonian and Persian Empires, there is absolutely no trace in contemporary records" (Porteous, *Daniel*, 47). "The weakest spot in the whole structure of the Maccabean theory," states Archer, "is to be found in the identification of the fourth empire predicted in chapter 2" (Archer, *Survey of Old Testament*, 396).

47. Virtually all critical scholars see this passage as late and not from the Isaiah of Jerusalem. It is probably to be dated to the time of the Babylonian exile or later (Tucker, "Book of Isaiah 1–39," 155).

They have generally been seen as Babylon, Persia, Greece, and Rome, or Babylon, Media, Persia, and Greece, just as above. The principal difference between chapters 2 and 7, in this respect, is the latter closes with a little horn power that emerges out of the fourth kingdom and oppresses the "people of the holy ones" (vv. 23–27).

In Dan 8, there is a sequence of three empires, a ram, a goat, and the little horn. The ram is specifically identified as the kings of Media and Persia; the goat, the king of Greece; the little horn, "a king of bold countenance" (vv. 20–23). The little horn arises out of one of the divisions of the Greek empire (vv. 9–10). A sequence of Media-Persia, Greece, and a king out of the divisions of the Greek empire may thus be recognized. Cyrus II had conquered Media some years prior to the fall of Babylon and made it part of his Persian empire.

Finally, in Dan 11, a vision with little explicit apocalyptic symbolism, the sequence is Persia (v. 2a), Greece (vv. 2b–4), the king of the south (vv. 5–19), and finally the king of the north, who considers himself "greater than any god" (vv. 21–45). The king of the south is no doubt Egypt under the Ptolemies, while the king of the north is the Seleucid (Syrian) kings, culminating in Antiochus IV.

Each of the visions in chapters 2, 7, 8, and 11 thus seems to cover essentially the same ground. Chapters 8 and 11 end on the same note: the oppressive reign of an evil king who arises from the ruins of the Greek empire and who is subsequently condemned by God and brought to judgment. Chapter 8 ends with the work of this evil king under the symbolism of a little horn (vv. 23–25), identical to the little horn in Dan 7:23–27. It is reasonable to assume, then, that both little horns (chs. 7–8) are the same entity, namely, a malevolent king who rises from the divisions of the Greek empire. Significantly, the latest gentile ruler mentioned anywhere in Daniel is the prince of Greece (10:20). The age of Greece—the Hellenistic age—is apparently the terminal point of all the apocalyptic visions in Daniel. The author, who evidently lived during the middle of the second century BCE, felt the climax of history to be imminent. If Greece, then, is the fourth empire, then the third would have to be Persia, the second, Media, and the first, Babylon. If this interpretation is correct, these four empires—Babylon, Media, Persia, Greece—are probably the ones represented in the stories and apocalyptic prophecies in the book and thus most likely those corresponding to the successive metals in the image.[48]

In our own day, identifying the four empires has continued to vary widely. Some scholars posit the four as four individual kings, rather than

---

48. J. Collins, *Daniel* (Hermeneia), 168; Porteous, *Daniel*, 46–47.

kingdoms or empires, succeeding Nebuchadnezzar. According to Löwinger, they are four Assyrian kings.[49] Others find four Persian kings[50] or the four Ptolemaic kings.[51] Goldingay favors identifying them as the four kings mentioned in Daniel: Nebuchadnezzar, Belshazzar, Darius, and Cyrus.[52]

The four-kingdom motif, however, may not actually designate four specific, successive empires or even kings. Widespread throughout the ancient Mediterranean world, as we have seen, was the idea of a four-kingdom schema as comprehensive of the course of history.[53] Hesiod, the Greek poet (eighth century BCE), imagines the world as unfolding in four generations—one golden, another silver, a third bronze, and a fourth iron—like the metals in Nebuchadnezzar's visionary statue.[54] The Greek historian Herodotus (c. 485-425 BCE) writes: "The Assyrians had held the empire of upper Asia for the space of 520 years, when the Medes set the example of revolt from their authority." Later, "the Medes were brought under the rule of the Persians."[55] The Babylonian Dynastic Prophecy from the Hellenistic period mentions the rise and fall of the nations in an alternating pattern of good and evil, including Assyria, Babylon, Persia, and Macedonia.[56] Aemilius Sura, in a fragment preserved by Vaelleius Paterculus, also refers to the full four-kingdom motif, but adds a fifth: "The Assyrians were the first of all races to hold power, then the Medes, after them the Persians, and then the Macedonians. Then when the two kings, Philip and Antiochus, of Macedonian origin, had been completely conquered, soon after the overthrow of Carthage, the supreme command passed to the Roman people."[57] In Daniel, the fifth empire—the kingdom of God—is the great stone that fills the whole earth.

From this it appears the four-kingdom motif is quite flexible and resists a straight linear designation of specific powers. Baldwin, given this fact, does not try to identify the nations in the sequence. She pinpoints Babylon, then passes on to the fourth kingdom, which she leaves unidentified as well.

49. Löwinger, "Nebuchadnezzar's Dream," 1:336-52.

50. Schedl, *Geschichte des Alten Testaments*, 5:79-80.

51. Gammie, "Spatial and Ethical Dualism," 356-85. The four proposed Ptolemaic kings are Ptolemy I Soter (305-283 BCE); Ptolemy II Philadelphus (283-247); Ptolemy III Euergetes (247-221); Ptolemy IV Philopator (221-203).

52. Goldingay, *Daniel*, 174.

53. Cf. Hasel, "Four World Empires," 17-30.

54. Hesiod, *Works and Days*, lines 110, 127, 144, 176. An interpolation in Hesiod gives a fifth, an age of demigods.

55. Herodotus, *Hist.* 1.95, 130.

56. See the text of the Dynastic Prophecy in *COS* 1.150, 481-82.

57. Cited in Swain, "Theory of Four Monarchies," 2.

Then she directs attention to the fifth power, the God of heaven, just as in Daniel 2 (vv. 44–45).[58]

Perhaps we should think of the four-kingdom trope along the same lines as we do the four directions on the compass or the four seasons of the year. Analogous to the four Edenic rivers (Gen 2:10–14) and the four horns in Zechariah (Zech 1:18), the four kingdoms represent the Near Eastern world in general.[59] It seems to be a comprehensive image of history—so understood in antiquity—without necessarily identifying all the participating empires.

Turning back to the statue itself, we notice the feet, composed of iron mixed with the clay (v. 43), following the sequence of empires, may refer to political intermarriage, manifested especially in the attempts of the Ptolemaic and Seleucid rulers to align themselves politically through marital alliances. Antiochus II, for example, married Berenice in 252 BCE. Ptolemy Epiphanes wed Cleopatra in 193/194.[60] Daniel mentions such marital alliances (Dan 11:6, 17). Alternatively, the phrase may refer to the intermarriage of different cultures encouraged by Alexander and his successors, a practice repugnant to the Jews.[61] The incompatible elements of iron and clay mixed in the feet of the image point to serious, fatal divisions in the fourth kingdom. Upon the death of Alexander the Great in 323 BCE, with no clear successor, the Greek empire was divided among Alexander's generals, two of whom controlled the Ptolemaic empire, centered in Egypt, and two of whom controlled Seleucid in Syria. These two empires struggled for dominance over the territory of Judea, which lay uncomfortably between them, for more than a century. The Seleucid king Antiochus III defeated the Ptolemies at the Battle of Paneion in 198 and seized control of the province of Judea, thus setting the stage for the Antiochene crisis of 167–164 BCE, the historical context of the book of Daniel. Since the Seleucids proved stronger than the Ptolemies, Porteous suggests the iron in the feet represents the Seleucids; the clay, the Ptolemies.[62]

This brings us to the climax of the dream (v. 44). All attention is now focused on the stone that becomes a mountain. The stone is cut out from the mountain without hands—with no human assistance (v. 45). It represents the unending kingdom of God that will not be dominated by any other. Although the term messianic is not found here, there can be little doubt that

---

58. Baldwin, *Daniel*, 93.
59. von Rad, *Old Testament Theology*, 2:312n25.
60. Smith-Christopher, "Book of Daniel," 7:55.
61. Russell, *Daniel*, 53.
62. Porteous, *Daniel*, 49.

the stone represents the long-awaited messianic kingdom. The other nations preceding it, symbolized by iron, bronze, clay, silver, and gold, will be smashed, but the stone grows into a great mountain. The dream, however, does not go on to specify who will benefit from the deity's entrance onto the historical stage.[63]

The growth of the stone into a great mountain compares to the oracle in Isa 2:2–4 and Mic 4:1–4.

> In the days to come
>> the mountain of the LORD's house
> shall be established as the highest of the mountains,
>> and shall be raised above the hills,
> all the nations shall stream to it.

Christian tradition, or course, has usually understood the stone as the Messiah and the forthcoming messianic kingdom.[64] In seventeenth-century Cromwellian England, as we have seen, the non-conformist Puritan sect calling themselves the Fifth Monarchists took the fourth kingdom in this vision as the Roman pope (as the antichrist). The great stone signified the second coming of Christ, which would inaugurate a millennial reign upon earth, as indicated in Rev 20.

The shattering of the great statue, Daniel informs Nebuchadnezzar, occurs in the days of those kings. Who are these kings? The phrase may point to the kingdoms that arise following the fourth empire or, alternatively, to the whole network of nations in the ancient world. Is the phrase "in the days of those kings" an attempt to pinpoint more precisely the end or climax of human history? Consider the dream from Nebuchadnezzar's perspective. He is informed his kingdom will decline, but the event apparently is not imminent. "After me, the deluge!" There is yet to be a sequence of empires. The coming kingdom of God—the great stone—thus lies indefinitely in the future, when another earthly kingdom is dominant. For Nebuchadnezzar, the eschatological climax is thus practically delayed or deferred.[65] However, no date is assigned this climatic event. Later in the book, we hear of several different time periods at which eschatological deliverance is expected. A time, two times, and half a time; 2300 evenings and mornings; seventy weeks; 1290 and 1335 days—all appear as yardsticks marking the limits of the persistence of evil, but in Dan 2, no such figure is given. The latter two numbers—1290 and 1335 days—seem to be calculations extending or

---

63. Crenshaw, *Story and Faith*, 364.
64. Young, *Prophecy of Daniel*, 79. Cf. Mark 12:1–12; Eph 2:18–22; 1 Pet 2:4–8.
65. J. Collins, *Daniel* (Hermeneia), 174–75.

recalculating the end of days (Dan 12:11–13). Attempts to fix the date for the coming of God's eschatological kingdom, however, constitute a sad and tragic history of failed hopes and bitter disappointment.

A few years ago, near the exit ramp on one of Atlanta's busy interstate highways appeared a slovenly dressed man holding a large white sign with a carefully lettered message: "The world will end on September 27!" He stood at the exit ramp for several weeks. The bold, audacious prediction caught my attention every time I approached. The constant flow of traffic prevented my asking the man how he had reached this bold conclusion. Even though I never got to ask the question, everyone knows how the story comes out. September 27 came and went. The man vanished. I do not know what happened to him. But his prediction ended miserably—like all the other predictions of the end of history before him.

The large stone Nebuchadnezzar sees, of course, is a symbol of God's rule. "In the days to come, the mountain of the Lord's house," Micah predicts, "shall be established as the highest of the mountains . . . peoples shall stream to it" (Mic 4:1–2). This mountain of God "will end the reign of terror perpetuated by humans." It comes without human assistance. While it refers to the end of evil, it also makes room for the healing of those victimized by evil. "When humans try to cut the stone, even if they do so in God's name, the result is inevitably violent destruction with no healing."[66]

NEBUCHADNEZZAR HONORS DANIEL (2:46–49)

> [46] Then king Nebuchadnezzar fell prostrate and did obeisance to Daniel, and he ordered a grain offering and incense be made to him. [47] The king spoke to Daniel, "Of a truth your god is God of gods and Lord of kings. He reveals secrets, for you have been able to reveal this secret!"
>
> [48] Then the king promoted Daniel and awarded him many excellent gifts, making him ruler over all the district of Babylon and chief of prefects over all the wise men of Babylon. [49] Daniel requested of the king and he appointed over the administration of the province of Babylon Shadrach, Meshach, and Abednego, but Daniel remained at the king's court.

Nebuchadnezzar's response is unusual (v. 46). Having just been assured his own kingdom was going to come to its end, replaced by another, and then the entire edifice of nations brought to a crashing end, instead of opposing

---

66. Smith-Christopher, "Book of Daniel," 55.

the interpretation given by a Jewish captive, he rewards Daniel. Is he relieved all this will happen after he is gone? Without denouncing his own gods, he praises Daniel's God as God of gods and Lord of kings. Exalted thus over all the gods of Babylon, Daniel's God is the One who reveals secrets. He orders an offering to Daniel, a move that has troubled both Jewish and Christian commentators, for it implies worship. Jewish tradition accordingly resists the idea that Daniel accepted these sacrifices. Nebuchadnezzar falls prostrate and does obeisance to Daniel, apparently in an act of reverence. This, however, does not seem to bother our author. Is not Nebuchadnezzar bowing to Daniel's God, rather than Daniel himself? Moreover, the king rewards Daniel by making him administrator or chief of prefects (a prefect is an administrative district) over all Babylon's wise men and diviners (v. 47). He also grants Daniel's request that Shadrach, Meshach, and Abednego be placed over the administration of the province of Babylon (v. 49). That Daniel is promoted ruler over the province of Babylon, and his three friends as administrators, invokes the literary pattern of three plus one. The pattern whereby a unit of three is capped by a fourth of special standing is well-known from other ancient Near Eastern literature, as well as the HB.[67] As successful modern politicians do, Daniel brings his friends with him into public office.

Several of the stories in the book end like this. The king acknowledges the God of Judah and changes his attitude toward the Jewish captives. Conversion to the Jewish faith or monotheistic transformation would be too strong a word for this. Nevertheless, the king is favorably disposed toward the Jewish subjects and their God, whom he concedes—at least momentarily—as superior to his own. On Nebuchadnezzar's part, this is a shift toward henotheism.[68] The purpose of these narratives is to show the superiority of Israel's God over all competitive deities, especially those encountered during the diaspora. Divine deliverance of the Jewish exiles demonstrates God's mighty power to rescue those harassed and persecuted.

Daniel's perceptive superiority over the soothsayers of the Babylonian court and, behind that, the preeminence of Daniel's God, the seemingly random rise and fall of empires, directed from behind the scenes by the God of gods, leading to the final denouement of the divine kingdom that will never be destroyed: these are the themes converging in this epic story. It sets the stage for the rest of Daniel, particularly the apocalyptic visions to follow.

---

67. Talmon, "Daniel," 347–49; e. g., "For three transgressions of Damascus, and for four, I will not revoke punishment" (Amos 1:3). Cf. also Amos 1:6, 9, 11, 13; 2:1, 4, 6; Prov 30:15–31.

68. Henotheism is the belief there is one principal deity for a community, tribe, or nation, without denying the existence of other gods. One god is held to be preeminent over all other gods.

The God of Gold

Daniel 3

Nothing is more difficult and nothing requires more character than to find oneself in open opposition to one's time and to say loudly: No.

—Kurt Tucholsky, *Schnipsel*

In this story, God astonishingly snatches Daniel's three Jewish colleagues from the jaws of death. The chapter reminds us of the stories in *Foxe's Book of Martyrs*. As in Esther, the Jewish exiles, perhaps too hastily promoted to high positions in the government, become clear targets of prejudiced, jealous ambition. The Jewish heroes are put in danger and sentenced to death. Only through divine power are they rescued. The movement in the court tale goes from "scurrilous accusation to unjust punishment, and from imminent death to miraculous rescue."[1]

The story of the great image on the plain of Dura connects with the previous chapter about the great metallic image through the catchword צֶלֶם (*tselem*, image or statue), the fourth word in the sentence at Dan 3:1. Like Dan 6, this story reveals the rivalry between the Judean exiles and the established members of the royal court.

Strangely, Daniel is absent from the narrative. Hardly mentioned in Dan 1 and 2, but on center stage here, the three Jewish youths do not appear again in the rest of the stories in Dan 4–6. Daniel's absence has been variously explained. According to one Jewish tradition, Nebuchadnezzar had

---

1. Anderson, *Signs and Wonders*, 27.

dispatched him to Tiberias to build a canal.[2] Other traditions claim that, like the three companions, he was initially commanded to worship the image, but refused. Perhaps because of his high regard for Daniel (Dan 2:46-49), however, Nebuchadnezzar declined to impose the same penalty his companions received. Daniel observed the entire spectacle from a distance, Hippolytus claims, and from this vantage point encouraged his companions to resist.[3] That Daniel is omitted from the narrative may simply indicate that these six stories (Dan 1-6) were originally independent and only later brought together by the editor.

The story begins with a lengthy introduction (Dan 3:1-7), which sets up a loyalty test, then moves quickly to the accusation against the Jews (vv. 8-12) and their interrogation before the king (vv. 13-18). They are then condemned to death and thrown into a blazing furnace (vv. 19-23). To the king's astonishment, a fourth person appears amid the flames, shielding the three Jewish youths from harm (vv. 24-27). At the conclusion, in a kind of reversal of errors, Nebuchadnezzar acknowledges the God of the Judean exiles and promotes them to high office in the Babylonian province (vv. 28-30).

After a brief connecting sentence, the LXX has added to the story the Prayer of Azariah (vv. 24-45) and the Song of the Three Young Men (vv. 46-90). These Additions will be discussed in part 3 of this commentary.

THE LOYALTY TEST (3:1-7)

> Nebuchadnezzar the king made an image of gold, its height was sixty cubits, its breadth six cubits. He set it up on the plain of Dura in the province of Babylon. ² Then Nebuchadnezzar the king sent to gather the satraps, prefects, governors, counselors, treasurers, judges, and magistrates, as well as all rulers of the provinces to come to the dedication of the image that Nebuchadnezzar had set up. ³ Then were gathered the satraps, prefects, governors, counselors, treasurers, judges, and magistrates, as well as all rulers of the provinces to the dedication of the image that Nebuchadnezzar the king had set up. They were standing in front of the image that Nebuchadnezzar had set up. ⁴ Then the herald loudly proclaimed, "To you command is given, O peoples, nations, and languages, ⁵ at the time that you hear the sound of the horn, pipe, lyre, trigon, harp, stringed

---

2. See b. Sanh. 93a.
3. Cited in J. Collins, *Daniel* (Hermeneia), 179n1.

instrument, wind instrument, and every sort of music, you shall fall down and worship the golden image that Nebuchadnezzar the king has set up. ⁶ But whoever will not fall down and worship, in that instant will be thrown into the midst of the furnace of blazing fire." ⁷ Thus, in the moment when all peoples heard the sound of the horn, pipe, lyre, trigon, stringed instrument, wind instrument, and every sort of music, all peoples, nations, and languages fell down and worshipped the golden image that Nebuchadnezzar the king had set up.

The LXX and Theodotion Greek texts preface this story with a chronological note, "in the eighteenth year of Nebuchadnezzar," thus dating the incident to the year when Nebuchadnezzar carried out the third Judean deportation (582 BCE). This gives the story an implicit brutal, repressive setting.[4] It certainly reads like an occasion to separate, isolate, and then eliminate disloyal subjects. Unlike the statue in the previous story, we are given the dimensions of this one (v. 1). It stands sixty cubits or about ninety feet tall, and only six cubits or nine feet wide, giving the statue a slender, column-like appearance. Such height—approximately seven to eight stories—would have been surpassed in antiquity only by the famous Colossus of Rhodes, which stood seventy cubits tall.

The disproportional size of the statue has led some to question whether it had a human shape. It was rather more like a stela, obelisk, or pillar, such as ancient kings typically erected to promote their accomplishments. However, since the image is called a *tselem*, it probably had a human shape, particularly in view of the metallic, human-shaped *tselem* in Dan 2, of which this image may be an imitation. It is portrayed as an object of worship associated with Nebuchadnezzar's gods (vv. 12, 14, 18). To obey the king's command to worship the image would provide evidence of loyalty to the king, as well as to his gods.

That the image was of gold suggests a further connection with Dan 2, where Nebuchadnezzar is the head of gold on the great metallic image of the nations. Unlike the statue in Dan 2, this statue is entirely of gold, although not solid gold. Typically, such iconic statues had wooden cores, or in smaller statues, clay overlaid with gold.[5] Similar composite metallic figures are known from ancient Syria, including a god modelled in bronze, with a head covering and head of gold and a body plated in silver.[6]

---

4. J. Collins, *Daniel* (Hermeneia), 180; see Jer 52:28–30.
5. "An idol?—A workman casts it, and a goldsmith overlays it with gold" (Isa 40:19).
6. For examples, see *ANEP*, figs. 466–67, 482–84.

Nebuchadnezzar erects the statue at Dura, a Mesopotamian term, derived from the Akkadian *dūru* (city wall, fortified place),[7] which sometimes appears in compound names. The location is unknown, although it probably was not an area within the walls surrounding Babylon.[8] The text places the plain of Dura somewhere in the province of Babylon, probably near the city environs. Such statues were not lacking for temples during the reign of Nebuchadnezzar. Nor was it unusual for a person to lie at the feet of such a towering statue to seek guidance from an oracle.[9]

The occasion may have marked the dedication of a new temple. Nebuchadnezzar is known to have restored the temple of Nanna at Ur, an old Sumerian city, clearing out the rooms where priests privately made offerings to the gods and replacing them with an open area where an altar had been set up in full public view. Here this was evidently done so worshipers could witness and participate, at least vicariously, in the ritual acts of the priests.[10]

To this dedication of the image, Nebuchadnezzar assembles the satraps, prefects, governors, counselors, treasurers, judges, and magistrates, as well as all rulers of the provinces, as official representatives of his empire (vv. 2-3). The function of all these officials is uncertain, but the satraps, at least in the later Persian empire, oversaw the main divisions of the empire. The prefects were high officials directly under the satraps, and the governors were heads of the divisions of the satrapies.[11]

Once these officials had gathered, a herald gives the order (vv. 4-6): When the assembly hears the horn, pipe, lyre, trigon, harp, stringed instrument, wind instrument, and every sort of music, they are to fall prostrate and worship the golden image. The entire musical ensemble includes stringed as well as wind and percussion instruments. The designation of three of the instruments have passed from Greek into Aramaic: the lyre (קַתְרוֹס, *qatros*), harp," (פְּסַנְתֵּרִין, *pesantarin*), and wind instrument (סוּמְפֹּנְיָה, *sumponeyah*). Since these terms are Greek, they may provide a clue as to the date of the writing of this story. *Sumponeyah*, for example, is not mentioned even in Greek literature before the Hellenistic period (c. 300 BCE). This suggests chapter 3 was probably not committed to writing prior to the Hellenistic era, when the Greek language became widely dissimulated.[12]

---

7. Hartman and Di Lella, *Daniel*, 160.
8. E. Cook, "In the Plain," 115-16.
9. Baldwin, *Daniel*, 96.
10. Harrison, *Old Testament Times*, 271-72.
11. Hartman and Di Lella, *Daniel*, 156. Compare the list of Nebuchadnezzar's officials in the clay prism now in the Istanbul Museum ("Neo-Babylonian Empire and Its Successors," translated by A. Leo Oppenheim [*ANET* 307-8]).
12. Citing the presence of Greek culture in Syria and Palestine from as early as the

Should anyone in the convocation fail to bow down and worship the image, he or she would be thrown into the midst of the furnace of blazing fire. Burning criminals alive as a form of execution was rare in the ancient Near East. Jeremiah predicts Nebuchadnezzar would roast the prophets Ahab and Zedekiah in the fire. For prostitution, a Levitical priest's daughter was to be burned in fire, as was the man who incestuously married both mother and daughter.[13] Asshurnasirpal II, the ninth-century BCE Assyrian king, is reputed to have burned some prisoners. The closest parallel to this story, however, comes from the Maccabean era, the same period to which we have dated the book of Daniel. Antiochus Epiphanes executed the high priest Menelaus by throwing him alive into the burning ashes in a kind of incinerator.[14] It may be the author of this tale wanted readers to find in Antiochus IV Epiphanes an echo of Nebuchadnezzar. Antiochus had set about destroying the Jewish faith and erected an idol of Zeus at the altar in the temple courtyard, insisting the Jewish people worship his gods.[15]

The furnace in our story appears to have been like a kiln. At its top was an opening through which combustible fuel could be added and from which the men were thrown. An opening at the bottom permitted the cinders to be raked out and observers to witness what happened within.[16]

When the herald gives the command, then, everyone is to bow obediently in humble worship of the golden image that Nebuchadnezzar the king had set up (v. 7).

THE ACCUSATION (3:8-12)

> [8] Therefore, at this time the Chaldeans approached and maliciously accused the Jews. [9] They said to Nebuchadnezzar the king, "O king, live forever! [10] You, O king, made a decree that every person who hears the sound of the horn, pipe, lyre, trigon, stringed instrument, wind instrument, and every sort of music shall fall down and worship the golden image, [11] and whoever does not fall down and worship will be thrown into the midst of the furnace of burning fire. [12] There are men of

---

seventh or sixth centuries, Young takes issue with this. "The presence of Greek words ... is no argument against the early date for the authorship of the book" (Young, *Prophecy of Daniel*, 87).

13. Jer 29: 21–23; Lev 21:9; 20:14.
14. See 2 Macc 13:4–8; J. Collins, *Daniel* (Hermeneia), 185.
15. Russell, *Daniel*, 60.
16. Hartman and Di Lella, *Daniel*, 164; Russell, *Daniel*, 62–63.

the Jews whom you appointed over the service of the province of Babylon—Shadrach, Meshach, and Abednego—these men have paid no attention to your mandate, O king. Your god they have not served, nor the golden image you have set up have they worshiped."

All fall reverently prostrate—except Shadrach, Meshach, and Abednego. No doubt because these three Jewish foreigners had been given important responsibilities within the government, certain Chaldeans (v. 8), the professional class of diviners, accuse them of several infractions, all connected to their Jewish identity. They disobey the king's orders (vv. 10–11), refuse to worship the golden image, and thus fail to serve Nebuchadnezzar's gods (v. 12). Worship of such an image, of course, was forbidden in Hebrew law.[17] As in most ancient monarchies, there were sycophants ready to pounce upon anyone perceived to deviate from allegiance to the potentate. אֲכַלוּ קַרְצֵיהוֹן (*akalu qartseho*, literally, "they ate their sides") is a particularly vivid Aramaic idiom for vicious slander or defamation.[18] Haman in the story of Esther accuses the Jewish Mordecai and ends up condemning the entire Jewish people (Esth 3:8–11). Tobit is likewise betrayed by an Assyrian informer (Tob 1:19). Such tragic anti-Semitism has been all too frequently the brutal lot of the Jewish people. Human nature being what it is, things have changed little since Daniel. Absolute monarchs generally expect complete subservience, at least externally. Yet they cannot read the heart, however, nor control it, no matter how foolishly they try.

THE INTERROGATION (3:13–18)

[13] Then in furious rage, Nebuchadnezzar commanded to apprehend Shadrach, Meshach, and Abednego. So, these men they brought before the king. [14] Nebuchadnezzar said to them, "Is it true, Shadrach, Meshach, and Abednego, to my gods you do not pay reverence and to the golden image that I have set up you do not worship? [15] Now, if you are ready, at the time when you hear the sound of the horn, pipe, lyre, trigon, harp, drum, and every sort of music, you fall down and worship the image that I have made. But if you do not worship at that moment, you will be

---

17. "You shall have no other gods before me . . . you shall not bow down to them or worship them" (Exod 20:3, 5; Deut 5:8–9).

18. This expression means "to eat what has been pinched off someone." Idiomatically, it signifies "to denounce someone, to make accusations to the authorities because of alleged crime" (Kaddari, "אכל (I, II)," 27).

thrown into the midst of the furnace of burning fire! Who then is the god who can rescue you from my hand?"

¹⁶ Shadrach, Meshach, and Abednego answered king Nebuchadnezzar, "We do not need to give you a response concerning this matter. ¹⁷ If our God whom we serve is able to rescue us from the burning furnace of fire, he will also rescue from your hand, O king. ¹⁸ If not, be it known to you, O king, your gods will we not serve, nor the golden image you have set up will we worship!"

Nebuchadnezzar now interrogates the three accused Jews (v. 13). He is furious (see Dan 2:12). Such an interrogation—confrontation with an antagonistic authority figure—is part of the stuff of martyr legends. In 2 Macc 7, a mother and her seven sons are callously questioned by the tyrannical potentate (Antiochus IV) before being sadistically tortured and murdered. Nebuchadnezzar offers the three young men an additional chance to bow down before the image (v. 14.) Is it true, he asks. While it is one thing to avoid bowing down in worship when surrounded by a crowd with everyone milling about, it is quite another when confronted directly by the king. If these three Jewish young men are to defy the royal cult of Babylon, they must be prepared for the brutal consequences.

Another opportunity, reiterated with the same threat of lethal punishment, will go far to confirm where their allegiance lies (v. 15). The king repeats the decree, almost in its entirety, as though to delay the final sentence. Who then is the god who can rescue you from me? What god exists—anywhere—capable of saving from my royal power? Nebuchadnezzar is the sole ruler of the empire. All peoples—at least in his universe—are subjects. His power, he hubristically assumes, is equal or superior to any deity one might conceivably reverence, and especially to the lowly, vanquished deity of the Jews. The question echoes the challenge of the Assyrian Rabshakah in Hezekiah's day. "Has any of the gods of the nations ever delivered its land out of the hand of the king of Assyria?" (2 Kgs 18:33).

We do not need to give you a response may refer to the offer of a second chance at compliance (v. 16). A second opportunity is not necessary, the three men respond. The opening expression in Aramaic in verse 17, a conditional phrase, proves difficult to render. אִיתַי (*itay*) is the Aramaic particle of existence, literally, "there is" or "there exists." This may convey the sense of "if there is the God whom we serve" or "if the God whom we serve exists," either of which implicitly challenges the reality of the Jewish God. The phrase probably does not reflect any uncertainty about God's existence, but rather hesitation about whether God in this instance would deliver from Nebuchadnezzar. "Any Jew of the post-exilic period," Collins observes, "must have known that God, for whatever reason, does not always deliver the faithful."[19] Another rendition of this sentiment, proposed by Montgomery, reads, "If our God can save us, he will."[20] The sense seems to be "if God wills, God is capable of rescuing us from the furnace and from your, hand, O king."

So understood, the sentence sets up the defiant reply of the Jewish youths in verse 18, where the calm demeanor of the three contrasts sharply with Nebuchadnezzar's furious rage: if the Jewish God cannot or will not deliver, your gods will we not serve, nor the golden image you have set up will we worship.

THE CONDEMNATION AND SENTENCING (3:19-23)

> [19] Then Nebuchadnezzar was filled with rage and his expression changed toward Shadrach, Meshach, and Abednego. He commanded to heat the furnace seven times more than customary. [20] He ordered some of the most valiant men in his army to bind Shadrach, Meshach, and Abednego and throw them into the furnace of burning fire. [21] Then these men were bound in their trousers, garments, head coverings, and clothing and thrown into the furnace of burning fire. [22] Because the order of the king was harsh and the furnace overheated, the men who hauled up Shadrach, Meshach, and Abednego were killed by a flame of fire. [23] Then these three men, Shadrach, Meshach, and Abednego, fell bound into the midst of the furnace of burning fire.

Enraged by having his second offer rebuffed, Nebuchadnezzar has Shadrach, Meshach, and Abednego hurled into the blazing, incinerating fire. His initial clemency rejected, he quickly snaps in anger (v. 19). Irate, he orders the furnace heated seven times than customary (v. 20)—as hot as possible. He orders the three men bound with ropes and in tight, festive clothing, covering head, upper body, and legs (v. 21), not stripped of clothes as customary, and entrusts his most valiant attendants to throw them helplessly to their death into the furnace. The scene satirically mocks the king's powerlessness to compel submission and emphasizes the miraculous nature of the deliverance to follow. But Nebuchadnezzar's extreme measures are no match for the God of heaven.

---

19. J. Collins, *Daniel* (Hermeneia), 188. Collins cites the defiance of Mattathias in 1 Macc 2:19-22: "Even if all the nations that live under the rule of the king obey him . . . yet I and my sons and my brothers will live by the covenant of our fathers." Some psalms of lament (e.g., Ps 88) contain no indication of God's deliverance from mortal illness, despite the desperate pleas of the psalmist.

20. Montgomery, *Critical and Exegetical Commentary*, 93.

The king's rash orders tragically cost the attendants their lives, as a flame of fire surges from the furnace and devours them (v. 22). The attendants, sadly, are collateral damage. Bound tightly, Shadrach, Meshach, and Abednego tumble into the deadly red-hot flames (v. 24).

At this point (following v. 23), the Greek LXX and Theodotion insert three additional pieces: the poetical Prayer of Azariah, preceded by a short prose introduction; a prose introduction to the young men in the furnace; and then the Song of the Three while in the furnace. These Additions will be discussed in part 3 of this commentary. The prose introduction before the Song of the Three gives a little taste of how this Addition works:

> ⁴⁶ All this time, the king's servants, who had thrown them into the furnace, had been stoking it with crude oil, pitch, tow and brushwood ⁴⁷ until the flames rose forty-nine cubits above the furnace ⁴⁸ and, leaping out, burnt those Chaldeans to death who were standing round it.⁴⁹ But the angel of the Lord came down into the furnace beside Azariah and his companions; he drove the flames of the fire outwards from the furnace ⁵⁰ and, in the heart of the furnace, wafted a coolness to them as of the breeze and dew, so that the fire did not touch them at all and caused them no pain or distress (3:46–50 NJB).

In the face of such an extraordinary, astonishing scene, the king is stunned. The fate of the three men is beyond belief.

THE DELIVERANCE (3:24-27)

> ²⁴ Then Nebuchadnezzar the king was astonished and rose in haste. He said to his counselors, "Were not three men thrown bound into the midst of the fire?" They answered the king, "True, O king!" ²⁵ He replied, "Lo! I see four men walking around loose in the midst of the furnace, and they are unharmed! The appearance of the fourth is like a son of the gods." ²⁶ Then Nebuchadnezzar approached the door of the furnace of burning fire and said, "Shadrach, Meshach, and Abednego, servants of the Most High God, come out! Come here!" So Shadrach, Meshach, and Abednego came out from the furnace of fire. ²⁷ The satraps, prefects, governors, and counselors of the king gathered and observed these men over whom the fire had no power, nor was the hair of their heads singed, their trousers harmed, nor had the odor of fire passed over them.

The king is evidently positioned in such a way he can peer into the furnace. If structured like a kiln, used for firing bricks needed in construction, open near the top and bottom, one could conceivably gaze into the red-hot blaze (v. 24). The king sees four men walking around in the midst of the furnace—apparently unharmed (v. 25)! That they are now loose—unbound— is significant. A symbol of police, state, or other authority, binding coerces persons into humiliating subjection. Now for the three, that authority has been loosened. It no longer restrains the three men.

The appearance of the mysterious fourth person is said to be like a son of the gods. We are not given a description, only that the individual was like a בַּר־אֱלָהִין (*bar-elahin*, son of [the] gods). The Aramaic phrase is equivalent to the Hebrew בְּנֵי הָאֱלֹהִים (*benay-ha-elohim*, sons of the gods), appearing in Job and several other places for divine or heavenly beings.[21] Collectively, these sons of the gods are known as the host of heaven.[22] Canaanite texts often refer to such a heavenly assembly.[23] Son of god would therefore signify a member of the class of gods or heavenly beings. Such a designation, Collins argues, stems from ancient Near Eastern polytheistic mythology.[24] The LXX renders this in a genitive phrase as ἀγγέλου θεοῦ (*angelou theou*, angel of God), while Theodotion has the dative expression υἱῷ θεοῦ (*uio theou*, [likened to] a son of God). The Latin Vulgate has the equivalent dative *filio Dei*, a son of God. The Greek versions equate this figure with an angel, as does verse 28 in the Aramaic (מַלְאַךְ, *malak*, angel). Elsewhere in the HB, the angel of the Lord protects and guides Israel, even inflicting damage on an Assyrian army amassed against Jerusalem. Later in Daniel, we hear of Michael as the protector of the people of Israel.[25]

Christian tradition usually understands this son of god as the pre-existent Christ. "Since the language of the text would have us understand that a supernatural Person was present," Young says, "we must ask whether this supernatural Person was merely an angel or whether we are face to face with a pre-incarnate appearance of the second Person of the Trinity."[26] From this text, how would one recognize in this angelic being the pre-existent Christ? More insistently, how would the initial readers of Daniel become

21. See Gen 6:2, 4; Job 1:6; 38:7; Ps 8:2; 29:1.
22. 1 Kgs 22:19; Ps 148:2.
23. See Mullen, *Assembly of the Gods*.
24. J. Collins, *Daniel* (Hermeneia), 190.
25. Exod 14:19; 23:20; 2 Kgs 19:7, 35; Dan 10:13; 12:1.
26. Young, *Prophecy of Daniel*, 94. "As for its typical significance, this angel of the Son of God foreshadows our Lord Jesus Christ, who descended into the furnace of hell . . . [to] deliver those who were held imprisoned by chains of death" (Jerome, *Jerome's Commentary on Daniel*, 3.92).

aware, living as they did before the incarnation of Jesus? It seems anachronistic to read into this ancient text an awareness of the second Person of the Trinity—Christ. Admittedly, the equation of son of the gods with the Christ will be made in the NT, some two hundred years in the future.[27] Minimally, there is no indication in Daniel—or the NT—that this son of the gods in the furnace is anything other than a heavenly figure like an angel.

Upon seeing this stunning heavenly personage, Nebuchadnezzar thinks immediately of the professed God of the three, whom he calls the Most High God (אֱלָהָא עִלָּאָה, *elaha illaah*) (v. 26). The Hebrews have risked their lives out of devotion to the Most High God. This epithet, found only here and in Dan 4:2, 17, 24–25, 32, 34; 7:25, became a popular expression for God in the postexilic era. Out of profound respect, Jewish writers in Hellenistic times and later tried to circumvent or substitute other expressions for the sacred divine name (YHWH = Yahweh), the Tetragrammaton. Most High God is the equivalent of an ancient title found in the HB, as well as in Ugaritic, Phoenician, and Aramaic sources.[28] In Genesis, Melchizedek, king of Salem, in the name of the Most High God (אֵל עֶלְיוֹן, *el elyon*) blesses Abram (Abraham) after Abram had rescued Lot from his captors. The Most High God in this text is equated with Yahweh. "I have sworn to Yahweh, God Most High, maker of heaven and earth," replies Abram (Gen 14:22, AT). It is understandable to a Hebrew audience that such a title would seem more proper on the lips of a non-Israelite such as Melchizedek—or Nebuchadnezzar—than the sacred name YHWH.

Nebuchadnezzar cautiously approaches the opening in the furnace and commands the three men to come out, evidently through the opening at the base. The king's officials gather round, shocked by the sight of three men who had been hurled into the blazing hot fire (v. 27), yet survive without the hair of their heads singed, their trousers harmed, or the odor of fire having passed over them. Amazing! Unbelievable!

Herodotus mentions an aborted burning of Croesus, king of Lydia (560–546 BCE), and seven others by the Persian king Cyrus, which is the closest ancient parallel to this experience.[29] In the case of Croesus, Cyrus

---

27. See Rom 1:1–4. It is possible to understand the son of the gods in Dan 3 as Jesus the Christ by invoking the hermeneutical principle of *sensus plenior*, namely, that a deeper (Christian) meaning was embedded in the text more than the original pre-Christian writer was aware. Whether such Christological meanings were embedded in the text, they were only recognized much later when the entire HB came to be regarded as an anticipation of Jesus the Christ. On this, see 1 Pet 1:10–12.

28. Newsom, *Daniel*, 135. See Gen 14:18–20, 22; Deut 32:8–9; 2 Sam 22:14; Pss 7:17; 97:9.

29. Herodotus, *Hist.* 1:86.

may have wanted to test whether the gods would come to Croesus's rescue. Once the fire was lit on the pyre where Croesus and the others were bound, Cyrus heard Croesus groan aloud and cry out three times. He took pity on Croesus and changed his mind about the execution. Cyrus ordered his servants to extinguish the flames. But the flames were now too hot to be snuffed out. In a panic, Cyrus desperately called to the god Apollo. Out of a clear sky, dark clouds suddenly gathered, the wind began to blow, and a storm burst out. Rain quickly put out the flames; Croesus was amazingly spared.

We have no way of verifying Herodotus's story, just as we have no way of confirming the story of the three Hebrews in the furnace. As a matter of faith, the biblical tradition accepts the story of the three as a divine miracle and regards it as a supernatural deliverance.[30]

At a deeper level, the fire in this story elicits the Babylonian exile as a symbol of refining fire. Israel was tested in a "furnace of adversity" (Isa 48:10). More explicit is the imagery in Second Isaiah: "When you pass through the waters, I will be with you, and through the rivers, they shall not overwhelm you; when you walk through the fire you shall not be burned, and the flame shall not consume you" (Isa 43:2).

THE REVERSAL OF ERRORS (3:26–30)

> [28] Nebuchadnezzar said, "Blessed be the God of Shadrach, Meshach, and Abednego, who sent his angel and delivered his servants who trust in him and altered the order of the king. They yielded their body without self-regard and did not worship any god other than their God. [29] Therefore, I am issuing a decree that any nation, people, or language, who utters contempt for the God of Shadrach, Meshach, and Abednego, he will be dismembered, and his house made a ruin, because there is no other god who can deliver like this." [30] The king immediately promoted Shadrach, Meshach, and Abednego in the province of Babylon.

In view of this extraordinary phenomenon, Nebuchadnezzar honors the God of Shadrach, Meshach, and Abednego, even conceding their God has sent his angel and delivered his servants (v. 28). He praises their devotion to God. We should not understand this as a genuine conversion to the Jewish faith. Like most in antiquity, Nebuchadnezzar accepted a plurality of gods

---

30. 1 Macc 2:51–59; 2 Macc 6:6–7; Heb 11:33–34. See below.

and believed "some had to be treated carefully."[31] It is a significant acknowledgement of the power of the God of the three young men.

The impetuous king now issues a decree countering the original one honoring the golden image. No one anywhere in his vast empire is to mock or treat with disrespect the God of Shadrach, Meshach, and Abednego (v. 29). Should anyone do so, the king mandates severe punishment: he will be dismembered, and his house made a ruin.[32] Then, as happens to Daniel in the previous story, the three men, in contradistinction to their accusers, are given promotions in the government of Babylon (v. 30).

The story of the faith and courage of the three Jews certainly resonated with the faithful during the Antiochene oppression, when their faith was challenged to its core by the Seleucid king. They were inspired by this very story. "Remember the deeds of the ancestors," the writer of 1 Maccabees recalls, then goes on to mention Abraham, Joseph, Joshua, David, Phinehas, Elijah—heroes of faith all—before coming to the three: "Hananiah, Azariah, and Mishael believed and were saved from the flame" (1 Macc 2:51-59). In 3 Maccabees, Daniel and his friends are mentioned as models of faithful courage: "The three companions in Babylon who had voluntarily surrendered their lives to the flames so as not to serve vain things, you rescued unharmed, even to a hair, moistening the fiery furnace with dew and turning the flame against all their enemies" (3 Macc 6:6-7). Over two hundred years later, the courage and faith of the three inspired the early Christians. In Hebrews they are mentioned as those "who through faith . . . quenched raging fire" (Heb 11:33-34).

If we read this story as simply directed against idolatry, we fail to grasp something of its far-reaching impact. Nebuchadnezzar and his decree to honor the golden image stands as representative for any dominant power who demands absolute submission from its subjects. The decree demanded the three Jews abandon what was to them most sacred to conform to the ideology of the dominant empire. True, the momentary bowing to the image could have been regarded as a mere gesture of respect expected by the captor. They could have feigned allegiance. Most people, sad to say, would have. But for the three Jews, the veneration asked of them required a fundamental turning away from the God of Abraham, Isaac, and Jacob. "Hear, O Israel: the Lord is our God, the Lord alone" (Deut 6:4).

The Hebrews looked—by faith—to a day when all nations would bow in acknowledgement to the God of Abraham, Isaac, and Jacob.

---

31. Hoerth, *Archaeology*, 374n7.

32. This same penalty is threatened against anyone who alters the decree of the Persian king Darius enacted for the rebuilding of Jerusalem after the exile (Ezra 6:11). See also Dan 2:5.

The Mad King

Daniel 4

Power tends to corrupt and absolute power corrupts absolutely.

—JOHN EMERICH EDWARD DALBERG-ACTON (LORD ACTON)

A powerful Middle Eastern king, bereft of reason, ejected from the luxurious trappings of his stately palace, expelled from the halls of justice, stripped of all dignity, now roaming the fields, chomping on sparse blades of grass, hair a tangled mess, jumbled and spilling across his face, obscuring eyes and nose, loping around on all fours rather than standing poised and erect, this is the illustrious Nebuchadnezzar II—greatest of the Neo-Babylonian king.

Here is the fascinating tale of Nebuchadnezzar's madness, humiliation, and ultimate restoration. The Aramaic (MT) text, arranged in slightly different order than the English translation, goes directly from Nebuchadnezzar's affirmation of the superiority of the Hebrew God following the spectacular deliverance of the three Hebrews from the furnace to Nebuchadnezzar's even more eloquent affirmation of the Most High God. What appears in the Aramaic text to be the conclusion of the story of the golden image (Dan 3:28–30) is thus really the beginning of the new story in chapter 4. Then the confession in 4:1–3, introduced as an epistle, or formal official letter, is in effect joined back to back with the doxology concluding chapter 3 in the Aramaic text (vv. 28–30).

Daniel 4 witnesses Nebuchadnezzar's self-aggrandizing boast. The tipping point comes when he recognizes his personal and political success is fundamentally a gift of the Most High God. Triggering this awakening is the sudden, unexpected madness of Nebuchadnezzar. The story is linked with chapter 5, where Nebuchadnezzar's animalistic experience is recounted as a cautionary tale for the inebriated Belshazzar (Dan 5:18-23).

That the arrangement in the Aramaic text of chapter 4 is different than in the English Bible deserves explanation. Keep in mind that when these stories were combined in a scroll, there were no physical or literary breaks like our modern chapter divisions. A shift in content would suffice to alert readers that a new story had begun. Chapter numbers were added to the NT by Stephen Langton (c. 1150-1228), later archbishop of Canterbury, and applied to the HB in the fourteenth century CE. Division into verses came even later (sixteenth century). This commentary follows the standard English versification, which may be traced back to the Latin Vulgate and the LXX. For convenience, the Aramaic versification is indicated in brackets following the more familiar English verse number. Additionally, differences in arrangement of the story may indicate that the MT and LXX preserve variant or separate recensions (editions) of the same story.[1]

Daniel 4 is framed as an epistle or official public letter directed to the subjects in Nebuchadnezzar's empire.[2] Since it represents public proclamation, more formal than a letter, it is best considered an epistle. The epistle form was anciently used as a means of official communication. Certain stylistic features, such as placing the sender's name before the recipient, bear close resemblance to other such documents extant from Neo-Babylonian and especially Persian times. The first person epistolary style, however, is not maintained throughout. It begins with a doxology (Dan 4:1-3) and closes with a liturgical act of praise (4:31-34).

Between these doxologies, we read of Nebuchadnezzar's dream of the great world tree (Dan 4:4-18), The dream report, its interpretation, and its fulfillment form the core of the story: Daniel's startling interpretation of the dream (4:19-27), Nebuchadnezzar's fall from normalcy in fulfillment of the dream (4:28-33), and Nebuchadnezzar's restoration (4:34-37).

---

1. J. Collins, *Daniel* (Hermeneia), 220-21. Thus, neither recension may be the *Vorlage* (source) of the other. Some scholars think diverse traditions have been woven together in Dan 4. The story of the king's dream and its interpretation, according to Haag, has been combined with the story of the king's loss of kingship, each from a different source (Haag, *Errettung Daniels*, 14-25). Lawrence Wills finds three different traditions (Wills, *Jew in the Court*, 87-121).

2. J. Collins, *Daniel* (FOTL 22), 61-62. On this form of salutation, see Ezra 4:11, 17; 5:7-8; 7:12; 1 Macc 10:18, 25; 14:20; 15:2; 2 Macc 1:1, 10.

A DOXOLOGY FOR THE MOST HIGH GOD (4:1-3)

> [3:31 in Aram.] Nebuchadnezzar the king to all people, nations, and languages who dwell upon the earth, may you have abundant prosperity. ² [3:32] The signs and wonders that the Most High God did with me, it seems acceptable for me to declare.
> ³ [3:33] How great are his signs, and how mighty his wonders!
> His kingdom is an eternal kingdom,
> and his rule from generation to generation!

Nebuchadnezzar begins by addressing his subjects: all people, nations, and languages (v. 1). At its height, the Neo-Babylonian empire stretched from the Zagros Mountains southward to the Persian Gulf, the western border of modern-day Iran, to the Nile Valley in Egypt—the entire Fertile Crescent, heart of ancient civilization. Over this territory, Nebuchadnezzar, like many of his ancient counterparts, claims universal rule, here typically expressed in ancient royal ideology. The theme of his epistle is the signs and wonders performed by the Most High God (v. 2), which immediately leads to a doxology by Nebuchadnezzar about the greatness of this God (v. 3). The stress falls on God's eternal rule running continuously from generation to generation. While Nebuchadnezzar claims universal sovereignty over the earth, his doxology, in effect, concedes the authentic dominion to the Eternal One. According to the chapter arrangement in the Aramaic text, this doxology looks back ("signs and wonders") to the deliverance of the three Hebrews in the furnace and forward to the story of Nebuchadnezzar's humiliation.

Nebuchadnezzar's admission does not represent a conversion. He does not here convert to the Jewish religion. Strictly speaking, the epithet אֱלָהָא עִלָּאָה (*elaha illaah*, the highest god) is henotheistic. It recognizes that the Hebrew God, who has effectively demonstrated divine power, is the greatest of the gods. Nebuchadnezzar has tacitly come to acknowledge the sovereignty of the Most High God. Here is an issue already raised in previous stories: the sovereignty of the God of Israel versus the religio-political power of the Gentile kings and their gods (see Dan 2:31–35, 44). Divine trustworthiness distinguishes the divine from transitory human sovereignty.

DREAM OF THE GREAT TREE (4:4-18)

> ⁴ [4:1 in *Aram.*] I, Nebuchadnezzar, was at ease in my house, flourishing in my palace. ⁵ [4:2] I had a dream and it startled me; the imaginations on my bed and the visons of my head terrified

> me. ⁶ [4:3] I gave an order to bring in before me all the wise men of Babylon so that they might make known to me the interpretation of the dream. ⁷ [4:4] Then the magicians, the enchanters, the Chaldeans, and the diviners came in, and I told them [the dream], but its interpretation they could not make known to me. ⁸ [4:5] Afterwards, Daniel—whose name is Belteshazzar, after the name of my god and in whom is the spirit of the holy gods—came before me and I told the dream to him.

Another dream! While outwardly at peace in his palace, the affairs of state going well, Nebuchadnezzar has another disturbing dream (vv. 4–5). Startled and terrified, he summons all his diviners and courtiers to help him understand the dream (v. 6). They could not (v. 7). At the very outset, as in Dan 2:9–11, the impotence of the Babylonian diviners becomes apparent. A short while later, in comes Daniel (v. 8). His delay heightens the drama. The king meanwhile exhausts assistance available at the court.

The king readily acknowledges that Daniel's remarkable insight into such matters is due to the spirit of the holy gods within him (v. 9). Something of the divine resides in Daniel. Pharaoh uses the same language to describe Joseph.³ Here Nebuchadnezzar calls Daniel by his Babylonian name, *Belteshazzar*, which we noted earlier, may signify "protect his life" or "protect the life of the prince." Because of the quality of Daniel's spirit or his divinely given ability—or both—no secretive dream distresses Daniel. If Daniel is seen here as a psychodynamic interpreter of the unconscious (e.g., dreams), it is a credit to his objectivity or therapeutic neutrality that he can interpret such a distressing dream without himself becoming enmeshed. Daniel's God, after all, is a revealer of mysteries (Dan 2:47). The dream report follows.

> ⁹ [4:6] "O Belteshazzar, chief of the magicians in whom I know is the spirit of the holy gods, no secret distresses you, declare the visions of my dream that I saw and its interpretation.
> ¹⁰ [4:7] "I saw the visions of my head upon my bed,
> and lo, a tree stood in the center of the earth,
> and its height was great.
> ¹¹ [4:8] The tree grew and became strong.
> Its top reached to the heavens and its visibility
> to the end of all the earth.
> ¹² [4:9] Its foliage was lovely, its fruit bountiful,
> and food on it for all.

---

3. "Pharaoh said to his servants, 'Can we find anyone else like this—one in whom is *the spirit of God*?'" (Gen 41:38; italics added).

Underneath it animals of the field and birds in its branches find shade,
>   on its branches the birds of heavens dwell,
>   and from it all flesh is nourished."

The dream, set off in rhythmic, poetical style, is recounted in two segments (vv. 10–12; 13–17). In the first (vv. 10–12), Nebuchadnezzar sees a majestic, tall tree standing like a giant sequoia in the center of the earth. It grows so tall its boughs, loaded with fruit, touch the sky. Not only is it visible to the whole landscape, but its fruit also nourishes all living creatures, who find shade and protection from the hot desert sun under its luxurious boughs.

That the tall tree, covered with luxurious foliage, stands in the center of the earth and is visible to the end of all the earth expresses its ascendancy. To Nebuchadnezzar, the landscape would appear flat, like a pancake, stretching out in every direction, with the gigantic tree ascending high in the center of the flat circle of the horizon. This tree is no doubt the so-called cosmic tree, known in many ancient mythologies.[4] Such a tree is often depicted with a winged sun above it, situated on a stylized cosmic mountain or, in some instances, a tree providing nourishment, its trunk in the form of a goddess.[5] In Assyrian iconography, it became a symbol of royal power and dominance. Ezekiel likens the Egyptian Pharaoh to a great tree whose "height was loftier than all the trees of the field," and "under its branches all the beasts of the field gave birth" (Ezek 31:5–6 NASB), a symbol of Pharaoh's universal superiority (v. 10). The ancient historian Herodotus tells us the Median king Astyages had a vision of a vine—rather than a tree—growing out of his daughter's body. It grew to such a height, it overshadowed the whole of Asia. The vine was Cyrus the Great, whose empire stretched from Asia to the Mediterranean. In another passage, Herodotus mentions that Xerxes, one of the later Persians kings, had a dream in which he was covered with a branch of an olive tree, whereupon the boughs spread out and covered the whole earth. The dream meant "all mankind would become his servants."[6] Each image—whether tree or vine—indicates dominance and universal rule. Absolute monarchs, such as Nebuchadnezzar, no doubt found such imagery especially congenial to their narcissistic ambitions.

---

4. Widengren, *King and Tree of Life*, 442–68.
5. Keel, *Symbolism of Biblical World*, 51, 186–87.
6. Herodotus, *Hist.* 1:108; 7:19.

¹³ [4:10] "I saw in the visions of my head upon my bed and lo, a watcher, even a holy one from heaven, descended, ¹⁴ [4:11] calling in a loud voice. Thus he said,

'Hew down the tree, cut off its branches,
>strip off its foliage, scatter its fruit,
>disperse the animals from under it
>and the birds from its branches.

¹⁵ [4:12] Only leave the stump of its roots in the ground,
>with a band of iron and copper,
>in the grass of the field.

Let him be wet with the dew of heaven,
>and his lot be with the animals of the field
>and the plants of the earth.

¹⁶ [4:13] Let his mind be changed from a human,
>and let the mind of an animal be given to him
>and let seven times pass over him.

¹⁷ [4:14] By the decree of the watchers is the sentence,
>and by the word of the holy ones is the affair.

Concerning the matter, may the living know
>that the Most High rules over the kingdom of human beings
>and to whomever he wills he gives it
>and the lowly among human beings he establishes over it.'

¹⁸ [4:15] "This is the dream I, king Nebuchadnezzar, saw. Nevertheless you, Belteshazzar, explained the interpretation because none of the wise men of my kingdom could make known to me the interpretation, but you were enabled because the spirit of the holy gods is in you."

In the second part of the dream, a watcher, even a holy one, descends from heaven and like a royal herald, calls out loudly (v. 13). This watcher, from the Aramaic root עיר (*ir*, waking or wakeful one), is evidently a heavenly being, as the phrase *holy one from heaven* indicates. This is the only place in the HB where the word *ir* signifies a heavenly being. In Jewish literature of Hellenistic and early Roman times, it represents both good and evil watchers.[7] We should take this as an angelic intermediary, perhaps a

---

7. E.g., in 1 Enoch 1–36, the Book of the Watchers, roughly contemporary with Daniel, it is used as the term for fallen angels. In Jubilees 4:15, it denotes the angels of the Lord. The word occurs frequently in Aramaic texts from Qumran, such as 1 Enoch 10:9; 12:3; 13:10; 22:6; 93:2; 1QapGen 2:1, 16; 6:13; 7:2.

"distinct class of angelic being."[8] Like the angelic messengers in the book of Revelation (Rev 8:13), this watcher is the harbinger of judgment upon the giant cosmic tree.

The tree, whose top reaches the heavens, is chopped down, its branches stripped, its fruit scattered, and the sheltered animals under it who eat from its fruit, dispersed. Only the stump, literally, root or rootstock (עִקַּר, *iqqar*), together with an iron and copper band, is left (vv. 14–15). The significance of the band is unexplained. Is it a protective device to keep the stump from splitting? Is it instead the band or fetter by which a mad person would be restrained? This latter view is interesting, given that psychotic individuals were often restrained this way, and are still shackled in some parts of the world today.[9] The symbolism of the metal band may thus be a foreshadowing of Nebuchadnezzar's own madness. Incidentally, it was only in the early 1960s that psychiatrists in the United States began the use of chemical restraints, such as phenothiazine medications, to replace mechanical restraints for psychotic patients.[10] As the following explanation indicates, cutting down the tree, yet preserving the stump, represents Nebuchadnezzar's fall, not only from political sovereignty, but from a "superhuman status" to "subhuman rank."[11] Yet it also foreshadows the possibility of restoration (see v. 26). As a Hebrew sage observed with characteristic, understated wit, "Pride goes before destruction, and a haughty spirit before a fall" (Prov 16:18).

DANIEL INTERPRETS THE DREAM (4:19–27)

> [19] [4:16] Then Daniel—whose name is Belteshazzar—became distressed for a time and his thoughts terrified him. The king answered, "Belteshazzar, do not let the dream or the interpretation trouble you." Belteshazzar responded, "My lord, may the dream be against those who hate you and its interpretation against your adversaries. [20] [4:17] The tree you saw that grew up and became strong, and whose top reached the heavens and its visibility to all the earth, [21] [4:18] its foliage beautiful, its fruit plentiful, its food for all in it, underneath it the animals of the field dwell and the

---

8. J. Collins, *Daniel* (Hermeneia), 225. Collins notes "interest in such intermediary beings was widespread in pagan as well as Jewish circles in the Persian and Hellenistic periods" (225). See 1 Enoch 20:1.

9. The Gerasene demoniac in Jesus's day "had often been restrained with shackles and chains" (Mark 5:4).

10. William F. Doverspike, PhD, e-mail to author, January 9, 2020.

11. Newsom, *Daniel*, 141.

birds of the heavens live in its branches. ²² [4:19] You are the king who has grown great and strong. Your greatness has increased so that it now reaches to the heavens and your sovereignty to the end of the earth. ²³ [4:20] Then the king saw a watcher, even a holy one, descend from heaven and say, 'Chop down the tree and destroy it. Only the stump of its roots leave in the ground with a band of iron and copper in the grass of the field. It will be wet with the dew of heaven and with the animals of the field will be its portion until seven times pass over it.'"

Ancient rulers did not appreciate their diviners' revealing bad news in their interpretation of dreams and visions. This troubles Daniel, as he anxiously for a time ponders the king's dream. He cautions Nebuchadnezzar not to allow the dream to unsettle him (v. 19). Although this seems deferential on Daniel's part, designed to prepare the king for an unpalatable interpretation, it may reflect genuine concern—even affection—for the king and his welfare. Daniel may well have realized such bad news in dream analysis could get him not only fired but executed. Daniel wishes instead he could shift the baleful message from Nebuchadnezzar onto his enemies and adversaries. He wants to ward off the threat to the king and, like a good court physician, heal the king's malady.

The giant cosmic tree, Daniel explains, under which all the animals of the field dwell and the birds nest in its branches (vv. 20-21) represents Nebuchadnezzar, or more precisely, the greatness of the king. You are the king who has grown great and strong. Your greatness has increased until your sovereignty extends to the end of the earth (v. 21).

Daniel repeats the watcher's judgment, adding once the tree has been cut down and its stump left, seven times will pass over with the dampening dew (v. 23). Elsewhere in Daniel the word times (עִדָּנִין, *iddanin*) coupled with a number, seems to indicate solar years (see Dan 7:25). Since seven in the Bible often suggests completeness, here the expression seven times probably indicates a complete or full period, not seven literal years. It is the period pedagogically necessary for Nebuchadnezzar to concede fully the sovereignty of the Most High (v. 25).

> ²⁴ [4:21] "This is the interpretation, O king, and it is a decree of the Most High that has come upon my lord the king. ²⁵ [4:22] You will be chased from human society and among the animals of the field you will dwell. They will feed you grass like oxen, and you will be bathed from the dew of the heaven, and seven times will pass over you, until you recognize that the Most High is sovereign over the kingdom of humanity and to whomever he wills he gives it. ²⁶ [4:23] And as they commanded to leave the stump

of the roots of the tree, your kingdom will be re-established for you when you acknowledge that Heaven is sovereign. ²⁷ [4:24] Therefore, O king, may my advice be acceptable to you. Break off your sins by right doing and your iniquities by showing favor to the poor; perhaps there will be an extension of your prosperity."

Nebuchadnezzar would be banished from human society and make his abode with the wild animals. He would eat grass like oxen, while the dew of heaven bathes him (vv. 24–25). At the time the degradation has reached its lowest point or hit bottom, as we say, and the king acknowledges God's sovereignty, there would come a turning point. Then Nebuchadnezzar would be restored (v. 26). Since this is Nebuchadnezzar's fate, insofar as the dream and the heavenly decree is concerned, Daniel urges the proud king, break off your sins by right doing and your iniquities by showing favor to the poor (v. 27). Such social justice ideals were generally expected of ancient monarchs. "He [the king] delivers the needy when they call ... he has pity on the weak and the needy ... from oppression and violence he redeems their life," intones the psalmist of the obligations of the monarchs (Ps 72:12-14). Since this passage urges the king to break off his sins by right-doing, it has become a flashpoint for the debate between Protestants and Catholics over the prospect of salvation by means of human cooperation. Daniel, however, is not concerned here with salvation in the Christian sense, but with ethical performance in the tradition of the Torah and the Prophets. "If the king is to have a lengthening of prosperity, he must give up his injustice and cruelty to the poor and must practice righteousness and mercy."[12] The fate of the king is set, but Daniel holds out that by practicing mercy, Nebuchadnezzar's prosperity might be extended.

Human history bears relentless witness to cruel, human oppression. The poor usually bear the brunt of such cruelty. The gap between the rich and poor in most cultures, including the United States, seems to grow wider with each passing decade. Graft and corruption enable the socially powerful to oppress the unfortunate. The calloused, harsh treatment of a nation's citizens by its rulers deserves the strong rebuke Daniel levels against Nebuchadnezzar. People of conscience expect—even demand—better of their rulers. But in many nations people still groan under the tyrannical impulses of their leaders. "When the righteous triumph, there is great glory," wrote one of Israel's wise. "But when the wicked prevail, people go into hiding" (Prov 28:12).

Nebuchadnezzar evidently does not respond to Daniel. Nor does Daniel speak again in the story. Did Nebuchadnezzar heed Daniel's advice?

12. Young, *Prophecy of Daniel*, 108–9.

Did he take Daniel seriously? That twelve months that went by before the sentence was executed makes it seems as though for a time, at least, he may have responded favorably. But we do not know.

NEBUCHADNEZZAR'S FALL (4:28-33)

> [28] [4:25] All this happened to Nebuchadnezzar the king. [29] [4:26] At the end of twelve months, he was walking about upon the royal palace of Babylon. [30] [4:27] The king exclaimed, "Is not this great Babylon that I have built as a royal residence by the strength of my power and for the splendor of my majesty?" [31] [4:28] While the word was in the mouth of the king, a voice fell from heaven saying, "To you, O king Nebuchadnezzar, the kingdom has passed from you! [32] [4:29] From human society you will be driven, and with the animals of the field you will dwell. Grass like oxen will they give you to eat, and seven times will pass over you, until you recognize that the Most High is sovereign over the kingdom of mortals, and to whomever he wills, he gives it. [33] [4:30] In that same moment the sentence was fulfilled concerning Nebuchadnezzar, and from human society he was driven. Grass like oxen he ate, and from the dew of heaven his body was wet, until his hair grew long like eagles' feathers and his nails like birds' claws.

Then all comes crashing down! The urgency of the moment passes. Nebuchadnezzar, once again obsessed with his own greatness, disregards the admonition (v. 28). A year later, while strolling about on the flat roof of the imperial palace, he looks out on Babylon, capital of his vast empire, and boasts, "Is not this great Babylon that I have built?" (v. 29). Great Babylon (בָּבֶל רַבְּתָא, *Babel rabbeta*) could be translated as Babylon the great to emphasize the intertextual connection of this phrase with the mythical archenemy of God, Babylon the great, in the book of Revelation (Rev 18:2). In both cases the phrase indicates arrogant defiance of God. In Revelation as in Daniel, the phrase refers to a city, representing an empire, set against the sovereignty of God. In Revelation, it is Rome; in Daniel, Babylon, in the form of the Neo-Babylonian empire.

Nebuchadnezzar is known to history as a prolific builder.[13] Many kiln-fired bricks went into his building projects. Bricks bearing his inscription

---

13. See Josephus, *Ant.* 10:11.1, *Ag. Ap.* 1:19; Young, *Prophecy of Daniel*, 109; Newsom, *Daniel*, 146-47; Kitchen, *On the Reliability*, 69.

may even today be picked up by archaeologists in the ruins of Babylon.[14] To him is attributed the famous Ishtar Gate of Babylon, with its deep blue tiles and alternating figures of dull yellow bulls and white and yellow lions and dragons, portions of which are now preserved in the Pergamon Museum in Berlin; the restored Esagila temple (temple of Marduk); a grand palace for himself; the so-called hanging gardens, ostensibly erected for his Median wife, and counted by the Greeks among the Seven Wonders of the World; the massive fortification walls; and many other temples and state buildings in and around Babylon, making him the greatest builder among all the Neo-Babylonian kings. Herodotus, the ancient Greek historian, goes on and on about the size and splendor of Babylon. "While such is its size, in magnificence there is no other city that approaches to it."[15]

Nebuchadnezzar looks with overweening pride upon the magnificence of Babylon and the empire it represents and attributes to himself—to what he has accomplished—power, might, and splendor. These words are used of Nebuchadnezzar in Dan 2:37, only there it is God who credits them to the king. Here Nebuchadnezzar smugly claims the attributes for himself. This is a boast of hubris (insolent pride), a turning away from the very divine sovereignty by which Nebuchadnezzar himself reigns. In Daniel, all kings owe their dominion to the God who "changes times and seasons, deposes kings and sets up kings" (2:21). By now, Nebuchadnezzar has forgotten this basic truth.

Nebuchadnezzar's boast—seen as religiously offensive by our writer—is not unusual for a proud ancient Near Eastern monarch. In the cuneiform Assyrian Annals (858–825 BCE), which glorify the Assyrian kings and their exploits, Shalmaneser III boasts, "[I am] Shalmaneser, the legitimate king, the king of the world, the king without rival, the 'Great Dragon,' the [only] power within the [four] rims [of the earth], overlord of all the princes . . . the strong man, unsparing, who shows no mercy in battle."[16]

Scarcely were the words out of Nebuchadnezzar's mouth when—in a classic reversal of fate—the sentencing decree falls from heaven. "The kingdom has passed from you!" (v. 31). He is to lose his kingdom. He is to be driven from human society into the steppe land, where in company with wild and domestic animals he eats grass like oxen (v. 32), a penalty he must in a liminal state endure until ironically, he comes to his senses and recognizes God's sovereignty. His disheveled hair grows long, his finger and toenails become like birds' claws of a vulture (v. 33). "When humans

---

14. Hoerth, *Archaeology*, 377.
15. Herodotus, *Hist.* 1:178.
16. "Historiographic Documents," translated by A. Leo Oppenheim (*ANET*, 276b).

image God, they have the right to rule in his name," Lucas warns. "When they try to *be* God, they forfeit that right and may become 'bestial.'"[17] God is the true Sovereign, insists this text. Human leaders, who may think of themselves in grandiose terms, soon pale into insignificance. In view of the "great panorama of Yahweh's cosmic rule," they disappear as though they had never existed.[18] Nebuchadnezzar, as psychiatrist Carl Jung indicates, becomes here "a complete regressive degeneration of a man who has overreached himself."[19] The Neo-Babylonian empire had been built on violence, extortion, robbery, and the pillage of people and nations throughout the Near East. Now Nebuchadnezzar, head of this rapacious empire, in a strange reversal of fortune must undergo what he has inflicted on so many others— a deathlike, ruined state. Ralph Waldo Emerson compares all humanity to Nebuchadnezzar's experience: we are all like "Nebuchadnezzar, dethroned, bereft of reason, and eating grass like an ox . . . . A man is a god in ruins."[20]

The text does not tell us what happened in Babylonian statecraft during Nebuchadnezzar's absence. Who presided over state affairs? Who governed the empire? Did these humiliating events really happen to Nebuchadnezzar? If so, it seems, he would certainly have been deposed, as the text says, and driven into exile. As reasonable as this sounds, he would not have been the first ruler to have been considered insane and yet kept on the throne. Caesar Nero comes to mind, as does the British King George III during the American Revolution. Closer to our time, a maniacal and unstable Adolf Hitler plunged the whole world into a ghastly war.

Many think the story in Dan 4 is really about Nabonidus (556–539 BCE), one of Nebuchadnezzar's successors (a usurper) and the last official ruler of the Neo-Babylonian empire, rather than Nebuchadnezzar.[21] According to the Harran inscriptions,[22] discovered in northern Mesopotamia in 1956, Nabonidus was disturbed by various dreams, which he figured had come from the lunar god Sîn. Prior to the dream, in his third regnal year (c. 554/553), Nabonidus had gone to great lengths to rebuild the temple of Sîn at Harran in northwestern Mesopotamia, erecting a statue of Sîn in

---

17. Lucas, "Daniel, Book of," 159; italics in original. Note that the ancient empires in the apocalyptic section of Daniel are depicted in animalistic fashion.

18. Sims, "Daniel," 329.

19. Jung, *Symbolic Life*, 110.

20. Emerson, *Ralph Waldo Emerson*, 53.

21. Riessler, *Buch Daniel erklärt*, 43; see also Hommel, "Abfassungszeit des Buches Daniel," 145–50. Note the backstory of Nabonidus in Saggs, *Babylonians*, 119–24.

22. Gadd, "Harran Inscriptions of Nabonidus," 35–92; "Verse Account of Nabonidus," translated by A. Leo Oppenheim (*ANET*, 312–15); McNamara and Di Lella, "Daniel," 4:512; Newsom, *Daniel*, 131–32.

the temple, and urging devotion to Sîn by extolling upon him epithets like Lord/King of the Gods and God of Gods.[23] Provoked by this, the resentful Marduk priests accused him of neglecting the god Marduk, the chief deity of Babylon, in favor of Sîn. Facing strong opposition from priests, state officials, and even the citizenry, he withdrew to the desert oasis of Tema, more than four hundred miles southwest of Babylon. He remained absent from Babylon for ten years.

The parallels in Nabonidus's Harran inscription and the narrative plot in Dan 4 are striking, suggesting the two stories may be versions of the same incident. If so, traditions about Nabonidus may underlie Dan 4. The protagonist of the story would have been shifted from Nabonidus to Nebuchadnezzar, who was far more notable. In the verse account of Nabonidus, evidently written by a Babylonian priest who opposed Nabonidus and preserved today in the British Museum, Nabonidus stands up in the assembly to praise his own military conquests, "I am wise, I know, I have seen (what is) hidden,"[24] a boast that compares easily with Nebuchadnezzar's claim in this chapter (v. 30). The verse account also mentions Nabonidus's withdrawal to Tema.

Suspicion about a connection to Nabonidus has been partially confirmed by the discovery among the Dead Sea Scrolls of the Prayer of Nabonidus (4QPrNab^{ar}).[25] This brittle, fragmentary text tells of "the prayer uttered by Nabunai [Nabonidus] king of the l[and of Ba]bylon, [the great] king, [when he was afflicted] with an evil ulcer in Teiman by decree of the [Most High God]." Nabonidus was stricken for seven years. He prayed to the "gods of silver and gold, [bronze and iron], wood and stone and clay." An anonymous Jewish exorcist from among the Judean exiles appeared, pardoned Nabonidus, and advised him: "Recount this in writing to [glorify and exalt] the name of the [Most High God]."[26] Again, the parallel with Dan 4 is remarkable. A Babylonian king is afflicted for seven years. A Jewish diviner intercedes. And in both documents, the king speaks in first person. While there are significant differences between the Prayer of Nabonidus and Dan 4, it seems likely the two documents are in some way related.

Have popular traditions about Nabonidus been transferred in the tradition to the more renowned Nebuchadnezzar? The description of the madness of Nebuchadnezzar better fits the reputation of Nabonidus than

23. Beaulieu, *Reign of Nabonidus*, 43–65.

24. "Verse Account of Nabonidus," translated A. Leo Oppenheim (*ANET*, 313b–14a).

25. See F. Cross, *Ancient Library of Qumran*, 166–68; Milik, "Prière de Nabonid," 407–17.

26. Citations of this text are from Vermes, *Complete Dead Sea Scrolls*, 573.

of Nebuchadnezzar. The Prayer of Nabonidus also shows the Jewish people were familiar with traditions about Nabonidus's illness. All this may contribute to the confusion in Dan 5 between Belshazzar as the son of Nebuchadnezzar rather than Nabonidus, his actual father (see Dan 5:18).

Still, neither the Prayer of Nabonidus nor the story in Dan 4 may constitute the source of the other. The Prayer of Nabonidus, it would appear, does not represent a literary (or oral) source for Daniel. Both may instead draw on a "common stock of traditions" about Nabonidus, perhaps "different developments of a common tradition."[27] We do know from extrabiblical sources that Nebuchadnezzar, who was taken ill near the end of his reign, never vacated his throne.[28] It was rather Nabonidus who abdicated, leaving the province of Babylon under the authority of delegated officials. The Prayer of Nabonidus, along with the Additions to Daniel in the LXX, causes scholars to think there existed anciently a cycle of stories about Daniel, only some of which were eventually edited and collected in the book bearing his name.

How are we to understand this story's portrayal of Nebuchadnezzar's physical and mental deterioration? Does he suffer from a form of psychosis, a psychopathological condition? The ancients, of course, had a horror of mental illness. Superstitious and apprehensive, often attributing the pathology to demons, they tried to isolate victims of mental illness from society. "You will be chased from human society" (v. 28). Scholars have interpreted Nebuchadnezzar's animalization in at least four different ways.

To some, the animal imagery—eating grass like an ox, hair long as eagle feathers, nails like bird's claws, driven from society—is typical of mythic depictions of the netherworld, the place of the dead.[29] These netherworld metaphors appear frequently, especially in ancient cultic prayers. A person afflicted with a deadly illness might speak as though already in the grave. "Like those forsaken among the dead," cries one poet, "like the slain that lie in the grave, like those you remember no more, for they are cut off from your hand . . . in regions dark and deep" (Ps 88:5-6). Use of netherworld

---

27. Newsom, *Daniel*, 128; J. Collins, *Daniel* (Hermeneia), 218. See also F. Cross, *Ancient Library of Qumran*, 167-68.

28. Josephus, *Ag. Ap.* 1.20. Archer claims there is no extant Babylonian record of any governmental activity on the part of Nebuchadnezzar between 582 and 575. Archer's claim is an argument from silence, however, and should not be taken as confirmation or disconfirmation (Archer, "Daniel," 15). Eusebius of Caesarea mentions a tradition independent of the HB about Nebuchadnezzar's madness. On this see Young, *Prophecy of Daniel*, 110-11; Smith-Christopher, "Book of Daniel," 71-72.

29. Hayes, "Chirps from the Dust," 305-25. See Ps 22:12-18; Isa 14:12-20.

metaphors was one way of speaking of people afflicted by God. Nebuchadnezzar's affliction, then, may be understood in the context of netherworld imagery.

The animalistic imagery used about Nebuchadnezzar is to others more consistent with the wild man trope found in the mythic lore of the ancient Near East.[30] Our modern Tarzan myth—a man reared by wild animals in the jungles of Africa—is similar. Enkidu is thus depicted in the famous Sumerian tale of Gilgamesh.[31] Nebuchadnezzar, dominant over most of the civilized world, lives in splendor and majesty in his ornate palace. "Isn't this Babylon, the magnificent city that I built as the royal house by my own mighty strength and for my own majestic glory?" (Dan 4:30 CEB). An equitable punishment, it seems, would be to humiliate, decivilize him, and force him into the wilderness, where wild animals live. Our text (v. 33) does not say he became an ox or eagle, only that, disheveled, he behaved like one (כְּתוֹרִין, *ketorin*, like oxen).

In examining Mesopotamian magico-medical texts, Hector Avalos notes a parallel to Nebuchadnezzar's condition.[32] An incantation text, known by its initial line as *dingir.šà.dib.ba*, indicates the belief that a bestial nature might be imposed on a human being as a curse for violating a temple. In such an incantation, one so tormented intoned:

> I am an ox, I do not know the plants I eat
> I am a sheep, I do not know the absolution rite in which I take part
> I am river water,
> I do not know where I am going
> I am a ship, [I do not know] at which quay I put in
> The iniquities of mankind are more numerous than the hairs on his head
> I have trodden on my iniquities, sins, and transgressions,
> [which] were heaped up [like leaves]
> On this day let them be released and absolved.[33]

Under a cultic curse, a person might be disgraced, humiliated, and turned into a bestial condition, all to symbolize lack of common wisdom and humility. "Do you see persons wise in their own eyes? There is more hope for fools than for them" (Prov 26:12), The victim may be humbled to

---

30. Henze, *Madness of Nebuchadnezzar*, 3.

31. "Gilgamesh and the Land of the Living," translated by S. N. Kramer (*ANET* 47–50).

32. Avalos, "Nebuchadnezzar's Affliction," 497–507.

33. Lambert, "dingir.šà.dib.ba Incantations," 285, lines 2–8, cited in Avalos, "Nebuchadnezzar's Affliction," 503.

become like one eating grass; disheveled with long stringy, matted hair; and nails sticking out like an eagle's claws. Similarly, Nebuchadnezzar is urged to atone for his sins through exercising mercy to the oppressed (v. 27). The experience of Nebuchadnezzar resembles someone upon whom a divine curse has been ritually uttered and who is thus reduced to brutish existence.

In probably the most persistent interpretation of the king's illness, the behavioral symptoms manifest in the text, taken literally, suggest Nebuchadnezzar may have suffered from a rare form of clinical zoanthropy, in which the victim imagines being an animal. Although this diagnosis was suggested as early as the seventeenth century,[34] in his review of the international scientific literature from 1850 to the present, Blom discovered only fifty-six cases of clinical zoanthropy, thirty-four men and twenty-two women, many of which were also capable of other diagnoses, such as schizophrenia, psychotic depression, and bipolar disorder.[35] The diagnosis in present-day life is extremely rare. Variations of this delusion are boanthropy, where a victim imagines being a bovine cow or bull; lycanthropy, the delusion of being a wolf or other animal; and avianthropy, where the victim assumes birdlike behavior, even attempting to roost in trees. The American Psychiatric Association's *Diagnostic and Statistical Manual* (DSM-5) includes these disorders under *bizarre delusions*, psychotic beliefs of experiences that are impossible.

Roland Harrison tells of witnessing a victim of boanthropy while he worked briefly in a British psychiatric hospital.[36] The patient, with disheveled hair and long nails, wore little clothing, and roamed the grounds of the institution, rain or shine, feeding on the grass, but always refusing to eat ordinary institutional food. Another case is known in medieval Persian tradition. The Buyid prince, Majd al-Dawla, suffered from a delusion where he believed he was a cow. He imitated the sounds of a cow and asked to be slaughtered like a cow so his flesh could be consumed like beef. According to tradition, he was subsequently cured of this illness by the famous philosopher/physician Avicenna (980–1037 CE). European werewolf legends are also based on possible instances of lycanthropy.

Modern psychologists warn such modern diagnoses of ancient persons, based on symptomatology solely contained in non-scientific, anecdotal documents, without direct clinical examination of the persons involved, is tentative and risky.[37] Given we do not know how literally the language de-

---

34. Newsom, *Daniel*, 155.
35. Blom, "When Doctors Cry Wolf," 87–102.
36. Harrison, *Introduction to Old Testament*, 1115–17.
37. Doverspike, "Boanthropy, Lycanthropy, and Zoanthropy," 1. Much of the foregoing is indebted to Doverspike, 1–4, and Avalos, "Nebuchadnezzar's Affliction," 497–507.

scribing Nebuchadnezzar's symptoms is to be taken, such a diagnosis would be inappropriate. The same goes for the other three interpretations we have discussed: metaphor of the netherworld; the wild, uncivilized man; or the person under a curse. We do not know enough about what happened to Nebuchadnezzar (Nabonidus?) to be certain of any of these interpretations. Suffice it to say, he was humbled on account of his overweening hubris, but through his bitter experience ended up acknowledging the true King of heaven (v. 37). His story is a cautionary tale for every autocrat or would-be despot who seeks absolute power.

NEBUCHADNEZZAR'S RESTORATION (4:34-37)

> 34 [4:31] At the end of the days, I, Nebuchadnezzar, lifted my eyes to heaven, and my understanding returned to me.
> I blessed the Most High,
>> and praised and honored the living Eternal One,
>> because his rule is an eternal rule and his sovereignty
>> from generation to generation.
> ³⁵ [4:32] All the inhabitants of the earth are accounted as nothing,
>> and according to his will by power he made the heavens
>> and those who dwell on earth.
> There is none who can deter his hand,
>> or say to him, "What are you doing?"
> ³⁶ [4:33] At that time my understanding came back to me, the majesty of my kingdom, honor, and splendor also returned to me, and my counselors and lords sought me out, over my kingdom I was re-established, and pre-eminent greatness was added to me. ³⁷ [4:34] Now I, Nebuchadnezzar, praise, exalt and honor the King of heaven,
>> of whom all his acts are truth
>>> and his ways justice,
>>> and whoever goes about proudly
>> he is able to humble.

The story ends like it began (Dan 4:3), with a doxology. This is a structural literary device, known as an inclusio or ring composition, where the end of a document echoes how it began. At the end of his period of banishment, Nebuchadnezzar's reason (sanity?) returns to him (vv. 34-35). His suffering endures for a time, just as it had been predicted. At the end, he is transformed and restored. He acknowledges this in a doxology, the first lines of which closely resemble the doxology appearing at the beginning in v. 3. He blesses the living Eternal One,[38] whose sovereignty over the earth is from generation to generation, and whose will toward humanity cannot be hindered. At the same time, Nebuchadnezzar's reign, splendor, and honor—attributes earlier he arrogantly claimed exclusively for himself—return to him, and once more his counselors seek his advice (v. 36). The business of being king continues. The king praises the King of heaven as One whose acts are true, faithful, and just, precisely as the One who humbles the proud has declared (v. 37). Interestingly, the epithet King of heaven (מֶלֶךְ שְׁמַיָּא, *melek shemayya*) occurs only here in the HB.[39]

This doxology drives home the point of the story. The God of heaven is sovereign over all humanity. God rules the world. God's will, whether exalting or humbling human rulers, cannot be resisted. God establishes kings and nations, but also deposes them according to God's will. The sovereignty of God, we may say, is the central theme running through Dan 1–6.

Civilization since Daniel would appear to contradict these convictions. Oppressive, violent regimes have come and gone with chilling, persistent regularity. The Caesars, Genghis Khans, Napoleons, Hitlers, Stalins, and Joseph Mugabbis have wreaked havoc on their subjects and devastated entire cultures, before disappearing ignominiously into the scrapheap of history. How can it be said that particularly evil rulers are the result of God's will? In the NT, Paul seems to concur with this apocalyptic judgment when he writes to the Roman Christians, "There is no authority except from God, and those authorities that exist have been instituted by God" (Rom 13:1). By instituting such authorities, is God implicated in the evils they perpetrate? Even if we grant that for the times of Daniel and Paul, God appointed certain kings, how can it be urged that God universally selects national leaders, when many—perhaps most—continue to exploit their subjects? How can the idea that God sets up and deposes kings be considered a universal truth?

In the apocalyptic visions to follow in Daniel, we get a partial answer to this question. Even the beastly empires of earth are astonishingly allowed to rise and even flourish for a restricted, determined time. The fourth empire in Dan 7, with large iron teeth, devours, breaks in pieces, and tramples what was left of other peoples as it dominates the earth (Dan 7:7). When the probationary eschatological time expires, however, judgment comes.[40] Final

---

38. Dan 12:7; Gen 21:33; Sir 18:1.

39. The epithet (ὁ βασιλεὺς τοῦ οὐρανοῦ, *ho Basileus tou ouranou*, "the king of heaven") appears in Tob 1:18; 13:7, 11, 16; 1 Esd 4:46, 58, suggesting it may be postexilic in origin.

40. For judgment upon Babylon, see Jer 27:5–7.

justice—ultimate accountability—will be eventually applied, if not within history, at its end. In some way, God remains sovereign.

> Truth forever on the scaffold,
> > Wrong forever on the throne—
> Yet that scaffold sways the future,
> > and, behind the dim unknown,
> Standeth God within the shadow,
> keeping watch above his own.[41]

Nebuchadnezzar's experience, Newsom suggests, may be likened to a rite of passage.[42] Although he reigns as a ruler over all his empire, he is stripped of his royal—and human—status and segregated from society. Through seven seasons he suffers deprivation. This is a liminal period of humiliation. At the end of the time, he receives new self-awareness and understanding, and is transformed and reintegrated into society, convinced now he holds his status only as one under God, the real Monarch of the world.

---

41. James Russell Lowell, "The Present Crisis," stanza 8.
42. Newsom, *Daniel*, 149.

Handwriting on the Wall

Daniel 5

Terrific energy is expended—civilizations are built up—excellent institutions devised; but each time something goes wrong. Some fatal flaw always brings the selfish and cruel people to the top and it all slides back into misery and ruin. In fact, the machine conks. It seems to start up all right and runs a few yards, and then it breaks down. They are trying to run it on the wrong juice. That is what Satan has done to us humans.

—C. S. Lewis, *Mere Christianity*

The story in Dan 5 gives us the famous catchphrase for a star-crossed fate, the "handwriting on the wall." In Robert Louis Stevenson's famous tale *The Strange Case of Dr. Jekyll and Mr. Hyde*, Dr. Jekyll writes to his friend Utterson about his discovery of the personality of Mr. Hyde, "This inexplicable incident, this reversal of my previous experience, seemed, like the Babylonian finger on the wall, to be spelling out the letters of my judgment." Daniel 5 depicts a king who has his doom spelled out in cryptic characters, appearing mysteriously on the plaster wall of the royal palace.

Throughout Daniel, writing—words—symbolizes the power exerted by the one inscribing a text, whether in the form of decree, edict, vision, or inscription on a plaster wall, as in this story. "In the book of Daniel," points out Donald Polaski, "writing is used not merely to give a degree of verisimilitude to the court tales, it marks the exercise of political power, by emperor and the deity alike."[1] In this story, the writing on the wall confounds

---

1. Polaski, "*Mene, Mene, Tekel, Parsin*," 649.

king and advisors, and thus royal power, requiring the assistance of a scribe (Daniel), imbued with the "spirit of the gods" and exercising an authority that comes only from God. The Authority represented in the mysterious writing on the wall subverts and undercuts the regime of Belshazzar and spells its doom.

A celebratory banquet opens the story. During the festivities, a detached human hand slowly etches the mysterious writing on the wall (vv. 1-6). The terrified king calls for his advisors, who utterly fail to interpret the riddle-like omen (vv. 7-9). Recalling Daniel's earlier prowess in interpreting dreams, the elderly queen mother urges Daniel be summoned (vv. 10-12). Daniel appears before the king and courageously interprets the strange writing (vv. 13-28). Finally, after Daniel has been duly rewarded, Babylon tragically falls to the conquering Persians (vv. 29-31).

Collins considers Dan 5 a legend because it reports the miraculous writing on the wall, the panic of the king, and draws a moral lesson. It also resembles a tale of court contest.[2] Such tales have the monarch confronted by mysterious omens or riddles the royal courtiers do not comprehend, but which another courtier, usually of inferior status, succeeds in unraveling. The courtier is then elevated to high office or rewarded. Within this tale, the writer has placed Daniel's indictment of Belshazzar (vv. 17-28), which resembles a prophecy of disaster, like the ones commonly found in the prophets.[3]

This well-known story of an ill-fated king is closely related to the previous tale in chapter 4. In both chapters 4 and 5, a king is humbled and, in the latter, loses his life. Both stories tell of divine judgment upon kings who fail to acknowledge God's sovereignty. Both stories move from the illusion of absolute political power to the reality such fragile power is strictly temporary. While the terrified king in chapter 5 shudders before the mysterious writing on the wall, Daniel recalls the earlier experience of Nebuchadnezzar's madness (ch. 4). One difference between these court tales is that in this one, Belshazzar loses his life (Dan 5:30).

BELSHAZZAR'S FEAST (5:1-4)

> Belshazzar the king made a great feast for a thousand of his lords, and in the presence of the thousand he was drinking wine.
> ² Under the influence of the wine, Belshazzar commanded to

---

2. J. Collins, *Daniel* (FOTL 22), 67.

3. Cf. Elijah's confrontation with Ahab (1 Kgs. 21:20-24) or Jeremiah's with Hananiah (Jer 28:12-16).

bring the vessels of gold and silver which Nebuchadnezzar his father had confiscated from the temple, which was in Jerusalem, so that the king, his lords, his consorts, and his concubines might drink from them. ³ Then they brought the vessels of gold that they had taken from the temple of the house of God in Jerusalem, and the king, his lords, his consorts, and his concubines drank from them. ⁴ They drank wine and praised the gods of gold, silver, bronze, iron, wood, and stone.

Belshazzar, his royal coterie, wives, and concubines, enjoy a great imperial feast, the occasion of which is not mentioned. A thousand guests chatter, laugh, and join in revelry (v. 1). The Assyrians, Babylonians, and Persians were known to host extravagant state banquets like this. Lavish banquets elevated the king's status as a "powerful benefactor and bound his subordinates more closely to him."[4] One thousand may be a round figure for a large number, but the Assyrian king Ashurnasirpal (883–859 BCE) is said to have dedicated his new capital in a ten-day festival with 69,574 guests in attendance![5] According to Herodotus, Belshazzar and his attendants were "engaged in a festival . . . dancing and revelling" when Babylon fell to the Persians.[6] In the large banquet hall of the royal palace in Babylon, in or near the throne room, the king, eating and drinking, sits with his back to the wall, facing the revelers.

Present not only are the king's subordinates, but his consorts (שֵׁגַל, shegal, wives) and concubines (לְחֵנָה, lehenah), women of the royal harem, their presence evocative of Belteshazzar's royal authority. The company of women and wine in such royal festivities suggests drunken carousing and sexual libertinism.[7] Greek and Roman writers, generally moderate in use of wine, often ridiculed the excessive drinking at these Oriental festivals.[8]

As Belshazzar becomes inebriated from the wine, he impetuously orders the vessels originally confiscated from the Temple of Yahweh in Jerusalem be brought in so the assembly could drink wine in them in honor of the Babylonian gods, whom they regarded as obviously superior to the God of the subjugated Hebrews (v. 2). Hebrew faith was aniconic; it had no physical image for God. "You shall not make for yourself an idol . . . You shall not bow down to them or worship them" (Deut 5:8–9). Because they were intimately associated with Yahweh, the sacred vessels in the temple, the ark,

---

4. Newsom, *Daniel*, 165.
5. "Banquet of Ashurnasirpal II," translated by A. Leo Oppenheim (*ANET*, 560b).
6. Herodotus, *Hist.* 1:191.
7. Newsom, *Daniel*, 167. See 1 Esd 4:29–31.
8. J. Collins, *Daniel* (Hermeneia), 244. See Esth 1:10; Herodotus, *Hist.* 5:18.

the candlesticks, and so on, acquired an aura of sanctity. In the absence of a physical image, these sacred vessels were proxy for the Lord. They pointed to Yahweh's sovereign power. By profanely using them as drinking vessels and thereby praising Babylon's gods with them (v. 3), Belshazzar defames and mocks God (see v. 23) and thereby asserts his superiority over the vanquished God of Israel.

The writer tells us, unlike the invisible, living God of the temple in Jerusalem, the Babylonian gods were made of gold, silver, bronze, iron, wood, and stone, the very metals, except for wood and stone, which comprised the image of the nations in Dan 2 (v. 4). Anti-idol polemics found in the HB rightly insist that such idols do not see, hear, or smell, and are without divine or even human abilities.[9] The sacrilege in Belshazzar's action involves idolatry, the ironical praising of impotent gods.

Such a scene no doubt resonated with the Jews during the second century. They were suffering oppression and persecution under the Seleucid king Antiochus IV, who dared to desecrate the sacred temple, as Belshazzar does with the temple vessels, and erect an image to the Olympian Zeus in the Ttmple courtyard.[10] Antiochus IV, like Belshazzar, indulges in sacrilegious mockery of the God of Israel.

THE HANDWRITING ON THE WALL (5:5-9)

> [5] In that moment, the fingers of a human hand appeared and in view of the lampstand wrote on the plaster of the wall of the king's palace. The king was watching the palm of the hand that wrote. [6] Then the brightness of the king's countenance changed, and his thoughts terrified him, his hip joints went slack, and his knees knocked one against another. [7] The king cried out to bring in the enchanters, the Chaldeans, and the soothsayers. The king spoke to the wise men of Babylon, "Whoever can read this writing and make known its interpretation to me, will be clothed in purple and a golden chain placed on his neck, and he will be the third ruler in the kingdom." [8] Then all the king's wise men came in, but they could not read the writing, nor make known the interpretation to the king. [9] Then king Belshazzar grew extremely alarmed, his countenance changed, and his lords were confounded.

9. In the Additions to Daniel, note Bel and the Dragon (Dan 14:6-7, 23-27). Cf. Deut 4:28; Isa 44:9-20; Jer 10:2-11.
10. See 1 Macc 1:41-61; 2 Macc 6:1-11.

Who was Belshazzar? The Belshazzar known to history was a Babylonian prince, son of Nabonidus, who had appointed him co-regent over Babylon while Nabonidus was absent from Babylon in Tema in the southern part of the empire.[11] His name, Belshazzar (בֵּלְשַׁאצַּר), the Aramaic form of the name *bēlšaṣṣar*, may be a corruption of the Akkadian *bēl-šarra-uṣur*, "O Bel, protect the king!" There is no evidence he ever served as the king, although he is called such in this story, perhaps based on his co-regency. Note he promises Daniel will be the third ruler in Babylon, implying that he, Belshazzar, is second (v. 16).

His father is said to be Nebuchadnezzar, although Beshazzar was not a descendant of Nebuchadnezzar, except possibly on his mother's side.[12] Nabonidus (556–539 BCE), his real father, Babylon's last king, was a usurper to the throne, not of royal lineage. There had been three kings following Nebuchadnezzar, each of whom reigned only a brief time: Amel-Marduk (562–560), called Evil-Merodach in 2 Kgs 25:27; Neriglassar (560–556); and Labashi-Marduk (556), who was killed in a conspiracy. One of the assassins, Nabonidus, then a Babylonian military commander from Haran, seized the throne. He shifted the state's religious devotion from the god Marduk, the patron god of Babylon, to the lunar god Sîn, angering the priests of Marduk. Nabonidus soon departed Babylon, under pressure, no doubt, to gain firmer control over the southern region of his empire. In the late 1990s, an imperial inscription commissioned by Nabonidus was discovered high on a mountainous promontory in what was anciently known as Edom. This inscription appears to commemorate Nabonidus's southern conquest of Edom.[13]

In his absence from Babylon, he elevated Belshazzar to co-regency and put him in charge of the northern frontier of the Babylonian empire, which included the city of Babylon. The Nabonidus Chronicle, now in the British Museum, puts it this way: "He [Nabonidus] let [everything] go, entrusted the kingship to him [Belshazzar], and himself, he started out for a long journey... towards Tema [deep] in the west."[14] For as long as a decade, Nabonidus remained absent from Babylon. The descriptive terms in this story, father and son (Dan 5:18, 22) are thus not to be taken literally as indicating

---

11. See Daugherty, *Nabonidus and Belshazzar*; McNamara, "Nabonidus," 131–49.

12. Hartman and Di Lella, *Daniel*, 183, 186. See Gruenthaner, "Last King of Babylon," 406–27.

13. See Da Riva, "Dangling Assyriology," 25–32. The ten-foot-high bas-relief carving shows Nabonidus holding a staff and lifting the other hand to his mouth in a gesture of prayer. The accompanying inscription seems to refer to the conquest of Sela and Edom.

14. "The Nabonidus Chronicle," translated by A. Leo Oppenheim (*ANET*, 313b).

direct ancestry from Nebuchadnezzar.[15] In ancient semantics, the term son often referred to a royal successor in office, even though there was no blood relationship. In this case, father equals predecessor.[16]

In the middle of the great royal banquet, on the plaster wall behind the king in the glow of the lampstand, a human hand—detached from the body—begins to etch mystifying words. The effect on the king was immediate. Color drained from his face, his hip joints went slack, and his knees knocked one against another (v. 6). The curious phrase "his hip joints went slack," literally, "the knots of his loins were loosened" (קִטְרֵי חַרְצֵהּ מִשְׁתָּרַיִן, *qitre hartseh mishtarayin*), may refer to the sphincter muscles, which control the release of bodily wastes.[17] If so, the king embarrasses himself by becoming incontinent—in public!

In terror and humiliation, he summons his court scribes and diviners, just as Nebuchadnezzar in the earlier stories (Dan 2:2-8; 4:6-7). These advisors, skilled in the reading, translation, and interpretation of texts, supported the political authority of the empire. He desperately promises that should they interpret this omen, they would receive royal clothing (purple being the royal color) and a golden chain and, more importantly, be promoted to the status of third ruler in the kingdom (v. 7), evidently next in line behind Nabonidus and the co-regent Belshazzar, or alternatively, as one of three main princes of the realm (see Dan 6:1-2). Such clothing and jewelry were symbols of dominant social status.

Try as they may, they cannot unravel the riddle (v. 8), not because the writing was a strange script, but because the individual words, probably Aramaic or Akkadian, were cryptic. They did not make sense. They were coded verbal riddles, omens with embedded messages from the gods. In a period valuing written texts, writing was mysterious even to highly educated scribal diviners. For dramatic effect, the author cleverly holds back what was specifically written until the very end of the story. The reader learns the meaning only when Belshazzar does. Confusion reigns.

The king, his courtiers, and diviners would have taken this baffling writing as an omen. The Babylonians were well-known for their fascination with omens of all sorts. They cultivated experts, known as *baru*(s), who

---

15. Archer, *Old Testament Introduction*, 382-83. Archer gives several examples of the conventional use of son and father in ancient royal contexts. In the HB, Elisha called Elijah "my father," even though there was no direct kinship (2 Kgs 2:12). The sons of the prophets, who appear in the narratives about Elijah and Elisha, were their disciples, not children or grandchildren (2 Kgs 4:1). See Soggin, *Introduction to Old Testament*, 476; Baldwin, *Daniel*, 22.

16. Harrison, *Old Testament Times*, 274; Kitchen, *Ancient Orient*, 38-39.

17. Wolters, "Untying the King's Knots," 117-22.

worked with extispicy, the examination of the entrails of sacrificial animals; heptoscopy, the reading of dissected animal livers; and astronomical omens, concerned with stellar phenomena. They compiled collections of the data and methods for the interpretation of omens. Note this example of heptoscopy from one of these collections: "If there are two 'palace gates' and three kidneys and at the right of the gall bladder there are two breaches, and they go all the way through, it is an omen of Apišalim whom Naram-Sin took prisoner when breaching (the wall of his city)."[18]

Portentous dreams also drew attention, as in the story of Nebuchadnezzar and the metallic image (Dan 2). The designation *baru*, an older term for a professional diviner, was probably still in vogue for such diviners at the time of the Neo-Babylonian empire.

Failure to read such omens as the writing on the wall would have tried the patience of the court diviners. Everybody's anxiety would have skyrocketed (v. 9), since to leave an omen undeciphered would not prevent its mysterious, dangerous effect. Several explanations have been given why the otherwise skilled diviners could not read the writing. The set of Aramaic abbreviations, Albrecht Alt suggests, would not have been readily known to the diviners.[19] Possibly the words were written from left to right, thus turning the Aramaic backwards, as Aramaic (like Hebrew) normally runs right to left. Or they may have been positioned vertically from top to bottom, or with the letters out of order.[20] "But the reason the sages cannot read," astutely observes Polaski, "is not nearly as important as the fact they cannot read."[21]

THE QUEEN MOTHER CALLS FOR DANIEL (5:10-12)

> [10] The queen, because of the words of the king and his lords, entered the banquet hall. The queen spoke, "O king, live forever! Do not let yourself be disturbed, nor your thought or countenance be changed. [11] There is a man in your kingdom in whom is the spirit of the holy gods. In the days of your father, illumination, insight, and wisdom like the wisdom of the gods was found in him. King Nebuchadnezzar, your father, promoted him as chief of the magicians, enchanters, Chaldeans, and diviners. [12] Because an excellent spirit, knowledge, understanding, dream

---

18. A. Goetze, *Old Babylonian Omen Texts*, 24.9, as cited in R. Wilson, *Prophecy and Society*, 94.

19. Alt, "Zur Menetekel Inschrift," 304-5.

20. b. Sanh. 22a.

21. Polaski, "*Mene, Mene, Teqel, Parsin*," 655.

interpretation, the explanation of riddles, and the unraveling of difficulties is found in him, in Daniel, whom the king named Belteshazzar. Now let Daniel be called and he will make known the interpretation."

Overhearing the confusion in the banquet hall, the queen mother enters (v. 10). According to Josephus's account, now corroborated by the discovery of the basalt stele of Eski-Harran, this is probably Belshazzar's grandmother.[22] In the ancient Near East, the importance and influence of the queen mother is widely attested. The Harran inscription, mentioned earlier, tells of the queen mother of Nabonidus and grandmother of Belshazzar, Adda-guppi, and her influence on her son's career.[23] From long memory, the queen mother calms the king by recalling that in the past, in the days of your father, there was a certain man in possession of the wisdom of the gods who could explain such omens and riddles (v. 11). His name was Belteshazzar, almost like the king's own. He will make known the interpretation, she promises (v. 12). The text does not explain why such an extraordinarily gifted person remains unknown to the king, but political leaders have short memories. Belshazzar's own role in the Babylonian state was also vague. This motif—the forgotten wise man—is conventional.[24] A new king arises in Egypt who does not know Joseph (Exod 1:8). The king of Assyria had to be reminded there once was a wise man named Ahikar who was good at "resolving questions like these."[25] That Daniel possesses the spirit of the holy gods recalls what was said about him in Dan 4:8 ("the spirit of the holy gods is in him"). Daniel's ability to interpret dreams, explain riddles, and unravel difficult omens—such as the mysterious writing—is emphasized. This ability links this chapter to chapters 2 and 4 and accentuates Daniel's most renowned trait.

Aside from the queen mother, in the book of Daniel, women play almost no role. The book, like much of the HB, is patriarchal. Men do all the speaking and acting; women are only incidentally mentioned. Offstage, women are marginal characters, peripheral to what is going on in the main drama. When onstage, they play only bit pieces. Only the queen mother and

---

22. Josephus, *Ant.* 10.11.2; "Family of Nabonidus," translated by A. Leo Oppenheim (*ANET*, 312a). Other possibilities are that she was Belshazzar's mother or the grandmother of Nabonidus (Hartman and Di Lella, *Daniel*, 188; Newsom, *Daniel*, 172).

23. Gadd, "Harran Inscriptions," 47, 90. See also Andreasen, "Role of the Queen Mother."

24. J. Collins, *Daniel* (Hermeneia), 248–49.

25. See Ahiqar 1.23–28. "He is a wise [counselor and scribe], on whose counsel and ad[vice] all Assyria used to rely" (lines 1.27–28).

Susanna, in the Additions, have a speaking voice.[26] What is true in Daniel, however, is true of much of the biblical text, including the NT and the deuterocanonicals. Almost all biblical authors and editors were no doubt men, so they wrote with an implicit masculine bias. Gender bias does not preclude the biblical text from being the bearer of a divine message.[27] "On the one hand, the Bible is written in androcentric language, has its origin in the patriarchal cultures of antiquity, and has functioned throughout its history to inculcate androcentric and patriarchal values," notes Elizabeth Schüssler Fiorenza. "On the other hand, the Bible has also served to inspire and authorize women and other nonpersons in their struggles against patriarchal [and other forms of] oppression."[28]

DANIEL INTERPRETS THE OMEN (5:13-28)

> [13] Then Daniel was brought before the king. The king proceeded to say to Daniel, "Are you Daniel who is one of the captives from Judah, whom my father the king brought from Judah? [14] I have heard concerning you that the spirit of the gods is in you, and that enlightenment, understanding, and exceptional wisdom are found in you. [15] Now, the wise men, the conjurers, have been brought in before me so that this writing they might read and make known its interpretation to me, but they could not make the matter known. [16] I have heard concerning you that you can give interpretations and solve problems. Now, if you can read the writing and make known its interpretation, you will be dressed in purple, have a golden chain around your neck, and as the third in the kingdom you will rule."

The king interrogates Daniel, inquiring about his reputation—one who has within himself the spirit of the holy gods—and thus one skilled in omen interpretation (vv. 13–14). He reminds Daniel of his foreign social status—he is one of the captives from Judah—before going on to ask about his professional reputation (cf. Dan 2:25). He tellingly points out his own counselors have been unable to explain the matter, but he has heard what Daniel could do (v. 15). If Daniel can unravel the riddle, he pledges, Daniel would be outfitted in royal purple, with a golden chain about his neck (royal status symbols), and be promoted to a high level in the kingdom (v. 16). Being the

---

26. See Dan 5:10–12 (queen mother); 13:22–24, 42–43 (Susanna).

27. For a good overview of the problem of gender bias in interpretation, see Brown, *Handbook to Old Testament*, 247–77.

28. Fiorenza, "Transforming the Legacy," 5.

third in the kingdom may refer to a high position alongside the co-regency Belshazzar occupied with Nabonidus, or Daniel would be one of three high governmental officials or, more generally, simply a high official or close aide to the king.[29]

> [17] Then Daniel answered before the king, "Let your gifts be for yourself or your rewards give to another; however, I will read the inscription for the king and will make known to him the interpretation. [18] O king, the Most High God gave to Nebuchadnezzar your father the kingdom, greatness, glory, honor, and majesty. [19] Because of the greatness that he gave him, all peoples, nations, and languages trembled and feared before him. Whomever he willed, he slew; whom he willed, he let live; whom he willed, he exalted; and whom he willed, he humbled. [20] When his heart was exalted and his spirit became presumptuously arrogant, he was deposed from the royal throne and his majesty removed from him. [21] From mortals he was expelled, and his mind became like that of an animal and his abode was with the wild asses. They fed him grass like oxen, and his body was bathed with the dew of heaven, until he recognized that the Most High rules over the kingdom of mortals and to whomever he wishes he establishes over it. [22] But you, Belshazzar his son, have not humbled your heart even though you were aware of all this. [23] Against the Lord of the heavens you have exalted yourself. The vessels of his house they have brought before you; your nobles, wives, and concubines have been drinking wine from them, and the gods of silver, gold, copper, iron, wood, and stone, who do not see or hear or know you have praised. But the God in whose hand is your breath and to whom all your ways belong you have not honored."[30]

Rejecting out of hand the king's rewards for a proposed interpretation (v. 17), Daniel indicts Belshazzar by recalling Nebuchadnezzar's psychopathic affliction (vv. 18–21), mentioned earlier (Dan 4:19–26). Daniel's recapitulation, in tone more like prophet than sage, sharply criticizes Nebuchadnezzar's ambitious behavior. He had claimed God's prerogatives, the

---

29. See J. Collins, *Daniel* (Hermeneia), 247; Newsom, *Daniel*, 171.

30. This section (Dan 5:17–23) is missing from the OG text, the source text of the LXX, and largely absent from the LXX itself. The OG text is sometimes called the Ur-Septuagint or the Proto-Septuagint. Collins explains vv. 17–23 as an editorial addition in the MT intended to draw a contrast between Nebuchadnezzar and Belshazzar, illustrating the different ways God deals with gentile kings (J. Collins, *Daniel* [Hermeneia], 249).

power to give or take life, death, and prosperity. Nebuchadnezzar ironically "*thought* he had this ability, but in reality he did not."[31]

Instead of heeding the cautionary tale about Nebuchadnezzar, of which Belshazzar has evidently been aware all along (v. 22), he has taunted God by sacrilegiously drinking wine in the sacred vessels of the temple, while at the same time glorifying gods of silver, gold, copper, iron, wood, and stone. The sovereign God you have not honored, Daniel accuses Belshazzar (v. 23). There is no mention of a reprieve from this condemnation. In Daniel's fourth vision (chs. 10–12), a pretentious king—usually identified with Antiochus IV Epiphanes—"will do as he pleases. He will exalt himself and consider himself great over every god, and against the God of gods he will speak presumptuous words" (Dan 11:36). Belshazzar "had the opportunity to know something but neglected it in his devotion to gods who know nothing."[32] He is at fault because he had Nebuchadnezzar's corrupt example and failed to heed its lesson.

> [24] "Therefore, from his presence the palm of the hand was extended, and this writing inscribed. [25] This is the writing that was inscribed: *Mene, mene, teqel,* and *parsin.* [26] This is the interpretation of the matter: *Mene*: God has numbered your kingdom and brought it to an end. [27] *Teqel*: you have been weighed in the scales and found deficient. [28] *Peres*: your kingdom is divided and given to the Medes and Persians."

After considerable delay, the reader now hears exactly what the mysterious hand had inscribed on the wall. It consists of three cryptic Aramaic words with a double meaning, one of which is repeated (v. 25), probably for emphasis. *Mene, teqel,* and *peres* (*parsin* is the plural form of *peres*) are the names of weights, as we can tell from the verbs used with them: numbered and weighed (vv. 26–27)]. Daniel interprets the *mene* (מְנֵא) or *mina* as a Babylonian stone weight, giving it the sense "God has numbered your kingdom and brought it to an end." *Teqel* (תְּקֵל), the Aramaic equivalent of the Hebrew shekel (שֶׁקֶל), stands for the weighing of the kingdom in the balance scales and finding it deficient. The shekel, of course, was also a monetary weight, usually a stone, used for weighing silver and gold of equivalent weight.[33] Finally, the term *peres* (פְּרֵס) is a half-*mina* but also

---

31. Smith-Christopher, "Book of Daniel," 83; italics in original. Cf. Deut 32:39; 1 Sam 2:6–8; Ps 75:7.

32. J. Collins, *Daniel* (Hermeneia), 250. See Dan 8:11, 25; Isa 14:12–20; 37:29; 2 Kgs 19:28.

33. Cornfeld and Freedman, *Archaeology of the Bible*, 234. The Israelite shekel, not the Babylonian or Persian, weighed 11.4 grams. Metal ingots served as currency before

almost equivalent to *Paras* (פְּרַס, Persia). The name for the *peres* weight is a wordplay on the nominal designation for Persia. *Paras* is the very empire that would vanquish Babylon in this story. "Your kingdom is divided and given to the Medes and Persians" (v. 28). Thus, the interpretation of the three cryptic words contains a terse message of doom for Belshazzar and Babylon. "Suddenly Babylon has fallen and is shattered . . . forsake her, and let each of us go to our own country" (Jer 51:8–9).

Several interpreters understand the diminishing value of the weights to represent the diminishing quality of the final Neo-Babylonian kings. This would be either Nebuchadnezzar II (602–562), Nabonidus (556–539), and Belshazzar (coregent with Nabonidus); or Evil-Merodach (561–560), Neriglissar (560–556), Labashi-Marduk (556), and Nabonidus (with Belshazzar).[34] "What is the worth of the kings of Babylon?" asks Frost, punning on the diminishing weight values. "The answer is that God has weighed them and found them to be steadily losing weight."[35]

Daniel however does not interpret the weights in exactly this manner. Instead, he recognizes the punning, double meaning of the words,[36] which in effect declare, "God has numbered and found lacking your kingdom and given it over to the Persians."

The mysterious writing assures the judgment of which it speaks. But it is not understood until Daniel interprets it. Both its encoding in indecipherable letters and its decoding by Daniel are acts implied in power relations. The deity is doing more here than communicating a judgment in a riddle. God is expressing divine authority, mastery over the empire and its minions.[37]

DANIEL REWARDED AS BABYLON FALLS (5:29–31)

> [29] Then Belshazzar gave command, and they clothed Daniel in purple garments and put the chain of gold around his neck and

---

the introduction of coins in the Achaemenid empire.

34. Freedman, "Prayer of Nabonidus," 32; Kraeling, "Handwriting on the Wall." As early as 1886, C. Clermont-Ganneau suggested this sequence offered an evaluation of the last kings of Babylon (Clermont-Ganneau, "Mané, Thécel, Pharès," 44–45).

35. Frost, "Mene, Mene, Tekel, and Parsin," 349.

36. Newsom, *Daniel*, 177. Newsom points out that in antiquity, "words were understood to participate in the reality of the thing they described," so the punning of the cryptic words was not mere wit, but a "perception of hidden realities" (178).

37. Polaski, "*Mene, Mene, Teqel, Parsin*," 657.

proclaimed regarding him that he should be the third ruler in the kingdom.

³⁰ In that very night Belshazzar, the Chaldean king, was slain. ³¹ [*Aram.* 6:1] Thus, Darius the Mede received the kingdom, being about sixty-two years old.

We know nothing of Belshazzar's immediate, emotional reaction to this dreadful news. It must have been one of shock and dismay; he could hardly have felt grateful for the fearsome interpretation he had been given.[38] The last night of Babylon's empire—stretching from the Tigris and Euphrates Rivers to the Mediterranean—had come to a bitter end. Belshazzar nevertheless stoically follows through with the rewards to Daniel, dressing him in royal purple, placing the chain of gold around his neck, and having him proclaimed as the third ruler in the kingdom (v. 29), despite Daniel's earlier refusal of reward (v. 17).

Whereas the handwriting on the wall tells of the judgment upon Babylon in three terse Aramaic words, the text now spells out the fate of Belshazzar in six (v. 30). Nabonidus, it appears, had returned to Babylon prior to these events. Belshazzar's status after Nabonidus's return remains unclear. The Greek historian Xenophon (430–354 BCE) relates that, on this occasion, a group of Persian soldiers entered the palace and slaughtered the king and those in attendance.[39] Xenophon's description seems to be generally consistent with Daniel.

Implied in the six words about the fate of Babylon is that the Persians made a surprise entrance into the city. Historical reconstruction of this, except in the most general terms, has eluded historians. According to the ancient Greek historian Herodotus, when Cyrus neared Babylon, the Babylonian army engaged him in a battle, but subsequently retreated into the fabled protective walls of the city. Cyrus then had his troops dig canals and partially divert the river which flowed directly into Babylon, so troops could then stealthily march through the shallow waters and into the city, surprising the startled Babylonians who were preoccupied in the great banquet.[40]

Xenophon also mentions the diverting of the river while the Babylonians were engaged in a night festival, but the Babylonian writer Berossus (c. 290 BCE) tells that Nabonidus engaged Cyrus upon his approach, and

---

38. Hartman and Di Lella, *Daniel*, 190. Josephus says that Belshazzar "was in great sorrow and affliction . . . the interpretation was so heavy upon him" (Josephus, *Ant.* 10:11.4).

39. Xenophon, *Cyr.* 7.5.24–30.

40. Herodotus, *Hist.* 1:190–91.

after being repulsed, fled to Borsippa. Cyrus then razed the walls of Babylon and captured the city.[41]

These accounts cannot be entirely reconciled with the contemporary Nabonidus Chronicle and the Cyrus Cylinder. The Nabonidus Chronicle puts it this way:

> In the seventeenth year [of Nabonidus] . . . . In the month of Tashritu, when Cyrus attacked the army of Akkad in Opis on the Tigris, the inhabitants of Akkad revolted, but he [Nabonidus] massacred the confused inhabitants . . . . The fourteenth day . . . Nabonidus fled. The 16th day, Gobryas (*Ugbaru*), the governor of Gutium, and the army of Cyrus entered Babylon without battle. Afterwards, Nabonidus was arrested in Babylon when he returned.[42]

After conquering Babylon, Cyrus (557–529 BCE) had a decree inscribed on the so-called Cyrus Cylinder, an artifact discovered by Hormuzd Rassam in the nineteenth century. This decree tells of the misdeeds of Nabonidus, particularly his neglect of the principal god of Babylon (Marduk) and how Marduk chose Cyrus instead as the legitimate ruler. The Cyrus Cylinder describes the fall of Babylon:

> Marduk, the great lord, a protector of his people/worshipers, beheld with pleasure his [Cyrus] good deeds, and his upright mind . . . [and] ordered him to march against his city Babylon. He made him set out on the road to Babylon going at his side like a real friend. His widespread troops—their number, like that of the water of a river, could not be established—strolled along, their weapons packed away. Without any battle, he made him enter his town Babylon, sparing Babylon any calamity. He delivered into his hands Nabonidus, the king who did not worship him [Marduk]. All the inhabitants of Babylon as well as of the entire country of Sumer and Akkad, princes and governors [included], bowed to him [Cyrus] and kissed his feet, jubilant that he [had received] the kingship.[43]

In the absence of sufficient data, I will not attempt to reconcile these accounts. The greatly abbreviated description of this night of Babylon's

---

41. Xenophon, *Cyr.* 7:5.1–36; Berossus, *Babyloniaca* 1:20, as cited in Young, *Prophecy of Daniel*, 128.

42. "Nabonidus Chronicle," translated by A. Leo Oppenheim (*ANET*, 306b). Note that the chronicle attributes the taking of Babylon to Ugbaru, the governor of Guttium and commander of the Persian army.

43. "Cyrus Cylinder," translated by A. Leo Oppenheim (*ANET*, 315–16).

fall—without a battle—in the book of Daniel is essentially supported by the historical records of the time.[44] The writer must have had a general awareness of the unusual fate of Babylon.

There may be a literary connection between the story in Dan 5 and Jeremiah's reference to Babylon's fall coming at a time when "her officials and her sages" are drunk along with "her governors, her deputies, and her warriors" (Jer 51:56) and Isaiah's oracle, "Fallen, fallen is Babylon; and all the images of her gods lie shattered on the ground" (Isa 21:9). It is conceivable Dan 5 may have been composed as the fulfillment of these two prophetic oracles.

The final verse of this chapter (v. 31) is Dan 6:1 in the Aramaic text. It mentions when Babylon fell on this fateful night, Darius the Mede received the kingdom. This verse introduces one of the great puzzles of the book of Daniel: who is Darius the Mede? The stage is now set for the next episode in the drama, the testing of Daniel's faith. That episode involves the mysterious Darius.

---

44. See Cogan, "Into Exile," 361–64. For a more negative appraisal, see Newsom, *Daniel*, 163–64.

The Plot against Daniel

Daniel 6

Courage is almost a contradiction in terms. It means a strong desire to live taking the form of a readiness to die.

—G. K. Chesterton, *Orthodoxy*

Like his three colleagues, tested to the point of death at the dedication of Nebuchadnezzar's golden idol (ch. 3), so Daniel must also face his time of trial. This is probably the most popular story in Daniel. Children's Sunday School classes everywhere tell it over and over. In Daniel, it complements the story of the burning furnace and the deliverance of the three. The NT, interestingly, mentions these two stories in the same line. The faithful "obtained promises, shut the mouths of lions, quenched raging fire" (Heb 11:33–34). In structure as well as plot, the two stories are also similar. Both begin with a loyalty test set by a king. The protagonists are maliciously accused of violating a loyalty test contrary to their religious convictions. Found guilty, the protagonists are then hurled to their awaiting deaths in fire or in the lions' pit, from which they are amazingly delivered. Their executioners end up perishing by the same means of execution as they exacted. The king ends up acknowledging the sovereignty of the God of the Hebrews.

Yet the interaction between the king and the Jewish heroes differs. In Dan 3, the confrontation with the king presents an opportunity for a bold, frank confession of faith (3:16–18); in Dan 6, there is no such confrontation. Here the king, evidently more sympathetic, instead expresses assurance Daniel's God could deliver him. Daniel speaks only after he has been delivered, not before (6:22).

The English, most modern translations, and the Aramaic MT versions have a slightly different versification. This commentary follows the English versification, but for convenience, the Aramaic verse numbers are indicated in brackets.

Preserved among the deuterocanonical Additions to Daniel is another story about Daniel in the lions' pit, known as Bel and the Dragon (Dan 14). In this story, Daniel arouses popular hostility by destroying the serpent deity of the Babylonians. While in the lions' pit, Daniel is miraculously fed by the prophet Habakkuk, who is astonishingly transposed from Judah to Babylon.

Daniel 6 is classified as a court legend. Stereotypical folkloristic elements, such as the king's utter passivity, the use of hyperbole and exaggeration, and the concerted mob behavior of the 120 satraps mark the story as legend.[1] Daniel 6, set in the court of the Achaemenid empire, probably originated either toward the end of this empire (fourth century) or later in the third century BCE.

After an introduction (Dan 6:2-4), a conspiracy, provoked by jealousy, arises against Daniel (vv. 5-10). Daniel is subsequently condemned to be thrown into the lions' pit (vv. 11-18). There he spends the night but is astonishingly delivered by God (vv. 19-25). The king then makes a royal proclamation that all in the realm should honor—"tremble and fear"—Daniel's God (vv. 26-27). A postscript giving the extent of Daniel's successful career marks the end of the story (v. 28).

THE CONSPIRACY AGAINST DANIEL (6:1-9)

[*Aram* 6:2] It seemed good before Darius that he set over the kingdom one hundred twenty satraps, who would be over the realm. ² [6:3] He placed over them three officials of whom Daniel was one. These satraps were to give account so that the king suffer no loss. ³ [6:4] Then this Daniel distinguished himself over the officials and satraps because an extraordinary spirit was in him, and the king planned to appoint him over the whole realm. ⁴ [6:5] Then the officials and satraps sought to find grounds for complaint against Daniel with respect to the kingdom. But they were unable to find any corruption because he was trustworthy, and no neglect or corruption was found in him. ⁵ [6:6] Then these men said, "We will not find in this Daniel any grounds for complaint unless we find it with the law of his God."

---

1. J. Collins, *Daniel* (Hermeneia), 272-73.

As part of the administrative restructure of the new realm, Darius sets up 120 satraps and seven supervisory officials, of whom Daniel is one (vv. 1–2). The number of satraps (from the Persian *sarkin*, chief administrator) and supervisory personnel mentioned is inconsistent with other biblical references to the Persian administrative polity. Esther instead mentions 127 provinces and seven supervisors (Esth 1:1, 14). First Esdras has three nobles who advise the Persian king (1 Esd 3:9), which is more in keeping with this story. The numbers should probably be taken as estimates or ideal numbers.

These verses, however, present us with a lingering problem: who is Darius the Mede? Unfortunately, no one by the designation Darius the Mede is known to ancient or modern historians. He cannot so far be documented in any extra-biblical record. Darius the Mede is mentioned only in the book of Daniel, nowhere else in the HB.[2] According to Daniel, Darius was of Median ancestry, the son of Ahasuerus (Dan 9:1). At the time he set up his administration, he was about sixty-two years old (5:31), an advanced age at the time. He appointed 120 satraps over the kingdom, with three presidents or presiding officials. Although only his first regnal year is mentioned (11:1), Cyrus II is said to have succeeded him as monarch (6:28).

Since we know Cyrus conquered Babylon and continued as sole monarch of the Achaemenid (Persian) empire—including Babylon—some scholars assume Darius the Mede is really a fictional character introduced into the story on account of the prophetic tradition that the Medes would one day destroy Babylon. "I am stirring up the Medes against them . . . and Babylon, the glory and pride of the Chaldeans, will be like Sodom and Gomorrah" (Isa 13:17–19).[3] In the four-kingdom sequence in Nebuchadnezzar's dream (Dan 2:36–45), it is argued, there was a need for a Median rule interposed between the Babylonians and Persians; hence, the necessity for this story featuring Darius the Mede. However briefly the Median empire may have prevailed, in other words, it would sequentially precede Persia among the four empires: Babylon, Media, Persia, Greece.[4]

Rather than insert a fictional character, others claim the Danielic author has confused Darius the Mede with Darius I (522–486), a later Persian king, the son of Hystaspes, the successor of Cambyses (530–522). Darius I was known as a skilled administrator of affairs of state. Herodotus mentions his setting up of twenty satrapies.[5] If Darius the Mede has been confused

---

2. Dan 5:31; 6:1, 28; 9:1; 11:1.

3. See also Isa 21:1–10; Jer 51:11, 28.

4. Rowley, *Darius the Mede*, 59; Smith-Christopher, "Book of Daniel," 88; Newsom, *Daniel*, 192; Newsom, "Daniel and Additions," 160.

5. Herodotus, *Hist.* 3.89.

with Darius I Hystaspes, however, the author has introduced a glaring anachronism into the text. This would make Darius the successor of Cyrus II, not his predecessor.

Although some have considered Darius another name for Astyages, the last ruler of the Medes, this is unlikely since Cyrus deposed Astyages in 553/552, over a decade before the fall of Babylon. There is no hint of Astyages's association with Cyrus in the conquering of Babylon. Nor can he be identified with Cambyses, Cyrus's son, who later succeeded him.[6] Cambyses was not Median, nor could he have been sixty-two years old at the time. Cyaxares II, the son of Astyages, the last ruler of the Medes, has also been proposed,[7] but again, there is no record of his association with Cyrus at the fall of Babylon. Wiseman and Kitchen identify Darius the Mede and Cyrus as the same person under a double name. Cyrus was known to have used the title king of the Medes as well as king of Persia and to have been about sixty years old around the time Babylon fell. Daniel 6:28 may thus be translated: "So this Daniel prospered during the reign of Darius, that is, in the reign of Cyrus the Persian."[8]

The Babylonian Nabonidus Chronicle mentions a certain "Gobryas (*Ugbaru*), the governor of Gutium, and the army of Cyrus entered Babylon without battle." This report has led many to identify Gobryas (the Greek spelling of *Gubaru* or *Ugbaru*, both given in ancient sources) with Darius the Mede. The Chronicle goes on to tell how Cyrus installed Gobryas as governor, and Gobryas, in turn, appointed "(sub) governors in Babylon," a comment that accords well with Daniel: Darius "set over the kingdom one hundred twenty satraps" (Dan 6:1). However, Gobryas (Ugbaru) died about three weeks later in the "month of Arahshammu," and a period of official mourning followed.[9] Despite this, there are references in other cuneiform

---

6. So Boutflower, *In and Around*, 142.

7. Cyaxares II is the tentative preference of Nichol, *Seventh-Day Adventist Bible Commentary*, 4:814–17.

8. See Baldwin, *Daniel*, 26; Kitchen, *On the Reliability*, 74; Wiseman, "Some Historical Problems," 14; Walvoord, *Daniel*, 134. Similar is the view that Darius is an old Persian royal title such as Augustus or Caesar in the Roman empire (Hoerth, *Archaeology*, 384). The LXX of this verse reads: "Daniel was in (his) position in the reign of Darius, then Cyrus the Persian received his kingdom," suggesting that Cyrus succeeded Darius and thus was not identified with him.

9. "Neo-Babylonian Empire and Its Successors," translated by A. Leo Oppenheim (*ANET*, 306b). The problem may be more complicated. Whitcomb distinguishes between Ugbaru, the one who led the Persian troops to victory and died three weeks later, and Gubaru, who was appointed governor of Babylon, a post he appears to have held for at least fourteen years. Whereas Ugbaru and Gubaru are generally recognized as the same person, Whitcomb resists combining these two individuals into Gobryas (Whitcomb, *Darius the Mede*, 26). See Harrison, *Introduction to Old Testament*, 341–43.

records to a Gubaru as the governor of Babylonia and Ebir-nari, an area to the west of Babylon, in the period 535–532 BCE.[10] The historical problems notwithstanding, this is the most attractive option for Darius's identity,

If Darius is identified as Gobryas (Ugbaru), why then has the author designated him Darius the Mede? Is Josephus correct when he says of Darius, "he was the son of Astyages, and had another name among the Greeks"?[11] Unfortunately, Josephus does not indicate what this other name may have been. Is Darius possibly another name—perhaps a throne or royal name—for Gobryas? We know Cyrus followed the policy of appointing a reliable deputy as temporary administrator over certain regions when it was necessary for him to give attention to another part of the empire. These appointees received the title of *Dāreyāwēš*, apparently signifying the royal one, from *dara*, an Avestan Persian term for king. Thus, according to W. F. Albright:

> Gobryas, who, as we know from cuneiform sources, was appointed governor of Babylonia by Cyrus, had been governor of Gordyene (Gutium), and was almost certainly a Mede, since earlier in his career he was a general of Nebuchadrezzar, the ally of the Medes. The statements of Daniel and the Cyropaedia regarding the advanced age of the first Iranian ruler of Babylonia are thus confirmed by the cuneiform records. It seems to me highly probable that Gobryas did actually assume the royal dignity along with the name "Darius," perhaps an old Iranian royal title, while Cyrus was absent on an Eastern campaign.[12]

While we cautiously accept the identification of Darius the Mede as Gobryas, the actual identity of Darius remains shrouded in mystery. The question must remain open.

Once appointed to his supervisory post by Darius, as we have come to expect, Daniel excels (v. 3). In him resides an extraordinary spirit (רוּחַ יַתִּירָא, *ruah yatira*), evidenced in his legendary discernment and wisdom (see Dan 1:17; 5:12). This very trait provokes the jealousy of his more mediocre colleagues. Unable to find any basis for censure in his work, they turn to his religious practice, the law of his God (vv. 4–5), which here probably denotes the legislation now found in the Torah (Pentateuch). Although there is no reference in the Torah to praying three times a day, the psalter

---

10. Archer, "Daniel," 18; Whitcomb, *Daniel*, 80; Wood, *Daniel*, 153–55. For a full discussion of this identity, see Whitcomb, *Darius the Mede*. Miller summarizes the evidence (S. Miller, *Daniel*, 172–73).

11. Josephus, *Ant.* 10:11.4.

12. Albright, "Date and Personality," 112–13n19.

does mention the practice: "I will call upon God . . . evening and morning and at noon" (Ps 55:16–17).

> ⁶ [6:7] Then these officials and satraps came storming into the king, and thus said to him, "O King Darius, live forever! ⁷ [6:8] All the officials, prefects, satraps, counselors, and governors of the kingdom have taken counsel together in order to establish a royal statute and enforce an injunction that whoever seeks a petition from any god or mortal for thirty days except from you, O king, will be cast into the pit of lions. ⁸ [6:9] Now, O king, establish the injunction and sign the writing so it cannot change, according to the law of the Medes and Persians that may not be abrogated." ⁹ [6:10] Therefore King Darius signed the document and injunction.

The officials manipulate the king's vanity (vv. 6–7). They regard the king as "someone who is weak and can be manipulated, perhaps even bullied."[13] They subversively propose an injunction forbidding an appeal, as in a prayer or petition, to any person or god for thirty days, except the king. This injunction seems broadly directed against the petition of any deity, but its effect grants divine status to the king. The king is the only person—human or divine—to whom such petition may be made. As in Dan 5, a written document in this story is a symbol of authority. The story pits the royal injunction against the law of Daniel's God. Which is the most authoritative? At the end, Darius settles this question by writing an epistle to his empire that all should respect and honor the God of Daniel (Dan 6:25–27).

The royal injunction sets a clever trap for Daniel. Such a decree runs counter to the tendency of the early Achaemenid (Persian) monarchs, who were generally tolerant of the religious practices of their subjects. Not only this, but the Persian monarchs, in contrast to the Egyptians, did not claim divine attributes for themselves. Despite these considerations, anyone who violated this injunction would be cast into the pit of lions. In a sense, Daniel becomes representative of the Jewish people, the king, typical of paganism or non-Jewish religion. Judaism demands the exclusive worship of Yahweh, which sets Daniel at odds with the pagan king. A conflict is set up between the דָּת (*dat*, law) of God and the state (also דָּת) of the king. Two cultures collide. In Dan 7, the little horn, symbolizing the Seleucid king Antiochus IV Epiphanes, attempts to "change the sacred seasons and the law [דָּת]," presumably, the law of God, setting up a similar conflict (Dan 7:25).

At the courtiers' insistence, the hoodwinked, clueless king signs the legislation (vv. 8–9), which now becomes binding, according to the law of

---

13. Newsom, *Daniel*, 193.

Persia that may not be abrogated. That the law of Persia cannot be changed is noted elsewhere in postexilic biblical literature[14] as well as in the Greek historian Diodorus Siculus (first century BCE). Diodorus tells of an incident in which an innocent man was condemned and put to death under Darius III (336–330) on account of the rigidity of Persia law, which could not be revoked, even though the condemned man was clearly innocent.[15] The laws of two realms—those of Persia and those of Daniel's God—jarringly collide. Ironically, the unalterable law of the Persians is up against the God who can change the unchangeable (Dan 2:21). The unchangeable law that sends Daniel to his death will be changed by the Eternal God into Daniel's deliverance from death.

DANIEL'S CIVIL DISOBEDIENCE (6:10-15)

> [10] [6:11] Although Daniel realized that the written decree had been signed, he went to his residence and with his windows open in the roof-chamber facing Jerusalem, three times a day he knelt on his knees, prayed, and praised before his God, just as he had done previously. [11] [6:12] Then these men came by prior arrangement and found Daniel praying and seeking mercy before his God. [12] [6:13] Then they approached the king and spoke about the injunction, "O king, did you not sign an injunction that any person who prays to any god or mortal for thirty days, except to you, O king, will be cast into the pit of lions?" The king replied, "The matter stands firm according to the law of the Medes and Persians that cannot be abrogated."

Knowing full well the injunction had been signed, Daniel calmly ignores it (v. 10). Returning to his residence, he resumes his routine practice of praying three times a day facing Jerusalem, much as Muslims turn toward Mecca during their five daily prayers. Through the open window he turns in the direction of Jerusalem, a custom mentioned in Solomon's prayer at the dedication of the Jerusalem temple. Tobit also mentions praying at an open window in an upper room.[16] In exile, Jerusalem was venerated as a symbol of hope and promise of the return of the exiles. Worshipers in exile generally turned in that direction when they prayed. Such personal private

---

14. Ezra 6:11-12; Esth 1:19; 8:8; Dan 6:13.

15. Diodorus, *Hist.* 17:30. Herodotus, to the contrary, states "that the king of the Persians might do whatever he pleased" (*Hist.* 3:31), but this refers to a potential conflict in the Persian law, which the king could resolve by following his own predilection.

16. 1 Kgs 8:35-36; Ps 138:2; Tob 3:10-11.

prayer may well have been coordinated with the regular times of the temple morning and evening sacrifices.

In his roof-chamber, a room in the corner of a flat roof, often with latticed windows to let air circulate freely, Daniel prays. Such a structure would permit an open view to bystanders in the street below. We read of Ehud "sitting alone in his cool roof-chamber" (Judg 3:20). By leaving the windows open, was Daniel deliberately engaging in civil disobedience? The verb in the Aramaic (פְּתַח, *petah*, opened) is passive, implying the windows were usually left open. Theodotion's Greek translation also uses the passive voice, following the Aramaic. The LXX instead has the active voice; in other words, Daniel throws open the windows when he prays. Whether active or passive, it is possible to take this as an act of civil disobedience.[17] Daniel openly, courageously defies the edict and thus resists the legal authority behind it. The charge levelled against Daniel by the antagonists in v. 13 calls attention to Daniel's intentional resistance.

Daniel's antagonists, however, are shrewdly monitoring Daniel's religious practice, and subversively report back to the king (v. 11). They remind him of his injunction, now put into law. The matter stands, the king annoyingly states, because it is the law of the Medes and Persians, that cannot be abrogated (v. 12).

> [13] [6:14] Then they answered before the king, "Daniel, who is from the captives of the Judean exile, has not paid due regard to you, O king, or to the injunction that you have signed, but three times a day requests his petition." [14] [6:15] Then the king, when he heard the matter, became greatly displeased. He determined regarding Daniel to deliver him, and so until sunset he struggled to rescue him. [15] [6:16] Then these men came by prior arrangement before the king and said to the king, "Know, O king, it is the law of the Medes and Persians that any injunction or statute which the king establishes is not to change."

Daniel's political enemies slander him as a captive of the Judean exile. Not only is Daniel of a different, inferior culture, they assert, he has scorned the edict and has done so not once, but three times per day (v. 13). Now that a criminal charge is specifically made against Daniel, the king is horribly upset, because he previously had held Daniel in high regard (v. 14). He had in fact planned to promote Daniel to chief of the officials and satraps. Yet his hands are now legally tied, since the law of the Medes and Persians cannot be altered (v. 15). At some level it probably dawned on him these wily officials had manipulated him to turn the law against Daniel, which may

---

17. Smith-Christopher, "Book of Daniel," 92.

explain why he now sets out to try to rescue Daniel. Through the entire day, until the sun sets in the west, Darius struggles—within the law—to make this happen.

Some interpreters, anxious to show the relevance of these stories for the Jewish struggle under Antiochus IV, suggest the kings in Dan 1–6 are representative of Antiochus. Darius in this story, however, is not antagonistic toward Daniel. Nor is he eager to compel submission or even eliminate him but is favorably disposed—even emotionally—toward Daniel. Unlike Antiochus and even Nebuchadnezzar, Darius seeks to protect Daniel from the consequences of what he now realizes is a reckless ultimatum.

DANIEL THROWN INTO THE LIONS' PIT (6:16–18)

> [16] [6:17] Then the king commanded, so they brought Daniel and cast him into the pit of the lions. The king said to Daniel, "May your God, to whom you pay reverence continually, deliver you!" [17] [6:18] A stone was brought and placed over the opening of the pit and the king sealed it with his signet ring and the signet ring of his nobles that nothing might be changed concerning Daniel. [18] [6:19] Then the king went to his palace and passed the night fasting; no diversions came in before him, and sleep fled from him.

Darius, forced by his own edict to carry out the sentence, has Daniel cast into the pit of lions (v. 16). He does so imploringly. "May your God, to whom you pay reverence continually, deliver you!" In keeping with several translations, we render this sentence subjunctively. It is not a promise nor even a pledge, but a wish or hope that Daniel's God would deliver him from a hopeless situation. The odds are long, however, and for the king probably futile. This story is about to show that even this—deliverance from ravenous lions—is possible with God.

To be thrown into a pit of lions as punishment is not attested elsewhere in the ancient Near East. We have no corroborating evidence from ancient sources of such a use of a lions' pit. Mesopotamian kings generally kept lions in cages and zoological parks so they could be released to provide the thrill of a royal hunt. A stone bas-relief, now in the British Museum, shows the warlike Assyrian king Ashurnasirpal II (884–860 BCE) in his chariot, hunting lions. Two lions lie on the ground beside the chariot, pierced by arrows, and a third, already wounded by arrows, charges the chariot from behind.[18]

---

18. A photograph of this relief may be found in *ANEP*, fig. 184.

Lions were thus trapped in pits or fenced in gardens, but the use of such enclosures for punishment is unknown outside Daniel.

On a figurative level, lions were often used as images for vicious forces arrayed against the innocent. Ezekiel describes the Judean king Jehoiachin as a young lion captured by the Babylonians in a pit (Ezek 19:2–9). The only other ancient Near Eastern mention of a pit of lions occurs in a letter from Urad-Gula to the Assyrian king Ashurbanipal: "Day and night I pray to the king," says the desolate Urad-Gula, "in front of the lion's pit." Van der Toorn suggests this pit of lions may be a metaphor for Urad-Gula's hostile colleagues.[19] Several commentators prefer this metaphorical interpretation. The Danielic author, Newsom submits, may have literalized the metaphor for artistic reasons.[20] Similarly, Bentzen thinks the background to this story is the motif of plunging the hero into the realm of death, into Sheol.[21] Smith-Christopher regards this story of the lions' pit as a metaphor for the exile and deliverance from it.[22]

The pit where the king caged the lions in this story seems to have been a cavern or deep pit of some kind, with an opening at the top, and perhaps a side entrance where the signet seal stone was placed (v. 17). The lions' pit as a place of punishment, again with Daniel as the victim, appears in Bel and the Dragon, where Daniel is once more thrown into the pit, and delivered by the Lord (Dan 14:31–42). More likely, the two stories refer to the same tradition, and have been edited to fit the plot of their own respective story.

What happened to the king shows how upset he is by this whole affair (v. 19). He spends the sleepless night fasting, as though performing some sort of ablutionary rite for Daniel. Even the diversions, whether food or entertainment, such as dancing girls or even prostitutes,[23] brought in to relieve his anxiety, have no effect. He is perhaps angry with himself for having been duped by his officials and at the same time truly distressed over the fate he has inadvertently brought upon the innocent Daniel.

---

19. Urad-Gura, cited in van der Toorn, "In the Lion's Den," 632.
20. Newsom, *Daniel*, 195.
21. Bentzen, "Daniel 6," 58–64, as cited in Barr, "Daniel," 597. See also Ps 22:12–15.
22. Smith-Christopher, "Book of Daniel," 93.
23. There is no consensus about the meaning of the term דַּחֲוָה, *dahawah*, translated here as diversions.

DANIEL DELIVERED FROM THE LIONS (6:19-24)

[19] [6:20] Then the king arose at break of day and with haste went to the pit of the lions. [20] [6:21] When he approached the pit, with a pained voice he cried out. The king said to Daniel, "Daniel, servant of the living God, has your God whom you reverence continually been able to deliver you from the lions?" [21] [6:22] Then Daniel said to the king, "O king, live forever! [22] [6:23] My God sent his angel and shut the mouth of the lions, so they did not harm me, because before him I was innocent; also, before you, O king, I have not committed a crime." [23] [6:24] Then the king was very pleased, and commanded that Daniel be taken up from the pit. So, Daniel was taken up from the pit, but no injury of any kind was found on him, because he trusted in his God. [24] [6:25] The king commanded, and these men, who had maliciously accused Daniel, were brought in and cast into the pit of lions—they, their children, and their wives. They had not reached the bottom of the pit until the lions overwhelmed them and broke all their bones in pieces.

Darius has apparently met the minimum amount of time for Daniel's execution to be carried out before he rushes in haste to the lions' pit (v. 19). When he arrives, anxiously he calls to Daniel in an unusual manner. He refers to him as a servant of the living God (v. 20). This title reveals a measure of respect for the God of Daniel, particularly for the potency of Daniel's God. Darius will repeat this same title in his proclamation at the end of this chapter (v. 26). In the HB, the living God stands in contrast to the idols of the gentiles, who are regarded as the lifeless works of human craftsmanship (Isa 44:9-20; Jer 10:6-11).

Daniel addresses the king deferentially, then tells of the miraculous deliverance that has taken place. "God sent his angel and shut the mouth of the lions, so they did not harm me," he says, because he is innocent of the charges before God and the king. He does not admit to violating the king's edict. Even though he has broken the letter of the law, Daniel does not accept the edict as legally binding, perhaps because he knows its dubious origin. He simply says he has done nothing criminal (חֲבוּלָה, *habulah*, crime) before the king (vv. 21-22). Yet there was not a scratch on his body, just as there was no odor of smoke on the Daniel's three companions after their ordeal in the fiery furnace (Dan 3:27).

What happened in the lions' pit? Whereas Daniel claims an angel shut the lions' mouths to keep them from devouring him, as the Babylonian god Marduk is said to have done on another occasion, Schmidt objects that lions in captivity receive food during the day; at night they do not hunt for prey, but only sleep.[24] Daniel is thus tossed into the pit during the evening when the lions normally sleep. Thus, he escapes harm. These two views are not necessarily incompatible. What Daniel interprets theologically as a divine act, Schmidt gives a naturalistic explanation.

The reason Daniel escapes harm, like Shadrach, Meshach, and Abednego, is because he trusted in his God (v. 23). It is worth noting the word for trust in Aramaic is אֲמַן, *aman*, which is related to the word amen, a Hebrew expression we often repeat in worship, "May it be so!" *Aman* means to put one's trust in someone regarded as faithful. God is declared trustworthy. Daniel has resolutely put his trust in the faithful God and has prevailed. "For in him [Christ] every one of God's promises is a 'Yes,'" writes Paul. "For this reason it is through him that we say the 'Amen,' to the glory of God" (2 Cor 1:20).

So relieved, yet so enraged is Darius at Daniel's antagonists, he orders them, their wives, and children, cast into the pit of now hungry lions, where they are gruesomely torn to pieces before they touch the pit's bottom (v. 24). From our perspective, this is excessively vengeful. For Daniel's readers, it may have been understood in the light of the Torah's provision that when a person falsely accuses another and is discovered, "then you shall do to the false witness just as the false witness had meant to do to the other" (Deut 19:18–19).[25] The perpetrators of malicious allegations against Daniel themselves receive the capital penalty they had in mind for Daniel. This execution probably did not include all the satraps and their families, but only the other two administrative officials (Dan 6:2). Still, not only do the perpetrators perish, but so do their innocent family members, including children.

THE KING'S PROCLAMATION (6:25–28)

> [25] [6:26] Then Darius the king wrote to all peoples, nations, and tongues who dwell in all the land: "May you prosper abundantly! [26] [6:27] I make a decree that in all the realm of my kingdom everyone should tremble and fear before Daniel's God,
> > for he is the living God,
> > > enduring forever,
> > > and his kingdom one that will not be destroyed,

---

24. N. Schmidt, "Daniel and Androcles," 4.
25. See also Esth 9:25; Ps 140:9–11.

nor his sovereignty end.
²⁷ [6:28] Who delivers and rescues,
and works signs and wonders
in heaven and on earth,
who delivered Daniel
from the power of the lions."
²⁸ [6:29] This Daniel prospered in the reign of Darius and in the reign of Cyrus the Persian.

Darius ends up issuing a decree. All his subjects must honor Daniel's God, called here the living God, who endures forever (vv. 25-26). His decree differs from Nebuchadnezzar's in chapter 4 in that, while Nebuchadnezzar only expresses personal praise of Daniel's god, Darius requires universal recognition. Darius's decree brings the cycle of narratives in chapters 1-6 to a satisfying conclusion. That this God delivered Daniel from the power of the lions is proof enough for Darius to urge such reverence and fear (v. 27). Like Nebuchadnezzar in Dan 4:1, 34, Darius concludes the whole episode by praising and honoring the Hebrew God. Both kings acknowledge the sovereignty of God, but neither should be taken as converting to the Hebrew faith.

The editor adds a postscript about Daniel's success during the reigns of Darius and Cyrus (v. 28). By linking Darius and Cyrus, the verse implies Darius was succeeded by Cyrus, the founding monarch of the Achaemenid empire. Here in the postscript is the problem of Darius the Mede (see above). The wording of this postscript is like Dan 1:21 ("Thus, Daniel continued until the first year of Cyrus the king") and suggests, when taken with 6:28, that the original end of the book of Daniel, at least as a collection of stories, may have occurred here. At some time after this editorial collection was essentially complete, probably the third century BCE, the apocalyptic section of the book (chs. 7-12) was added.

Smith-Christopher mentions Mahatma Gandhi's fascination with the story of Daniel in the lions' pit. Gandhi (1869-1948) saw Daniel as "one of the greatest passive resisters that ever lived." He took Daniel as a model of resistance against South African apartheid laws. Alluding to Daniel's throwing open his windows at times of prayer, Gandhi urged Indians to "sit with their doors flung wide open" to inform South African authorities "whatever laws they passed were not for them unless those laws were from God."[26]

In this story from the Achaemenid period, Daniel certainly appears as a model of resistance against unjust laws of state. The deliverance of Daniel

26. Gandhi, as cited in Smith-Christopher, "Book of Daniel," 94-95.

from the lions' pit became for later Jews a "symbol of God's miraculous intervention in time of trouble." It appears in a synagogue mosaic found at Naaran, near Jericho.[27] While this story has resonance wherever unjust laws are enacted, it would certainly have read as resistance and affirmation during the Maccabean Revolt in the days of Antiochus Epiphanes.

This brings us to the end of the collection of stories about Daniel and his Judean friends. Why does the book begin with a series of stories placed before an apocalypse? We should note the book of Revelation follows a similar pattern. A group of letters (chs. 1–3) precedes the apocalyptic section (chs. 4–22). This mixture of other genres with apocalyptic is also found in other apocalypses, such as the Apocalypse of Abraham.

The stories so situated now set the stage for the apocalyptic section. The stories have the Judean exiles among the nations and in various degrees of conflict with the pagan rulers, laws, religions, and culture. Although generally at peace with their cultural surroundings, from time to time the exiles must resist—even on pain of death—their pagan rulers. The stories demonstrate God "changes times and seasons, deposes kings and sets up kings; he gives wisdom to the wise and knowledge to those who have understanding" (Dan 2:21). Daniel 7–12 speaks of these same notions in apocalyptic style. The sovereignty of God over kings, nations, and the very course of human history stands out, even in the stories. With the stories, the search to unravel the mysteries of heaven and of the nature of God's relationship with the human story begins. Once we have heard these inspiring stories, we are ready to hear Daniel's apocalyptic visions of the future destiny of God's people and of the nations.

---

27. Kraft et al., *IFE*, 11:15.

A Vision of Four Beasts

Daniel 7

Study the past if you would divine the future.

—Patrick Henry

The book now shifts from narrative to apocalyptic discourse as the visions begin. Such abruptness—without an adequate transition—indicates the two parts of the book were once independent. Instead of relating the experiences of a Babylonian king, Daniel now personally experiences dreams and visions. He also becomes the primary narrator. In the previous stories, the dreams come to the king while Daniel occupies the role of court interpreter. Now, one of the attendants (Dan 7:16), a celestial being, assumes the interpretive role. Instead of a Babylonian or Persian setting, chapters 7–12 seem to reflect closely the second-century conflict between the Syrian Seleucids and the Jewish people that sparked the Maccabean revolt. The reader is suddenly catapulted onto a world stage and hears the march of armies, the clash of swords, and the bitter struggle of nations.

Despite these differences, the chapter is linked to Dan 1–6 in other ways. An apocalyptic parallel is found among the stories in Dan 2—the dream of the metallic image and the four kingdoms. There are four kingdoms in Dan 7, too, but the climax comes with the divine judgment upon the nations. The stone cut out without human assistance in Dan 2, which falls upon the feet of the metallic image and breaks it into pieces, is also a form of divine judgment. The judgment in Dan 7, however, goes further. It not only hands the nations over to destruction, but also bestows everlasting dominion upon the holy ones of the Most High.

At the verbal level, there are parallels. The Aramaic verb דְּקַק (*deqaq*, crush in pieces—in causative haphel form), found in Dan 7:7, 19, 23, describing the hideous beasts tearing at their prey, is also found in 2:34, 40, 44, where it portrays the smashing of metals and clay terra cotta into pieces.[1] This may also tell us something about why Dan 2:4b—7:28 is in Aramaic. The two chapters—Dan 2 and 7—act as bookends, we might say, for the series of dramatic Aramaic stories encompassed within these two. Even if the vision report in Dan 7 was composed independently of the stories, as is generally assumed, its author no doubt knew of Nebuchadnezzar's dream in Dan 2 and has been careful to link the two. The vision in Dan 7 is an advance in detail and complexity over Dan 2.

The four visions in chapters 7–12 chronologically parallel the stories in Dan 5–6. Belshazzar appears in Dan 5, and again in Dan 7:1 and 8:1, the first and third years of his reign, respectively. The first year of Darius the Mede (9:1) recalls 5:30–31 and the fall of Babylon. And the Persian monarch Cyrus appears in 10:1, as well as in 6:28.

Daniel 7 thus occupies a crucial, pivotal role in this arrangement. Not only does its Aramaic text overlap the Aramaic of the stories (2:4b—7:28), but the apocalyptic vision in chapter 7 sets the essential literary structure for the visions in chapters 8–12, all in Hebrew.

It has become evident over the past century, as more literary texts have become available from the ancient Near East, that the author of Dan 7 has drawn upon mythical images from Babylonian, Canaanite, and possibly Persian origin.[2] These shed considerable light on the imagery found in Dan 7.

The chapter begins with an introduction in 7:1–2a, followed by the report of a vision (vv. 2b–14), then the interpretation of the vision by one of the heavenly attendants (vv. 15–18). Like a laser, attention then shifts to the bizarre fourth beast and its pretentious little horn (vv. 19–27). A concluding note (v. 28), revealing Daniel's ongoing concern about the mysterious vision, ends the chapter. Here we will follow the natural order of the chapter by first describing the vision, then go on to discuss the interpretation provided Daniel by the heavenly attendant.

---

1. The verb is also used in Dan 6:25 with the lions as the subject.
2. See the detailed discussion of these important mythic motifs in J. Collins, *Daniel* (Hermeneia), 280–94.

INTRODUCTION (7:1)

In the first year of Belshazzar, king of Babylon, Daniel saw a dream and visions of his mind upon his bed. Then he wrote the dream and related the sum of the matter:

An editorial comment opens the chapter. Like other visions, this one is given a royal date, the first year of Belshazzar.[3] The editor evidently regards Belshazzar as a monarch, not the co-regent he seems really to have been in the ancient cuneiform records. Aside from the fact that king was normally used as a title for someone in Belshazzar's position (co-regent of Babylon during Nabonidus's absence), the previous story ends with two kings, Darius and Cyrus (Dan 6:28). It would seem appropriate for the editor to transition between the two chapters by referring to Belshazzar as king.

Daniel has a night dream or vision (v. 2).[4] He records the *sum* of the matter: a report of the vision and its interpretation (see v. 28). The awkward words (he "related the sum of the matter") are missing from 4QDan^b, one of the fragments from the Dead Sea, and Theodotion, but are preserved in the MT and the LXX. This is the first reference in the book to Daniel's authorship, implying that what has preceded, namely, the stories in chapters 1–6, may come from other authors. In this commentary (see the introduction), we have assumed the visions have been pseudonymously ascribed to Daniel, one of Israel's heroic, visionary figures, but they, like the stories, are anonymous. Most Jewish apocalypses follow this conventional practice of attribution to an ancient, widely admired celebrity. Fortunately, resolving the question of authorship makes little difference in the interpretation of this or any other vision in Daniel.

THE VISION OF THE FOUR BEASTS (7:2-8)

² Daniel said, "I saw in the visions in the night and, lo, four winds of heaven were stirring up the great sea. ³ Four mighty beasts came up from the sea, different from one another. ⁴ The first was like a lion, and it had eagles' wings. I watched until its wings were plucked off and it was lifted from the earth and

---

3. Cf. second year of Nebuchadnezzar (Dan 2:1); third year of the reign of King Belshazzar (8:1); first year of Darius (9:1); third year of King Cyrus (10:1). For first year in 10:1, Theodotion has third year, as does 8:1.

4. There appears to be no distinction between a vision (חֵזוּ, *hezu*) and a dream (חֵלֶם, *helem*) in this passage, nor in the rest of the book. See Koch, "Vom profetischen zum apokalyptischen Visionsbericht," 413-46.

made to stand upon two feet like a human being, and a human mind was given to it. ⁵ Then, lo, another beast, a second one, like a bear, and it raised up on one side and three ribs were in its mouth between its teeth, and they said thus to it, 'Arise, devour much flesh.' ⁶ After this, I watched and, lo, another like a leopard, and it had four wings of a bird on its back, the beast also had four heads, and dominion was given to it. ⁷ After this, I watched in the visions of the night, and lo, a fourth beast, frightening and terrible, extraordinarily powerful, and it had large iron teeth. It was devouring, breaking in pieces, and trampling the rest with its feet. It was different from all the beasts which came before it, and it had ten horns. ⁸ I was considering the horns, and lo, another little horn came up among them and three of the former horns were plucked out from before it. Lo, eyes like human eyes were in the horn, and a mouth speaking great things.

Four powerful, horrific wild beasts ascend from the depths of the great sea, a reference to the Mediterranean. In Hebrew tradition, the sea and the mysterious creatures in its depth had come to symbolize the enemies of Yahweh and Israel (Ps 74:13-14; 89:9-10). From the sea now come the four terrifying beasts, unfolding the political history of the nations, with the four winds of heaven representing the extent of their sovereignty. One of Isaiah's oracles enlists comparable imagery: "The nations roar like the roaring of many waters, but he [God] will rebuke them, and they will flee far away, chased like chaff on the mountains before the wind and whirling dust before the storm" (Isa 17:13).

In part, such imagery is rooted in Canaanite mythology.⁵ In Canaanite myth, the god Baal slays Yamm, the god of the sea. The Ugaritic name Yamm (*ym*) designates the god Sea.⁶ The Aramaic word for sea (יָם, *yam*), used in verse 2, is the same as the Ugaritic. Just as Yahweh dispatches the Leviathan in the sea, the god Baal slays Lotan, the monstrous, writhing serpent in the sea, who may personify the god Yamm. Motifs known in ancient Canaanite myth are here applied to the historical sequence of the Gentile nations.⁷

---

5. See Isa 27:1; 51:9-10; Ps 74:13-14; 89:9-10. Lotan (Ugaritic: *ltn*) and Leviathan (לִוְיָתָן, *liwyatan*) are semantically cognate. While these images appear in ancient Near Eastern mythology, their role in the composition of this vision is not certain. The author may have drawn upon them as Near Eastern stock images without advocating the myths from which they come (Newsom, *Daniel*, 218-20).

6. Olmo Lete and Sanmartin, *Dictionary of Ugaritic Language*, 2:965.

7. "The author overwrites the mythic plot of battle and defeat with a schema of political historiography," Newsom notes, "which describes the divine plan for the succession of imperial kingdoms until they are displaced by the eternal divine kingdom" (Newsom, *Daniel*, 221-22).

Distinct from each other, these hideous beasts are bizarre, composite creatures (v. 3). The first, a lion, had eagles' wings rising from its back. But the wings are finally torn out, and the lion made to stand like a man on two feet, with a human consciousness given to it (v. 4). Ancient Near Eastern iconography (pictorial art) offers many artistic examples of similar lionlike creatures, often with wings and human faces. A shell inlay from an ancient lyre sound box found in the ancient Mesopotamia city of Ur, shows a lion standing upright on two legs, like the one here, with a cup in its right paw and a wicker-covered vase in its left. The same artifact shows a bear dancing while a donkey plays the lyre.[8] In Iraqi Kurdistan in 1970, archaeologists noticed a bas-relief carving of seven gods and goddesses facing the Assyrian king Sargon II (c. 722–705 BCE). When archaeologists later excavated the site, the seven gods and goddesses could be seen riding mythical dragons, horses, and what appears to be winged and horned lions, like the lion in this vision.[9]

Such animal imagery—even grotesque, exaggerated imagery—was no doubt familiar to the readers of Daniel. There is something of a cartooning effect in the imagery. The eagles' wings on the lion's back signal the eagle as the noblest of birds, while the lion is the noblest of beasts. When the wings are ripped out, the lion loses its noble powers and becomes more like a human. That it is given a human mind (לְבַב אֱנָשׁ, *lebab enash*, human heart) alludes to chapter 4, where Nebuchadnezzar's reason—the cognitive ability that distinguishes human from animal—returns to him and he finally blesses God (Dan 4:34–35).

A bear arises with three ribs in its mouth. "Arise," it is urged, "devour much flesh" (v. 5). The bear represents the next empire, with little more than passing reference given the fact it rises on one side and has three ribs in its mouth. The metaphor evokes a vicious, wild animal ravenously devouring its prey, jagged flesh and bloody gore dripping from its mouth.

Then comes a ferocious leopard with four birds' wings and four heads (v. 6). Leopards in the biblical tradition are noted for both speed and rapacity (Hab 1:8; Jer 5:6). The number four probably denotes universality. Lion, bear, and leopard in Hosea are mentioned as divine threats of judgment. "I will become like a lion to them, like a leopard I will lurk beside the way. I will fall upon them like a bear robbed of her cubs . . . as a wild animal would mangle them" (Hos 13:7–8). The wild animal in Hosea's oracle may be the antecedent for the fourth, hideous beast in Daniel. Hosea's lion, bear,

---

8. *ANEP*, fig. 192; see also figs. 644–646, 651.
9. Cargill, "Strata," 16.

leopard, and wild animal are the most plausible source for the metaphorical beasts in Daniel's vision.[10]

What gets main attention, however, is the fourth beast, a mysterious, powerfully built monster with iron teeth (vv. 7–8). It rips open and crushes the other beasts, trampling them with its feet. From its head protrude ten horns. There, amid the horns arises a little horn (קֶרֶן אָחֳרִי זְעֵירָה, *qeren ahari zeerah*, horn, another little [one]) that uproots three others. The horn oddly has eyes and a mouth which speaks insolent, profane words. This beast is hideously repulsive, even more than the others. The iron teeth betoken its vicious, destructive power. The ten horns—horns are often a biblical symbol of power—depict its sovereign might.[11] In ancient Near Eastern iconography (graphic art), horns often appear on monsters and gods,[12] and there is Seleucid or Hellenistic coinage with royalty wearing horned head gear. Such Seleucid coinage offers a clue as to the identity of this little horn.

Daniel next sees the heavenly judgment. Because these poetical lines seem out of place in a vision text about four hideous beasts, some scholars think vv. 9–10, 13–14 have been secondarily inserted, possibly drawn from an older source, such as a poem or hymn.[13] It is easy to see how one might reach this conclusion. Unlike the prose surrounding them, these verses are in poetical style. When read consecutively from v. 8, then vv. 11–12, finally moving on to vv. 15–22, the text reads smoothly without fissures, often a good indication something has been inserted into the text that disturbs the literary flow. Whatever their origin, these verses (vv. 9–10, 13–14) now fill in the details of a final judgment scene.

JUDGMENT UPON THE FOUR BEASTS (7:9-14)

> [9] "I watched until thrones were placed,
>   and an Ancient of Days was seated,
> his clothing was white as snow,

---

10. J. Collins, *Daniel* (Hermeneia), 295–96. The fourth beast in Daniel is much more ferocious than Hosea's wild beast—lit., animal of the open field (חַיַּת הַשָּׂדֶה, *hayyat hasadeh*).

11. See Zech 2:1–4; 1 Enoch 90:9.

12. *ANEP*, figs. 525–26, 646–47.

13. Niditch, *Symbolic Vision*, 195–99; Montgomery, *Critical and Exegetical Commentary*, 296; Porteous, *Daniel*, 93. Hartman and Di Lella (*Daniel*, 210) consider all the references to the little horn to be secondary insertions (vv. 11a, 20b, 21–22, 25), but the description of the divine judgment is "wholly the work of the author of the primary stratum" (217).

and the hair of his head like pure wool,
his throne a flame of fire,
    its wheels a burning fire.
[10] A river of fire flowed forth from before him,
    a thousand thousands served him,
and ten thousand times ten thousand stood before him.
    The judgment was set,
    and the books opened.

[11] "I watched then because of the sound of the arrogant words that the horn was speaking. I watched until the beast was slain, and its body destroyed and given to the burning fire. [12] As for the rest of the beasts, their dominion was taken away, and a lengthening of their lives was given to them until a season and a time. [13] I watched in the visions of the night,
and lo, with the clouds of heaven
    one like a human being was coming,
and he came to the Ancient of Days
    and was escorted before him.
[14] Then to him was given dominion,
    honor, and kingly authority,
that peoples, nations, and languages
    should serve him.
His dominion is an everlasting dominion
    that will never pass away,
and his kingly authority
    will never be destroyed."

The Ancient of Days (עַתִּיק יוֹמִין, *attiq yomin*), with pure white hair and garments, sits in judgment upon a glittering, fiery throne, surrounded by an innumerable multitude of heavenly attendants (vv. 9–10). The judgment was set, and the books opened. This scene clearly belongs to the tradition of biblical throne visions, found for example in Micaiah's vision of Yahweh sitting upon the throne (1 Kgs 22:19), Isaiah's vision while in the Jerusalem temple (Isa 6:1–5), and Ezekiel's vision of the four living creatures and the divine throne, surrounded by fire and great splendor (Ezek 1:26–28). The NT parable of the judgment of the nations in Matt 25:31–46 also draws upon this imagery. Perhaps the most notable parallel appears in the apocalypse of 1 Enoch, where Enoch on his heavenly journey passes through a heavenly temple:

> I observed and saw inside it a lofty throne—its appearance was like crystal and its wheels like the shining sun, and (I heard) the voice of the cherubim; and from beneath the throne were issuing streams of flaming fire.... And the Great Glory was sitting upon it—as for his gown, which was shining more brightly than the sun, it was whiter than any snow ... the flaming fire was round about him, and a great fire stood before him. No one could come near unto him from among those that surrounded the tens of millions (who stood) before him.[14]

This epic language is symbolic, of course. Daniel's vision depicts a court scene of unspecified location, presumably upon the earth, while Enoch's is clearly situated in heaven. In the HB, when God sits in judgment of human beings, the location is generally the earth, as here.[15] The unique title Ancient of Days, while paralleled in 1 Enoch,[16] finds its closest analogy earlier in Ugaritic literature where the high God El is called *mlk ab shnm*, king, father of years.[17] The title emphasizes the infinity of God, who is here both eternal king and judge. In Canaanite myth, while El sits upon his throne, the human figure who comes before him to receive kingship is the young god Baal.[18] Our author has skillfully adapted this mythic imagery to forge a dynamic tableau of divine judgment.

The burning fire surging and surrounding the throne is typical imagery used for most royal and divine thrones in the ancient Near East. It is reminiscent of the traditional image of the fire of judgment at the end of the world.[19] In the presence of the Ancient of Days, surrounded by admiring multitudes, the heavenly books are opened, containing the record of all

---

14. 1 Enoch 14:18-22 *OTP*. This text may have influenced the author of Daniel. Among the fragments of 1 Enoch found at Qumran is one containing this throne vision, a text considered to be older than our book of Daniel. Whether there is direct influence, the texts are certainly closely related (J. Collins, *Daniel* [Hermeneia], 300; Stone, "Book of Enoch and Judaism."). See 1 Enoch 90:20: "I kept seeing till a throne was erected in a pleasant land; and he sat upon it for the Lord of the sheep; and he took all the sealed books and opened those very books in the presence of the Lord of the sheep."

15. See Jer 49:35-38; Joel 3:12-14. This imagery comes from the convention of victorious kings to sit at the gate of conquered cities as they reviewed their troops and sentenced the vanquished (Newsom, *Daniel*, 228).

16. "The One to whom belongs the time before time" (1 En 46:1-2); "the Antecedent of Time" (47:3).

17. Olmo Lete and Sanmartin, *Dictionary of Ugaritic Language*, 2:834; Lacocque, *Book of Daniel*, 142-43.

18. F. Cross, *Canaanite Myth*, 16-17.

19. See Isa 66:24; Mal 4:3; Ezek 1:15-28; 2 Pet 3:10.

human deeds, whether good or bad.[20] The court sits, as the next verses indicate, to hold the gentile nations accountable for their violent, destructive ways, and to decide in favor of the holy ones, who have too long suffered their ire.

Judgment deals first with the fourth beast and its little horn, which cannot refrain from uttering insolent words. The Aramaic participle מְמַלֱלָא (*memalelah*, speaking) implies continuous action, "the arrogant words the horn kept speaking." The little horn's scorn results in the destruction by fire of the fourth beast (v. 11). Whereas the monstrous fourth beast emerges from the chaotic sea, it is ironically finally destroyed by fire, echoing the fiery furnace of Dan 3. The remainder of the beasts are given a reprieve until a season and a time, a period left unspecified (v. 12). Did the author expect three of these four kingdoms to remain viable for a period even after their apparent demise? Did he thereby project the hope that eventually all nations would one day become subservient to the people of God and so must continue to remain viable?[21] Whatever the case, the three beasts are stripped of their sovereignty in contrast to the fate of the fourth beast. The fourth beast is then summarily destroyed.

The vision moves quickly to the verdict given in favor of the mysterious one like a human (v. 13). Our translation, an attempt at gender-neutrality, ends up obscuring the traditional Aramaic phrase בַּר־אֱנָשׁ (*bar enash*, son of man). Who is this son of man, this humanlike figure? Is he a celestial or heavenly being? Is he an allegorical symbol like the preceding four beasts? The human imagery sharply contrasts with animalistic portrayal of the four beasts. The identity of the son of man has been widely debated. Since this figure comes with the clouds of heaven to the Ancient of Days, evidently to receive everlasting dominion, is he considered a divine being? The Aramaic phrase *bar enash* offers little help, for it merely indicates a humanlike figure, namely, one like an ordinary human being.[22]

That this humanlike figure comes with the clouds of heaven reminds us of the image of the Canaanite Baal as the *rkb rpt*, rider of the clouds, a title given Baal sixteen times in various Ugaritic texts.[23] The apocalyptist

---

20. See Isa 65:6–7; Mal 3:16; Ps 56:8–9; Luke 10:20; Rev 20:12.

21. See Rowley, *Darius the Mede*, 123; Isa 14:1–2; 49:22–23; 60:12; Zech 8:22; Ps 89:9; Tob 13:11.

22. See the Hebrew equivalent, בֶּן־אָדָם, *ben-adam*, son of man, in Num 23:19; Isa 56:2; Jer 32:19; Ps 8:4; 144:3.

23. The same image, applied to Yahweh, appears in Deut 33:26; Isa 19:1; Ps 68:4 ("lift up a song to him who *rides upon the clouds*" [רֹכֵב בָּעֲרָבוֹת, *rikab baaraboth*]). See Garfinkel, "Face of Yahweh?" 32; Wyatt, "Titles of Ugaritic Storm-God"; Weinfeld, "Rider of the Clouds."

has again drawn upon ancient mythic imagery to portray the dramatic approach of the humanlike figure before the Ancient of Days.

In Daniel's vision, this son of man receives the glory and kingship (v. 14). According to vv. 17, 21, he represents the holy ones of the Most High who receive the kingdom. In v. 27, it is the *people* of the holy ones of the Most High who receive the dominion. Thus, the son of man in some sense stands for the people of God. The son of man or one like a human seems to be the "personification of the righteous people," who in turn reflect the "perfect image of the righteous individual."[24] In ancient Israel, there was a reciprocal identification between the people as a corporate entity and the individual. The individual embodied the essence of the community; the community, the essence of the individual. There was frequent oscillation between community and individual. The community summed up or encompassed the individual, without denying the reality of the individual's uniqueness. This way of conceiving community in relation to the individual is known as corporate personality.[25] A king or another prominent representative, such as David, may thus embody the entire group and vice-versa.

Among the Dead Sea Scrolls, the text known as the Community Rule (1QS) sheds some light on the son of man image. The Community Rule envisions an eschatological age when the saints will inherit an "everlasting possession." They will "inherit . . . the lot of the holy ones." The language is like Dan 7:18, 27, suggesting the righteous will be exalted to share the status of the heavenly angels.[26] The imagery blends the heavenly and the earthly. Indeed, Jesus makes the same point: "Those who are considered worthy of a place in that age and in the resurrection . . . cannot die anymore, because they are like angels and are children of God, being children of the resurrection" (Luke 20:35-36; cf. Dan 12:1-3).

It is only a short step from the idea of corporate personality to the son of man as a messianic figure standing for the whole of faithful Israel. "The person of the Messiah," notes Riesenfeld, "is inseparable from his Kingdom."[27] Although Dan 7:13-14 does not explicitly mention the Mes-

---

24. Lacocque, *Book of Daniel*, 146, who is describing, not advocating this view. Noticing the cloud motif here, reminiscent of the entourage of the god Baal in Canaanite literature, Cross notes this figure "is evidently young Ba'l reinterpreted and democratized by the apocalyptist as the Jewish nation" (F. Cross, *Canaanite Myth*, 17).

25. See Robinson, *Corporate Personality*, 15, 25-30, 45-47; Knight, "Book of Daniel," 446.

26. Carey, *Ultimate Things*, 91. "What we have here in essence," Barr notes, "is an eschatological appearance of an angelic being as man in heaven" (Barr, "Daniel," 598).

27. Riesenfeld, *Jésus transfiguré*, 78. Cf. House, *Old Testament Theology*, 509. Klausner offers a contrary view: "There is no *individual* Messiah in Daniel: the entire people Israel is the Messiah that will exercise everlasting dominion throughout the whole

siah, the son of man figure seems to play a messianic role. This passage has accordingly been understood as messianic in both Jewish and Christian tradition.[28] We note, for instance, in the Synoptics, Son of Man is a title used for Jesus and in words attributed to him.[29] The Synoptic Gospels certainly make the connection with Dan 7 in the account of the trial of Jesus. "Are you the Messiah?" the high priest asks Jesus. "I am," he replies. "You will see the Son of Man seated at the right hand of the Power and coming with the clouds of heaven" (Mark 14:61–62; pars. Matt 26:64; Luke 22:69). Jesus's response to the high priest embodies a citation from Dan 7:13, which is neatly blended with Ps 110:1 ("sit at my right hand"). Jesus refers to the same Danielic text when he promises the disciples, "When the Son of Man is seated on the throne of his glory, you who have followed me will also sit on twelve thrones, judging the twelve tribes of Israel" (Matt 19:28).

Although in Daniel the son of man figure is probably a heavenly being, more likely the angel Michael,[30] Daniel's first readers may have recognized in the figure who approached the Ancient of Days a messianic promise particularly appropriate during the almost unendurable religious oppression of Antiochus IV. The judgment scene announces the ultimate victory of the Lord on behalf of God's people.

Puzzled and confused by the sudden arrival of the four horrific beasts and their inevitable fate, Daniel now insistently asks the heavenly attendant to explain the mysterious vision.

THE EXPLANATION OF DANIEL'S VISION (7:15–28)

> [15] As for me, Daniel, my spirit was troubled within me, and the visions of my mind alarmed me. [16] I approached one of those standing nearby and asked him the truth concerning all this. He said to me that he would make known the interpretation of the matter. [17] "These mighty beasts, which are four, are four kingdoms that will arise from the earth. [18] But the holy ones of the

---

world" (Klausner, *Messianic Idea in Israel*, 230; italics in original).

28. Talmudic references include b. Sanh. 98a; Num. Rab. 13:14; 'Ag. Ber. 14:3; 23:1. Later Jewish and Christian interpretation assume the passage refers to an individual rather than corporate entity. Christians generally have taken the passage as the Second Coming (Talbot, *Prophecies of Daniel*, 133). Daniel 7 supplies the background for much of Jesus's thinking about his mission (Knight, "Daniel," 444). Justin Martyr (*Dialogue with Trypho*, 76) and Tertullian (*Against Marcion*, 4.10) are good examples of treating the appearance of the son of man in Dan 7 as the second advent.

29. Matt 16:27; Mark 2:10; Luke 21:36; cf. John 3:14.

30. Adela Collins, "Son of Man," 342–43. See Dan 10:13, 20–21; 12:1.

Most High will receive the kingdom and possess the kingdom forever—forever and ever."

In response, the heavenly attendant explains the four beasts are four kingdoms that arise out of the earth (vv. 15-17). The Aramaic מַלְכִין (*malkin*, kings) refers to kingdoms or empires (see v. 23). Who are these four kingdoms?

Like Dan 2, our text does not identify the four beasts beyond stating they are kings or kingdoms. It is conceivable the author never intended to identify them, but rather expressed the struggle of nations under a fourfold animal symbolism. If so, we should not expect to find here detailed historical information. Although their individual identity remains obscure, they are commonly understood as the same four kingdoms mentioned in Nebuchadnezzar's dream of the great metallic statue (Dan 2:31-46). The kingdoms depicted by the metallic statue—with one exception—were not specified either. The lack of specification has led, as we expect, to a variety of opinions regarding the identity of these kingdoms. The original sequence of the four empires in Dan 7, like Dan 2, accordingly, is Babylon, Media, Persia, with the fourth kingdom as Greece. Out of the latter comes the little horn entity.

The first beast is a lion sporting an eagle's wings. Since Nebuchadnezzar II, king of Babylon, is likened to a powerful lion in several biblical passages,[31] the lion in this vision probably represents the Babylonian empire, as does the symbolic head of gold on the statue in Dan 2.[32] The wings of an eagle, while not explained, may indicate the swiftness of the Babylonian military, which under Nebuchadnezzar in just a few short years came to dominate much of the ancient Near East.[33] The lion standing on two feet with human cognition may perhaps allude to a chastened Nebuchadnezzar, as in Dan 4.

As for the terrifying bear with three bloody ribs between its teeth, most modern interpreters identify the Median empire, represented in Daniel by Darius the Mede.[34] The three ribs, also left unexplained, may point to the three Babylonian kings preceding Persia—Nebuchadnezzar, Evil-Merodach, and Belshazzar.[35] Considering this kingdom as Media, however, cre-

---

31. See Jer 4:7; 49:19; 50:17.
32. "You [Nebuchadnezzar] are the head of gold" (Dan 2:37-38).
33. See Hab 1:8; Ezek 17:3-6.
34. Hartman and Di Lella, *Daniel*, 212-13.
35. Lacocque, *Book of Daniel*, 140. Belshazzar was not the last monarch. That distinction goes to Nabonidus, with whom Belshazzar was co-regent over a portion of the empire.

ates a historical problem. Ancient history, as we have seen, does not know of a dominant Median empire interposed between the Neo-Babylonian and Persian. The Persians, who under Cyrus had already subdued the king of Media (c. 554/553 BCE), then absorbed the Neo-Babylonian empire at the fall of Babylon (539 BCE).[36] The Median empire was contemporary with the Babylonian. It had lost sovereignty a decade before the collapse of Babylon. Since this vision ends with the Greek empire and the rise of the little horn, it seems the author, thinking there had to be a kingdom of Media in this position, inserted it between Babylon and Persia.[37] Media, if anything, was more provincial and not as universal as were the other three kingdoms. To place the Median empire in this position, however, may be taking the apocalyptist a little too literally. Rather than aiming for exact historical alignment, the author may instead be appealing to the traditional four-ages trope symbolizing the course of history, as we find in Hesiod, the eighth-century BCE Greek poet.[38] At any rate, Daniel appears uninterested in the second and third powers. His major concern lies with the fourth. The sequence assumed here then is Babylon, Media, Persia, and Greece, which makes up a total sequence of four empires reaching down to Hellenistic times, just before the expected arrival of God's kingdom.[39]

With birdlike wings and four heads, a leopard swiftly moves over the earth.[40] The leopard symbolizes the Persian empire. What the four heads represent is uncertain. Some take them as the four Persian kings known to the apocalyptist: Cyrus, Ahasuerus, Artaxerxes, and Darius II.[41] Daniel 11:2 mentions four *Persian* kings in the sequence of nations, but they are not specifically identified. Still others have taken the four heads to represent the four corners of the earth, thus signifying the extent of the Persian empire,[42] which dominated the largest span of territory of any of the ancient empires prior to Greece and Rome.

The dreadful, Godzilla-like fourth beast, different from all the other beasts, with large iron teeth, ravenously crushing and stamping down all the

36. J. Cook, *Persians*, 38–46.
37. Crenshaw, *Story and Faith*, 365.
38. Hesiod, *Op.* 109–201.
39. McNamara and Di Lella, "Daniel," 511.
40. A white marble frieze from the middle third millennium BCE in Mesopotamia depicts a leopard fighting a horned creature. Such scenes of violent contest between human, superhuman beings, animals, and monsters are common in Mesopotamian glyptic art (*ANEP*, fig. 678).
41. Hartwell and Di Lella, *Daniel*, 213. Cyrus (Ezra 1:1), Ahasuerus (Ezra 4:6), Artaxerxes (Ezra 4:7, 11, 13), and Darius II (Neh 12:22).
42. J. Collins, *Daniel* (Hermeneia), 298.

others, if we follow the sequence suggested here, must be the Greek empire, which swept with astonishing swiftness over the Mediterranean world under Alexander the Great (336-323 BCE). The fourth empire is thus Greece under Alexander and his successors. Alexander's dominion stretched from Macedonia in the west to the river Indus in the east, and south to encompass Egypt. Before Rome, such a vast empire was unparalleled in the ancient world.

What about the ten horns on the beast's head? Taken literally, the ten horns may signify the ten kings remaining from the splintering of the Greek empire after Alexander's death, three of whom were plucked out after being defeated by Antiochus IV Epiphanes (175-164 BCE). The figure ten, however, may merely indicate fullness.[43]

Among these ten horns now comes a little horn which uproots three others. This represents the Seleucid king Antiochus IV Epiphanes,[44] even though literally he would represent the eleventh horn. This little horn strangely has eyes and a mouth issuing arrogant, profane, scornful words. The little horn receives further description in vv. 24-25.

Following the rise and fall of the four kingdoms and the appearance of the little horn, the heavenly attendant mentions the triumph of the holy ones,[45] who finally gain an eternal kingdom, not subject to human whim,

---

43. Anderson, *Signs and Wonders*, 81. A suggested list of the ten kings is as follows: (1) Alexander the Great [336-323]; (2) Alexander Aegus [323-312]; (3) Seleucus I [312-280]; (4) Antiochus I [280-261]; (5) Antiochus II [261-246]; (6) Seleucus II [246-223]; (7) Seleucus III [226-223]; (8) Antiochus III [223-187]; (9) Seleucus IV [187-175]; (10) Antiochus IV Epiphanes [175-164]. The three kings overthrown probably include the two sons of Seleucus IV, who were legitimate heirs to the throne (Lacocque, *Book of Daniel*, 153). Already in the Sibylline Oracles (3:381-400), c. 140 BCE, the ten horns are said to be the ten kings preceding Antiochus IV Epiphanes.

44. J. Collins, *Daniel* (Hermeneia), 299, 320-21. This interpretation, which is inherent in the text of Dan 7 and its historical setting, appears again in the fourth century CE interpreter Ephrem the Syrian (*Opera omnia*, 2:216).

45. The term קַדִּישִׁין, *qaddishin* (holy), and its Hebrew equivalent are used most often to refer to heavenly beings (Deut 33:2; Job 5:1; 15:15; Ps 89:6, 8; Zech 14:5; Dan 4:17), so there is a question as to whom it refers here. Collins sees it as a reference to the heavenly angels, to whom the people are akin or are on the same side (J. Collins, *Daniel* [Hermeneia], 313-17). It may also be a symbol of Israel. There is a close, almost reciprocal relationship between the holy ones and the people of Israel. The Jewish Essene sect, who established a religious community at the north end of the Dead Sea and preserved the famous Dead Sea Scrolls, made the claim from Daniel that they were the holy ones of the Most High. They would be victorious over the wicked (1QM 6:4-15). The fate of the holy ones in these visions is intended also to show the fate of the Jewish people suffering under Hellenistic oppression (Smith-Christopher, "Book of Daniel," 105). "As is the case with the humanlike figure," Goldingay reminds, "Daniel 7 is too allusive to enable us to decide with certainty whether the holy ones are celestial beings,

oppression, or temporality (v. 18). God will prevail over all the hostile earthly kingdoms, and God's kingdom will be everlasting. The Aramaic emphasizes the enduring quality of this holy kingdom by the repetitive alliterative phrase עַד־עָלְמָא וְעַד עָלַם עָלְמַיָּא (*ad-alma wead alam almaya*), literally, unto the eternal, even to the eternality of the eternal (ages).

Daniel finds this graphic explanation of the beasts, particularly the fourth beast and its peculiar little horn, woefully inadequate. His interest especially focuses on the little horn. He asks for further clarity.

> [19] Then I desired to make certain concerning the fourth beast, which was different from all of them, extremely terrifying, its teeth of iron, its claws of bronze, it devoured and broke in pieces and trampled the rest with its feet, [20] and concerning the ten horns which were on its head and another which came up and before whom three fell. This horn also had eyes and a mouth speaking arrogant things, and its appearance seemed more imposing than its fellows. [21] As I watched, this horn made war with the holy ones and was able to prevail against them, [22] until the Ancient of Days came and judgment was given for the holy ones of the Most High, when the time arrived and the holy ones took possession of the kingdom.

The little horn is more imposing and menacing than the other horns or beasts. Not only does it act with hostility toward the holy ones, but it also prevails, at least for a time, until the judgment of the Ancient of Days cuts it short (vv. 19–21). These lines sound as though in the vision the holy ones are near defeat and going down, about to give up. But then comes the intervening judgment (see vv. 9–12), when the verdict will be given in favor of the holy ones, and they will take dominion (v. 22). Why then is this little horn so menacing? The heavenly interpreter explains:

> [23] Thus he said,
> "The fourth beast will be the fourth on the earth,
>   which will be different than all the kingdoms,
> and it will devour all the earth,
>   and trample it down and break it to pieces,
>   [24] and concerning the ten horns,
>   from which the ten kingdoms arise,
> and another which arose after them,
>   and was different from the former,
>   and brings low three kings.

---

earthly beings, or both" (Goldingay, *Daniel*, 178).

> ^{25} He speaks words against the Most High,
>> and wears down the holy ones,
> and seeks to change appointed times and the law,
>> and they have been given into his hand
>> until a time and times and half a time.
> ^{26} Then the judgment will be seated,
>> and his dominion taken away
>> to be consumed and destroyed until the end.
> ^{27} The kingdom and the dominion
>> and greatness of the kingdom under the whole heaven
>> will be given to the people of the holy ones of the Most High.
> Their kingdom is an everlasting kingdom
>> and all its dominions will serve and obey them.

Repeating what has been said about the fourth beast, its ten horns, and the three horns uprooted in its wake (vv. 23–24), the heavenly attendant focuses like a laser on the little horn. Since the little horn ultimately arises out of the fractured Greek empire, particularly after Alexander, the three horns undoubtedly represent kingdoms conquered by Antiochus IV Epiphanes en route to dominating the region. The remaining seven are probably to be identified as the various other kings in the eastern Mediterranean region, although it is also possible the number ten, as well as the number three, is a representative number, as we have noted.[46] Given its historical setting, the little horn represents Antiochus IV Epiphanes, who is vividly portrayed from the perspective of his virulent hostility toward the Jewish people.

Following a futurist dispensational interpretation, quite common among American and British evangelicals, Whitcomb identifies the little horn as the future eschatological antichrist, who is to rule the entire world in the first half of the seventieth week (see Dan 9:27), immediately following the removal of the church from the world through the rapture.[47] This will happen, according to the dispensationalist scheme, just before the end of time. Hence it is still in the future for us.

---

46. The division of history into ten periods is common in apocalyptic literature. See 1 Enoch 91:12–15; Sybilline Oracles, bks. 1–2, *passim*; and 11Q13 (Melchizedek), line 10.

47. Whitcomb, *Daniel*, 102–3; S. Miller, *Daniel*, 214–16. The rapture of the church refers to the dispensationalist, premillennialist, or midtribulationist view that the church will be taken up from earth before the last great tribulation and the rise of the antichrist. At the end of the tribulation and millennium, Christ will return in power.

Because he sees the fourth beast as the Roman empire, not Greece, Young also identifies the little horn as the future antichrist. This leads him to mark the terminal point of this vision at the second advent of Christ. In the symbols of this vision, he insists, the "entire course of history is given from the appearance of the historical Roman empire until the close of human government."[48] A similar historicist interpretation may be found in the *Adventist Bible Commentary*, where the little horn is identified as Roman Catholicism.[49]

Both the futurist and historicist interpretation of the little horn tend to ignore the primary Hellenistic setting of Daniel. They project from the time of writing into the far distant future. In the case of historicism, there is also an inclination to seize upon persons or events contemporary with the interpreter's own time and mark them as the fulfillment of ancient apocalyptic. The view that the little horn is Roman Catholicism, for instance, has its roots in the anti-Catholic animus of the sixteenth-century Protestant Reformation,[50] rather than in the context of Daniel.

No doubt the earliest interpretation—the primary interest in this commentary—of the malicious acts of the little horn concerns the oppressive Seleucid king Antiochus IV Epiphanes, who tried to suppress the Jewish religion beginning in the year 167 BCE. The parallel vision in Dan 8 also draws attention to the little horn and greatly illuminates the identity of this symbol. Even a cursory reading of 1 Macc 1:10–64, with its generous appropriation of Danielic language, confirms the contemporary identification of the little horn with Antiochus IV. The Seleucid kingdom, of course, was one of the four main divisions of the Greek empire that emerged after Alexander the Great. Of Antiochus's actions, 1 Maccabees draws on Daniel: "Now on the fifteenth day of Chislev, in the one hundred forty-fifth year, they erected a desolating sacrilege on the altar of burnt offering" (1 Macc 1:54; 2 Macc 6:1–6). "Desolating sacrilege" directly alludes to Daniel. "How long will be vision of the regular sacrifice and the transgression of the desolator, and the giving over of the sanctuary and the host for trampling?" (Dan 8:13; see also 9:27; 11:31). Maccabees evidently understands Dan 7–8 to refer to Antiochus and thus to the Greek empire as manifest in the Seleucid kingdom.

---

48. Young, *Prophecy of Daniel*, 150.

49. Nichol, *Seventh-Day Adventist Bible Commentary*, 4:831–38; Haskell, *Story of Daniel*, 102.

50. "The most marked characteristic of the Reformation period is the virtually unanimous belief that the Papacy is assuredly the predicted Antichrist . . . called the Little Horn of Daniel 8" (Froom, *Prophetic Faith*, 2:528–29).

On his official coinage, Antiochus relished self-aggrandizing, divine epithets.[51] He speaks words against the Most High, evidently hostile, scornful, blasphemous words that malign the deity (v. 25). Such language may refer, at least in part, to the titles used on the coinage issued by Antiochus: ΒΑΣΙΛΕΩΣ ΑΝΤΙΟΧΟΥ ΘΕΟΥ ΕΠΙΦΑΝΟΥΣ (*Basileos Antiochou Theou Epiphanous*, King Antiochus, the Manifestation of God). Later (169/168 BCE), he appended to this ΝΙΚΗΦΟΡΟΥ (*Nikephorou*, Bringer of Victory). Although some of this language was not included on all coins, it is hard to overestimate the outrage—the blasphemy—they represented to the Jewish apocalyptist.[52]

The blasphemy is further portrayed in the parallel vision of Dan 8:10–12, where the little horn goes up against the host of heaven; in 9:26–28, where the desolator defiles the temple; and in 11:21–45, where he exalts himself as greater than any god. Antiochus deposed from office the Jewish high priests, looted the temple treasury, ordered savage reprisals against the people of Jerusalem who opposed him, and even erected an altar to the Greek god Zeus near the large altar of sacrifices in the temple courtyard. Upon this altar on Kislev 15, 167 (December 6), swine were offered, turning the temple into what Daniel aptly calls the "abomination of desolation."[53] Statues of other Greek gods were set up in the temple and elsewhere in Jerusalem. These punitive actions helped trigger the famous Maccabean revolt, an insurgent movement which soon erupted in the Judean countryside. Not until Kislev 25, 164 (December 14), near the end of the Maccabean revolt, was the profane statue removed, the temple cleansed from this blasphemous defilement, and the sacred lamps relit.[54] This December event is celebrated to this day by the Jewish people as the festival of Hanukkah (dedication of the temple).[55]

Moreover, the little horn sought to change appointed times and the law. Antiochus, zealous to impose Hellenistic culture upon the Jews, banned the reading of Torah and outlawed the traditional Jewish sacrifices. He

---

51. Note that Antiochus IV "spoke with great arrogance" (1 Macc 1:24).

52. J. Collins, *Daniel* (Hermeneia), 322–23.

53. Dan 9:27; 11:31; 12:11. In Hebrew, this expression is שִׁקּוּצִים מְשֹׁמֵם, *shiqutsim meshomem*, "detested thing(s) causing horror." This is a derisive distortion of the Semitic name the Lord of Heaven, another designation for the Olympian Zeus.

54. Dan 8:13–14; 1 Macc 1:20–64; 2 Macc 5:1—6:11; Anderson, *Signs and Wonders*, 89; Pfeiffer, *History of New Testament*, 13–15.

55. "Then Judas [Maccabeus] and his brothers and all the assembly of Israel determined that every year at that season, the days of dedication of the altar should be observed with joy and gladness for eight days, beginning with the twenty-fifth day of the month of Chislev" (1 Macc 4:59).

abolished the Sabbath and other religious festivals and persecuted, sometimes to death, those who dared defy him. The reference to appointed times (v. 25), sometimes taken to refer to his wreaking havoc with the Jewish sacred calendar, may refer instead to Antiochus's impudent defiance of the divinely determined period for his dominance.[56] One of the themes "deeply rooted" in Daniel is the idea that God has predetermined the times allotted for nations to rule.[57] Once a nation runs out the clock, its demise is assured.

The little horn is thus allotted a certain period to exercise tyrannical rule: a time and times and half a time. If a time is one year, as Dan 4:16 suggests, then a time, (two) times,[58] and half a time would equal three and a half years. This is approximately the time between the desecration of the second temple by Antiochus IV and its cleansing or restoration a little more than three years later. In Dan 8:14, this same period is given as 2300 evenings and mornings, or the number of daily evening and morning sacrifices that would have been offered at the temple had they not been banned. Computed as two such sacrifices per day, this equals 1150 days, or a little more than three years.[59] "Then the sanctuary will be put right" (Dan 8:14b). Daniel 11:45 speaks of the death of Antiochus IV sometime after this. However, it is futile to try to make these periods precisely fit the historical record. Later references in the book indicate the difficulty of assigning such spans of time to historical events (see 12:7, 11–12).

The fate of the little horn is the same as the four beasts. It will be brought to judgment, condemned, consumed and destroyed (vv. 26–27), then its dominion taken by the people of the holy ones of the Most High. This phrase seems to identify the holy ones of the Most High with the faithful people of God. Yet, there would appear to be some blending of the holy ones as celestial beings with the human people of God. Perhaps the sense

---

56. Barr, "Daniel," 598; Newsom, *Daniel*, 240–41.

57. Newsom, *Daniel*, 240.

58. The Aramaic word for times is עִדָּנִין, *iddanin*, a plural noun. It should probably be read here as a dual, two times. Most commentators assume a time equals a year. According to the lunar calendar in use in Judea at the time, a year consisted of 354 days, divided into twelve months of alternatively thirty and twenty-nine days each. The time or year in question in this vision is probably a year consisting of a rounded number of 360 days, hence 3½ x 360 equals 1260, as the same figure is understood in Rev 11:2 ("they will trample over the holy city for forty-two months . . . for one thousand two hundred sixty days"). In Revelation, there are several references to this 3½ years as 42 months or 1260 days (Rev 11:2–3; 12:6; 13:5). By NT times, the figure 3½ had become stereotypical (Luke 4:25; Jas 5:17). In rabbinic literature, the expression merely signifies a long time (Lacocque, *Book of Daniel*, 154).

59. The period between Dec. 6, 167, when the temple was desecrated, and Dec. 14, 164, when it was re-consecrated, is three years and eight days, or a total of 1103 days. On the morning and evening sacrifices, see Num 28:1–8.

is that the people of Israel belong to the eternal kingdom, just as do the celestial ones.

> [28] Thus is the conclusion of the matter. For me, Daniel, my thoughts greatly troubled me, and my countenance changed, but I kept the matter in mind.

Daniel remains troubled. He is still concerned about understanding what he has envisioned. Daniel's perplexity over the interpretation of the vision should offer us some consolation for our own puzzlement. Although he has good news for the faithful, oppressed people, the magnitude of the earthly evil it portrays understandingly disturbs his thoughts for days to come. While the mysteries of this vision linger, the Aramaic portion of the book ends, but not without anticipating what is to come.

The Abomination of Desolation

Daniel 8

Whosoever studies Divine providence, whether it be in relation to the events that concern us, our families, the cities and nations to which we belong; whosoever studies the rise and fall of nations and empires, whoever looks at the clashing of armies, will perceive that these are only parts of one grand movement. God is marching on to the accomplishment of an appointed end; namely, the subjugation of the world to Himself.

—J. M. REID

Once more in this vision, we encounter the great kingdoms of antiquity and the dreaded little horn. The author again skillfully uses ancient iconic animal imagery to craft the vision. Because the same literary pattern is followed, there are clear parallels with Dan 7. The introduction to the vision in Dan 8 makes this connection. The "one that appeared to me in the beginning" (Dan 8:1), is a reference to the previous vision in chapter 7. Interpretation of chapter 8 is greatly augmented by comparison with chapter 7. The two visions cover the same historical ground. Symbolized as monstrous animals in both visions, empires move in succession from one to another—Media, Persia, and Greece—finally arriving at the decisive power, the little horn. Because of its hubris (insolent pride), the little horn is singled out for divine condemnation and, like the metallic statue in Dan 2, finally shattered.

Besides a shift in symbolism, there are other differences between the two visions. The most obvious is that Dan 7 is written in Aramaic, Dan 8 in Hebrew. The two languages suggest separate authors, or at least an author more at home in Aramaic than Hebrew. Although they cover the same ground—the rise and fall of the great empires—Dan 8 especially highlights the victimization of the Jerusalem temple. In contrast to chapter 7, where three of the empires receive divine authorization, as it were, in chapter 8 all the empires appear to act on human initiative.[1] Daniel 8 also spells out more extensively the malevolent work of the little horn.

As to its literary form, Dan 8 consists mainly of a symbolic dream vision, exhibiting a full example of the genre. Within the symbolic dream vision may be found the epiphany or divine appearance of an interpreting angel and a regnal or dynastic prophecy.[2] In addition, Daniel borrows several motifs from other biblical texts and creatively weaves these together into a new pattern.[3]

Although the unity of Dan 8 has been questioned,[4] in its present form an editorial introduction assigns a date and location (Dan 8:1-2). A vision report follows (vv. 3-14), then its interpretation (vv. 15-25). Like chapter 7, there is a concluding statement (vv. 26-27).

THE VISION OF THE TWO GOATS (8:1-14)

> In the third year of the reign of Belshazzar the king, a vision appeared to me, I, Daniel, after the one that appeared to me in the beginning. ² I was watching in the vision—now it happened in my vision that I was in Susa the palace, which is in the province of Elam. I observed in the vision that I was by the river Ulai. ³ I raised my eyes and observed, and behold, a ram was standing before the river, and it had two horns. The two horns were tall, but one was taller than the second, and the taller one came up after it. ⁴ I saw the ram thrusting toward the sea, toward the north, and toward the south country, and no living beast could stand before it, nor could any deliver from its power. It did as it wanted and became strong.

---

1. Newsom, *Daniel*, 256.

2. A comparable example of dynastic prophecy is the Babylonian Dynastic Prophecy, dated to the Hellenistic period, just as Daniel. Like Daniel, this prophecy predicts the rise and fall of Assyria, Babylon, Persia, and Macedonia (Grayson, *Assyrian and Babylonian Chronicles*, 2-37).

3. J. Collins, *Daniel* (FOTL 22), 86-87.

4. The principal passage in dispute is Dan 8:11-14 (J. Collins, *Daniel* [Hermeneia], 328-29).

The vision is dated to the third year of Belshazzar (v. 1), which would be c. 551/550 BCE, creating a hiatus of about two years between it and chapter 7, which is dated to the first year of Belshazzar (Dan 7:1). An editor has no doubt supplied this date.[5] Daniel finds himself in Susa, in the province of Elam, by the river Ulai (v. 2). This is odd, because Susa was one of the royal residences of the Achaemenid empire, while Daniel, according to the assigned date, is still serving in Babylon during the time of Belshazzar (v. 27). Since he was a high official in the Babylonian government, however, Daniel could have had occasion to visit Susa in Elam, which was under Babylonian control for a time. On the other hand, the text may indicate Daniel's presence in Susa was in the vision, not physically, but in a visionary state, like Ezekiel, who while physically in Babylon was transported in vision to Jerusalem.[6] The location by the river Ulai is also problematic, for the Hebrew term translated river is אוּבָל (*ubal*, watercourse or canal). Although Susa was located on this river, *ubal* may refer to a canal or tributary.[7]

Daniel sees a ram standing beside the ubal, with two horns. One horn was taller than the other and came up after it (v. 3). The ram, which represents the kings of Media and Persia (v. 20), is charging and striking in every direction, toward the sea, the north, and the south. No living beast can withstand it or overpower it. Significantly, the ram freely does as it wants, whatever it wishes. It possesses enormous strength (v. 4). In antiquity, the ram, a favorite icon in Persian art, was a well-known symbol for the Persian empire.

> [5] I was considering, and behold, a male goat came from the west over the face of the whole earth without touching the ground. The goat had a conspicuous horn between its eyes. [6] It came toward the ram, the owner of the two horns that I saw standing beside the river, and it ran into it with furious force. [7] I saw it approaching close to the ram. It was enraged against it and struck the ram and shattered its two horns. There was no strength in the ram to stand before it. It threw the ram to the ground and trampled it, but there was no one to rescue the ram from its power. [8] The male goat grew exceedingly great, but while it was at full strength the great horn was broken and four conspicuous horns came up in its place toward the four winds of the heavens.

5. According to Collins, this dating is a "transparent fiction" (J. Collins, *Daniel* [FOTL 22], 87).

6. "The spirit lifted me up between earth and heaven, and brought me in visions of God to Jerusalem" (Ezek 8:5).

7. Hartman and Di Lella derive this term from a different root, *abul*, city gate (Hartman and Di Lella, "Daniel," 417).

A male goat moves swiftly from the west, so swiftly it never touches the ground. What is most noticeable about this goat, however, is not the goat itself, but the horn between its eyes (v. 5). Running into and battering the ram, in great fury it throws the ram to the ground, tramples upon it, and splinters its two horns (vv. 6–7). No one comes to the ram's rescue. Then, as the male goat, representing the kingdom of Greece (v. 21), grows great, reaching full strength, the prominent horn between its eyes is broken. Four other conspicuous horns come up in its place, dominant in every direction, as reference to the four winds of the heavens suggests (v. 8). The author further distinguishes between the two goats by using different terms for each. The ram is called an אַיִל (*ayil*), a term usually designating a male goat or ram as flock leader. For the male goat who tears along across the earth, the author uses a rather unique expression, צְפִיר הָעִזִּים (*tsephir ha-izzim*), a compound phrase that may be tautologically or redundantly rendered "a goat (as distinguished from a female) goat," hence, a male goat or he-goat.[8]

> [9] Out of one of them came another smaller horn, and it became greater than the rest toward the south country, toward the east, and toward the beautiful land. [10] It grew great up to the host of heaven, and it threw down to the earth some of the host and some of the stars and trampled them.

Out of one of the winds or geographical directions, or out of one of the horns, arises another smaller horn (v. 9). It is uncertain whether this little horn emerges from one of the winds, or from one of the four horns. The syntax of the sentence is ambiguous. Both winds and horns are feminine nouns in Hebrew, but the pronoun in verse 9a referring to them (מֵהֶם, *mehem*, from one of *them*) is a masculine plural. It is not unusual to find a Hebrew masculine pronoun referring to a feminine antecedent, but here the grammatical construction only leaves more ambiguous the origin of the little horn. Interestingly, several medieval Hebrew manuscripts change this pronoun to a feminine form, making it correspond to both horns and winds. In other manuscripts, the masculine verb associated with the pronoun has also been changed to feminine. None of these changes solves the difficulty. Despite the resulting grammatical harmony, the ambiguity remains, perhaps intentionally so. The apocalyptist may have aimed to introduce an element of

---

8. Three different types of goats were domesticated in the region: the black-haired goat, especially adapted to desertlike terrain; the reddish-brown Damascene goat, known for its milk-producing qualities; and the black-and-white-haired goat of the higher, more mountainous altitudes (Borowski, "Goat, Goatherd," 585). It is impossible to distinguish among any of these three in the vision of Dan 8. For the male goat as a symbol of royal power, see Ezek 34:17–22; Zech 10:3.

uncertainty. But it does seem reasonable to assume the little horn, a symbol probably borrowed from Dan 7, emerges from the male goat's bizarre four horns, not the four directional winds. In other words, the little horn comes out of the divisions of the Greek empire following Alexander's premature death (323 BCE). This corresponds to its origin—"out of this kingdom"—as in Dan 7:24.

The little horn prospers in every direction, but particularly toward the beautiful land, a reference to Israel, or perhaps Jerusalem. Not content with mere territorial acquisition, the little horn exalts itself against the heavenly powers, whether gods or angels, casting them down to the ground and trampling upon them (v. 10). The theme of revolting against the host of heaven and sweeping them away occurs in the book of Revelation, where the great red dragon, symbol of Satan, "swept down a third of the stars of heaven and threw them to the earth" (Rev 12:4).

> [11] Even against the prince of the host it became great, and the regular sacrifice was taken away from him, and the place of his sanctuary cast down. [12] The host was given over together with the regular sacrifice on account of transgression. It cast the truth to the ground and kept on acting and prospering. [13] Then I heard a holy one speaking, and another holy one said to the certain one who spoke, "How long will be the vision of the regular sacrifice and the transgression of the desolator, and the giving over of the sanctuary and the host for trampling?" [14] So he said to me, "Until two thousand and three hundred evenings and mornings, then the sanctuary will be put right."

The little horn adamantly opposes the prince of the host (v. 11), no doubt a reference to God (v. 25). By abolishing the regular sacrifices normally offered at the temple, it casts down the place of God's sanctuary. Moreover, it cast the truth to the ground and kept on acting and prospering (v. 12). What is meant by truth (אֱמֶת, *emeth*) in this verse remains unclear. *Emeth* in Hebrew has more the connotation of fidelity or reliability than of factual, logical reality, as we think of objective truth. The term may refer to the Torah, which the little horn prohibits, or the world order as divinely determined, against which it rails.[9] Hard questions come from among the holy ones: how long will this little horn continue its destructive, blasphemous rampage (v. 13)? The answer is forthcoming, but in cryptic, enigmatic form: "Until two thousand and three hundred evenings and mornings, then the

---

9. Newsom, *Daniel*, 266. See Dan 7:25. Lacocque prefers Torah as the meaning here (Lacocque, *Book of Daniel*, 163).

sanctuary will be put right" (v. 14).¹⁰ A length of time of some sort is allowed for the little horn to wreak devastation, even upon the temple itself.

Although the interpretation of this vision does not begin until vv. 15-26, it is difficult to make sense of it without some awareness of the events being described. The ram, we are told, represents the empire of Media and Persia; the male goat, Greece under Alexander the Great (see vv. 20-21), who is portrayed on some Ptolemaic coins as a god with horns protruding from his forehead and called Alexander of the double horns.¹¹ Following Alexander's untimely death, his empire, after a few years of internal discord, finally divided into four main successor kingdoms under four generals, corresponding to the four horns: Macedonia (Philip Aridaeus), Asia Minor (Antigonus Monophthalmus), Egypt (Ptolemy Lagus), and Syria (Seleucus Nicator). Acting and speaking like the little horn in Dan 7, the little horn in both visions is no doubt the same entity. As we saw in Dan 7, it represents the Seleucid or Syrian kingdom under Antiochus IV Epiphanes. Antiochus IV, who proudly dubbed himself the god manifest (*epiphanes*), was a perversely ambitious king who aspired not only to vanquish the nations around him, but also to impose Hellenistic culture, which he zealously favored, upon his empire.¹² It was especially this unwelcome imposition that sparked the conflict between him and the Jewish people.

Once the Romans had checked Antiochus's territorial ambitions toward the western Mediterranean region, Antiochus turned his attention to Egypt. Stymied there—again by the Romans—he turned back toward Palestine. To put down what he perceived as treason then brewing among the Jews, Antiochus harshly prohibited Jewish religious practices contrary to his vision of Hellenism. To repeat what was said above in our comments on Dan 7, Antiochus deposed and replaced the Jewish high priests, looted the temple treasury to support his military ambitions, ordered military reprisals against the dissenters in Jerusalem, and in a deliberate, sacrilegious act, erected a small altar to a Greek god, the Olympian Zeus, at the altar of sacrifices in the temple courtyard. On this altar in December 167, swine—unclean and defiling—were offered, debasing the temple into what Daniel calls

---

10. Some scholars challenge the authenticity of vv. 11-14. The angelic dialogue disrupts the vision, and there is a shift in syntax between the feminine forms used with the horn and the masculine forms used in the interpretation. However, should these verses be excised, v. 26 would also have to be called into question, because it refers to the evenings-mornings of v. 14.

11. Kraft et al., *IFE*, 11:11; Cornfeld and Freedman, *Archaeology*, 233.

12. "This is the God-given portrait of Antiochus Epiphanes," claims Talbot, "that terrible creature who was to come, and who long ago passed off the scene of this world's history." Talbot goes on, however, to interpret Antiochus as "a type of the [end-time] Antichrist" (Talbot, *Prophecies of Daniel*, 150-51).

the "abomination of desolation" (שִׁקּוּצִים מְשֹׁמֵם, *shiqqutsim meshomem*), an expression that sarcastically distorts the Semitic name Baal of heaven. The abomination of desolation seems to refer specifically to the altar Antiochus erected on the altar of sacrifices in the temple courtyard.[13]

Antiochus forbade under penalty of death the religious observances mandated in the Torah. Circumcision could no longer be practiced, the Sabbath observed, nor the festivals celebrated. Even to possess a scroll of the Torah was a capital offense. Copies of the Torah were confiscated and destroyed. In addition to Zeus, he set up statues of other Greek gods, not only in the temple precincts, but elsewhere in Jerusalem and the surrounding area. These hostile actions provoked the Maccabean revolt, led by Judas Maccabeus and his brothers, which erupted in the countryside of Judea at Modein. Not until 164, over three years later, after the Maccabean insurgents had successfully driven the Seleucid armies from the vicinity of Jerusalem, was the offensive altar removed, the temple cleansed, and the sacred lamps relit.[14] Such cruel, repressive hostility against subject peoples and their religion was deeply offensive to our author, and indeed, to all who cherish freedom to worship. This vision, then, deals with the same events as those described in 7:24–25, only here there is greater concern about the temple itself.

"How long?" goes up the cry from the holy ones. This is a traditional complaint, generally found in penitential literature. "How long, O Lord? Will you be angry forever?" (Ps 79:5). For apocalyptic, we have seen, the human world is temporarily in the thrall of evil, anxiously awaiting divine deliverance. In the meantime, evil must run its predetermined course. Hence the answer to the plaint comes in temporal form: 2300 evenings and mornings. This period, which is a little more than three years, apparently corresponds to the three and a half times (years) in Dan 7:25, the period allotted in Dan 7 to the little horn for its dirty work. However, the unit of measure is different. Instead of times, it is literally 2300 עֶרֶב בֹּקֶר (*ereb boqer*, evening-morning[s]), a phrase found only here in the HB. What does this expression indicate? Generally, it has been understood in at least two different ways, either of which could have been recognized by Daniel's original audience.

The first view, which takes the 2300 as 2300 literal days, points to the nearest parallel to *ereb boqer*, found in Genesis, where a similar phrase is

---

13. 1 Maccabees refers to this altar to Zeus as the "abomination [βδέλυγμα, *bdelugma*] that he had erected on [ἐπὶ, *epi*, upon, over] the altar in Jerusalem" (6:7). See also Dan 9:27 (LXX).

14. See 1 Macc 1:20–64; 4:36–59; 2 Macc 5:1—6:11; 10:1–8; Anderson, *Signs and Wonders*, 89; Pfeiffer, *History of New Testament*, 13–15.

used to mark the individual days of creation: e.g., "there was evening [*ereb*] and there was morning [*boqer*], the fourth day" (Gen 1:19). In Genesis, evening and morning mark the boundaries of individual days in the weekly cycle. Since the regular morning and evening offerings in the temple occur daily,[15] proponents consider the combined reference evening-morning to be equivalent to a single day.[16] Consistent with this view, the LXX and Theodotion of Dan 8:14 render *ereb boqer* as ἡμέραι (*hemerai*, days).[17]

Gaebelein, a proponent of this view, takes the period as 2300 literal twenty-four-hour days and commences it from 171 BCE, the date of Antiochus IV's appointment of Menelaus as high priest and the assassination of the popular high priest Onias III. The 2300 days, accordingly, then extends from 171 to 165, or about six years, three months, and a few days, when Judas Maccabeus cleansed and restored the temple in December of that year.[18]

Although several English translations concur in translating 2300 as days, such rendition is misleading, for this is not what the text precisely says. The Greek translations are primarily to blame for this confusion, which has subsequently been passed along to many later translations.

The second view claims the 2300 refers not to twenty-four-hour days, composed of an evening and morning, but rather to the regular daily sacrifices offered at morning and eventide at the Temple.[19] The NIV, for example, reads "it will take 2,300 evenings and mornings; then the sanctuary will be reconsecrated." The TNK has "for twenty-three hundred evenings and

---

15. Note Ezra: they "offered the daily burnt offerings by number according to the ordinance, as required for each day" (3:4).

16. Schwantes, "'*Erebbōqer* of Dan 8:14," 375–80. Whitcomb (*Daniel*, 113–14) takes these as literal days (based on Gen 1) and then relates them to a period from 170 to 164 BCE, six years and almost four months, from the time Antiochus began his suppression of the Jews to the time of the restoration of the temple. Cf. S. Miller, *Daniel*, 229–30; Wood, *Daniel*, 218–19. Accepting the interpretation as days, Nichol, *Seventh-Day Adventist Bible Commentary* (4:842–45), goes a step further and interprets the 2300 days based on the year-day principle as prophetic years—2300 years—allowing the Danielic text to predict the initiation of the eschatological judgment, believed to have begun in 1844. Despite the debate over the exact meaning of evening-morning(s), there is nothing in this text that indicates the 2300 should be thought of as prophetic years, much less a prediction of the nineteenth century beginning of the final judgment of humanity. See the discussion below.

17. Interestingly, the Latin Vulgate does not do this, but renders the expression quite literally as *ad vesperam et mane* (unto evening and morning).

18. Gaebelein, *Daniel*, 99–100.

19. Slotki, *Daniel*, 68; Talbot, *Prophecies of Daniel*, 153. Note also Num 28:3–4: "This is the offering by fire that you shall offer to the Lord: two male lambs a year old without blemish, daily, as a regular offering [*tamid*]. One lamb you shall offer in the morning, and the other lamb you shall offer at twilight." See also Num 4:16; 1 Esd 5:50.

mornings; then the sanctuary shall be cleansed." The number 2300, in short, refers not to twenty-four-hour days, but to the number of daily sacrifices (two per day) omitted during the ban. This regular offering, consisting of a lamb along with meal and wine offerings, was known as the תָּמִיד (*tamid*, continual), the same word used here (see v. 12). According to priestly law, each morning and evening on a given day a lamb was to be offered. "One lamb you shall offer in the morning, and the other lamb you shall offer in the evening." This is called the *tamid* offering (Exod 29:39-42). Ben Sira, active only a few years before the Antiochene desecration, mentions the two daily sacrifices as a constant staple in the temple of this time.[20] Since this sacrifice was offered in the morning and evening of each day, 2300 evenings-mornings would represent a total of 1150 such sacrifices, offered over a corresponding number of days.[21] Each day, two *tamid* offerings were offered.

The temple would continue to be in a state of defilement because of the sacrilegious actions of the little horn—in other words, for as long as the number of daily morning and evening *tamid* sacrifices that would have been offered had they not been banned. This would be true for 1150 days, a little less than the three and a half years indicated in Dan 7:25.[22] According to the vision, then, at the conclusion of this time, the temple would be put right or reconsecrated, cleansed of the idolatrous accessories placed there by Antiochus IV and restored to its normal operation.

This period of 2300 and the events associated with its terminus, as we would expect, has stirred the date-setting obsession of many apocalyptic interpreters down through the ages. One of the most fascinating interpretations of the 2300 evenings-mornings is that of New England farmer turned evangelist William Miller (1782-1847), leader of the famous apocalyptic Millerite Movement of the 1830s and 1840s. Miller used the 2300 evenings-mornings prophecy to predict the date of the end of the world, at first claiming it would come in 1843, and then, after this date had passed, in 1844.

---

20. "His sacrifices shall be wholly burned twice every day continually" (Sir 45:14).

21. Archer, "Daniel," 103. Note Jerome: "[Antiochus] even took away the . . . 'continual offering,' which was customarily sacrificed in the morning and at evening, and he prevailed to the casting down of the 'place of his sanctuary'" (*Jerome's Commentary on Daniel 8:11-12*). Cf. Jeffery, "Introduction and Exegesis" 476; Pfeiffer, *Introduction to Old Testament*, 759; Slotki, *Daniel*, 68.

22. The period between 6 Dec. 167, when the temple was desecrated, and 14 Dec 164, when it was reconsecrated, according to Collins, is three years and ten days, or a total of 1105 days. Historians differ on the precise date of the reconsecration. Collins suggests the difference in these numbers may be because ch. 8 was written a short while later than ch. 7, after some of the predetermined time has already elapsed (J. Collins, *Daniel* [Hermeneia], 336). See 1 Macc 4:52-54 for a slightly different calculation of three years.

Seventh-Day Adventists have adopted Miller's time calculations of Dan 8:14, but apply them instead to a heavenly rather than an earthly event: the great eschatological judgment.

The Adventist interpretation, like William Miller, starts with Dan 8:14 as rendered in the King James Version (KJV): "Unto two thousand and three hundred days; then shall the sanctuary be cleansed." Again like Miller, Adventists read the period in this verse according to the year-day principle. This is the interpretive idea that in many prophetic and apocalyptic texts—and even some narratives—in the Bible, a day stands for a year, viz., a lunar year of 360 days. A day becomes a symbol for one lunar year.[23] The 2300 days in Dan 8:14 are thus understood as 2300 years. At the end of this period, according to Dan 8:14, the sanctuary would be cleansed. Miller took this to indicate Jesus would return to cleanse the earth—the sanctuary—of sin and its effects. He expected the world as we know it to come to an end at the terminus of this period (1844). Adventists accept Miller's basic time calculation but place another event at its end.

When did the 2300 years begin? Adventists find the beginning point in Dan 9. "Know therefore and understand," says the angel Gabriel, "from the going forth of the word to restore and rebuild Jerusalem until an anointed ruler will be seven weeks; and for sixty-two weeks it will again be built with a plaza and moat, even in troublous times" (Dan 9:25). The going forth of the word to restore and rebuild Jerusalem, according to this view, occurred in 457 BCE when the decree of the Achaemenid king Artaxerxes I authorized an additional return of Judea from Babylonian exile. When 2300 years are projected from 457, the result is 1844 CE.[24] Drawing upon the Karaite Jewish calendar of 1844, considered the most conservative Jewish religious calendar of the time, Adventist scholars pinpoint the ending date of the 2300 years on October 22, 1844, which happened to be the date of the Day of Atonement (Yom Kippur) in 1844.[25]

What happened then? At this point, Adventists depart from Miller and claim the 2300 days come to fulfillment not at the second advent, but at the start of the final judgment of humanity. This awesome event, Adventists

---

23. The Hebrew lunar year was 354 days. Every five years, an extra month would be added to the year, making it approximate the solar time for the year. The 360 in this calculation is a round figure required to approximate the predicted time.

24. That is, 2300−457 = 1843, but one year must be added to this because there is no zero year between BCE and CE (2300−457) + 1 = 1844.

25. Adventist scholars have sought to establish that the decree of Artaxerxes I reauthorizing a return from Babylonian exile went into effect in late summer or early fall 457, not 458 BCE, as most scholars think (Horn and Wood, *Chronology of Ezra 7*, 107–17). An excerpt from this decree appears in Ezra 7:12–26.

believe, takes place in heaven, not upon earth. Christ as the great High Priest—on October 22, 1844—began a ministry of final judgment in the heavenly sanctuary, corresponding to the Day of Atonement in ancient priestly ritual. This utterly unique interpretation of Dan 8:14 constitutes the basis of what Adventists now call the doctrine of the investigative judgment.[26] Stephen Haskell explains:

> It was seen that the work of the high priest in the earthly tabernacle was but a figure of the service upon which Christ, the great High Priest, entered in 1844. At that time he entered into the presence of the Ancient of Days . . . and began the work of the investigative judgment, at the end of which work he will appear in the clouds of heaven.[27]

Some contemporary Adventist scholars have tried to soften the punitive, judgmental tone of this doctrine by emphasizing the vindication and grace at work in it. "In this word of injustice, oppression, abuse, suffering, slander, and evil," writes Richard Davidson, "the God of justice and mercy is in the heavenly sanctuary, working it all out to bring justice to all wrongs done in the universe, and salvation and vindication to all those who trust in Him."[28]

For those who have reviewed this doctrine, it involves a complicated pastiche of typology, theology, numerology, and eschatology and would take much more space than here to unravel. This interpretation remains controversial even among contemporary Adventists.[29] Here we must be content simply to note the 2300 evenings and mornings refers to the morning and evening regular sacrifices at the temple. Twenty-three hundred of these twice-daily sacrifices would occur over 1150 days, not 2300 years. Thus Dan 8:14 has nothing to do with the high priestly ministry of Christ or an extended chronology ending in 1844. In the context of Daniel, it is a forecast of how long the Jerusalem temple would linger in a desecrated state and the regular sacrificial ritual remain inoperative during the reign of Antiochus IV in the second century BCE.

26. See General Conference of Seventh-Day Adventists, *Seventh-Day Adventists Believe*, 347–69.
27. Haskell, *Story of Daniel*, 132–33.
28. Davidson, "Sanctuary Doctrine," 21.
29. See Farley, "Sanctuary Doctrine."

THE INTERPRETATION OF THE VISION (8:15-26)

> ¹⁵ Now it happened when I, Daniel, saw the vision, I also sought understanding; and lo, standing beside me was one in appearance like a man. ¹⁶ Then I heard a human voice between the banks of the Ulai. He called and said, "Gabriel, make this one understand the vision." ¹⁷ He came near where I stood. When he approached, I was terrified and fell on my face. But he said to me, "Understand, O mortal, that the vision is for the time of the end."

As we have seen, once a vision has occurred, the apocalyptist anxiously seeks to understand its meaning (see Dan 7:16). A heavenly interpreter is dispatched to clear up the mystery. Here, the angel Gabriel appears in this role. He reappears in the vision of Dan 9 (v. 21). An unnamed man—often identified as the archangel Michael—standing inside the canal banks of the Ulai (v. 15) and speaking in a human voice summons Gabriel to explain the vision (v. 16). As Gabriel approaches, Daniel falls on his face in terror, as he does at the beginning of the fourth vision, when greeted by a radiant, heavenly being. "My strength left me, and my complexion grew deathly pale.... I fell into a trance, face to the ground" (10:8–9 NRSV). Being overcome with trepidation is common in Scripture—especially in apocalyptic—wherever there is a heavenly epiphany.[30]

The vision, Gabriel explains, is for the time of the end (v. 17). This phrase עֵת־קֵץ (ets-qetz) has an obvious eschatological connotation. It appears several more times in Daniel (11:35, 40; 12:4, 9), all referring to a future period, an approaching era that seems to fall just shy of the ultimate end (but see v. 26). In verse 19, it appears again as מוֹעֵד קֵץ (moed qets, an appointed end time), apparently a time explicitly determined for the end, yet not revealed. For this author, like the NT, the eschaton (end of the world) always seems precipitously near, ready to break in upon the world. "Blessed is the one who reads aloud the words of the prophecy, and blessed are those who hear and who keep what is written in it," writes John in the late first century CE, "for the time is near" (Rev 1:3). Since all the visions in Daniel seem to culminate in the middle of the second century BCE with the Antiochene crisis, the author evidently expects the end of human rule and the final revelation of God's glory to occur in or around that time.

> ¹⁸ When he spoke with me, I fell on my face in a deep sleep on the ground. He then touched me and made me stand in my

---

30. J. Collins, *Daniel* (Hermeneia), 337. See Josh 5:14; Ezek 1:28; 3:23; Rev 1:17; 1 Enoch 14:14, 24; 2 Esd 10:29–30; Apocalypse of Abraham 10:2.

place. ¹⁹ And he said, "Behold, I am making known to you what will be in the end of the indignation, for at an appointed time is the end. ²⁰ The ram that you saw, owner of the horn, is the kings of Media and Persia. ²¹ The male goat is the king of Greece, and the great horn that is between his eyes is the first king. ²² As for the horn broken off and the four that stand up in its place, these are four kingdoms that arise from out of the nations, although not with his power."

Once again, in the face of all this Daniel collapses into a deep sleep. Then with astounding clarity and a heavenly touch, Gabriel offers the interpretation of the vision. The vision pertains to the appointed time given over to the defiant little horn (v. 19). It is explained the ram stands for the kings of Media and Persia, treated here as a dual kingdom, with Persia arising after Media, as symbolized in the two horns (v. 20). In Dan 2 and 7, the Persians were treated as a separate kingdom, albeit in chapter 7, the bear symbolizing Persia rises on one side, conceivably depicting the rise and triumph of the Persians over Media (Dan 7:5). The male goat is the king of Greece, with the conspicuous horn the first king, known to history as Alexander the Great (v. 21). When the horn is broken, four new horns come forth, symbolizing the four kingdoms arising from the ashes of Alexander's empire. These kingdoms, as we noted above, are the rulers of Macedonia, Asia Minor, Egypt, and Syria.

> ²³ "At the end of their reign, when transgressors have finished,
>   a king will arise, audacious and skilled in intrigue.
> ²⁴ His power will be mighty, but not in his own strength.
>   He will destroy to a remarkable degree,
>   prosper and accomplish,
>   and destroy mighty people and the people of the holy ones.
> ²⁵ By his cunning he will cause deceit to prosper under his own hand,
>   and in his own mind he will be great.
> While at peace he will destroy many,
>   and will even stand against the prince of princes.
> But without a hand he will be broken."

Gabriel now sketches the career of the audacious little horn, Antiochus IV. He appears near the culmination of the three preceding kingdoms (v. 23), a time when transgressors have finished, and quickly becomes enormously powerful (v. 24). Daniel is deterministic at this point.[31] Iniquity must run

---

31. J. Collins, *Daniel* (Hermeneia), 339. Note the determinism in Gen 15:16; 2

its course until the land has been filled with it. Wickedness must be allowed to work itself out. Wickedness is cumulative. It piles up like garbage until finally it reaches the limits of divine patience. When the moment is reached, judgment falls.

Near the very end of this accumulative evil arises the arrogant king. His reign, deceitful though it be, enjoys unusual success. He revolts against the people of the holy ones and finally even against the prince of princes (v. 25). His defiance is bold, audacious, even hubristic. He evinces a kind of brazen arrogance, in this case, against the holy ones, the celestial hosts, and then against the prince of princes, here no doubt a reference to God. Above, the hubris of Antiochus IV was expressed in terms of antagonism toward the temple and its worship. Here, it develops from his own attitude. "In his own mind he will be great" is the very definition of hubris. His rude, insolent attitude and behavior toward the sacred institutions of Israel bring him under the overwhelming condemnation of the apocalyptist.

Not only here but throughout this vision, the various kingdoms mentioned act out what Collins calls the "Lucifer pattern"—"hybris leads to a great fall"[32]—as seen in Isa 14:13-14:

> You said in your heart,
>   "I will ascend to heaven;
> I will raise my throne above the stars of God;
>   I will sit on the mount of assembly on the heights of Zaphon;
> I will ascend to the tops of the clouds,
> I will make myself like the Most High."

This hubristic "storming of the gates of heaven" appears in a prophetic oracle against Babylon (v. 4) and has been used traditionally (as in Milton's *Paradise Lost*) to flesh out the myth of Lucifer's (Satan's) fall from heaven.[33] In Dan 8, each beast indulges in self-aggrandizement. The ram "did as it wanted and became strong" (v. 4). The goat "grew exceedingly great" (v. 8). Its self-exaltation is progressive, until the climax when the little horn "grew great up to the host of heaven ... even against the prince of the host" (vv. 10-11). Then, like a self-glorifying Lucifer or an arrogant Babylon, it is

---

Macc 6:14; 2 Esd 4:36-37. The element of contingency in this determinism, however, is rooted on the quantity of the wickedness of the ungodly. More wickedness shortens the determination.

32. J. Collins, *Daniel* (FOTL 22), 88.

33. The myth of Lucifer's (Satan's) fall appears also in the NT (Luke 10:18-20; Rev 12: 7-12).

"brought down to Sheol, to the depths of the Pit" (Isa 14:15). Then comes a fall. "Without a hand he will be broken" (Dan 8:25).

"While at peace he will destroy many" is generally taken as a reference to the surprise attack on Jerusalem—on the Sabbath—by Antiochus's principal tax collector, Apollonius.[34] In the end, however, Antiochus would meet destruction without a hand, without human intervention. Antiochus did come to an untimely death in 164.[35] Our text, however, gives only a general statement of this fact, with no explicit details. "He has risen up against God and by God he will be overthrown."[36] Just as a tyrant may crush others without warning, so the holy God may, without warning and without human assistance, bring about the demise of the tyrant. Antiochus's downfall comes because he has so brazenly confronted the God of Israel.

Several conservative commentators read this vision differently. Whitcomb, for instance, agrees the little horn is Antiochus IV in verses 9–14, but the little horn appearing later in the chapter (vv. 23–26) is either the eschatological antichrist, "who will be destroyed supernaturally at the second coming of Christ" (see Rev 19:19–20) or his counterpart, the eschatological king of the north (cf. Dan 11:45). The king of the north—identified elsewhere as Gog of the land of Magog (Ezek 38:2–6)—will oppose the prince of princes and "will be broken without human agency" (Dan 8:22–23). According to Whitcomb, the little horn in this vision has a double identity, one in the days of the Maccabees, a second eschatological, just before the second advent.[37] There appears to be no basis in this text, however, to make a distinction between the little horn in Dan 8:9–14, which applies to Antiochus IV, and then 8:23–26, an expanded description of the same power as in 8:9–14, and apply it to a future antichristian power. Verses 9–14 and 23–26 are clearly speaking of the same entity, whom we identify as Antiochus IV. The correspondence between the actions of the little horn in Dan 7–8 and the activities of Antiochus IV in 167–164 is just too great to be minimized and reapplied, without warrant, far in the future, as commentators such as

---

34. See 1 Macc 1:29–32; 2 Macc 5:24–26.

35. Daniel 11:45, which mentions the death of Antiochus, seems also unaware of the actual circumstances of his death. See the comments on Dan 11:45 for the varied accounts of Antiochus's demise.

36. Young, *Prophecy of Daniel*, 181.

37. Whitcomb, *Daniel*, 113–19. For Stephen Miller, the little horn in ch. 8 is Antiochus IV, but in ch. 7 is the eschatological antichrist (S. Miller, *Daniel*, 225n22). Wood, preserving the double identity, takes the little horn primarily as the antichrist, but secondarily as Antiochus (Wood, *Daniel*, 226–27). Gaebelein sees in the little horn in Dan 8 as a power much like the ancient Assyrians, who in the last days comes from the region now known as Turkey. His identity is unknown, "whether a great Russian Czar or some other one, remains as a secret with God" (Gaebelein, *Daniel*, 110–18, citation from 118).

Whitcomb have done. Through the centuries, of course, because of its vagaries, apocalyptic writing has too easily lent itself to secondary and even tertiary application, but the primary referent of the little horn in this passage is clearly Antiochus IV Epiphanes.

CONCLUDING STATEMENT (8:26–27)

> [26] The vision of the evening and mornings that has been related is true. As for you, seal up the vision because it is for many days.
> [27] But I, Daniel, was exhausted and sick for days. However, I arose and went about the work of the king. I was appalled about the vision but did not understand it.

These lines certify the reliability of the vision of the evening-mornings. In accordance with the time span of the evening-mornings, the vision is to be for many days (v. 26). Daniel is therefore told to seal up the vision, a notion found often in apocalyptic (Dan 12:4, 9; Rev 22:10). The obscure, apocalyptic mysteries are not be revealed until a future time. In 1 Enoch, for instance, Enoch's visions "are not for this generation, but for a distant generation which will come" (1 Enoch 1:2 *OTP*). According to the implied narrative setting of this book, Daniel is living in the time of the Babylonian empire, during which period he received the visions.[38] The deeper meaning of his visions, however, was to be locked away until the times of Antiochus IV, the actual historical setting of the book. Daniel, in the time of the late Babylonian empire—following the apocalyptic style—anticipates the rise of Antiochus IV and the climax of history far beyond his implied moment in time.

The narrative closes with an admission. Although the vision troubles him (v. 27), Daniel does not understand it. It has been sealed—hidden—for a later time. He is not able to make sense of it.

---

38. J. Collins, *Daniel* (Hermeneia), 341–42.

The Seventy Weeks

Daniel 9

Our desire to do something must not blind us to the idea that the solution, finally, is eschatological . . . our problems are of such global and even cosmic proportions that only God enthroned in glory at the last day can truly set things right.

—Borsela Eale and William Wright, *Chalice Introduction*

With Dan 9, the usual vision arrangement within the chapter suddenly shifts. Instead of a vision, this chapter inserts a prayer. The prayer then introduces a reinterpretation of Jeremiah's prophecy of the seventy years allotted for the destruction of Jerusalem and its aftermath in the Babylonian exile. The entire chapter is obviously aimed at reassuring the Jewish people that their exilic sojourn will come to an end. In the prayer, Daniel seeks mercy for his desolated country, Judea, and the ruined temple in Jerusalem that once stood at its religious center.

The prayer is therefore fashioned as a communal confession of sin and a petition for divine mercy. It is an extraordinary prayer, worthy to stand alongside the other great prayers in the Bible.[1] Like all these prayers, there is about it a distinctly Deuteronomistic flavor—an echoing of themes in Deuteronomy.[2] Such prayers confess Israel's sin, accept the verdict of divine justice, and appeal for mercy for God's own sake. Like a good pastor, Daniel

---

1. See Ezra 9:6–15; Neh 9:5–37; Ps 79; Bar 1:15–3:8; the prayer of Azariah (Dan 3:24–45, LXX). The relationship between Bar 1:15–3:8 and Dan 9:4–19 is especially close.

2. E.g., Dan 9:11 compared with Deut 28:15–68; 29:10–29.

stands in solidarity with his people. He begins speaking in first person singular, then quickly identifies with his people by adopting the first person plural, we: "We have sinned and done wrong" (v. 5).

Why begin with a prayer rather than a vision? The vision in chapter 8 ended with Daniel told to seal up the vision, because it was yet for many days (Dan 8:26). Daniel's anxiety concerning the delay implicit in the vision, which according to the date lines in chapters 8–9 occurred a decade or so before the prayer, now resurfaces in chapter 9. Chapters 8–9 are linked by their focus on the fate of the sanctuary (temple), and both utilize similar vocabulary. Chapter 8 speaks of the "transgression that desolates" the sanctuary (8:13), while chapter 9 of "an abomination that desolates" (9:27).[3]

Without appealing to Israel's worthiness as a ground for his prayer, Daniel pleads for God no longer to delay bringing relief to Jerusalem. He refers to ending the seventy-year period of exile announced in Jeremiah's prophecy (vv. 3–19). In answer to Daniel's petition (vv. 20–23), the angel Gabriel is dispatched to lay out in an angelic discourse the course of events that will finally bring relief to the Judeans (vv. 24–27). In an obscure reinterpretation of Jeremiah's prophecy, the seventy years are transformed into seventy weeks of years, at the end of which the desolation will cease.

INTRODUCTION (9:1-2)

> In the first year of Darius, son of Ahasuerus, of Median descent, who was made king over the kingdom of the Chaldeans, ² in the first year of his reign, I, Daniel, discerned in the books the number of the years that the word of Yahweh had revealed to Jeremiah the prophet for the fulfillment of the desolation of Jerusalem, namely, seventy years.

The text is dated to the first year of Darius the Mede (v. 1), whose identity is historically debated (see comments on Dan 6:1-2). Darius is represented here as the son of Ahasuerus, another name for Xerxes I (486–465), who reigned after the date given in this text. This date would be c. 539/38 BCE, approximately the time when, according to Jeremiah's prophecy, the seventy years would end. "When Babylon's seventy years are completed . . . I will fulfil to you the promise and bring you back to this place [Jerusalem]" (Jer 29:10). The previous chapter 8, with which chapter 9 is linked, is dated to the third year of Belshazzar, or about twelve years earlier. Such chronology is confusing, but we remember the action in the book is set against the

---

3. For other parallels, see Newsom, *Daniel*, 287-88.

sixth-century transition between the Babylonian and Achaemenid empires, while the actual historical composition and redaction of the book took place in Palestine in the second-century Hellenistic era, when most of Dan 7–12 was probably written.

Here Daniel is concerned about oracles in the book of Jeremiah that predict the desolation of Jerusalem (587 BCE) would last seventy years (v. 2).[4] This is interestingly the first reference in the HB where books (סְפָרִים, *sepharim*) are spoken of in the sense of scriptural writings.[5] Does this allude to the process of canonization that two centuries later (late first century CE) would eventually shape the complete HB with its three familiar sections, the Torah, Prophets, and Writings? It is certainly worth pondering. The *sepharim* to which Daniel refers are certainly considered sacred prophetic writings.

Having read the scroll of Jeremiah, Daniel is evidently trying to figure out whether the end of the predicted seventy-year period is drawing near. "This whole land," Jeremiah had written, "shall become a ruin and a waste, and these nations shall serve the king of Babylon seventy years. Then after seventy years are completed, I will punish the king of Babylon and that nation, the land of the Chaldeans, for their iniquity" (Jer 25:11-12). Since Babylon had already passed off the scene, Daniel muses, the predicted time must be near an end.[6] Although neither of Jeremiah's references mention the temple, Daniel understands Jeremiah's prophecy to point to the restoration of Judah's independence and sovereignty as it had been before the Babylonians destroyed Jerusalem. Following Daniel's prayer, and in response to his concerns about the period of exile, the angelic intermediary Gabriel offers a complex reinterpretation of the seventy years, now understood as "seventy weeks [of years?]" (Dan 9:24-27).

The sacred name Yahweh now occurs for the first time in the book. All occurrences to Yahweh in Daniel appear in this one chapter.[7] I have left the name Yahweh in the text wherever it occurs in the translation. Why only here? Since the subject matter of the chapter concerns the temple, the holy city Jerusalem, and the people Israel, the author may feel comfortable

---

4. Jer 25:8-14; 29:10-11.

5. Lacocque, *Book of Daniel*, 179; Anderson, *Signs and Wonders*, 105. See 2 Pet 1:19-21; the prologue to Sirach.

6. The figure seventy in Jeremiah's prophecy is probably not to be taken literally, hence the difficulty of figuring out the starting point of the prophecy (605? 587?). The book of Daniel seems to take the beginning point as c. 605 BCE and its end point around c. 538-535. Being a multiple of seven, however, it probably indicates a complete or exhaustive period, perhaps something like an entire lifetime rather than an exact period. See also Jer 29:10-11; Zech 1:12; Ps 90:10; 2 Chr 36:20-22.

7. Dan. 9:2, 8, 10, 13, 14, 20.

enough to use the sacred Tetragrammaton (יהוה, YHWH = *Yahweh*). In the previous vision reports and other narratives, which deal with interaction with other nations, the Tetragrammaton is withheld in favor of more generic titles, such as the Most High, particularly as these appear on the lips of gentiles. In addition, since the chapter draws upon various scriptural texts, such as Deuteronomy and Jeremiah, books where the Tetragrammaton is much in evidence, the author employs it here. Daniel is unquestioningly praying to Yahweh, the only God of Israel, on Israel's behalf.

DANIEL'S PRAYER (9:3–19)

> ³ I set my face to the Lord God to seek by prayer and supplication with fasting and sackcloth and ashes. ⁴ I prayed to Yahweh my God, confessed and said, "Ah, Lord, great and awesome one, keeper of the covenant and kindness for those who love him and keep his commandments, ⁵ we have sinned and committed iniquity, acted culpably and rebelled, and turned from your commandments and judgments. ⁶ We have not listened to your servants the prophets who spoke in your name to our kings, our princes, and our ancestors, and to all the people of the land."

The penitential prayer (vv. 3–19) begins in first person (v. 3). It falls into two parts. The first (vv. 4–14) deals with confession of sin and guilt, while the second (vv. 15–19) contains a petition for mercy and the restoration of the holy city. Daniel prepares for prayer in the customary ritual manner, with fasting and sackcloth and ashes. From these opening lines, we note the prayer will be about penitence, confession, and forgiveness, sought on behalf of Israel and on behalf of Daniel himself as a constituent of Israel. Seeing himself as a representative (v. 20), Daniel humbly, penitently takes upon himself the sin of his people, and shifts to we instead of I. This prayer is unlike anything else in Daniel, and since its style of Hebrew prose is superior to the Hebrew in the rest of Daniel, some scholars think the prayer is a later addition.[8] Since Hebrew writers often inserted prayers into narratives where they felt prayers appropriate, it is entirely reasonable to find here an

---

8. Plöger, *Buch Daniel*, 135; Fohrer, *Introduction to Old Testament*, 477; Porteous, *Daniel*, 135; Lacocque, *Book of Daniel*, 178; Crenshaw, *Story and Faith*, 370. Note how seamlessly v. 21 follows v. 2, and that vv. 3 and 20 appear like seams to smooth the incorporation of the prayer into vv. 4–19. The prayer itself linguistically is a type of Hebrew uninfluenced by Aramaic, unlike the Hebrew in the rest of the book. That the Tetragrammaton in the book of Daniel is confined to this prayer also suggests the prayer may well come from another source and is incorporated here.

example of this practice. Other examples may be found in both the OT and NT.[9] In this case, whatever the source of the prayer, it has been adapted (redacted) to this context. The result is an almost seamless text.

Addressing Yahweh, Daniel draws upon themes central to Israel's faith (v. 4). Yahweh is great and awesome, he extols, the Keeper of the covenant, who exercises kindness toward those who love and keep his commandments.

Nevertheless, Israel has committed iniquity, turning from Yahweh's Torah. Everyone in the nation—our kings, our princes, and our ancestors, and to all the people of the land—is guilty (vv. 5–6). From high to low, royal elite to peasant, everyone stands guilt-ridden before Yahweh. Verbs describing Israel's past infidelities are piled high. We have sinned and committed iniquity, acted culpably, rebelled, and turned away from your commandments and judgments. We have failed to listen to your prophets who spoke in your name. "It reads almost like a lexicon entry," remarks Anderson, "yet this effusive confession of past misdemeanours was not without some basis."[10]

> [7] "Righteousness belongs to you, O Lord, but to us is confusion of face as at this day, to the people of Judah, the inhabitants of Jerusalem, and all Israel who are near and far in all the lands where you have banished them for their treachery that they have committed against you. [8] O Yahweh, ours is confusion of face, to our kings, our princes, and our ancestors, because we have sinned against you. [9] To the Lord our God belong mercy and forgiveness, for we have rebelled against him. [10] Nor have we obeyed the voice of Yahweh our God to walk in his laws that he set before us by the hand of his servants the prophets."

The prayer recalls the long history of rebellion which had shaped Israel's spiritual and moral life up until the exile. Behind these words we hear the stentorian voice of Amos, "For three transgressions of Israel, and for four, I will not revoke the punishment" (Amos 2:6); the pleading of Hosea, "My people consult a piece of wood . . . for a spirit of whoredom has led them astray, and they have played the whore, forsaking their God" (Hos 4:12); or the thunderous voice of Isaiah, "Ah, you who call evil good and good evil, who put darkness for light and light for darkness, who put bitter for sweet and sweet for bitter!" (Isa 5:20). "I have sent to you all my servants the prophets," cries Jeremiah, "do not go after other gods . . . but you did not incline your ear or obey me" (Jer 35:15). Blatant wickedness and treachery had so filled Israel's life, corrupting it, particularly among the leaders, the

---

9. E.g., 1 Sam 2:1–10; Jonah 2:1–10; Luke 1:46–55; 2:29–32.
10. Anderson, *Signs and Wonders*, 107.

future now looked confused and doomed (v. 7). The prayer recalls moments when our kings, our princes, and our ancestors had turned from following the Lord and entered devious paths. Israel had turned a deaf ear to the earnest pleas of its prophets (vv. 8–9). Failure to hear—and to obey—was the constant message of the prophets. The long history of apostasy takes many forms, but according to the Deuteronomistic history (Joshua—2 Kings), it eventually led to the downfall of the nation (v. 10), first of the northern kingdom, Israel, and then of the southern, Judah, a century and a half later.[11] The pattern of disobedience continued unabated "until the Lord removed Israel out of his sight, as he had foretold through all his servants the prophets. So Israel was exiled from their own land to Assyria until this day" (2 Kgs 17:23). There were, of course, political miscalculations that figured in the demise of both Israel and Judah, but the prophets understood these to be rooted ultimately in unfaithfulness, the fracturing of the sacred covenant.

Daniel, on his part, assumes in prayer the corporate sin of the people. But in the middle of his confession, we begin to hear the note of mercy, pardon, and grace that must be the last word in the human encounter with God.[12] Without divine mercy, no person can survive the confusion and moral decay of life.

Reference to the Torah (laws) and the prophets, as noted above, suggests these two collections of the HB were relatively complete by the second-century BCE writing of Dan 9 and may offer a clue regarding the date of this material. The Torah, of course, refers to what Christians call the Pentateuch (see v. 13), while the Prophets are the collection of prophetic writings represented in the books Joshua, Judges, Samuel, Kings, and Isaiah–Malachi. These two collections within the canon were complete by c. 175 BCE, the Torah having reached its completion earlier by around 450 BCE.[13] Because the prayer consists of a pastiche of citations and allusions (known as intertexts) largely from the prophets and the Torah,[14] these works must have

---

11. See 2 Kgs 17:7–23; on the Southern Kingdom, 25:1–21.

12. See Exod 34:6–7.

13. The earliest reference to the Torah and the Prophets as collections in the HB comes from ben Sira (Sirach) in the first part of the second century. The development of the third section of the HB, the Writings, was probably complete by the end of the first century CE.

14. Several allusions to Lev 26, a passage containing the rewards and penalties of the covenant, occur in Dan 9: Lev 26:13 (Dan 9:15a); Lev 26:14–15 (Dan 9:5); Lev 26:15, 42 (Dan 9:1–11); Lev 26:31–33 (Dan 9:17–18). Since Lev 26 plays a significant role in the interpretation of the vision in Dan 9:24–27, Newsom surmises, "perhaps the author is already foreshadowing the important conjunction of these two texts [Jer 29 and Lev 26]" (Newsom, *Daniel*, 293).

been known to the writer, which suggests this chapter probably dates to the second century.[15]

> [11] "All Israel has transgressed your law and turned aside so as not to obey your voice, so you have placed upon us the curse and the oath which is written in the law of Moses, the servant of God, because we have sinned against him. [12] He has confirmed his word which he spoke against us and against our judges who governed us, to bring upon us great calamity as was done in Jerusalem that has never been done under the whole heaven. [13] Just as written in the law of Moses, all this calamity has come upon us, but we have not entreated Yahweh our God by turning from our iniquities and comprehending your truth. [14] Yahweh has kept watch over the calamity, and he brought it upon us, for Yahweh our God is just concerning all his deeds he has done, but we have not obeyed his voice."

Daniel looks to the stipulations of the covenant defining Israel's relation to God. Specifically, he mentions the blessings and curses associated with the covenant.[16] Israel had violated the sacred covenant (v. 11). Justly then, God's verdict had fallen upon them through the destruction of the nation, its temple, and the subsequent exile to Babylon (v. 12). Moreover, despite all, Israel had not turned back to God, nor comprehended that Yahweh was faithful to his word (v. 13). So, the consequence for this treachery—the exile—continued unabated, as in Jeremiah, "I am going to watch over them for harm and not for good" (Jer 44:27).

> [15] "Now, O Lord our God, who brought out your people from the land of Egypt by a mighty hand, you have made a name for yourself as at this day—we have sinned, we have acted wickedly. [16] O Lord, according to all your righteousness, let your anger and wrath turn away from your city Jerusalem, your holy mountain; because of our sins and the iniquities of our ancestors, Jerusalem and your people are a disgrace to all those around us. [17] Now, O our God, listen to the prayer of your servant and to his supplication—for your sake—and let your face shine upon your devastated sanctuary. [18] Incline your ear, O my God, and listen! Open your eyes and look at our desolation and the city upon which your name is called, for we do not thrust our supplication before you on the ground of our righteousness, but on the ground of your great mercies. [19] My Lord, listen! My Lord,

---

15. Collins dates the chapter to the end of 167 or early 166 BCE (J. Collins, *Daniel* [FOTL 22], 92).

16. See Deut 28:2–68; Lev. 26:1–45.

forgive! Listen and do not delay for your sake, O my God, because your name is pronounced over your city and your people."

Nearing the climax of the prayer, Daniel sets forth his petition (vv. 15-16). The petition is grounded not in human worthiness, but in the divine righteousness that justifies even the ungodly (see Rom 4:5). With the deliverance of Israel from Egypt in mind, he pleads for the restoration of Jerusalem and its devastated temple (vv. 17-18). Three terse Hebrew mandates characterize this part of the prayer (v. 19): "My Lord, hear! My Lord, forgive! My Lord, listen!" There is sheer desperation in this cry, as though everything now hangs on this petition. Daniel is insistent he be heard. May this be granted, or he and his people will perish! He is like the importunate widow of Jesus's parable, who kept bothering the judge until he relented (Luke 18:2-5). In the end, the prayer appeals to God's honor.

These words, of course, recall the fall of Jerusalem and the demolishing of the temple in 587 BCE, when the Babylonian armies crashed through the city walls and ended up putting the torch to the magnificent temple, pride of Israel. Following the return from Babylonian exile, the temple had been rebuilt (515 BCE; see Ezra 6:13-15). By the time of the writing of Daniel's prayer, the second temple had been once more violated by the abolition of the sacred sacrificial rituals and the substitution for them by the altar to the Olympian Zeus erected on the altar of burnt offerings in the temple courtyard. Daniel's prayer thus focuses on the restoration of the neglected second temple and its rites. As the Maccabees approached the temple following the victories over the Seleucids, "they saw the sanctuary desolate, the altar profaned." In the courtyard they witnessed "bushes sprung up as in a thicket . . . the chambers of the priests in ruins" (1 Macc 4:38). Daniel pleads with Yahweh not to delay, not to hesitate any longer in restoring the temple and its services.

The prayer (Dan 9:3-19) in this chapter comes in place of a vision report, unlike other chapters in the apocalyptic section (chs. 7—12). This prayer focuses on the desolated temple and hopes for its purification and reconsecration. Emphasis falls upon national apostasy, here in true Deuteronomic fashion the reason why the temple has been desecrated. The prayer pleads for God's mercy and grace to be bestowed upon Israel and for the temple to be restored.

> [20] While I was speaking, praying and confessing my sin and the sin of my people Israel and presenting my supplication before Yahweh my God on behalf of the holy mountain of my God, [21] while I was speaking in prayer, the man Gabriel, whom I had seen in vision at the beginning, being utterly weary, touched me,

at the time of the evening sacrifice. ²² He gave me attention and spoke, "Daniel, I have now come forth to give you insight in understanding. ²³ At the beginning of your supplications a word went out and I have come to declare that you are precious. So, consider the word and understand the vision.

As in other chapters containing a vision report, a heavenly messenger—Gabriel—approaches Daniel. Verse 20 offers a summary of the prayer and a transition into what follows. The interpretation does not concern the content of the prayer but instead Daniel's plea that restoring the holy mountain of God be hastened (vv. 20–21). Gabriel is evidently dispatched at the beginning of Daniel's prayer, emphasizing God's rapid response to his petition.[17] In conjunction with this timely arrival, we come across a curious phrase, here translated "being utterly weary." Since we have no criterion for measuring the weariness of an angel, this must be a reference to Daniel's psychological and physical state. Our translation of מֻעָף בִּיעָף (*muaph biaph*) as being utterly weary is thus provisional. The phrase may be dittography, a word written a second time, usually by accident, or perhaps intentionally to intensify by repetition, as I have tried to reflect in the translation. The ancient Greek versions take it to refer to the rapidity of Gabriel's flight. The LXX translates the phrase as τάχει φερόμενος προσήγγισέ μοι (*tachei pheromenos prosegnise moi*, "being borne in speed he approached me").

Gabriel arrives at the time of the evening sacrifice, one of the two daily regular offerings prohibited by the little horn, Antiochus IV.[18] By the Hellenistic era, the routine of the daily offering had become an appropriate time for prayer for many of the devout.[19] Gabriel has come to give Daniel understanding about the word and the vision. These two terms must be equivalent, and no doubt refer to the revelation in verses 24–27. He speaks of Daniel as precious in God's sight, a particularly endearing term, חֲמֻדוֹת (*hamudot*, preciousness), like gold or something unbelievably valuable. Three times this adjective describes Daniel (9:23; 10:11, 19), putting emphasis on his resolute, faithful character (vv. 22–23). The court tales preceding the apocalyptic visions and even the Additions following in the LXX and Theodotion texts demonstrate Daniel's legendary, worthy character to receive a revelation about the course of human events. God values human trust and fidelity.

---

17. "Before they call I will answer, while they are yet speaking I will hear" (Isa 65:24). Some scholars question the relationship between Daniel's prayer and the context in which it is placed (see Jones, "Prayer in Daniel 9"). Our position is that the angel's interpretation in Dan 9:24–27 is precisely a response to Daniel's prayer about the duration of the Babylonian captivity.

18. See Dan 8:11–14; 2 Kgs 16:14; Ezra 9:4–5.

19. See Ezra 9:3–5; Jdt 9:1; Luke 1:10.

THE SEVENTY WEEKS (9:24-27)

> ²⁴ "Seventy weeks are decreed for your people, and for your holy city, to complete the transgression, to finish sin, to atone for iniquity, to bring in everlasting righteousness, to seal the vision and prophet, and to anoint the most holy place. ²⁵ Know therefore and understand from the going forth of the word to restore and rebuild Jerusalem until an anointed ruler will be seven weeks; and for sixty-two weeks it will again be built with a plaza and moat, even in troublous times. ²⁶ After the sixty-two weeks, the anointed one will be cut off and have nothing, and the people of the ruler will destroy the city and the sanctuary. ²⁷ He will confirm a covenant with many for one week, and for half of the week he will cause sacrifice and offering to cease. And upon the wing of the detested thing causing horror, even until the annihilation, and the decreed end is poured out upon the desolator."

We come now to the most challenging passage in the book. Montgomery calls it the "Dismal Swamp" of Old Testament research.[20] This obscure passage, complains Young, is "one of the most difficult in all the OT, and the interpretations which have been offered are almost legion."[21] "There is no more intricate problem in Old Testament study," Francisco adds, "than the interpretation of Daniel 9:24–27."[22] More cynically, Freedman questions the interpretation being offered within the passage itself. It incorporates an esoteric interpretation that moves away from a literal understanding of Jeremiah's words (in Jer 29:10) to a reinterpretation applying Jeremiah's seventy years to the entire history of Israel down to the Danielic author's own time. "It does not seem possible that scholars can accept this approach to an understanding of the Scriptures," he goes on to say, "and as men of faith and commitment to religious truth, we have no need to."[23]

Even a casual reading of verses 24–27 confirms what these scholars intuit: this passage becomes more confusing and murkier the further one reads, until the entire passage, it seems, lapses into almost complete obscurity. The passage has naturally been subject to a wide variety of interpretation.[24] Our approach is to set forth briefly the major contemporary interpretations, then

---

20. Montgomery, *Critical and Exegetical Commentary*, xxiii, 400.
21. Young, *Prophecy of Daniel*, 191.
22. Francisco, "Seventy Weeks of Daniel," 126.
23. Freedman, "On Method in Biblical Studies," 1:157.
24. For a review of the interpretation and reception history of Dan 9:24–27, see Newsom, *Daniel*, 309–20.

read these verses in the light of the historical circumstances of the book of Daniel. We may conveniently organize the various interpretations into four categories, each varying in understanding the overall sense of the passage and the dates assigned to the events mentioned.[25]

1. The *idealistic-symbolic* interpretation. Apocalyptic writing makes use of varied, complex symbolism. The numbers in this passage, sevens, tens, multiples of seven, etc., are frequently used with a symbolic function in apocalyptic texts. Taking a clue from this use of symbolism, some scholars accordingly regard Dan 9:24-27 as a highly symbolic text concerned with a view of the history of salvation (*Heilsgeschichte*) or the history of God's saving acts, as portrayed in the Bible, divided into three epochs. The first part, the seven weeks, commences with the decree of Cyrus (538 BCE) and extends to the first advent of Jesus. The sixty-two weeks then covers the history of the church—symbolized by the city of Jerusalem—and the last one week conveys the struggle with the deadly antichrist so forcefully expressed in Dan 9:27 leading to the consummation of human history. That Daniel "thus announces the times of the development of the future consummation of the kingdom of God and of this world according to a measure that is symbolical and not chronological, does not in the least degree lose its character as a revelation," concludes Keil, "but thereby first rightly proves its high origin as divine, and beyond the reach of human thought."[26] Daniel 9:24-27, in other words, does not offer "chronological information. It is not chronology but chronography: a stylized scheme of history used to interpret historical data rather than arising from them."[27] The time periods in this view are considered symbolic numbers; they do not require historical precision.

2. The *futurist-dispensationalist* interpretation. The popular futurist-dispensationalist interpretation of the seventy weeks, also known as the gap or parenthesis theory, draws upon the systematizing work of John N. Darby (1800-1882), a Plymouth Brethren leader whose ideas greatly influenced late nineteenth-century millenarianism (speculation about the millennium or one thousand years in Rev. 20).[28] This school of thought gets its name from Darby's organization of history into separate eras or dispensations.

---

25. I have here adapted the typology of Jacques Doukhan ("Seventy Weeks of Daniel 9," 1-3) and Gerhard Hasel ("Seventy Weeks of Daniel 9:24-27," 1D-21D).

26. Keil, *Ezekiel, Daniel*, 1:400. Other representatives of this general view are Klieforth, *Buch Daniel*; Leupold, *Exposition of Daniel*, 406-9.

27. Goldingay, *Daniel*, 257.

28. For the development of dispensationalism, see Froom, *Prophetic Faith*, 4:1220-27; 3:585-87, 655-65.

Each dispensation represents a different stage in the divine-human relationship, a "step in the revelation of God's truth."[29]

According to the dispensationalist schema, the seventy weeks, understood as seventy weeks of years, represent the period during which the pedagogy or spiritual training of Israel would come to an end, and the nation finally be re-established in everlasting righteousness. Dispensationalism, which is really a variety of the futurist approach (see the introduction), breaks down the seventy weeks of years into three parts: seven plus sixty-two plus one. The first seven weeks, or forty-nine (seven times seven) years, extends from the official Persian dispatch of Nehemiah (445/444 BCE) to the rebuilding and restoration of Jerusalem.[30] Sixty-two plus seven weeks (= 483 years) also reaches from this point (445/444) to the crucifixion of Christ (c. 33 CE). "Then after the sixty-two weeks the Messiah will be cut off and have nothing" (v. 26 NASB).[31]

Following all this comes an indefinite period, an interval between the sixty-nine weeks of years and the final week of years known as the great parenthesis or the Church Age. Dispensationalists, in other words, shift the seventieth week of Daniel's prophecy (Dan 9:27)—"by the well-accepted OT phenomenon of prophetic perspective"[32]—to the final period of earth's history, producing a gap or parenthesis in the seventy-week prophecy extending for more than two thousand years. "During the interim between the sixty-ninth and seventieth weeks," states the *New Scofield Reference Bible*, "there must lie the whole period of the Church set forth in the N.T., but not revealed in the O.T."[33] In this period occurs the great tribulation, referred to by Jesus (Matt 24:21). The mysteries of the kingdom of heaven will be accomplished, and the calling out of the church from the world completed. When this long period or gap ends and the final, seventieth week of years begins, is

---

29. Erickson, *Contemporary Options in Eschatology*, 110.

30. Neh 2:1–10. Most historians date Nehemiah's arrival in Jerusalem to 445 BCE. On the history of this event, see J. Miller and Hayes, *History of Ancient Israel*, 469–72.

31. Wood, *Daniel*, 254–56. The above calculations are those of Thomas Ice, "Seventy Weeks of Daniel," 319–45.

32. S. Miller, *Daniel*, 269. By prophetic perspective, Miller means "gaps such as that between the first and second advents were not perceived." The prophecy, in other words, may have in view a significant event such as the Christ event, and then pass over other events of lesser importance to telescope into a second significant event such as the second advent. Miller provides an extensive discussion of this interpretation (S. Miller, *Daniel*, 269–73).

33. Scofield et al., *New Scofield Reference Bible*, Dan 9:24n1. See also Archer, "Daniel," 113; Walvoord, *Daniel*, 235–37; Wood, *Daniel*, 261–63. This view is based on the idea that the last week of this vision is "projected beyond history's horizon" (Sims, "Daniel," 333).

not revealed. During this final seven-year period, the struggle with the Antichrist (the same entity as the little horn in Dan 7), the conversion of the Jews to Christ, and earth's final great cataclysmic tribulation transpire.[34] Either preceding this seventieth week, or during it, a secret rapture, a preliminary arrival of Christ, will occur to gather all true believers into the kingdom of God.[35] Christ will later return to establish a literal thousand-year kingdom on earth.[36] "With Israel today back in the land," writes Walvoord, "the fulfillment of these prophecies may not be too long distant."[37]

The futurist-dispensationalist interpretation has been widely popularized by the *Scofield Reference Bible* (1909/1967) and in more recent times by the *Left Behind* series of Christian novels (1995–2003) by Tim LaHaye and Jerry Johnson. It represents, no doubt, the most intricate, complicated calculation of the seventy weeks. The dispensationalist interpretation has widely influenced evangelical and fundamentalist eschatological speculation,[38] probably because it gives assurance of the fulfillment of Daniel (and Revelation) and thus of the eschatological hopes of fundamentalist and evangelical Christians.

3. The *historicist-messianic* interpretation. This view represents a longstanding, traditional reading of Dan 9. Most of the Church Fathers and many of the older commentators find the Messiah in these verses. In this view, the first two chronological divisions in chapter 9 (seven plus sixty-two weeks of years) start with the seventh year of Artaxerxes I (458/457 BCE), rather than with Nehemiah's official arrival in Jerusalem (445/444), and culminate with the baptism of Jesus (c. 27 CE). The seventieth week then divides into two parts, the first part—half of the week or three and a half years—extends to Christ's crucifixion (c. 31 CE), the second three and a half years terminates at c. 34 CE with the stoning of Stephen, the first Christian

---

34. Scofield et al., *New Schofield Reference Bible*, 914–15; Archer, "Daniel," 116–19; Gaebelein, *Daniel*, 143–51. Cf. Robert C. Fuller, who offers a description of this view without advocating it (Fuller, *Naming the Antichrist*, 122). For a discussion of dispensationalism and its relation to the millennium, see Robert G. Clouse, *Meaning of the Millennium*.

35. On the rapture, see Barbara Rossing, *Rapture Exposed*, 19–25.

36. Hoffecker, "Darby, John Nelson," 292–93. See J. Pentecost, *Things to Come* (1958); Ryrie, *Dispensationalism Today* (1965); Walvoord, *Daniel*, 234–37.

37. Walvoord, *Daniel*, 237; cf. S. Miller, *Daniel*, 270; Wood, *Daniel*, 260; Talbot, *Prophecies of Daniel*, 168–73.

38. Note Erickson: "Because the rise of dispensationalism roughly paralleled that of the fundamentalist movement, it became virtually the official theology of fundamentalism . . . . Some have made it a test of orthodoxy" (*Contemporary Options in Eschatology*, 109).

martyr.[39] Thus, the seventy weeks terminate in the Christ-event,[40] that is, the coming of the Messiah into history.

4. The *historical-critical* interpretation. Critical scholars assume all Daniel's visions, including Dan 9:24–27, conclude with events in or closely following the time of Antiochus IV Epiphanes (175–164 BCE),[41] the Seleucid king who suppressed the Jewish religion by proscribing the Torah and eliminating the sacrificial rituals at the temple (Dan 7:23–25; 8:9–14).[42] This, of course, is the historical setting of Daniel, as we have noted.

None of these principal interpretations of Dan 9:24–27 is without difficulties. Chronological, semantic, theological, textual—intractable exegetical issues—hamper interpreters at every turn. None can make the time calculations fit exactly known historical events. Even with our present knowledge of apocalyptic literature, consensus on the precise meaning of this passage still eludes us. In general, it concerns affairs transpiring in the Maccabean era, the times of Antiochus IV (175–164. BCE), and indicates the impending ruin of this tyrannical ruler. If this assessment is correct, the critical interpretation is the most viable since it makes a serious effort to understand the vision against the historical background of the composition. Accordingly, we will follow the historical-critical approach in these verses (vv. 24–27).

"Seventy weeks are decreed for your people" (v. 24). The people mentioned here are the Jewish exiles, for whom a period of שָׁבֻעִים שִׁבְעִים (*shavuim shivim*, seventy sevens or seventy weeks), has been decreed.[43] How are we to understand the seventy weeks? (The Hebrew term שָׁבוּעַ, *shabua*, indicates both seven and a week of seven days.) Three traditional motifs combine in this vision. The number seventy recalls the seventy years allotted in Jeremiah for the exile of Judah,[44] mentioned at the beginning of Daniel's prayer (Dan 9:2). The figure seventy, originally applied to the Babylonian exile, is intensified here by a multiplication of seven (seventy times seven).

---

39. The dating of the stoning of Stephen is approximate (see Acts 7:54–60).

40. The precise dates of Jesus's life are uncertain. He was probably born c. 7 or 6 BCE, a few years before the death of Herod the Great (4 BCE). He began his ministry near the end of 27 or 28 CE. He was crucified in April of 30 CE (Meier, *Marginal Jew*, 1:406–9).

41. This interpretation (see J. Collins, *Daniel* [Hermeneia], 352–57) is supported by many Jewish scholars (see Slotki, *Daniel*, 77–79). Cf. Russell, *Daniel*, 183–92.

42. See Niskanen, "Daniel's Portrait."

43. Decreed is a translation of חָתַךְ, *hatak*, which only appears here in the HB. In later rabbinical literature it usually has the sense of cut off, dissect, or sever, but also decide, which arguably is its sense in Dan 9:24 (Jastrow, "חָתַךְ," *Dictionary of the Targumim*, 1:513). The LXX translates this as ἐκρίθησαν, *ekrithesan*, decided.

44. Jer 25:11–12; 29:10.

We find a similar intensification in Leviticus. "If in spite of this you will not obey me, I will continue to punish you sevenfold [שֶׁבַע, *sheba*, seven(fold)], for your sins" (Lev 26:18).

The number seven also suggests the sabbatical year, the seventh year in which the land had to remain fallow. "Six years you shall sow your field . . . but in the seventh year there shall be a sabbath of complete rest for the land" (Lev 25:4). Seventy weeks would equal ten such sabbaticals. "You shall count off seven weeks of years, seven times seven years, so that the period of seven weeks of years gives forty-nine years" (v. 8). During the Jubilee year, which came at the end of a cycle of forty-nine years (in the fiftieth year), the "land shall enjoy its sabbath years so long as it lies desolate, while you are in the land of your enemies [in exile]" (v. 34). Most interpreters thus take the seventy sevens or seventy weeks in Dan 9:24 to refer to seventy weeks of years, or hebdomads, as they are called.[45] Seventy weeks is thus to be understood as seventy weeks of years, rather than days, or in other words, 490 years, or ten times the Jubilee cycle of forty-nine years.

The Chronicler brings together these three motifs—the seventy years of captivity, the sabbatical year, and the Jubilee—to form the backdrop for the calculation in Dan 9. "He [Nebuchadnezzar] took into exile in Babylon . . . to fulfil the word of the Lord by the mouth of Jeremiah, until the land had made up for its sabbaths. All the days that it lay desolate it kept sabbath, to fulfill seventy years" (2 Chr 36:20-21). The seventy weeks in the vision are equal to ten times the sabbatical year, the 490 years equal to ten times the Jubilee period of forty-nine years. As Daniel begins his prayer, he is concerned about the seventy-year period—prophesied by Jeremiah—for the devastation of Jerusalem (Dan 9:2). The answer he receives, in short, is that the period will be lengthened tenfold.

The seventy weeks of years (490 years), we are told, begins from the "going forth of the word to restore and rebuild Jerusalem." We do not know exactly what this means, hence the "starting point [of the 490 years] is uncertain."[46] Is the word (דָּבָר, *dabar*) in this line considered to be of divine or human origin? Is this a divine decree, hidden from humanity, or a human one, and thus apparent to the reader? Verse 23 leads us to believe it is a

---

45. This usage is found in m. Sanh. 5.1; b. B. Meṣ. 9:10 and may have been prompted by the seven-year periods in Lev 25-26 (Porteous, *Daniel*, 140). The example of Jacob having to serve Laban another week before he could marry Rachel, may be cited. In this example, the one week, or seven days, of Jacob's service is understood as seven years (Gen 29:19-30). Doukhan points to the chiastic relationship between seventy years in Dan 9:2 and seventy weeks in v. 24 as an indication the seventy weeks are to be taken as seventy weeks of years ("Seventy Weeks of Daniel 9," 17). See also Brugmann, "Interkalation in den Sieben Jahrwochen," 67-81.

46. J. Collins, *Daniel* (Hermeneia), 354.

divine word, for Gabriel comes from heaven to Daniel to announce it. If so, it is a divine word that directly affects the human realm, where it is carried out by human agency.[47] Human initiative becomes the method by which a heavenly decree is carried out.

The edict of the Persian monarch Cyrus II in 539/538 BCE, which effectively ended the Babylonian exile, authorizing the Judean exiles to return to their homeland, is understood by the biblical writers as such a divine word mediated through human agency. Ezra describes the decree: "In the first year of king Cyrus of Persia, in order that the word of the Lord by the mouth of Jeremiah might be accomplished, the Lord stirred up the spirit of King Cyrus of Persia so that he sent a herald throughout all his kingdom" announcing a return of Judah to Jerusalem (Ezra 1:1–4). The famous Cyrus Cylinder, while not specifically mentioning this decree, tells how Cyrus restored many of the sanctuaries and holy sites of other nations and "gathered all their (former) inhabitants and returned (to them) their habitations."[48] Because of the importance of this edict for the Judean exiles, many interpreters have identified the decree of Cyrus as the one alluded to in Daniel.[49] The decree of Cyrus II, allowing the Judean exiles to return to Jerusalem, thus seems best to fit the start of the seventy weeks.[50]

According to verse 24, seventy weeks of years (490 years) is the time decreed or marked out in the vision, at the end of which six divine actions—three negative, three positive—are to be accomplished.[51] The three negative actions have to do with iniquity; the three positives, "restorative transformation."[52] Negatively, there is to be (1) a completion of the transgression; (2) a finishing or end of sin; and (3) an atoning for iniquity. Positively, there will be (4) a bringing in everlasting righteousness; (5) a sealing of the vision and prophet; and (6) an anointing of the most holy place.

---

47. Young, *Prophecy of Daniel*, 201–2.
48. "Cyrus Cylinder," translated by A. Leo Oppenheim (*ANET*, 316).
49. Porteous, *Daniel*, 141. According to Doukhan, the decree could theoretically refer to any of the three decrees mentioned in Ezra authorizing restoration of Jerusalem and the temple: that of Cyrus (Ezra 1:1–4) [538 BCE]; Darius I (6:6–12) [520 BCE]; or Artaxerxes I (7:12–26) [458 BCE]. Doukhan prefers the latter, which he dates to 457 BCE ("Seventy Weeks of Daniel 9," 15–16).
50. All told, there would be three returns from Babylon: 538–536; 458/457; and 445 BCE, corresponding to the dates mentioned above.
51. The obvious determinism in this prediction contrasts sharply with the conditional volition in the prayer that precedes it. This tension is never fully resolved. See Jones, "Prayer in Daniel 9," 493.
52. Newsom, *Daniel*, 301–2.

Taking all six events together, they seem to represent the actions necessary to fulfill an eschatological ideal.[53]

Although the text does not disclose what the completion of the transgression or the finish of sin entails, the two infinitives employed may be related. They may refer to the desecration of the temple by the Syrians under Antiochus IV, along with the abandonment of the covenant by the complicit Jewish Hellenizers at the same time.[54] According to Dan 8:23, "at the end of their rule, when the transgressors have reached their full end, a king of bold countenance will arise." Evil acts on the part of foreign rulers must run their course and exhaust themselves.

By using the word כִּפֶּר (*kipper*, atone), to atone for inquity, with God as the implied subject, this indicates the covering, canceling, or absolving of iniquity. To "bring in everlasting righteousness" (צֶדֶק עֹלָמִים, *tsedek olamim*) is a phrase occurring only here in the HB. It must be somewhat equivalent to the expression צֶדֶק לְעוֹלָם (*tsedek le-olam*): "Your righteousness is an everlasting righteousness and your law is the truth" (Ps 119:142). It stands in positive contrast to the putting to an end of sin and iniquity. To seal the vision and prophet refers to verifying or authenticating the vision, or prophecy of Jeremiah, which is under discussion here.[55] The two terms in this line, vision and prophet, are synonymous.[56]

Finally, to anoint the most holy place (קֹדֶשׁ קָדָשִׁים, *qodesh qadoshim*, most holy things or most holy site) no doubt refers to the purification and rededication of thetTemple in 164 BCE by Judas Maccabee from the Antiochus IV's desecration, an event described in 1 Macc 4:36-51 and 2 Macc 10:1-8. "See, our enemies are crushed; let us go up to cleanse the sanctuary and dedicate it . . . . They cleansed the sanctuary and removed the defiled stones" (1 Macc 4:36-43). While the expression "most holy" is used generally of consecrated things, it is also used of the temple or parts thereof,[57] which seems to be its significance here.

Gabriel now places these events in a chronological structure of seventy weeks. From the going forth of the word to restore and rebuild Jerusalem until an anointed ruler establishes the *terminus a quo* (beginning point) of the seventy weeks (490 years) (v. 25). The 490 weeks of years are further

---

53. J. Collins, *Daniel* (Hermeneia), 353.

54. "In those days certain renegades came out from Israel and misled many, saying, 'Let us go and make a covenant with the Gentiles around us . . .' They joined with the Gentiles and sold themselves to do evil" (1 Macc 1:11-15); cf. Gen 15:16.

55. Newsom, *Daniel*, 302. See Dan 9:2; 1 Kgs 21:8; Jer 32:9-12.

56. Collins suggests this sealing or authentication may include not just Jeremiah but all eschatological prophecy (J. Collins, *Daniel* [Hermeneia], 354).

57. See Exod 30:10; Ezek 45:3.

broken down into distinct periods: sixty-two and seven weeks of years which, if added together, are sixty-nine weeks of years. The seven weeks or forty-nine years leads to an anointed ruler, while the sixty-two weeks of years (434 years) sees an anointed ruler cut off and the city and sanctuary (temple) destroyed. Finally, in the seventieth week, the hostile prince would make an agreement or alliance, and for half of the week (three and a half years), sacrifice and offering would cease. After this apparently comes the end of the prophecy.

Does this seem bewildering? Confusing?[58] Trying to make these numbers precisely fit the known facts of history is probably futile.[59] The numbers seven and ten and multiples thereof are often used symbolically in Scripture. Consider the dialogue between Jesus and Peter, as recounted in Matthew's gospel. "Lord, if another member of the church sins against me," Peter asks, "how often should I forgive?" Jesus replies, "Not seven times, but, I tell you, seventy times seven" (Matt 18:21–22). This passage uses the same calculation (70 x 7 = 490) appearing in Daniel, but Peter is not expected dutifully to check off his forgiveness list until he reaches exactly 490, then abruptly cease. The number 490 is a symbol of completeness both in Daniel and in the gospel text. That the 490 years does not fit exactly any known events in history is further reason to regard the period as a round number.[60]

Moreover, throughout the ancient Near East—as well as in the Bible—the number seven was regarded as significant, even sacred to the Egyptians, Assyrians, Persians, and the Vedic (Indian) peoples, as well as to Israel. Seven carried with it the implication of completeness.[61] In multiples, completeness is emphasized. Ten was also symbolic of fullness. The biblical writers often added seven (and ten) to a large number to multiply its size. Hence the seventy years of exile, mentioned at the beginning of this chapter, suggests a complete, full period of exile, covering a whole generation.[62] The original prophecy of Jeremiah—seventy years—itself a combination of seven and ten

---

58. As this interpretation stands, we do well to heed Newsom's words: "While the contemporary readers would have known the complex series of events referred to, the schematic details . . . are almost unintelligible to the modern reader without historical background" (Newsom, *Daniel*, 306).

59. See Adela Collins, "Numerical Symbolism."

60. Porteous, *Daniel*, 140.

61. Boring, "Numbers," 4:298–99. For seven, see Exod 20:13; 25:31–37. For ten, see Gen 28:22; Exod 20:2–17. For forty-nine, see the law of the jubilee: "You shall count off seven weeks of years, seven times seven years . . . forty-nine years" (Lev 25:8). In the jubilee year, slaves were freed, properties reverted to their original owners, and freedom proclaimed throughout the land. The theme of jubilee liberation flows through Dan 9:24–27.

62. Note 2 Chr 36:20–21, cited above.

is further extended by the multiple of seven to reach 490. Multiples of seven and ten are combined, evidently based on the covenant curse "If you continue to be hostile to me . . . I will continue to plague you sevenfold for your sins" (Lev 26:21).[63] The number 490 equals ten Jubilee years, the numbers ten and forty-nine both having symbolic significance.

What about the precise numbers in verses 25–27? The text further subdivides the seventy weeks: it will be seven weeks, and for sixty-two weeks. There will be seven weeks and then sixty-two weeks, for a total of sixty-nine. It is not clear whether these represent two separate, distinct periods, or whether they should be added together to make sixty-nine, at the end of which would come an anointed ruler (מָשִׁיחַ נָגִיד, *mashiah nagid*). If distinct periods, the sentence may read: "From the going forth of the word to return and build Jerusalem until the anointed ruler will be seven weeks." This means the anointed ruler—whoever is meant by this term—would come forty-nine years (seven times seven) after the mandate to rebuild Jerusalem. Following this, obviously from a different starting point, would come the sixty-two weeks of years.

The uncertainty over how the seven and sixty-two weeks of years are related stems from the placement of accents in the MT Hebrew text. When the Masoretic scribes during the medieval period placed vowel signs and accents in the Hebrew text (Hebrew was originally written without vowels or accents), they put a pausal accent, a small subscript wishbone-shaped mark, known as an *athnah*, equivalent to our semicolon or comma, under seven weeks,[64] separating this number from the sixty-two weeks. Young contends this accent mark must have been incorrectly placed. The two periods of time are to be read together without any pause. "The appearance of an anointed one, a prince, is a period of 69 sevens which is divided into two periods of unequal lengths, 7 sevens and 62 sevens." The first seven weeks of years, he reasons, extends to the end of the period of Ezra and Nehemiah (c. 445 BCE), the sixty-two weeks of years from the time of Ezra and Nehemiah to the time of Jesus.[65]

---

63. Waltke and Yu, *Old Testament Theology*, 550–51.

64. This accent, known as an *ahnah*, usually divides a sentence into two logical parts. In English, it would be equivalent to a semicolon, comma, or even a period.

65. Notice that the date 445 does equal the terminal point of the forty-nine years, which would literally be 489 BCE, if the first year of Cyrus (538) is the terminus a quo of the period. Young recognizes this difficulty but takes the seven sevens as a "symbolical number." He seems also to take the sixty-two weeks of years as symbolical when it designates the time of the messiah (Young, *Prophecy of Daniel*, 205–6). Cf. Waltke and Yu, *Old Testament Theology*, 552.

By removing the accent, Young exposes a messianic prediction. He adds the sixty-two and seven weeks together to make sixty-nine weeks of years (483 years) to reach the time of Christ. The anointed one (מָשִׁיחַ, *mashiah*, Messiah) in verse 26 is thus for Young and many conservative Christian scholars the Messiah (Jesus). If the accent mark is left in place in verse 26, on the other hand, the initial seven weeks would reach to the anointed one. Thus, "there is no justification for the Early Church's view that there is here a reference to Messiah, however natural at the time such an interpretation must have seemed."[66] Moreover, since the date of the commencement of the seventy weeks is unknown, the beginning dates of the seven and sixty-two weeks would likewise be undetermined.

The failure to find a messianic prophecy in verse 26 no doubt disturbs many Christian readers, who have long looked to find such a prediction in Dan 9.[67] One way of checking is to investigate whether the NT looks to this passage as a messianic prophecy. This is usually a reliable way of determining what passages in the HB spoke to the early Christians as messianic. To be sure, there are some vague allusions to words or phrases found in Dan 9:24–27 in the NT.[68] But they are so imprecise, they cannot be considered messianic prophecies. Significantly, never do the NT writers cite Dan 9:24–27, or any part of it, as messianic, which would have to be the case had the NT writers so regarded it.

Who then is the anointed ruler (מָשִׁיחַ נָגִיד, *mashiah nagid*) mentioned in verse 25? Is this the same as the anointed one (מָשִׁיחַ, *mashiah*) mentioned in verse 26? Some interpreters, like Young, take verse 25 as a messianic prediction of Christ and identify the anointed prince in verse 25 with the anointed one cut off in verse 26.[69] In verse 25, the anointed ruler is understood by most scholars as the Persian king Cyrus II;[70] Joshua, the

---

66. Porteous, *Daniel*, 140, 142. E.g., Clement of Alexandria considered the sixty-two weeks to take in Christ's incarnation and the seven final weeks to embrace the Roman emperors Nero, Vespasian, and Titus, who were involved in the destruction of Jerusalem in 70 CE (Clement, *Strom.* 1:125–26).

67. "Who but *this Messiah* could well be thought of, when here . . . the violent death of *an Anointed One* is announced, to take place after the completion of the seven and the sixty-two weeks?" (Hengstenberg, *Christology of the Old Testament*, 415–17; italics in original).

68. See Matt 11:3; 24:15; Mark 13:14; Heb 9:12.

69. Doukhan also represents this interpretation ("Seventy Weeks of Daniel 9," 21), as does House, *Old Testament Theology*, 509; Hengstenberg, *Christology of the Old Testament*, 416.

70. Cyrus II is literally called מָשִׁיחַ, *mashiah*, messiah, in Deutero-Isaiah: "Thus says the Lord to his *anointed* [מְשִׁיחַ], to Cyrus," who is authorized to subdue nations and "cut through the bars of iron" (Isa 45:1–3).

high priest of the Judean exiles; or even Zerubbabel, the leader of the Judean exiles.[71] More likely, it refers to Joshua the postexilic high priest. Along with Zerubbabel, Joshua is mentioned in Zechariah as one of the "two anointed ones [בְנֵי־הַיִּצְהָר, *benei-hayyitshar*, sons of oil] who stand by the Lord of the whole earth" (Zech 4:14).

At the end of the sixty-two weeks of years (434 years), the anointed one will be cut off and have nothing (v. 26), which may refer to the assassination of the anointed high priest Onias III by Andronicus in 171 BCE.[72] Onias's assassination, which came on the heels of his exposé of Menelaus's theft of some of the golden vessels in the temple, ushered in a period of persecution that lasted until 168.[73] The final week of years, beginning with c. 171, concludes with the reconsecration of the temple previously desecrated by Antiochus Epiphanes. "He will confirm a covenant with many for one week, and for half of the week he will cause sacrifice and offering to cease" (v. 27), may refer to the alliance Antiochus made with the Hellenizing Jews,[74] while prohibiting the sacrifice and offering for half the week corresponds to the three and a half times of Dan 7:25 and the 1150 individual daily sacrifices of Dan 8:14.

Following Onias's assassination, the people of the ruler, a reference to the Syrian soldiers stationed in Jerusalem by Antiochus or the Jewish Hellenizers allied with Antiochus, will destroy the city and the sanctuary. Although they did not destroy the city, they harmed it by desecrating the temple and placing idolatrous images around the city. Alternatively, this may have reference to the expedition of Apollonius in 168 BCE, when Jerusalem was sacked, many homes destroyed, and the controversial fortress known as Akra built to control the area around the Temple. As a result, Antiochus IV's troops—people of the ruler—soon poured into Jerusalem.[75] The last line of this verse is extremely obscure. Literally, it reads: "His end will be in a flood, and until the end there will be wars. Desolations are decreed." This appears

---

71. Ezra 2:2; 3:2; Hag 1:1-14; Zech 3:1-5; 4:14; 6:9-14.

72. Dan 11:22; 2 Macc 4:33-38. The chronology of this period does not compute. If the starting date of 539/38 is used to calculate the 434 (62 x 7) years, the terminal date is not 171, but 105/4 BCE. According to G. R. Driver, whose study of this prophecy is considered definitive, the author may have been working with incorrect chronological data and did not bother with being exact (G. R. Driver, "Sacred Numbers"). "His chronology for the Persian period was probably quite erratic," says Barr of the writer, "and he had very little biblical data to help him here" (Barr, "Daniel," 599-600).

73. 2 Macc 4:23-38; Young, *Prophecy of Daniel*, 207; Jeffery, "Introduction and Exegesis," 498.

74. See 1 Macc 1:11-15.

75. Porteous, *Daniel*, 143.

to summarize the eschatological events, while verse 27 gives further details of the events about to transpire.[76]

The covenant confirmed with many for one week (v. 27) may well refer to the perfidious alliance Antiochus struck with the afore-mentioned Hellenizing Jews in Jerusalem, revealed in 1 Maccabees. These renegades urged, "Let us go and make a covenant with the Gentiles around us, for since we separated from them many disasters have come upon us" (1 Macc 1:11). They then arranged to "observe the ordinances of the Gentiles" by removing the marks of circumcision and abandoning the holy covenant (vv. 12–15).

Causing the sacrifice and offering to cease for half of the week, or three and a half days, reminds us of the offensive behavior of the little horn, who attempts to change times and seasons and holds sway for three and a half times, the exact period mentioned here (see Dan 7:25). The same little horn desecrates the sanctuary for 2300 evenings and mornings, or 1150 days, approximately the same length of time (8:11–14) as the reprisal against the rebellious Judeans.

The detested thing causing horror, according to 1 Maccabees, is the "desolating sacrilege on the altar of burnt offering," the altar of the Olympian Zeus placed there by Antiochus (1 Macc 1:54), utterly profaning the temple. Apparently, the Judeans who supported Antiochus IV's Hellenizing project had already been associating Yahweh with the Olympian Zeus, a tendency known as syncretism (i.e., the Olympian Zeus is another manifestation of Yahweh). Just as the seventy weeks was decreed for the Jewish people, so now for the great perpetrator of defilement an end is decreed and poured out upon the desolator.

In sum, then, Dan 9 starts with a heartfelt prayer for God's deliverance from the seventy-year sentence of Babylonian exile. The heavenly answer to the prayer is a reinterpretation of this seventy-year period that lengthens or intensifies the exilic sentence tenfold and tells of a tyrannical ruler who will desecrate Jerusalem and its temple and make matters far worse than expected. Once again, as with earlier visions in Dan 7–8, this vision centers on Antiochus IV and the atrocious acts committed during his reign, the very era in which Daniel was evidently composed. Like Dan 7–8, this vision also points to Antiochus IV's ignominious ruin. The next vision (Dan 10–12), which sketches the decades-long struggle between the Ptolemies and the Seleucids, greatly expands the role of Antiochus IV in this bitter conflict.

---

76. Newsom, *Daniel*, 307.

Prelude to a Final Vision

Daniel 10

One does not need to fast for days and meditate for hours at a time to experience the sense of sublime mystery which constantly envelops us. All one need do is to notice intelligently, if even for a brief moment, a blossoming tree, a forest flooded with autumn colors, an infant smiling.

—Simon Greenberg, *A Jewish Philosophy and Pattern of Life*

Daniel 10-12 represents the most intricate, comprehensive vision in the book. In our modern Bibles, it has been divided into two chapters (10-11) and part of a third (12:1-4). Scholars often refer to this vision as the fourth vision in the sequence. It consists of a brief vision account introducing a long visionary narrative. For this comprehensive vision, Daniel 10:1—11:1 is the prologue. The body of the vision (11:2-45), unlike earlier visions in the book, contains a minimum of apocalyptic symbolism and extends almost to the end of the MT text of Daniel (12:4). Daniel 10-12 contains what may be considered a historical apocalypse in the form of an epiphany (divine appearance) revealed to Daniel by an angelic messenger.[1]

Daniel 10 opens with Daniel caught in the throes of a mystical encounter with a heavenly messenger who has been dispatched to share a vision of the rise, turmoil, reversals, and toppling of nations occurring before the end of days. For the author, the end of the troubled sequence of nations is imminent. Offering a rather detailed account of Hellenistic history—a

---

1. J. Collins, *Daniel* (FOTL 22), 99.

"meditation on the structure of history"[2]—the angel's narration spans the Achaemenid empire down to the demise of the Seleucid monarch Antiochus IV Epiphanes (Dan 11:2-45) and climaxes with the deliverance of the Jewish people (12:1-4). Here occurs the HB's only clear reference to a general resurrection from the dead. An epilogue (12:5-13), which represents a brief new vision, then closes the Hebrew/Aramaic book of Daniel. Given the many remarkable parallels between this vision and Dan 8,[3] the vision of Dan 10-12 is offered as a new interpretation of the events leading up to the long-expected restoration of Israel and, as such, makes an appropriate conclusion to the entire book. To this, the LXX and Theodotion texts of Daniel—not the MT—add two additional stories about Daniel (Dan 13-14).

This fourth vision no doubt offered considerable encouragement to the persecuted Jews of the Maccabean era, who were sharply oppressed under the restrictive policies of Antiochus IV Epiphanes. His death forms the just climax of the vision (Dan 11:40-45) and would be followed by the resurrection of "some to everlasting life, and some to shame and everlasting contempt" (12:1-4 NRSV).

INTRODUCTION TO THE VISION (10:1)

> In the third year of Cyrus, king of Persia, a word was revealed to Daniel, whose name is Belteshazzar. The word was true and concerned great conflict. He understood the word and had understanding in the vision.

The date attributed to the vision is the third year of Cyrus, king of Persia (c. 536/535 BCE) (v. 1). This is the latest date mentioned in the book. According to Dan 1:21, however, Daniel's career extended only to the first year of Cyrus II (539/538). The LXX of 10:1 is consistent with 1:21 ("in the first year of Cyrus"). Theodotion's translation, however, renders this the third year, which is probably the correct reading. The choice of third year in the Hebrew may offer a parallel to the vision in 8:1, dated to the third year of Belshazzar.

The variation between the first and third year of Cyrus is puzzling. Perhaps the fault lies, as Newsom suggests, with the incomplete editing of the apocalypses in Dan 7-12 in conjunction with the court tales in Dan

---

2. Newsom, *Daniel*, 326.

3. E.g., the description of the evil king, Antiochus IV, acting with subtlety and deception (Dan 11:24, par. 8:25); references to the end and appointed time (11:27, 35, 40; par. 8:17, 19). For a full listing, see Willis, *Dissonance and Drama*, 159n28.

1–6.[4] When the court tales were joined to the apocalypse, the chronological references were not integrated seamlessly into the text. Whether the first or third year of Cyrus, the reference reminds us the vision commences with the Achaemenid empire.

In the first year of Cyrus II, the king issued a decree that allowed Israel to return from exile. "The Lord stirred up the spirit of King Cyrus of Persia so that he sent a herald throughout all his kingdom, and also in a written edict," allowing the Judeans to "go up to Jerusalem in Judah, and rebuild the house of the Lord" (Ezra 1:1–3).[5] This act is recalled in the prophetic words of Second Isaiah. "Thus says Yahweh to his anointed, to Cyrus, whose right hand I have grasped to subdue nations before him . . . to open doors before him" (Isa 45:1).[6]

Intriguingly, and perhaps significantly, Daniel's experience in this third year of Cyrus is called a *word* (דָּבָר, *dabar*). The Hebrew term is broader in significance than our English equivalent, which we employ for both oral and written messages. Since *dabar* is often used for divine communication in the form of commandments or prophecy,[7] there is nothing unusual for it to be equivalent to a vision, mentioned here. Although it is possible that the word refers to the word of deliverance offered in Isa 40,[8] anticipating Cyrus's decree, it is more likely that it embraces the entire vision narration in chapters 10–12.

This word concerns a great conflict. It is unclear whether צָבָא (*tsaba*) refers to physical warfare or military conflict, or to intense hardship and struggle in a general sense.[9] If the latter, it may refer to the hard work (conflict?) of Daniel in comprehending the vision and its implications,[10] the onerous struggle vividly depicted in this chapter. Anyone reading chapter 11 immediately realizes how difficult it is to sort out the various characters who appear here. In this vision, Daniel is obviously deeply distressed by what he sees and hears.

---

4. Newsom, *Daniel*, 328–29.

5. See also 2 Chr 36:22–23. A version of the decree is also cited in Ezra 6:3–5. The Cyrus Cylinder, one of the Persian royal inscriptions from the ancient Near East, mentions the policy of Cyrus in resettling the various gods of the conquered nations to their sacred cities (*ANET*, 316b). It is probably the decree of Cyrus appearing on the Cyrus Cylinder that is alluded to in Ezra. See Bickerman, "Edict of Cyrus."

6. See also Isa 41:14–16; 43:1, 14, 44:6–8, 22–28.

7. 1 Sam 15:10; 1 Kgs 6:11.

8. Lacocque, *Book of Daniel*, 204.

9. Slotki, *Daniel*, 80.

10. J. Collins, *Daniel* (Hermeneia), 372.

THE REVELATION (10:2-9)

² In those days, I, Daniel, had been mourning three full weeks. ³ No rich food had I eaten, neither meat nor wine had come into my mouth, nor had I applied an ointment for a full three weeks. ⁴ In the twenty-fourth day of the first month, I was on the bank of the great river, that is, the Tigris. ⁵ I lifted my eyes and looked, and lo, a man clothed with linen, his loins girded with a belt of gold from Uphaz. ⁶ His body was like chrysolite, and his face like the appearance of lightning, his eyes like flaming torches, his arms and feet like the gleam of polished bronze, and the sound of his words like the roar of a tumult. ⁷ I, Daniel, alone saw the vision. The men who were with me did not see the vision. Of a truth, great trembling fell upon them and they fled to hide themselves. ⁸ So I was left alone, and I witnessed this great vision, but no strength was left in me. My stamina was devastated, and I retained no strength. ⁹ Then I heard the sound of his words, and when I heard the sound of his words, I fell into a deep sleep on my face, with my face to the ground.

Daniel is fasting and mourning, presumably about the troubled situation in the devastated city of Jerusalem. During the period of three weeks wherein he has been humbling himself on behalf of his people (see Dan 9:15–19), he has avoided partaking of rich food, meat, or wine, and has avoided even the use of perfumed unguent oils, ordinarily used in mourning rites (v. 2). His diet may be compared to what he ate during the initial period of royal training. Earlier, as a young man "Daniel resolved in his mind that he would not defile himself with the king's food or with the wine which he drank" (1:8). Here the self-restraint of an elderly Daniel represents his preparation for a visionary experience (v. 3).[11]

Suddenly, a radiant being appears (v. 4), a man clothed with linen, girded with a gleaming golden belt or sash (v. 5). His body—in human form—glimmering like chrysolite, his face like lightning, his eyes burning like flaming torches, his arms and feet like the gleam of polished bronze (v. 6).[12] Chrysolite or topaz may be what is meant by תַּרְשִׁישׁ (tarshish), a precious gem, yellow or greenish in color, named for the location where it was

---

11. Note the experience of Ezra in 2 Esdras: "These are the signs that I am permitted to tell you, and if you pray again; and weep as you do now, and fast for seven days, you shall hear yet greater things than these" (5:13). See also 2 Esd 5:20; 6:35; 9:24; 12:51; 2 Bar 9:1; 12:5; 20:5–6; 21:1; 47:2.

12. This description may draw from Ezekiel, who also depicts an angel clothed with linen (Ezek 9:2–3, 11; 10:2, 6–7). See Rev 1:12–16.

anciently quarried, the southern tip of Spain (Tarshish). It parallels other references to yellow hues of gold, bronze, and fiery flames. This angelic being may be Gabriel but is left unidentified (see Dan 9:21).

At the time, the twenty-fourth day of the first month, Daniel is standing on the bank of the great river, evidently the Tigris, here called חִדֶּקֶל (*Hiddeqel*), which flows parallel to the Euphrates southward through Mesopotamia. Significantly, it is the first month (Nisan), the time of Passover, the festival celebrating Israel's liberation from Egypt, which traditionally required only one week of fasting, not three, as here (Lev 23:4-8).

Overcome by the awesome, unnerving presence and sound of this heavenly messenger, Daniel experiences a numbing weakness. He collapses to the ground (vv. 7-8). A trancelike state overcomes him (v. 9). Although he is in the company of others, presumably with him on official business, they are terrified and flee the scene, not hanging around to watch the apparition. Like Paul in the NT (Acts 9:3-7), Daniel alone has access to the vision; others flee. During the vision, Daniel requires revivification, not once, but three times (vv. 8-10, 15, 18-19).

Daniel apparently undergoes what today would be called a mystical experience. This is the most extensive account of such an experience in the book. Daniel encounters the Holy, mediated by an angelic being in human form. Mystical or ecstatic religious experiences,[13] known in all religions, are of at least two types. Unitive mystical experiences result in a sense of profound oneness with God, such as found among the Christian mystics or in Buddhism and Hinduism. A second type, communitive mysticism, seems to be more the case in Daniel. In communitive mysticism, a divine being in some form encounters the subject through auditions, visions, and often flashes of brilliant light.[14] This kind of mysticism is found frequently in the apocalyptic writings.[15] Mystical experiences deeply affect the psyche, and though they are difficult, if not impossible, to put into words, they communicate depths of mystery transcending cognition. Often, as here, the subject is rendered completely passive, but the experience itself is transient and lasts only a short while.[16]

---

13. I recommend Marcus Borg's fascinating discussion of these mystical experiences in the *God We Never Knew*, 37-51.

14. Hick, *Interpretation of Religion*, 165.

15. E.g., see 2 Esdras, where Ezra mentions "my heart was troubled within me . . . my spirit was greatly aroused, and my soul was in distress" (6:36-37). "All these experiences are so true psychologically," Russell observes, "that it is difficult to see in them nothing more than the expression of literary convention" (Russell, *Method and Message*, 165-66).

16. James, *Varieties of Religious Experience*, 371-72.

Such varied experiences are often cited as evidence of the reality of God. Are such experiences illusory or hallucinatory? Or do they point to a divine or supernatural order transcending yet impinging upon the psyche of a human subject? Given the sheer volume of such mystical experiences in the Jewish and Christian apocalypses, it must be asked whether these are actual mystical, visionary experiences or imaginary literary constructs. The question cannot be fully answered. I suspect the apocalypses reveal some of both real experience and literary art, perhaps even a combination of the two, with the apocalyptist using artfully crafted metaphorical language to describe what such an experience may have been like. In some instances, real mystical experiences do witness to the celestial realm. "It seems reasonable to suppose," C. D. Broad maintains, "that the whole mass of mystical and religious experience brings us into contact with an aspect of reality which is not revealed in ordinary sense-perception, and that any system of Speculative Philosophy which ignores it will be extremely one-sided."[17]

THE ANGEL'S DIALOGUE WITH DANIEL (10:10-21)

> [10] Then, lo, a hand touched me and set me trembling on my knees and the palms of my hands. [11] He spoke to me, "Daniel, man greatly beloved, consider carefully the words that I speak to you and stand in your position, for now I have been sent to you." When he spoke to me this word, I stood up, trembling. [12] He said to me, "Do not fear, Daniel, for from the first day that you set your mind to understand and humble yourself before your God. Your words have been heard, and I have come because of your words. [13] But the prince of the kingdom of Persia opposed me twenty-one days. Then, lo, Michael, one of the chief princes, came to help me, and I was left there with the kings of Persia. [14] I have come to help you understand what your people will encounter in the end of days, for the vision is yet for those days."

The angelic messenger, assuring Daniel, helps him to his hands and knees, then to an upright position (vv. 10-11). While Daniel shivers, he is told his prayers have been heard. In fact, the heavenly emissary has been dispatched at the beginning of his prayer, not the end of it, to bring him understanding (v. 12). The angel explains he has been delayed for twenty-one days—three

---

17. Broad, *Contemporary British Philosophy*, 1:99, as cited in Baillie, *Sense of the Presence*, 83. "This constant reference to visions coming during the night or in some state of sleep," notes Russell, "may suggest that we have here actual experiences and not merely expressions of literary convention" (Russell, *Method and Message*, 165).

weeks—by the opposition of the prince of the kingdom of Persia, the same period as Daniel's fast (v. 13). The prince of the kingdom of Persia is the patron angel of Persia. Widespread in the ancient world was the notion that different nations had their own patron deities. By the Second Temple period, when monotheism had generally prevailed in Judah, the gods of the nations had been relegated—demoted—to the subservient, angelic level. Each nation now had its own angelic representative (cf. Sir 17:17). This development can be noted in the LXX rendering of Deut 32:8. In the MT text, this reads, "When he [the Most High] separated the sons of man, he set the boundaries of the peoples with respect to the number of the sons of Israel [בְּנֵי יִשְׂרָאֵל, *benei yisrael*]." Instead of sons of Israel, the Qumran Hebrew text (*4QDeuteronomy*ʲ) has "when [the Most High] separated the nations . . . he set the bounds of the peoples according to the number of the children of God."[18] The Dead Sea scroll reading (בני אלים, *benei elim*, children of God) is probably correct. In transmission, the MT editors have evidently substituted "the sons of Israel" for this phrase, in part to downplay the existence of deities other than Yahweh.[19] But in translating this verse, the LXX makes another theological move and translates the Hebrew expression as ἀγγέλων θεοῦ (*angelon theou*, angels of God). This textual history may seem complicated, but this single instance allows us to sense something of the evolution in Hebrew consciousness from the earlier notion that each nation has its own god to the later idea each nation has only a patron angel, a lesser heavenly being—but not a god—to watch over its affairs.

This concept is at work in the vision of Dan 10. Michael is one of these heavenly angels or princes—"your prince" (v. 21). Here we get a glimpse of the elaborate angelology so characteristic of many apocalypses. Michael, who is mentioned here for the first time in the HB, is the name of the patron angel of Israel (Dan 12:1). He is one of the chief princes, evidently a hierarchical group of at least five archangels superior to other rank and file angels, according to 1 Enoch, who enjoy more intimate proximity to the divine throne.[20] His martial prowess appears in later apocalyptic writings, including the book of Revelation, where with the host of heaven, Michael

---

18. Abegg et al., *Dead Sea Scrolls Bible*, 191.

19. In the same context, note Yahweh's self-affirmation: "See now that I, even I, am he; there is no god besides me" (Deut 32:39).

20. First Enoch 20:1-7 supplies for these archangels the names Raphael, Raguel, Michael, Saraqael, and Gabriel, the last of whom also appears in Daniel. The passage in 1 Enoch and in Daniel reflects an angelology that emerged in the Hellenistic era and subsequently was elaborated in the extra-biblical writings over the following centuries. Michael and Gabriel are the only angelic names appearing in the Bible (Dan 9:21; 10:13, 21; 12:1; Jude 9; Rev 12:7). See Cousland, "Michael."

fights against Satan.[21] He is, in fact, the angel in charge of heaven, who in Jewish apocalyptic tradition leads the angels who bury Abraham's body and convey his soul to paradise.[22]

Of uncertain meaning is the last phrase in verse 13: "I was left there with the kings of Persia." Does this imply that, although Michael has arrived to assist, the angel sent to Daniel was left alone to contest the prince of Persia? The NRSV inserts the pronoun *him* into the sentence: "I left *him* [Michael] there with the prince of the kingdom of Persia," before coming to the aid of Daniel. A better solution, in my judgment, is to take the conjunction ו (*waw*), beginning the clause as explicative, and so render, "for *even* I had been left there with the prince of the kingdom of Persia."[23] Understood in this manner, the clause refers to a situation prior to the angel's arrival alongside Daniel.

According to these verses, in the celestial realm, there was conflict among the patron angels, such that affairs upon earth among the nations were directly affected. What was going on in the heavenly sphere, in other words, reflected affairs upon earth. There is an interplay between the heavenly and earthly realms. Here is the dualism for which apocalyptic is well-known. Apocalyptists pull aside the curtain separating heaven and earth, and visionaries witness this interaction, which may not be apparent to bystanders, as here (Dan 10:7). Bystanders need interpretation to unlock the symbolism as much or more than the visionaries themselves. From below, we observe and participate in earthly events, but remain unaware of the heavenly dimension. The apocalyptist shares in a view from above, and we see the two orders of reality, a heavenly and earthly. This is one important contribution that apocalyptic makes to religious life. God above is in control of the affairs of nations, even though the nations are unaware of this reality.

The vision concerns what will happen to the Jewish people, explains the angel, in the end of days (בְּאַחֲרִית הַיָּמִים, *beaharit hayyamim*) (v. 14). This phrase is clearly eschatological (having to do with the end of history). The phrase itself may be based on similar expressions from Genesis and

---

21. Second Enoch 22:6-9; 33:10; 3 Bar 11:4; Rev 12:7-9.

22. "They buried him [Abraham] in the promised land at the oak of Mamre, while the angels escorted his precious soul and ascended into heaven singing the thrice-holy hymn to God, the master of all" (Testament of Abraham 20:11-12 *OTP*). See 1 Enoch 24-25; Jude 8-9. On Michael, see Newsom, *Daniel*, 332-33.

23. This *waw* is also known as an epexegetical *waw*, generally translated as namely, even, or specifically (Williams, *Hebrew Syntax*, §434). Most of the modern English translations accept this same solution, e.g., "because I was detained there with the king of Persia" (NIV).

Habakkuk.[24] If we consider the larger context of Daniel, especially the concluding lines in the present vision (Dan 11:40–45), it refers to events surrounding the reign of Antiochus IV Epiphanes. The apocalyptist expects this malevolent king to flourish preceding the final deliverance of Israel and the resurrection of the dead (12:1–4). Although implicit here is some sort of delay, there is no reason to suppose this phrase looks to events far in the distance in the nineteenth, twentieth, or twenty-first centuries. Such an epochal span of time—more than two thousand years—would have been completely unimaginable to the writer (or readers), just as a long-range future extending two thousand years beyond would be to us. Like the NT writers, the author expected the climax of history to be imminent, close at hand, not to be revealed in some far distant event.

> [15] When he had spoken to me according to these words, I turned my face to the ground and was speechless. [16] Then behold, one in human form touched my lips and I opened my mouth and spoke. I said to the one standing in front of me, "My lord, because of the vision anguish has fallen upon me and I retain no strength. [17] How can the servant of my lord speak with my lord about this? For now, strength does not remain in me, nor is breath left in me."

Once more Daniel collapses, face to the ground, speechless (v. 15). The unidentified celestial being in human form intervenes again, touching his lips, much as Isaiah's were touched in his temple vision (Isa 6:6–7), rendering Daniel able to speak. Daniel complains of physical weakness enough to render him incapable of grasping what it is the angel wishes to reveal (v. 16). The experience of being confronted by a heavenly messenger is so overwhelming, he has no stamina left with which to grasp the vision about to be disclosed (v. 17). Although touching Daniel's lips does not appear to have a cleansing effect, we recall the anguished words of Isaiah, "Woe is me! I am lost, for I am a man of unclean lips . . . my eyes have seen the King, the Lord of hosts!" (Isa 6:5). Like Jeremiah, the touch enables Daniel to speak the word God has given (Jer 1:9).

> [18] Again, one in human form touched me and strengthened me. [19] He said, "Do not fear, O man beloved, peace be to you. Be strong, be strong!" While he was speaking to me, I was strengthened and said, "Let my lord speak, because you have strengthened me." [20] Then he said, "Do you know why I have come to you? Now I will return to fight against the prince of Persia, and

---

24. "Gather around, that I may tell you what will happen to you in days to come" (Gen 49:1); "For there is still a vision for the appointed time; it speaks of the end" (Hab 2:3).

when I have gone, behold, the prince of Greece will come. [21] However, I will tell you that which is inscribed in the book of truth. There is no one who shows himself courageous with me toward these except Michael, your prince."

A third time the one in human form touches Daniel, again bolstering him (v. 18). He calls him a man beloved (חֲמוּדָה, *hamudah*, precious treasure), an adjective also applied to Daniel in Dan 9:23; 10:11. To be referred to in this way would have a powerful, reviving effect, as we might imagine; hence the angel bids him שָׁלוֹם (*shalom*, wholeness or be well). He further urges Daniel to take courage, "Be strong, be strong!" (v. 19). This reassurance had the effect of reinvigorating Daniel.

It may look like this prelude has spent an obsessive amount of time on Daniel's emotional and physical state resulting from an encounter with the heavenly visitant. Three times he is overpowered, three times he must be revived, having been rendered speechless by the holy presence of the visitor or the portents of the vision he is about to receive. All this heightens the significance of the vision about to be unfold. The vision carries such solemn weight that its very announcement by a radiant heavenly visitor in human form proves excruciating.

Having done so in verse 14, the angel explains he has come to tell what is written in the book of truth (vv. 20–21). It is uncertain what this expression means. It may denote the book opened in judgment in the earlier vision of Dan 7:10, which appears to be identical with the book announcing the faithful who are to be delivered (12:1). On the other hand, as the angel begins to relate the vision, he declares, "Now I will announce the truth [אֱמֶת, *emet*] to you" (11:2). This is the same term used in the expression "book of truth" (אֱמֶת). Then the vision unfolds (11:2–45). The book of truth thus likely refers to the panorama of history about to be sketched in the vision. Similarly, the Babylonian Myth of Zu speaks of the deterministic Tablet of Destinies,[25] and Enoch learns "from the words of the holy angels," and understands "from the heavenly tablets" (1 Enoch 93:2–3).

Suddenly, without warning, the angel excuses himself, insisting he return to the struggle against the prince of Persia, with whom he has only Michael for support. In the meantime, Daniel is told the prince of Greece will come. We are then led directly into chapter 11:1, which is really a continuation of 10:21.

---

25. "Myth of Zu," translated by E. A. Speiser (*ANET*, 112b).

Finale

Daniel 11

Man is not God, and whenever he has claimed to be like God, he has been rebuked and brought to self-destruction and despair. When he has rested complacently on his cultural creativity or on his technical progress, on his political institutions or on his religious systems, he has been thrown into disintegration and chaos; all the foundations of his personal, natural and cultural life have been shaken.

—Paul Tillich, *Shaking of the Foundations*

Although this chapter falls under the broad designation of vision (מַרְאָה, *marah*, vision, revelation) (Dan 10:16), Dan 11 contains little of the apocalyptic symbolism we have come to expect. Here are no lions with wings, rams with large, protruding horns, or monsters with serrated iron teeth. We get a little taste of what apocalyptic would be like with little or no symbolism. This lack of distinctive apocalyptic coding is ironically a disadvantage. It renders the chapter even more difficult. Interpreting it is akin to unraveling the proverbial Gordian knot. The final vision in Daniel is the most difficult vision of all.

The chapter contains an extended visionary experience aptly described as a historical apocalypse, which begins with Dan 10:1 and continues until 12:4. Daniel 12:5–13 then forms the epilogue for the apocalyptic section (chs. 7–12) and the entire Hebrew/Aramaic book. For convenience, I have followed the conventional chapter divisions of Daniel.

Since little symbolism is used in Dan 11, the text is best read with one eye on the history of the eastern Mediterranean region in the Hellenistic period (fourth to first centuries BCE) and the other on the earlier visions in Dan 2, 7–9. The Hellenistic era is the period to which the text best seems to correspond. Numerous obscurities remain, but the vision contains many allusions to events during this era. The original readers would no doubt have had a basic knowledge of these events—not so most modern readers. Much of the history of this difficult period as it affected the Jews is preserved in the deuterocanonical books, especially 1–2 Maccabees. These books, along with other contemporary authors, such as Josephus, delineate many of the events narrated in Dan 11. To read Dan 11 intelligently hence requires a basic knowledge of the eastern Mediterranean region and the Near East during Hellenistic times. With such awareness, we can trace the persons and events on which this vision focuses. In the commentary, we will attempt briefly to sketch this history. Our interpretation will be anchored in the recounting of events in the author's own era. We will not read these events as though they actually refer to matters in the far distant future.

Daniel 11, in keeping with the apocalyptic style, is history written as prediction. Like other apocalyptists, the author inscribes the history leading up to the author's own time in a visionary mode. "The historical details are so precise and so generally accurate," notes Newsom, "that the author must have had access to a chronicle of Seleucid and Ptolemaic political and military interactions."[1] We can tell this because the closer the author comes to his own era, the more detailed the vision becomes. In this respect, the closest parallels to Dan 11 in ancient literature are the Akkadian pseudo-prophecies of political events. They are sometimes called pseudo-prophecies because they were written after the predicted events had already occurred, a technique known as *vaticinia ex eventu*. These Akkadian prophecies, many scholars think, are predecessors of the Jewish apocalypses, whose authors do the very same thing. In one of these, the Dynastic Prophecy, dated to the Hellenistic period—the same general period as the composition of Daniel—outlines with remarkable accuracy the rise and fall of dynasties, including Assyria, Babylon, Persia, and Macedonia. The Dynastic Prophecy offers a good example of history presented as prophecy,[2] which we now recognize as a stylistic technique used by apocalyptists. History thus presented as prophecy does not appear as a series of random, often chaotic events, as it does to

---

1. Newsom, *Daniel*, 336.

2. Sparks, *Ancient Texts*, 241–42; Newsom, *Daniel*, 336–37. For a translation of the Dynastic Prophecy, see Hallo, *Context of Scripture*, 1:149, 480–81.

us, but rather as a process under the direction of God, who both establishes and terminates the affairs of nations.

The chapter, which offers an amazingly detailed account of the Hellenistic period down to 165 BCE, begins with an introductory statement (10:21b—11:1), then gives a visionary review of Hellenistic history (11:2–45). The review starts with the Persian and Greek empires (vv. 2–4), then traces the wars between the Ptolemies and the Seleucids (vv. 5–9), the reigns of the Seleucid king Antiochus III (vv. 10–19) and Seleucus IV (v. 20), before turning to the exploits of Antiochus IV Epiphanes (vv. 21–45), who gets the lion's share of attention in the vision.

THE PERSIAN AND GREEK EMPIRES (11:1-4)

> "I, in the first year of Darius the Mede, stood up to strengthen and fortify him. ² Lo, yet three kings shall arise in Persia. The fourth shall be far wealthier than all, and when he has become strong through his wealth, he will stir up everyone against the king of Greece. ³ Then a mighty king will arise, rule with great authority, and act as he pleases. ⁴ When he arises, his kingdom shall be broken and divided to the four winds of heaven, but not to his posterity, nor according to his dominion with which he ruled, because his kingdom will be rooted up and go to others besides these."

At the start of the angel's discourse, we learn what has caused Daniel such emotional grief (Dan 10:17). It is a vivid account of seemingly endless wars, the rise and fall of numerous despots, particularly as their actions impinge upon God's people. The angel continues speaking to Daniel without pause, passing from one event to another and one chapter to another. The entire sequence (10:1—12:4) is understood as the word of the angel. "The word [דָּבָר, *dabar*, word, discourse] was true and concerned great conflict" (10:1). Daniel 11:1 continues directly from 10:21. Beginning in the Achaemenid period, the vision continues into the Hellenistic age, the time of the Maccabees, the stalwart Jewish insurgents who rebelled against the Seleucid king Antiochus IV Epiphanes—the very period of the writing of Daniel.

The date line, in the first year of Darius the Mede³ (v. 1) would be c. 539 BCE, when Persia overthrew the Neo-Babylonian empire (see Dan 5:30–31). The date assigned the entire vision—the third year of Cyrus

---

3. The LXX and Theodotion have Κύρου (Cyrus) in 11:1 instead of Darius. Darius is attested by 4QDan^c, one of the fragmentary texts from Qumran.

(10:1)—on the other hand, which would be three years later (c. 536/535 BCE), contrasts with the first year of Darius. Historians, we recall, are not aware of the existence of Darius the Mede, at least under this name (see comments on Dan 6:1-2). By inserting these dates, the author signals in true apocalyptic fashion the portrayal of the history of the Hellenistic era in predictive style. Here history is presented as the human counterpart to the perpetual heavenly struggle between Michael, Israel's patron angel, and the angelic patrons of Persia and Greece.[4]

The angelic narrator offers a terse summary of the later history of the Achaemenid empire and of its Greek conqueror, Alexander the Great (v. 2). In addition to the Persian king Cyrus II (c. 549-529), the first king alluded to in this text (Dan 10:1), the other three kings mentioned are probably Xerxes (486-465), Artaxerxes I (465-424), and Darius II (423-405), although this is uncertain.[5] The mighty king, however, is clearly Alexander the Great (356-323 BCE) (v. 3) who, in a series of lightning military strikes in a few short years conquered the world of his day, making Greece the dominant superpower of the time. Alexander aimed to spread Greek culture (known as Hellenism) throughout the empire as a mark of Greek superiority, a factor that would become decisive in Jewish relations depicted in this chapter. The decisive battle settling the mastery of the ancient world occurred near Issus in northern Syria in 333 BCE. There Alexander turned back the Persian army of Darius III. Alexander's goal had been announced earlier in the words of Aristotle, his teacher: "The Greeks could rule the world if they just associated themselves into one political society."[6] While still a young man, Alexander succumbed to malaria (?) on June 2, 323, and died prematurely eleven days later at age thirty-two.

No leader after Alexander proved capable of holding the great empire together. After a messy internecine struggle among his generals, known as the Diadochi, by 301 BCE, Alexander's empire had fractured and settled into four main divisions, "to the four winds of heaven" (v. 4). Lysimachus remained in charge of Thrace and Asia Minor; Cassander of Macedonia and Greece; Ptolemy I of Egypt, Palestine, and Phoenicia; and Seleucus I of Babylonia and Syria. This long struggle set the pattern for the numerous ongoing wars between the Ptolemies and the Seleucids (274-163 BCE) dominating the rest of Dan 11.

---

4. Henze, "Daniel," 1249. See 10:10-14.

5. Hartman and Di Lella, *Daniel*, 288-89. The text skips over several of the later kings to arrive at Alexander's conquest. The remaining kings between the four apparently mentioned here and Alexander are Artaxerxes II Mnemon (404-359); Artaxerxes III Ochus (358-338); Arses (337-336); Darius III Codomannus (335-330).

6. Aristotle, as cited in Lacocque, *Book of Daniel*, 217.

THE WARS BETWEEN THE PTOLEMIES
AND THE SELEUCIDS (11:5-9)

> ⁵ "Then the king of the south shall grow strong, but one of his officers shall even become stronger than he and have greater authority than his own dominion. ⁶ After some years, they will make an alliance, and the daughter of the king of the south will come to the king of the north to ratify the agreement. But she will not retain the strength of her arm, and his strength will not remain. She will be given up, her attendants, her child, and the one who supported her in those times.
>
> ⁷ "A branch from her roots will rise in his place. He will come against the army and will enter the fortress of the king of the north, and he will act against them and prevail. ⁸ Also their gods with their molten images, the silver and gold vessels of their desire, with the captives he will carry off to Egypt. And for some years he will refrain from [attacking] the king of the north. ⁹ Then he will enter the dominion of the king of the south but will return to his own land."

Since the vision concerns the nations directly involved in Jewish history, the rest of the angel's explanation focuses on the struggle between the two empires, the Ptolemies to the south (Egypt) and the Seleucids to the north (Syria) (vv. 5-45). Palestine was strategically positioned between these two empires and hence frequently the object of aggression by first one and then the other. In this vision, the king of the south (v. 5) refers to the various Egyptian Ptolemaic rulers, and the king of the north to the Syrian Seleucid kings. From the perspective of Palestine, since they occupied the southernmost region of the Levant (the lands from Greece to Egypt), the Ptolemies are designated the king of the south, while the Seleucids in the northern Levant are known as the king of the north. At the battle of Gaza in 312 BCE, the first of the Seleucid kings, Seleucus I Nicator (312-281), whose bronze bust has been found at Herculaneum near Pompeii (Italy), defeated Ptolemy I Soter (323-285) and inaugurated the Seleucid dynasty. This included the establishing of the Seleucid capital at Antioch, in what is now southern Turkey, a city that would later become a famous Christian center, the place where the followers of Jesus were first called Christians (Acts 11:26).

Around 250 BCE—"after some years"—Ptolemy II Philadelphus (285-246) attempted an ill-fated alliance with the Seleucid Antiochus II Theos (261-246) by arranging a political marriage to his daughter, Berenice

Syra (v. 6).[7] This meant only Berenice's son could legitimately succeed to the Seleucid throne. Consequently, Antiochus II had to divorce his otherwise politically powerful wife Laodice. Laodice's two sons were thereby excluded from royal succession. After Ptolemy II died, however, Antiochus II terminated the alliance with Ptolemy, thrust Berenice aside, and reconciled with his former wife Laodice. Such political maneuvering was not lost on Laodice, however. She took matters into her own hands, allegedly poisoned Antiochus, and flaunting her restored royal status, had Berenice and her infant son, the would-be heir, assassinated. The text witnesses to all this in one terse line: "she will be given up, her attendants, her child, and the one who supported her." Laodice's own sons were now once more contenders for royal succession. The eldest, Seleucus II Callinicus (246-226), consequently ascended to the throne.

Retaliation for this treachery came when Ptolemy III Euergetes (246-221), the "branch from her roots," a brother of Berenice (v. 7), marshalled his army against the Seleucid capital Antioch. "He will act against them and prevail," says our text. Contemporary monetary coinage depicts Ptolemy III as a deity, wearing a crown with rays of the sun coming from it, on his chest a golden breastplate of Zeus and Athena.[8]

Antioch was the fortress of the king of the north—now ruled by Seleucus II Callinicus—the son of Laodice. Through military assault, Ptolemy III conquered Antioch, together with the surrounding area, and even extended his influence as far east as Babylon. Seeking revenge, he executed Laodice. As the victor, Ptolemy III took spoil from the region (v. 8). Among the booty were the gods with their molten images, an indication the Seleucid's most important symbolic source of strength had now passed to the Ptolemies.[9] The so-called practice of godnapping—kidnapping a vanquished nation's gods—was widely practiced during warfare in the ancient Near East. It demonstrated the impotence of the vanquished nation's deities in contrast to the gods of the victors:[10] our gods are stronger than yours! When the Philistines defeated Israel, for instance, they made off with the ark of the covenant, which they assumed was the throne or image of Israel's God. The ark they relocated to the temple of Dagon, the chief deity of the Philistines, with disastrous consequences.[11] Among the gods confiscated by Ptolemy III

---

7. Hartman and Di Lella, *Daniel*, 289.
8. Kraft et al., *IFE*, 11:21.
9. Slotki, *Daniel*, 89. See Isa 46:1-2; Jer 48:7-8; 49:3-5.
10. Newsom, *Daniel*, 341.
11. See 1 Sam 4-5.

were some of the idols the Persian king Cambyses had previously captured (525 BCE) in Egypt and transported to Persia.

The next few years saw Seleucus II rebuilding his military forces. In 242, he mounted a counteroffensive to reclaim areas of southern Syria and Phoenicia. This campaign ended in disaster two years later, compelling Seleucus II to return to his own land (v. 9).

THE SELEUCID KINGS (11:10-20)

> [10] "His sons will mobilize and assemble a multitude of many forces and he will continue to advance, overflow, and pass through. He will again wage war up to his fortress. [11] Then the king of the south will become embittered and go and do battle with him, with the king of the north. He will raise a great multitude, but the multitude will be given into his hand. [12] When the multitude has been carried away, he will exalt his heart and cause ten thousand to fall, but he will not prevail. [13] The king of the north will return and raise up a multitude greater than the former, and after an interval of some years, he will continue to advance with a large army and much equipment."

Seleucus II was succeeded in 227 by his older son Seleucus III Ceraunus, who was tragically assassinated in 223. His second son, Antiochus III (223–187) then assumed the throne as the next king of the north. The next few verses (vv. 10–19) refer mainly to the exploits of Antiochus III (the Great). After putting down some of the political rivals, Antiochus set out to conquer Phoenicia and southern Syria, or as it was anciently known, Coele-Syria, including Palestine. Capturing Seleucia and the port of Antioch, he advanced, overflowed, and passed through (v. 10) Palestine and assaulted Raphia, on the border of Palestine, where he was met by the army of Ptolemy IV Philopator (221–203). The Ptolemaic army allegedly put in the field 50,000 infantry, 5,000 cavalry, and 73 war elephants, versus Antiochus III's lesser force of 65,000—a great multitude (v. 11). At the Battle of Raphia in 217, Ptolemy IV inflicted a terrible, humiliating defeat on Antiochus III, forcing him to vacate his claims to Coele-Syria.[12] Ptolemy regained control of Coele-Syria but strangely failed to follow up on his victory (v. 12).

For almost the next fourteen years—"after an interval of some years"— Antiochus III, smarting from defeat, turned attention to re-establishing control in the opposite direction, Asia Minor, Persia, and as far as the

---

12. Hartman and Di Lella, *Daniel*, 291; Grabbe, "Antiochians." A legendary account of this battle may be found in 3 Macc 1:1–7.

frontiers of India. Emboldened by successes in this endeavor, Antiochus III now felt prepared to reengage the Ptolemies. Opportunity presented itself when, upon the death of Ptolemy IV in 204, his six-year-old son, Ptolemy V Epiphanes, succeeded him. With a large army and much equipment (v. 13), Antiochus III, joined now by the army of Philip V of Macedon, finally confronted Egyptian troops under the command of the highly touted Aetolian mercenary general Scipio (Scopas) at Paneas (Caesarea Philippi), and in 200, soundly defeated the Ptolemaic army, compelling even Scipio's personal surrender in 199. With Antiochus III's victory at Paneas, Ptolemaic sovereignty over Palestine at last came to an end. In gratitude for Jewish support during the war, Antiochus issued a decree temporarily granting relief from taxation to Jerusalem.[13]

> [14] "In those times many will rise against the king of the south. The sons of the violent ones of your people will raise themselves up to establish the vision, but they will fail. [15] Then the king of the north will arrive and cast up siege works and capture a fortified city. And the forces of the south will not stand, even his choice people, nor is there strength to stand. [16] But he who comes against him will do as he pleases, and no one will stand before him. He will take a position in the beautiful land and destruction is in his hand. [17] He will set his face to come with the force of all his kingdom and upright ones with him; thus, he will do. And he will give to him the daughter of women to ruin it, but it will not endure, nor will it be for his advantage. [18] He will set his face against the coastlands and capture many. But a military commander will put a stop to his insolence; indeed, his insolence will return upon him. [19] Then he will turn back his face to the fortresses of his own land, but he will stumble and fall and be found no more.
> [20] "Then will arise in his place one who sends an exactor of tribute for the kingdom, but in a few days, he will be broken, not in anger nor in battle."

The sequence of events is interrupted by verse 14, "many will rise against the king of the south," which adds a parenthetical comment evidently referring to Egyptian insurgents opposed to the despotic policies of Agathocles, the acting regent for the child king Ptolemy V (204–181). "The sons of the violent ones of your people" may refer to a Jewish, pro-Seleucid party, generally identified with the Tobiads,[14] who originally formed to

---

13. Josephus, *Ant.* 12:12.3.

14. The Tobiad party was named after Joseph ben Tobiah and comprised the Jewish priestly aristocracy, the landed gentry, and rich merchants, all of whom readily adopted

obstruct and overthrow Egyptian domination of Palestine. The vision they were trying to establish, but at which they fail, is not indicated. It may refer to the prospect of the prophetic vision of Israel's restoration as predicted in the prophets.[15] In verse 14 also appears the first vague mention of time (in those times), repeated in various forms throughout the chapter (see vv. 20, 24, 27, 29, 35, 40). With verse 45, a new word is added to the expression, קֵץ (qets, end), indicating these expressions show the events as "steps on the way leading to the End."[16]

The account of the conflict between the king of the south and the king of the north resumes with verse 15. Antiochus III laid siege to the city of Sidon, a fortified city, and conquered it. He was now in control of all Coele-Syria. Emboldened, in 197, Antiochus seized Cilicia, Lycia, and Caria, all on the southern coast of Asia Minor, events alluded to in verses 16–17a. All the beautiful land (v. 16)—Judaea—now became an integral part of the Seleucid empire. The Jewish historian Josephus mentions a letter from Antiochus III to General Ptolemaios in which he granted numerous privileges to the Jewish people, including the right to live according to the Torah and other ancestral laws. "Let all of that nation live according to the laws of their own country," Antiochus wrote, "and let the senate and the priests, and the scribes of the temple, and the sacred singers, be discharged from poll-money and the crown-tax, and other taxes also."[17]

All this happened, however, under the ever-watchful eye of the emerging empire from the west—Rome. Antiochus III, wary of Roman intervention, thus avoided a direct attack on Egypt. It seemed more prudent first to make a peace treaty with Ptolemy V and seal it by giving his "daughter of women," Cleopatra, in marriage, a common practice in political dealmaking in antiquity. Many of Solomon's legendary wives were liaisons of this sort.[18] The marriage to Cleopatra took place in 193 at Raphia. Antiochus III, the text suggests, cunningly hoped to manipulate this marriage alliance to bring about ruin to Ptolemy V, but the scheme failed: "it will not endure, nor will it be for his advantage." Cleopatra, on her part, readily embraced her husband's cause and proved completely loyal to Ptolemy. She even urged a political alliance of Egypt with Rome.[19] Following Ptolemy's death (180),

---

the Hellenistic way of life. See Josephus, *J.W.* 12:160–236.

15. See, e.g., Ezek 37:24–28.
16. Lacocque, *Book of Daniel*, 224.
17. Josephus, *Ant.* 12:3.3.
18. See 1 Kgs 3:1–2; 11:1–8.
19. Hartman and Di Lella, *Daniel*, 292.

while remaining a powerful figure, Cleopatra I became the acting regent for her underage son.

Antiochus III now turned his attention against the coastlands of Asia Minor, capturing many previously Egyptian-controlled cities, despite the treaty with Egypt presumably in effect. Greece itself now enticed him, so he invaded in 192, ignoring Rome's warning to refrain from doing so. A year later, at Magnesia, the Romans routed and drove him entirely out of Asia Minor. The military commander who will put a stop to his insolence (v. 18) is no doubt Lucius Cornelius Scipio, who crushed Antiochus's forces at the Battle of Magnesia (189) near Smyrna, in what is now Turkey. As a result of this defeat, "insolence will return upon him." Forced to submit to humiliating peace terms, Antiochus had to pay a huge indemnity to Rome. Antiochus now had no other option but to give up his territorial ambitions, at least toward the west, where Rome's principal influence lay, and turn back to the fortifications of his own land (v. 19). Back on his home turf, but now as a subordinate vassal of Rome, in 187 he was assassinated while attempting to rob the treasury of Bel—one of his own deities—at Elamaïs, a Persian city, to pay the indemnity required by Rome. Thus ended the notorious career of Antiochus III the Great. "He will stumble and fall," the text says, "and be found no more."

His successor was Seleucus IV Philopator (187–175), whose twelve-year reign is said to have lasted only a few years (v. 20). Forced to raise critical revenue for his now nearly bankrupt empire, Seleucus IV sent an exactor of tribute, his foster brother and finance minister Heliodorus, to Jerusalem to pillage the Jerusalem temple treasury. Widespread rumor had it the temple contained vast treasures. According to 2 Maccabees, the majestic "power of God," in the form of a magnificent horse and rider wearing golden armor prevented the looting, striking Heliodorus helpless to the ground. Later, warning others not to attempt such pillage of the temple, he cautioned, "there is certainly some power of God about the place" (2 Macc 3:38). As for Seleucus IV, he "will be broken, not in anger nor in battle" is evidently a reference to Seleucus's assassination in 175, evidently as the result of a conspiracy planned by Heliodorus and assisted by Seleucus's younger brother, Antiochus IV. The major attention in the vision now focuses on Antiochus IV Epiphanes (175–164).

THE RISE OF ANTIOCHUS IV EPIPHANES (11:21-28)

[21] "Then will arise in his place a contemptible person on whom the honor of kingship has not been bestowed. He will come

in a time of peace and seize the kingdom through intrigue. ²² Armies will be utterly swept away and broken before him, and the prince of the covenant as well. ²³ And from the making of an alliance with him, he will act deceitfully, rise, and become strong with a few people. ²⁴ In a time of peace and into the richest parts of the province he will enter. He will do what none of his fathers and grandfathers have done. Booty, spoil, and property he will disperse among them. Against fortifications he will devise strategies, but only for a time. ²⁵ He will stir up his power and courage against the king of the south with a great army, and the king of the south will wage war with an exceedingly great army. But he will not stand, for schemes will be devised against him. ²⁶ Those who eat his provisions will break him, and his army will be swept away and the fatally wounded will fall. ²⁷ The two kings, their minds set on evil, at one table will speak of deception. But it will not succeed, for there is yet an end at the appointed time. ²⁸ He will return to his land with great booty, but his heart will be set against the holy covenant. He will act and then return to his own land."

Antiochus IV obtained the Seleucid throne illicitly—through intrigue—by ousting Demetrius, son of his brother Seleucus IV (v. 21), the legitimate heir, who was at the time a political hostage in Rome. With the empire nearing bankruptcy, Antiochus made a political arrangement with the Tobiads, the pro-Seleucid party in Jerusalem. In exchange for the removal of the official Jewish high priest, Onias III, the Tobiads agreed to contribute a substantial amount to Antiochus IV to relieve his indebtedness. After a bribe of "three hundred sixty talents of silver, and from another source of revenue eighty talents" (2 Macc 4:8), Jason, Onias's own brother, took the office of high priest, expelling Onias in the process. While living in exile, however, Onias's popularity grew so much among the Jewish people that they began wistfully to revere him as a kind of messianic figure.[20] Reflecting this sentiment, the text (v. 22) speaks of him as the prince of the covenant.

A few years later (172), another claimant for the high priesthood, Menelaus, in still a new act of betrayal, offered Antiochus three hundred talents of silver to grant him the high priesthood instead of Jason. When the interloper Menelaus pilfered the sacred golden vessels from the temple to pay the bribe he had offered Antiochus for the high priesthood, Onias publicly exposed him. In retaliation, in 171, Menelaus had Onias

---

20. "After the sixty-two weeks, an anointed one shall be cut off and have nothing" is probably a reference to Onias III (Dan 9:26 NRSV), as we have seen.

assassinated outside the sanctuary of Daphne, near Antioch, where he had taken refuge.[21]

The next few verses (vv. 23-24) depict Antiochus IV's exploits in Syria-Palestine during the early part of his reign. His double-dealing and treachery in consolidating his power were widely known. "Booty, spoil, and property he will disperse among them" refers to Antiochus's senseless, profligate squandering of war-time spoils upon his friends and supporters. "He used to give more lavishly than preceding kings" (1 Macc 3:30). Antiochus was by nature a genuine despot. According to contemporaries, he was at once eccentric and unreliable, sometimes extravagant and liberal. He often affectedly consorted with the common people, only to turn darkly cruel and tyrannical. The Judeans would soon learn it was no better having Antiochus as a friend than as an enemy.

The Ptolemaic empire was ruled by Ptolemy VI Philometor, at the time a minor under the supervision of his court guardians. At the end of 170, however, with tension again escalating between the Ptolemies and the Seleucids, the Ptolemaic army threatened. Antiochus responded by going to war against Egypt, "against fortifications, but only for a time." He defeated the Ptolemaic army and took Ptolemy VI prisoner even before his army had managed to escape the Sinai desert.[22]

Ptolemy VI's regents ("those who eat his provisions") then betrayed the young Ptolemy and turned the nation over to Antiochus (vv. 25-26). To accomplish this, according to Porphyry, Antiochus deceived Ptolemy VI, his nephew and now prisoner, by feigning interest in amity between the two empires. By this subtlety he got Egypt under his control. "The two kings, their minds set on evil, [while] at one table" speak deceptive words (v. 27), so the vision puts it. Such treachery and scheming were not to succeed. It was to end at the appointed time, at the time decreed by the God of heaven.

The sacred writer now speaks of Antiochus IV returning to his land, laden with great booty (v. 28). This seems to refer to Antiochus IV's return from his first campaign against Egypt. A second campaign is apparently described in verses 29-35. Here the sequence of events gets confusing. Did Antiochus invade Jerusalem twice, each time following his campaigns in Egypt? If so, during which invasion did he plunder the temple? Or did he do so twice?

Many modern scholars think there was only one such assault on Jerusalem.[23] However, Daniel, it seems, indicates two invasions (vv. 28-35).

---

21. See 2 Macc 4:30-35.
22. An account of this campaign may be found in 1 Macc 1:16-19.
23. "It appears that the author of Daniel has telescoped events somewhat and tried

It was after the second that a large Antiochene army entered Jerusalem and plundered the temple (vv. 31-32). There were evidently two attacks against Jerusalem, but the plundering and desecration of the temple occurred after Antiochus IV's second campaign against Egypt.[24]

As the words "his heart will be set against the holy covenant" signal, Antiochus IV was now embroiled in a bitter struggle against God. The Jewish temple, where Yahweh had placed the sacred name, now became the object of Antiochus IV's wrath.

THE DESECRATION OF THE TEMPLE (11:29-39)

> [29] "At the appointed time he will return and come into the south, but it will not be as it was at first or subsequently. [30] Ships of Kittim will come against him and he will be intimidated and turn back. Then he will be enraged against the holy covenant and act. He will turn back and pay heed to those who abandon the holy covenant. [31] And forces from him will stand and profane the sanctuary fortress. They will take away the regular burnt offering and set up the abomination of desolation. [32] Those who violate the covenant he will seduce with flattery, but the people who know their God will stand strong and act. [33] Those who have insight among the people will give understanding to many, but they will fall by sword and flame, by captivity and plunder, many days. [34] When they stumble, they will receive a little help, and many will join them with intrigue. [35] Some who have insight will fall, to test them and to purify and to cleanse until the time of the end, for it is yet for the appointed time."

Not long after returning to Antioch, Antiochus discovered that Ptolemy IV Philometer and Ptolemy VII Euergetes II Physcon, both sons of Cleopatra, had formed a coalition government. They had joined forces to oppose Antiochus and the Seleucids. Ironically, Antiochus IV happened to be their Syrian uncle (v. 29). The phrase "at the appointed time" (לַמּוֹעֵד, *lammoed*) subtly indicates that all these political machinations were under divine oversight (see vv. 14, 27). Behind the scenes, in the deep structures of human affairs, God was still in control. In the interest of human freedom, God allows

---

to tie them narratively to Antiochus's forced withdrawal from Egypt" (Newsom, *Daniel*, 350).

24. This sequence of events follows Bunge, "Untersuchungen zum zweiten Makkabäerbuch," 461-63, as cited in Schäfer, "Hellenistic and Maccabean Periods," 564-66. See also Josephus, *Ant.* 12:5.3-4.

the political and military intrigue to play out as it must. In the intersection between divine determination and human freedom—some might say in the clash between them—apocalyptic places the delicate balance between freedom and determination, paradoxically affirming both. Human freedom has limits, but neither is every single event divinely determined. God is in control, but not controlling.

Enraged at the Ptolemies, Antiochus seized the initiative and invaded Egypt again in 168, but "it will not be as it was at first or subsequently." The Romans checked Antiochus's invasion. Ships from Kittim (v. 30) arrived,[25] carrying a Roman delegation under Gaius Popillius Laenas. He brought orders from Rome: Antiochus was immediately to terminate hostilities and depart Egypt. Polybius (c. 200–120 BCE), the Greek historian, tells that when Popillius presented Antiochus the stringent Roman terms, Antiochus asked permission to consult his advisors. Quite annoyed, Popillius drew a circle in the sand around Antiochus and demanded he decide before he dared step outside the circle.[26] Intimidated and cowed, Antiochus angrily withdrew and retreated.

Antiochus subsequently turned to attack Jerusalem. His motives in doing so remain unclear. Previously, we recall, Antiochus had instituted a process of Hellenization in the region; now he assaulted the holy covenant, enlisting those who abandon the holy covenant (v. 30), the Jews who all along had favored Hellenization.[27] We do not know whether at this time Antiochus personally entered Jerusalem. We do know he appointed the Phrygian Philip as governor in Jerusalem, a person Maccabees claims was "more barbarous than the man who appointed him" (2 Macc 5:22). This arrangement did not work, at least to Antiochus's satisfaction, so he sent Apollonius in the summer of 167 with a large force directly to attack the city. On a Sabbath, easily catching the Jews by surprise, Apollonius's soldiers massacred "great numbers of people" (2 Macc 5:25–26). He erected a high wall with guard towers, known as the Akra, to accommodate Syrian troops occupying the city. The Akra became the controversial center of Hellenism in the city for a long time afterward.[28] Many Jews abandoned their homes and fled the city; soon, it became a military colony with a mixed gentile-Jewish

---

25. The Hebrew term כִּתִּיִּים, *kittiyim*, originally referred to the inhabitants of Cyprus and Macedonia. From the Qumran scrolls, however, we learn that in this period the term was also used for the Romans. The LXX translates it thus. Cf. the intertext in Num 24:24.

26. Polybius, *Hist.* 29:27.1–8.

27. See 1 Macc 1:11–15.

28. 1 Macc. 1:36 calls it "an ambush against the sanctuary, an evil adversary of Israel at all times." See 2 Macc 6:1–6.

population.[29] "She became a dwelling of strangers; she became strange to her offspring, and her children forsook her" (1 Macc 1:38).

Reinstating Menelaus as high priest, now with his support, Antiochus plundered the temple. He "took the golden altar, the lampstand for the light, and all its utensils . . . the table for the bread of the Presence, the cups for drink offerings, the bowls, the golden censers, the curtain, the crowns, and the gold decoration on the front of the temple," and carried the sacred booty back to Antioch (1 Macc. 1:21–22; cf. 2 Macc 5:11–21). Josephus graphically describes the whole incident:

> He left the temple bare, and took away the golden candlesticks, and the golden altar [of incense] and table [of shewbread,] and took away the golden candlesticks, and the golden altar [of burnt-offering;] and did not abstain from even the veils, which were made of fine linen and scarlet. He also emptied it of its secret treasures, and left nothing at all remaining.[30]

Subsequently, Antiochus imposed a series of anti-Semitic restrictions: "They will take away the regular burnt offering and set up the abomination of desolation" (v. 31). These restrictions aimed "to forbid burnt offerings and sacrifices and drink offerings in the sanctuary, to profane sabbaths and festivals, to defile the sanctuary and the priests, to build altars and sacred precincts and shrines for idols, to sacrifice swine and other unclean animals" (1 Macc 1:45–47). Circumcision, the sign of the covenant, was to be abandoned. To possess a scroll of the Torah was a capital offense. We are reminded of a time in later Christian history when Bibles translated into the popular languages were prohibited, or when vicious Nazi pogroms had Torah scrolls publicly burned. The Jews were to "forget the law and change all the ordinances" (v. 49).

The parallel of Dan 11:31 with the little horn in Daniel's earlier visions is obvious. Daniel 11 illuminates the role of the little horn in both Dan 7 and 8. The little horn was to "attempt to change the sacred seasons and the law" (7:25). Antiochus literally carried out what these visions indicate. Here, as in Dan 8:11 ("the regular sacrifice was taken away from him, and the place of his sanctuary cast down"), Antiochus removed the regular burnt offerings, the תָּמִיד (*tamid*), the daily morning and evening sacrifices at the temple. This would have had the effect of banning the daily services at the temple. Today, this would be like closing churches, synagogues, and mosques, forbidding worship, as was done in modern China or the old Soviet Union

---

29. Schäfer, "Hellenistic and Maccabean Periods," 584.
30. Josephus, *Ant.* 12:5.4.

under Joseph Stalin. Furthermore, Antiochus had an altar (or image) of the Greek Olympian god Zeus erected at the altar of sacrifices in the temple courtyard. On this altar on 15 Kislev (December) 167 BCE, swine—unclean and defiling—were offered, deliberately violating the temple with what Daniel calls the abomination of desolation (שִׁקּוּצִים מְשֹׁמֵם, *shiqqutsim meshomem*), a mocking distortion of the Semitic title *Baal Shamen* (Baal of heaven).[31] These heinous sanctions were to the Jewish people about as horrifying and sacrilegious as they could be, especially because they targeted the sacred temple and the Torah scrolls. Against this background we can better understand the intense language used in Dan 7, 8, 9, and 11, which focuses on Antiochus IV's bitter hostility toward the Jewish religion that he saw as standing in the way of his Hellenization project.

These events divided the Jewish people. They deepened the divisions already present. The ordinary citizen, "confused by the tumultuous events he had to live through," was "undecided whether he should go along with Hellenization as even some of the high priests had done."[32] One political faction—"those who violate the covenant"—cooperated with Antiochus's repression (v. 32). These were Hellenizers, who favored the adoption of the Hellenistic way of life. The Hebrew term for them is מַרְשִׁיעֵי בְרִית (*marshie berith*, literally, ones acting wickedly against the covenant). They sympathized with Antiochus's decrees, pretty much with his whole Hellenizing agenda. Others "who know their God will stand strong and act." This may be the Jewish armed resistance, those who supported the Maccabean revolt. The reference is vague, however, and leads us to ask why the author, evidently living at this very time, never refers to the Maccabean insurgency, led by Judas Maccabeus, against Antiochus, unless this verse is such reference. The little help these faithful receive (v. 34) is often regarded as an oblique reference to the Maccabean resistance.[33]

The text mentions those who have insight among the people (v. 33), who were the purveyors of understanding for the multitudes. This group is possibly related in some way to the wise of the wisdom tradition, the sages who gave us Proverbs, Job, and Ecclesiastes. Their counsel would no doubt have included the apocalyptic wisdom represented in the book of Daniel.[34]

---

31. See Dan 12:11; 1 Macc 1:54–57.

32. Hartman and Di Lella, *Daniel*, 299.

33. Slotki, *Daniel*, 97. For a contrary view, that the reference is to a yet unknown group, see Newsom, *Daniel*, 353.

34. This connection reminds us of von Rad's theory that apocalyptic literature finds its origin not in the prophets, as most assume, but in Hebrew wisdom (von Rad, *Old Testament Theology*, 2:301–8). In a work that came to my attention too late to be included in this study, Tim Meadowcroft contends that Daniel should be understood

The wise who impart insight are often associated with the *Hasidim*, who are called mighty warriors elsewhere. "There united with them a company of Hasideans, mighty warriors of Israel, all who offered themselves willingly for the law" (1 Macc 2:42). To identify the Hasidim too closely with the wise, however, is problematic, since the wise were known to be nonviolent and opposed to armed resistance.[35] Some suggest the author of Daniel may have belonged among the wise, because the book advocates passive nonresistance toward the hostile gentile powers. In Daniel, the "proper response to pressures of assimilation and threats and acts of violence from either Antiochus in particular or any ruler," Rillera emphasizes, "is patient and vulnerable faithfulness to the point of martyrdom."[36]

Despite the evil and injustice perpetrated by the great powers, the readers of the apocalyptic book are apparently encouraged passively to await the divine judgment expected at the end (Dan 12:8–10). Faced with Antiochus's spiteful anger, they "fall by sword and flame, by captivity and plunder, many days." Maccabees claims these faithful persons "chose to die rather than to be defiled by food or profane the holy covenant" (1 Macc 1:63). Pfeiffer notes how an earlier story in Daniel—the three Hebrews in the furnace of fire—finds resonance.[37] The three defy Nebuchadnezzar. "If our God whom we serve can rescue us from the burning furnace of fire, he will also rescue from your hand, O king. If not, be it known to you, O king, your gods will we not serve, nor the golden image you have set up will we not worship!" (Dan 3:17–18).

One of the stories of persecution and martyrdom from this era is the tale of Eleazar, the seven brothers, and their mother.[38] This story reminds us of *Foxe's Book of Martyrs*, indeed, the whole martyrdom tradition as it appears in Christian tradition. The king's agents brought in Eleazar, a ninety-year-old Jewish scribe, for interrogation. They promised him life unmolested if he would only pretend to ingest swine's flesh, forbidden by the Torah. He refused. Tortured, beaten, he was then executed.

The king, identified as Antiochus IV, then arrested seven brothers and their mother on a charge of defying the king's orders. At first, the brothers were tortured with whips and thongs and compelled to eat swine's flesh.

---

primarily as a Hebrew wisdom figure, as is already intimated in Dan 1:17 (Meadowcroft, *Like the Stars Forever*).

35. J. Collins, *Daniel* (Hermeneia), 385, contra Lacocque, *Book of Daniel*, 229; Newsom, *Daniel*, 352.

36. Rillera, "Call to Resistance," 776.

37. Pfeiffer, *History of New Testament*, 13.

38. See 2 Macc 6:18—7:42; 4 Macc 8–18.

They refused to transgress their religious principles. After seizing the first brother, cutting out his tongue, ripping off his scalp, and cutting off his feet and hands, the king horrifically fried him on a hot grill. Then he put the other six brothers to the same test—eating swine's flesh—and when they adamantly refused, he tortured and put them to death. Finally, he sought to coerce the mother to conform to his demands and forsake the Torah. By this time, she had been compelled to watch the agony of her sons. She obstinately refused to forsake Torah, choosing to perish at the king's merciless command.

Such horrific anti-Semitic persecution, our text claims, would test, purify, and cleanse the faithful, even though some would fall (v. 35).[39] The period of testing would extend until the appointed time of the end, evidently proximate, so close by it might even come within the lifetime of the apocalyptist (see Dan 12:8–12; 2 Macc 6:12–13). Just as the early Christians expected the second advent to come in their lifetime,[40] so this author no doubt expected the end of the age in his. Here the end is correlated with Antiochus's cruel reign. When Antiochus's reign ended, in other words, then the eschaton would appear. Many apocalyptic movements throughout history have cherished the fervent hope that the eschaton was imminent. So far, all have ended in disappointment. Still, God's faithful live in hope, despite what seems to be long, interminable delay—thousands of years. God's faithful look forward to the arrival of God's kingdom, whenever it takes place.

> [36] "The king will do as he pleases. He will exalt himself and consider himself great over every god, and against the God of gods he will speak presumptuous words. He will exalt himself and consider himself superior over every god, and against the God of gods he will speak presumptuous words. But he will prosper until the indignation is complete; for the decreed will be done. [37] And to the gods of his ancestors he will not give respect, nor to the desire of women. He will not give respect to any god, because he will make himself greater than all. [38] In their place, he will honor the god of fortresses, and he will honor the god whom his ancestors did not acknowledge with gold, silver, precious stone, and costly valuables. [39] He will act against the

---

39. Since the death of these faithful is expiatory, Lacocque regards v. 35 as a midrashic interpretation of the suffering servant song in Isa 53 (Lacocque, *Daniel*, 230). H. L. Ginsberg considers Dan 10–12 as the "oldest interpretation of the suffering servant," and as definitely collective rather than individualistic in scope (Ginsberg, "Oldest Interpretation.").

40. See 1 Thess 4:13–17.

strongest fortresses with [the help of] a foreign god. Whoever acknowledges him he will make wealthier, and he will appoint them to rule over many, and the land he will divide for a price."

The next few verses, while not in chronological order, offer a profile of Antiochus IV's arrogance, corrupt behavior (vv. 36–39). Acting self-interestedly, Antiochus does as he pleases, a criticism that could be leveled against many world leaders before and since (v. 36). Ancient writers tell how Antiochus grew insatiably bored with royal privileges. At night, he would shed the royal garb and wander freely through the dark streets and alleys. He would stay out late at night drinking wine with a few intimates. Often around noon, wine cup in hand, he would drunkenly toss coins by the handfuls into the street, amusingly watching people scramble to pick them up. At times, he would accost a stranger on the street and bestow upon him some object of great value, such as a large precious jewel, just to watch the shock on his face. He relished playing cruel, sadistic jokes on people. But underneath all his Neronic affability he had "fundamentally the nature of the tyrant . . . there was something horribly dangerous and panther-like in his caresses."[41]

On his freshly minted coins in the latter part of his reign, he inscribed BASILEOS ANTIOCHOU THEOU EPIPHANOUS NIKEPHOROU ("King Antiochus, the Manifestation of God, Bringer of Victory"). This is perhaps an instance of why the apocalyptist thought of Antiochus as one who would "exalt himself and consider himself great over every god." Like this accusation stands the boast of the Babylonian king, "I will make myself like the Most High" (Isa 14:14), and of the magnificent, personified city of Tyre, "I am a god; I sit in the seat of the gods, in the heart of the seas" (Ezek 28:2). Further back may be a Canaanite myth about similar hubris and self-deification.[42] For someone so pompous, it is little wonder many behind his back mockingly called him Antiochus *Epimanes*: Antiochus the mad (king).

Furthermore, "against the God of gods he will speak presumptuous words," just as did the little horn earlier in Daniel. "He speaks words against the Most High" (see Dan 7:8, 25) is a phrase remarkably similar to 11:36. There is no doubt the little horn power in both Dan 7 and 8 is identical with the king here envisioned, Antiochus IV Epiphanes. The God of gods (אֵל אֵלִים, *el elim*) is a Hebrew superlative expression for the greatest or highest God. Here it refers to the God of Israel.[43] Despite his boasts, Antiochus would not be allowed indefinitely to continue his blasphemous behavior.

41. Bevan, *House of Seleucus*, 2:129–30.
42. Clifford, "History and Myth," 25.
43. Deut 10:17; Ps 136:2–3.

Even though there is no indication Antiochus ever specifically vilified Yahweh, his suppressing the Jewish faith and practice was in the author's mind essentially the same thing (see 7:25; 8:23–25). Revolt against God, for the author, had to reach an extreme for divine anger to be unleashed.[44] The phrase "he will prosper until the indignation is complete" probably refers to the juncture at which Antiochus's animus had fully spilled over.

The next few verses (vv. 37–39) elaborate on what has been said in verse 36. Antiochus would disregard the gods of his ancestors; he would not respect any god (v. 37). How Antiochus would disdain other gods is not clear.[45] According to Polybius, Antiochus went through perfunctory motions, at least, of honoring all gods and spirits, not just Zeus and Apollo, both of whom Antiochus's coinage honored at different times.[46] His suppression of Yahwism was directed primarily at the region of Palestine as a punishment for Jewish opposition, but seems not to have been extended to other Jewish communities in the Seleucid empire. His main goal, it seems, was not religious, but political. He wanted to unify the various religions in his empire by establishing the cult of the Olympian Zeus as the principal deity.[47] Thus the statement that he disregarded the gods of his ancestors is an exaggeration. From a Jewish perspective, Antiochus acted on the worst possible motives, thus he was understandably demonized as the hated, bitter enemy. It is easy from our vantage point to minimize the genuine threat Antiochus posed to Jewish faith and culture. Had we lived in Judea during this time, I am sure, we would have felt much the same. The king's disrespect extended to the חֶמְדַּת נָשִׁים (*hemdat nashim*, the delight of women), probably a reference to Tammuz (also known as Dumuzi), the fertility god over whose demise Ezekiel sees the women of Israel ritually mourning at the entrance of the temple (Ezek 8:14–15). This deity was one of the most popular fertility gods in the ancient Near East.

In lieu of these deities, Antiochus considered himself greater than all and would in their place honor the god of fortresses (v. 38), sometimes identified with Jupiter Capitolinus or Zeus Akraios, the Zeus of the mountain of Acra. Antiochus imposed the cult of the Olympian Zeus on Jerusalem to "compel the Jews to forsake the laws of their ancestors and no longer to live by the laws of God." He sought to "pollute the temple in Jerusalem and to call it the temple of Olympian Zeus" (2 Macc 6:1–2). Hence the expression

---

44. See Gen 15:15–16; Isa 10:20–23.

45. Newsom points out Antiochus IV never abandoned the worship of the gods, including Apollo, the Seleucid ancestral deity (Newsom, *Daniel*, 353).

46. Polybius, *Hist.* 30.25–26.

47. Kraft et al., *IFE*, 11:25.

"the god of fortresses" may represent a "polemicized exaggeration"[48] for the abomination of desolation, the *shiqqutsim meshomem* mentioned in verse 31. Antiochus apparently did what his Seleucid ancestors had never attempted: set up the cult of the Olympian god Zeus in the temple at Jerusalem.

The "strongest fortresses" may refer to the Akra, the fortress in Jerusalem built by Antiochus as the military quarters for Syrian soldiers—the occupying force—and hence a very unpopular site (v. 39). There he established a base not only in the Akra, but in similar fortifications elsewhere. Like other tyrants, Antiochus was quick to lavish favors on loyalists. "Whoever acknowledges him he will make wealthier." In the story of the martyrdom of the faithful Jewish mother and her seven sons, Antiochus proposed to the seventh doomed son "he would make him rich and enviable if he would turn from the ways of his ancestors" which, of course, the young man would not do (2 Macc 7:24).

Many, particularly older commentators, see verses 36-39 as referring to the antichrist, who is expected to emerge in the latter days of earth's history. Instead, these verses have in view the career and malevolent activities of Antiochus IV Epiphanes. To apply them to the future antichrist, whether regarded as the Pope, Roman Catholicism,[49] or a sinister world leader, such as Adolf Hitler, is to go beyond what we find here. The antichrist myth was developed in Christianity much later than the book of Daniel, although it has roots in the NT.[50] The depiction of Antiochus has been projected by some interpreters as a prediction of how the eschatological antichrist is expected to speak and act. Nothing in these verses, however, originally referred to the antichrist of Christian eschatology.[51] This passage is not an eschatological forecast of the antichrist. Instead, the apocalyptist has in mind the historical Antiochus IV Epiphanes.

---

48. J. Collins, *Daniel* (Hermeneia), 388.

49. So Haskell, *Story of Daniel*, 235-49.

50. Note Paul, who cites Dan 11: "That day will not come unless the rebellion comes first and the lawless one is revealed.... He opposes and exalts himself above every so-called god or object of worship, so that he takes his seat in the temple of God, declaring himself to be God" (2 Thess 2:3-4). Cf. 1 John 2:18-25; 4:1-6; 2 John 7-11.

51. Cf. Di Lella: "The Antichrist interpretation of these verses is exegetically witless and religiously worthless" (Hartman and Di Lella, *Daniel*, 303). Whitcomb, contrary to Di Lella, finds in the eschatological king of the north a sinister character who prepares the ground for the antichrist, "the ultimate masterpiece of Satan," who will arise in the first half of the seventieth week (Dan 9:27), according to the dispensationalist schema (Whitcomb, *Daniel*, 160-61). Walvoord suggests a Russian force, along with others, may also be involved in the phrase *king of the north* (Walvoord, *Daniel*, 278).

THE TIME OF THE END (11:40-45)

⁴⁰ "At the time of the end the king of the south will attack him, but the king of the north will storm against him with chariotry, horsemen, many ships, and will enter countries and overflow and pass through. ⁴¹ He will enter the beautiful land, and many will fall, but these will escape from his hand—Edom, Moab, and the foremost of the sons of Ammon. ⁴² He will stretch out his hand against countries, and the land of Egypt will not escape. ⁴³ He will control the treasures of gold, silver, and the precious things of Egypt. The Libyans and Cushites will be in his train. ⁴⁴ But reports from the east and north will disturb him, and he will go out with great fury to destroy and eliminate many. ⁴⁵ He will pitch his palatial tents between the sea and the beautiful holy mountain, but he will come to his end and there will be no help for him."

With verse 40, we leave the section of the vision corresponding to the course of ancient history and begin a sequence of events that apparently goes beyond the historical awareness of the author. Whereas the preceding section (vv. 2-39) refers to the events in history, "nothing in these verses [vv. 40-45] matches the actual course of history as it is known from other sources."[52] This anomaly has long troubled interpreters. We are confronted in these verses with a prophecy never fulfilled, at least as written, naturally giving rise to several attempts at satisfactory interpretation.[53]

Some have explained verses 40-45 as the report of a third war against Egypt shortly after 168 BCE, despite the absence of historical documentation. Alternatively, the passage has been taken as a general summary of Antiochus's reign, including his various military campaigns, and a forecast of his untimely death. Such interpretations must still deal with the fact that virtually nothing here corresponds to what historically happened.

Others understand the passage as an apocalyptic prediction of the notorious eschatological antichrist and thus not about Antiochus IV at all. In this view, Antiochus becomes a type (example) of the future antichrist yet to come.[54] Thus the description of Antiochus typologically applies to the "An-

---

52. Hartman and Di Lella, *Daniel*, 303.

53. For a full discussion of these views, see Linder, *Commentarius in Librum Daniel*, 471-74; Hartman and Di Lella, *Daniel*, 303.

54. Young, *Prophecy of Daniel*, 251-53. Miller also connects the passage directly to the antichrist, not Antiochus, because the conflict mentioned in vv. 40-45 occurs just before the resurrection of the saints, hence at the end of the present (modern) age (S. Miller, *Daniel*, 309-11). See Wood, *Daniel*, 327-28; Talbot, *Prophecies of Daniel*,

tichrist, the Beast, or to the continuing opposition of evil."[55] In conservative Christian circles, the language about the Antiochene rule has been taken up into apocalyptic speculation about the end-time antichrist. Some futurist interpreters hold that Daniel even predicts the emergence in modern times of a ten-nation confederacy ruled by the antichrist.[56] A more generalized interpretation, applied broadly, takes Antiochus as a type of the "spirit of all kings who exalt themselves, doing whatever they please."[57]

Even if the symbols in Daniel reflect past historical figures like Antiochus IV, Sims argues, they may also be prophecies fulfilled "beyond the horizon of known history." He cites the way NT writers apply the self-aggrandizement of Antiochus in Dan 11:36 to a wicked ruler who "opposes and exalts himself above every so-called god . . . so that he takes his seat in the temple of God, declaring himself to be God" (2 Thess 2:4), and in Revelation as the one who "opened its mouth to utter blasphemies against God, blaspheming his name and his dwelling" (Rev 13:6). Both these intertexts of Daniel refer to the Roman empire, as does Jesus's reference to Rome as the "desolating sacrilege standing in the holy place" (Matt 24:15), the "abomination that makes desolate" (Dan 11:31). These passages are telescoped prophecy, explains Sims, a conflation of past or present phenomena and future prediction. The final fulfilment of Dan 11, accordingly, may thus still lie in the future.[58]

What these commentators really offer are reinterpretations of this apocalyptic text. In the introduction, we recognized, due to its peculiar metaphorical character, apocalyptic lends itself to reinterpretation that extends beyond what the apocalyptist may have had in mind. Such reinterpretation, not only of apocalyptic texts, but of other biblical texts as well, goes on repeatedly even within Scripture.

The main problem with the reinterpretation of the Antiochene references in Dan 11 as a prophecy of the eschatological antichrist is that it is not anchored in the literary, theological, and historical context of the apocalyptist. Quite simply, the picture of Antiochus drawn in these verses little resembles the eschatological antichrist of Christian speculation. One indication of this is the mention of Edom, Moab, and Ammon as escaping

---

200–201.

55. VanGemeren, "Daniel," 600; Walvoord, *Daniel*, 279.
56. See Fuller, *Naming the Antichrist*, 22–25.
57. VanGemeren, "Daniel," 600.
58. Sims, "Daniel," 328. See also Dan 7:3–12, 21, 25. Nichol thus regards Dan 11:31–39 as a prediction of the Roman Catholic Church, the "work of the papacy in the Christian centuries" (Nichol, *Seventh-Day Adventist Bible Commentary*, 4:874–76).

Antiochus's conquest (v. 41). These nations no longer exist and cannot therefore be elements of a forecast of the reign of the antichrist.

At minimum, perhaps the best way of reading these verses—setting aside unwarranted apocalyptic speculation—is to think of them as the author's visionary expectation of the final days of Antiochus's tyrannical rule and furthermore of the inbreaking of the reign of God (Dan 12:1–4) to follow his demise.

This section begins with a reference to עֵת קֵץ (*et qets*, the time of the end), which forms a preface to the lines following (v. 40). The day of eschatological reckoning has come (see vv. 27, 35). The king of the south, probably Ptolemy Philometor, would attack the king of the north, Antiochus IV. Antiochus would then counterattack with "chariotry, horsemen, many ships"—an overwhelming force. Aside from Porphyry's claim about an Egyptian campaign after 168 BCE,[59] there is no other indication of such a campaign in any ancient source outside the Bible.

This assault (on Judea) echoes the paradigm of the great eschatological battle depicted in the postexilic prophets.[60] The Lord "will gather all the nations against Jerusalem to battle, and the city shall be taken and the houses looted and the women raped; half the city shall go into exile, but the rest of the people shall not be cut off from the city. Then the Lord will go forth and fight against those nations" (Zech 14:2–3). With evil intent, nations surround Jerusalem, where they will summarily be defeated, not by human armies, but by the overwhelming power of God.

Following his assault, Antiochus would enter the beautiful land—Palestine—and many of its inhabitants will fall (כָּשַׁל, *kashal*, stumble, stagger, or totter) (v. 41). For some reason, the author exempts Edom, Moab, and "the foremost of the sons of Ammon" from this assault. This may be because during Antiochus's persecutions, both Edom and Ammon remained hostile to the Jews, but were friendly toward Antiochus (see 1 Macc 4:61–5:8). Since these nations were east of the Jordan Valley, mention of them indicates the invasion involves only the territory between the Mediterranean and the Dead Sea. Since Edom, Moab, and Ammon were the traditional enemies of Israel, the allusion to their exemption from hostilities may serve

---

59. Jerome attributes this claim to Porphyry (Jerome, *PL*, 25:572). Porphyry evidently based his comment on Dan 11:40. Most historians regard the comment as inaccurate.

60. This pattern is set in some of the later prophets by forecasting a final conflict between the nations and the Jewish people in the vicinity of Jerusalem (see Ezek 38–39; Joel 3:9–16; Zeph 3:8; Zech 12:2–9; cf. also Rev 16:12–16; 20:7–10). Based on this pattern, Talbot understands Dan 11:40–45 as descriptive of the battle of Armageddon in Rev 16 (Talbot, *Prophecies of Daniel*, 208–9).

as a backhanded reproach to Judea, the target of his hostilities.[61] The War Scroll (1QM 1.1–2) from Qumran portrays Edom, Moab, and the Ammonites, together with Philistia, as allies of the wicked army of Belial.

In this conflict, Egypt will not escape (v. 42), as it did when the Romans intervened on behalf of Ptolemy Philometor (v. 30). Antiochus would plunder the "treasures of gold, silver, and the precious things of Egypt," and go on to conquer the Libyans and the Ethiopians (v. 43). But "reports from the east and north will disturb him" (v. 43). This evidently refers to reports every ancient king while on campaign feared: disturbance at home or elsewhere in the empire. Such reports would merely intensify the king's anger. He therefore set out to eliminate the problem. Antiochus did spend the last months of his life campaigning against the Parthians in the eastern sector of his empire, as well as the Armenians, located in the north. The author surmises that on his way north from Egypt, Antiochus would pause long enough to exterminate many. The word used to describe this action is חָרַם (*haram*, devote to destruction), a cultic term for complete elimination of a people (religious genocide) as a righteous duty. This implies some type of pogrom-like violence against the Jewish people.

The campaign would end badly, however. The author boldly predicts Antiochus's death in verse 45. He will pitch his palatial tents between the Mediterranean and the beautiful holy mountain, Mount Zion, in the vicinity of Jerusalem.[62] There he will come to his end without any help from any quarter of his empire. Antiochus perished, not in Palestine in the vicinity of Jerusalem, as this text indicates, but at Tabae in Persia sometime between November and December 164 BCE.[63] This evidently happened shortly before Judas Maccabeus rededicated the Jerusalem temple in December. Antiochus had attempted to loot the temple of Artemis in Elymais, loaded with silver, gold, golden shields, breastplates, and weapons, but was driven back by the enraged citizens of the town. Withdrawing to Tabae, in the vicinity of Isfahan, Persia, he contracted a mysterious disease and died. "Here I am perishing of bitter disappointment in a strange land," he allegedly said as he lay dying (1 Macc 6:13; see vv. 1–17).

In addition to this account of the death of Antiochus IV, there are several ancient versions, each differing in detail. According to Polybius, his death occurred as follows:

---

61. See Ps 83:5–8; 2 Chr 20:1–2; Di Lella, *Daniel*, 304.

62. The author may have drawn the notion that Antiochus would die on the mountains of Israel from Ezek 39, where the archenemy of Israel, Gog, falls in the eschatological battle on the mountains of Israel (vv. 1–6).

63. See 1 Macc 6:1–4; 2 Macc 9:1–12.

In Syria, King Antiochus, wishing to provide himself with money, decided to make an expedition against the sanctuary of Artemis in Elymais. On reaching the spot he was foiled in his hopes ... and on his retreat he died at Tabae in Persia, smitten with madness as some people say, owing to certain manifestations of divine displeasure when he was attempting this outrage on the above sanctuary.[64]

According to 2 Macc 1:14–16, Antiochus was slain in the act of robbing a temple. In 2 Macc 9:1–29, he was repelled during a raid of Persepolis and then stricken with a disease. Despite the inconsistencies, all accounts agree Antiochus died in misery in Persia after an attempt to plunder a temple. According to a list of the second-century Seleucid kings, he died in late November or early December, 164, just prior to the cleansing of the very temple in Jerusalem he had notoriously desecrated.

Why, after offering such a detailed version earlier in the vision (vv. 20–39), did the apocalyptist fail to predict accurately the final events of Antiochus's life? The author must have been unaware of Antiochus's military foray into Persia in 165 or of his death in Persia in 164. It follows the author may have written the apocalypse, or at least this vision, in 165 or 164, without a real awareness of the circumstances of these events. Without the sure hand of the historical record, which he had evidently followed throughout verses 2–39, he casts an imaginary vision of the woeful end of Antiochus.

The historical differences between verses 2–39 and the fanciful predictions of verses 40–45 are the main reason that many scholars think the book of Daniel was written, compiled, and edited between 165 and 164. That the author spends so much time in this chapter describing the wars between the Seleucids and Ptolemies, and the rise and exploits of Antiochus IV Epiphanes, indicates these events were of special interest to his audience in the mid-160s of the second century. It is hard to see how these details would have been of interest—or relevance—to a writer in the sixth century, hundreds of years before. Why, had the author been predicting the events from that historical vantage point, would he have so badly missed the details of the final days of Antiochus, when he had portrayed accurately the bulk of his main career? It is hard to escape the conclusion that the final author of Daniel was active in the mid-160s—the era of Antiochus IV—rather than in the sixth century, as has been traditionally assumed.

The author predicts the ideal kingdom to come will follow soon after the death of Antiochus IV Epiphanes. The vision continues into the next chapter.

---

64. Polybius, *Strategica*, 31.9, as cited in J. Collins, *Daniel* (Hermeneia), 389.

Time of the End

Daniel 12

Believe those who are seeking the truth.

Doubt those who find it.

—André Gide, *lNews.co.uk*

Once finished with the long sequence of Seleucid and Ptolemaic wars, culminating in the demise of Antiochus IV, the vision moves swiftly to the hoped-for deliverance of Israel promised by the prophets. This is the destiny of the Israelite people who have suffered under Antiochus.

Daniel 10–12 is really one extended vision account. During the transmission of the text, chapter divisions interrupting the flow of the narrative have been introduced,[1] but the vision itself, as we have seen, runs from Dan 10:1 to 12:4. Then comes the climax of the book in a short epilogue (12:5–13). Due to its content and structure, 12:1–3 may be taken as the description of a judgment scene,[2] while the epilogue is really a revelatory dialogue, including a brief angelic epiphany (divine appearance).[3] Judgment scenes culminate the visions in Dan 7–9, and even chapter 2. This vision follows a familiar pattern.

---

1. Chapter divisions were first introduced by Stephen Langton (c. 1150–1228 CE), later archbishop of Canterbury and supplied for the HB in the fourteenth century.
2. Nickelsburg, *Resurrection, Immortality, and Eternal Life*, 12.
3. J. Collins, *Daniel* (FOTL 22), 100–101.

TIME OF THE END (12:1–4)

> "At that time will arise Michael, the great prince who stands up for the sons of your people. There will be a time of distress such has never been since the nations until that time, and at that time your people will be delivered, all who are found written in the book. ² Many from those sleeping in the dusty earth will awake, these to everlasting life, those to disgrace, to everlasting abhorrence. ³ Those who are wise will shine like the shining of the expanse of heaven, and those who lead many to righteousness like the stars forever and forever. ⁴ But you, Daniel, conceal the words and seal the book until the time of the end. Many will roam about and knowledge will increase."

At that time (בָּעֵת הַהִיא, *baet hahi*) provides a temporal marker for the following judgment scene (v. 41).[4] It refers specifically to the final activity of Antiochus IV Epiphanes, expected to occur near the "time of the end" (Dan 11:40). Immediately following the death of this arrogant, brutal king—itself an act of judgment—the angel Michael would stand up on behalf of "the sons of your people." The words "at that time" must indicate for this author the divine judgment and the final deliverance of God's people would take place shortly after the death of Antiochus (164) in the second century BCE. The author does not envision any lengthy, indefinite period to transpire before the events depicted in the vision.

Most apocalyptists expect eschatological events, particularly those surrounding divine judgment, to be near at hand in their day or, at most, in the proximate future. Apocalyptic enthusiasts—those who read and study apocalyptic texts—throughout history generally regard their own era as the time of the end and expect the final events of human history to be pressing urgently in upon them. When for our writer the eschaton did not appear, the epilogue lists three additional speculative attempts to discern more precisely when this fateful moment might arrive (Dan 12:6–7, 11–12). The crisis of delay implied by these temporal projections is also reflected much later in the NT expectation of the second advent. Skepticism about the second advent seems to have arisen quite early among the first Christians. "Where is the promise of his coming?" asks one critical voice, late in the first century CE. "For ever since our ancestors died, all things continue as they were from the beginning of creation" (2 Pet 3:4). "After Jesus' death," observes G. K. Berkouwer, "the delay became the problem of the whole

---

4. The phrase *baet hahi* is found often as an eschatological marker in post-exilic prophecy (see Jer 3:17; 4:11; 8:1).

Christian community." This delay eventually led to what Berkouwer calls the "de-eschatologizing of religion,"[5] something we see already in John's Gospel. Christianity, in other words, began to de-emphasize its apocalyptic hopes and focus instead on the present, earthly experience, the here and now. The epic apocalyptic climax envisioned in Daniel failed to appear. The timing of the prophecy, as evidenced in this chapter, was considerably off, which those who transmitted this book were evidently aware. They allowed these words to stand as they were, however, because they ultimately regarded God as "the victor in the struggle of history."[6] This does not mean, of course, these apocalyptic hopes would never materialize; only in the form set forth in Daniel have they not been fulfilled.[7]

In this decisive, eschatological time, Michael, the angel patron who appeared at the beginning of the vision (Dan 10:13), would stand "over [עַל, *al*] your people," like a military guard. He is a reassuring presence when "a time of distress such has never been since the nations until that time" surges over the land. Jeremiah refers to the Babylonian captivity in similar language. "Alas!" he writes, "that day is so great there is none like it; it is the time of distress for Jacob; yet he will be rescued out of it" (Jer 30:7). "In those days there will be suffering," Jesus's apocalyptic discourse predicts, "such as has not been from the beginning of the creation that God created until now" (Mark 13:19; Matt 24:21), so severe that few would escape, except for divine intervention. The "narrative arc of apocalyptic eschatology is similar in many ways to that of the modern thriller," notes Newsom. "Tension and conflict build over a long period of time, culminating in an almost unendurable scene of violent conflict, which is suddenly resolved in favor of the heroes."[8]

Dispensationalists apply the prophecy of the great tribulation—both in Daniel and in the Gospels—to the closing days of earth's history, immediately before the second advent,[9] hence, an event obviously still in our future. The prediction of our Lord just quoted, however, applies it to the horrific Roman war (66–73 CE) in which Jerusalem was destroyed and burned, its citizens slaughtered by the thousands.

---

5. "From such an exegetical conclusion one can understand the impasse in which Christian faith was caught as history continued. Every passing day contradicted the expectation; faith in a future coming of Christ slid into the abyss" (Berkouwer, *Return of Christ*, 68–69). See Carroll et al., *Return of Jesus*. See also Matt 10:23; 1 Thess 4:13–17; Phil. 4:5; Jas 5:7–9; Rev. 1:1–2.

6. Towner, "Daniel," 633.

7. Porteous, *Daniel*, 144.

8. Newsom, *Daniel*, 360.

9. Walvoord, *Daniel*, 282–83.

Daniel's words reflect the author's immediate eschatological concern. At that time—after the death of Antiochus IV (164 BCE)—the people of God would be delivered, those found written in the book, the book of future judgment. Other HB passages call attention to such a scroll. "The Lord took note and listened, and a book of remembrance was written before him of those who revered the Lord and thought on his name" (Mal 3:16).[10] The imagery of a book or scroll is metaphorical, of course. We are not to imagine the heavenly court literally equipped with parchment or papyrus scrolls containing by now billions of names. Earlier, Daniel envisions a scene when the Ancient One takes the throne, the court sits in judgment, and "the books were opened" (Dan 7:9-10).

In one most significant eschatological passages in the HB, the apocalyptist now hears of a resurrection. "From the dusty earth [some] arise to everlasting life, [some] to disgrace, to everlasting abhorrence" (v. 2). This is the only clear reference in the HB to a general resurrection to life—or to damnation. Would all be resurrected? Those written in the book—the redeemed—would awake to everlasting life (חַיֵּי עוֹלָם, *hayyei olam*). In the HB, this phrase occurs only here. It contrasts with an everlasting abhorrence (דִּרְאוֹן עוֹלָם, *diron olam*). Consideration of these abhorrent ones—the damned—seems to mean, as one of the martyred Jewish youths put it when he was about to die, "One cannot but choose to die at the hands of mortals and to cherish the hope God gives of being raised again by him. But for you [Antiochus IV] there will be no resurrection to life!" (2 Macc 7:14). In Isaiah, these two destinies are also contrasted. Those who "remain before me, says the Lord; so shall your descendants and your name remain," but the abhorrent ones (*diron*), "the people who have rebelled against me," would be loathed by all flesh (Isa 66:22-24). In John's Gospel, Jesus draws on Dan 12:2. "Do not be astonished at this, for the hour is coming when all who are in their graves will hear his voice and will come out—those who have done good, to the resurrection of life, and those who have done evil, to the resurrection of condemnation" (John 5:28-29). The book of Daniel thus witnesses to the reality of a resurrection from death in which "no limit to the resurrected life is envisaged."[11]

---

10. See also Exod 32:32-33; Isa 4:3; Ps 69:28.

11. J. Collins, *Daniel* (Hermeneia), 392. Collins traces the development of the resurrection in Jewish thinking in an enlightening excursus, with special attention to the apocalyptic literature (394-98). Surprisingly, Gaebelein claims this "passage has nothing to do with physical resurrection"; it is a "figure of the national revival of Israel in that day [the restoration of Israel in the last days]" (Gaebelein, *Daniel*, 200; cf. also Talbot, *Prophecies of Daniel*, 215-18).

Is the resurrection universal in extent? The text states, "many from those sleeping in the dusty earth will awake," many—but not all. In Hebrew, the word translated as many is רַבִּים (*rabbim*), a term signifying numerous, manifold, plentiful, but not literally all. The preposition מִן (*min*, from) that follows *rabbim*, is partitive, meaning only some of the dead.[12] The passage would appear to refer to a large but limited resurrection. This passage, of course, foreshadows the general resurrection of the dead in the NT, predicated on the resurrection of Jesus. "Christ has been raised from the dead," Paul writes, "the first fruits of those who have died . . . for as all die in Adam, so all will be made alive in Christ" (1 Cor 15:20–22).

Those resurrected are said to have been sleeping in the grave. Sleep often appears in the Bible as a metaphor for death. Ordinary sleep is seen as a mini death, albeit a temporary state from which one generally awakes. Unlike sleep, death is an irreversible condition.[13] A few resuscitations—returns from the grave—are mentioned, but not on scale such as Daniel envisions.

Verse 3 refers to the מַשְׂכִּילִים (*maskilim*, those who are wise), whom we met in Dan 11:35, where they provided guidance to the people, but nevertheless tragically fell by fire and sword. Following so closely after verse 2, this term appears to refer to those just resurrected. That the *maskilim* would shine like the starry expanse of the heavens, and those who lead many to righteousness like the stars forever and forever, may identify them with the angelic hosts. The stars are the host of heaven (see 8:10). In 1 Enoch appears a parallel: "You shall shine like the lights of heaven, and you will be seen; and the windows of heaven will be opened to you . . . you are about to be making a great rejoicing like the angels of heaven . . . for you are to be partners with the good-hearted people of heaven" (1 Enoch 104:2–6 *OTP*).[14] However, it seems as though our text merely compares the *maskilim* and those who lead many to righteousness with the angels; it does not state they become angels or are to be equated with angels. While they may be included

---

12. Williams, *Hebrew Syntax*, §324.

13. Levenson, *Resurrection and Restoration*, 186; Newsom, *Daniel*, 362. For the few resuscitations from death in the HB, see 1 Kgs 17:17–24; 2 Kgs 4:32–37; 13:21. Samuel returns as an apparition (?) in 1 Sam 28:11–20. See also Isa 26:19, sometimes taken as a reference to a resurrection.

14. Note the image of shining in connection with the stars in other apocalyptic literature: Testament of Moses 10:9 ("he will fix you firmly in the heaven of the stars"); 2 Enoch 1:5; 66:7 ("they will be made to shine seven times brighter than the sun"); 2 Esd 7:97 ("how their face is to shine like the sun, and how they are to be made like the light of the stars"). Association with angels may be found in 1 Enoch 39:5; Wis 3:7; 5:5–6; and Matt 22:30 ("For in the resurrection they neither marry nor are given in marriage, but are like angels in heaven").

among the resurrected, they evidently also receive a transformation somehow differentiating them from other resurrected ones.[15]

Daniel is now instructed to conceal the words and seal the book until the time of the end (v. 4). For the great vision about the desecration of the temple, Daniel was similarly told to seal up the vision (Dan 8:26). In both cases, the visions were to be sealed for the future, evidently an occasion when their vital messages would be most needed. The epilogue repeats this admonition (v. 9) but gives little indication as to why the message should be concealed. In antiquity, documents such as scrolls were sealed with wet clay or wax.[16] The owner's signet ring was then pressed into the clay or wax, thus protecting the document from tampering or opening by unauthorized persons. The time at which a prophecy was about to reach fulfillment was the critical time when such a classified document would be opened. Hence, when apocalyptists anticipate the immediate fulfillment of a vision, they are told, "Do not seal up the words of the prophecy of this book, for the time is near" (Rev 22:10). Generally, in apocalyptic, the trope of secret, esoteric knowledge passed down to those capable of understanding it is a common feature.[17]

Part of the reason for sealing may lie in the nature of the composition of this book.[18] The visions, we have seen, are represented as taking place in the sixth century BCE, during the Neo-Babylonian and Achaemenid empires. The visions, as we have seen, climax in the Hellenistic period, when the Seleucid king Antiochus IV Epiphanes unleashed a severe persecution against the Jews, more than three hundred fifty years after the implied setting of the visions. The intricate detail, particularly of this final vision (Dan 10–12), would have had little significance for a Jewish exile living in sixth-century Babylon. It would have been unintelligible, literally sealed off from such readers, like those in Isaiah's day. "The vision of all this has become for you like the words of a sealed document. If it is given to those who can read, with the command, 'Read this,' they say, 'We cannot, for it is sealed.' And if it is given to those who cannot read, saying, 'Read this,' they say, 'We cannot read'" (Isa 29:11–12). Even though the implied author is living in the sixth century, by sealing the message for a future generation, the book addresses its real audience in the second century, when the book of Daniel was actually written. Given the political and religious turmoil of this period in

---

15. Newsom, *Daniel*, 364.

16. See 1 Kgs 21:8; Esth 8:8–10; Isa 8:16; Dan 6:17.

17. Newsom, *Daniel*, 365. See 1 Enoch 1:2; 2 Esd 14:45–46; Rev 5:1–5.

18. J. Collins, *Daniel* (Hermeneia), 341–42; Hartman and Di Lella, *Daniel*, 310–11. Cf. 4 Ezra 14:45–46, where similar circumstances prevail.

Jewish history, the message of Daniel would have then been extremely relevant and deeply encouraging. At that moment, it was a tract for the times. Crenshaw offers this explanation:

> This sequestration also implies that the material is reserved for a special group of people and is therefore esoteric knowledge. In this way the long delay between the time of the original prophecy and its actual fulfillment is given a rational explanation, and a rationale is provided for the emergence of an old book years later.[19]

Since the word for knowledge in Hebrew (דַּעַת, *daat*) can easily be confused with the word for evil (רעה, *raah*), on account of confusion between the initial *d* (ד) and *r* (ר), it is uncertain whether verse 4b should read "many will roam about and knowledge will increase," which we have translated here, or "many will roam about and evil will increase." The LXX renders the phrase as πλησθῇ ἡ γῆ ἀδικίας (*plesthe he ge adikias*, the earth is filled with unrighteousness). The preferred textual reading, however, is probably knowledge. The line is remarkably similar to Amos 8:12, "They shall run to and fro, seeking the word of the Lord, but they shall not find it." So long as the vision remains sealed, people would not be able to understand it.[20] Whether this refers to the time when the book is initially sealed or when it is finally to be opened is not clear.

The vision ends with Dan 12:4. It is followed by an epilogue (12:5–13). Because 12:5–13 has the feel of an addendum or postscript, we ask, did the original author/editor of Daniel compose the epilogue, or was it added by another? This is uncertain. Verses 5–10, 13, according to Hartman and Di Lella, come from one redactor, verse 11 from another, and verse 12 from still a third.[21] Theoretically, of course, one or more editors is possible—biblical manuscripts were frequently touched up, supplemented, or altered in this way—but there is not enough indication here to be definitive.

THE EPILOGUE (12:5–13)

> [5] Then I, Daniel, looked, and two others were standing, one on the bank of the stream, and the other on the [other] bank of the stream. [6] One said to the man clothed with white linen, who

---

19. Crenshaw, *Story and Faith*, 366.
20. J. Collins, *Daniel* (Hermeneia), 399.
21. Hartman and Di Lella, *Daniel*, 261, 311. Ginsberg also finds multiple editors within the epilogue (Ginsberg, *Studies in Daniel*, 30–38).

was upstream, "How long until the end of the wonders?" ⁷ Then I heard the man clothed in white linen, who was upstream. He raised his right and his left hand toward heaven and swore by the One who lives forever, that for a time, two times, and a half, and that when the shattering of the power of the holy people has come to an end, all these things will be finished. ⁸ I heard but did not understand. So I said, "My lord, what will be the outcome of these things?" ⁹ He said, "Go, Daniel, for shut up and sealed are the words until the time of the end. ¹⁰ Many will be purified, cleansed, and refined, but the wicked will act wickedly. None of the wicked will understand, but those who are wise will understand. ¹¹ From the time the regular burnt offering is taken away and the abomination of desolation put in place, there will be one thousand two hundred and ninety days. ¹² Happy are those who wait and arrive at the one thousand three hundred and thirty-five days. ¹³ And you, go on to the end. You will rest and rise in your lot at the end of the days."

The epilogue begins, like the final vision (Dan 10:4) and the vision of the ram and the goat (8:1–3), on the bank of an unidentified stream of water (v. 5). Like the vision of the ram and the goat, the angelic dialogue here is similar (see 8:13–14). Found here, too, are additional, more precise dates for the elusive end of days. Two persons, no doubt angelic mediators, stand on the bank, one on either side, a little distance from each other. One is clothed with white linen, reminiscent of the apparel of the High Priest. The other asks the one clothed in linen, "How long until the end of the wonders?" (v. 6). This query sets up the rest of the epilogue, concerned with when the events in the final vision and probably the entire apocalypse would reach fulfillment.

The man clothed in white linen raises both hands toward heaven and takes an oath (v. 7). Ordinarily only the right hand is raised for an oath.²² That two are raised here underscores the gravitas of the oath. He swears by the One who lives forever—the God of Israel—that the wonders would climax in a time, two times, and a half. This is the same time span mentioned in Dan 7:25, three and a half years or 1260 days (a month = thirty days), also corresponding to the half of the week mentioned in 9:27.

Daniel does not understand what this means, any more than do we, so he asks, "My lord, what will be the outcome of these things?" (v. 8). He apparently wants to know when the end (אַחֲרִית, *aharit*, after part, end, outcome) of these critical matters would be reached. His curiosity is understandable. For the author, it seemed that "history was winding to a close, and

---

22. Gen 14:22; Deut 32:40.

every announcement of hostile engagement must have been electrifying for a community awaiting the end."[23] Having realized various time periods in his visions, he wants to know how long it would be until the divine plan for the deliverance of his people would be realized.

That the deliverance failed to take place as the author expected poses a critical challenge for interpreters. Here is a delay not unlike the eschatological delay of the second advent for Christians, as we have mentioned above.

The response Daniel receives is just as frustrating as it has been to all who through the centuries have asked the same question. *Go about your business, Daniel, because matters are sealed until the time of the end* (v. 9). He received the same advice in Dan 12:4, and at the end of the long vision about the temple (see 8:17, 27). During the time until the elusive terminus (v. 10), many will be purified, cleansed, and refined. These are to be identified with the *rabbim* (רַבִּים) mentioned in 11:33, 44, and 12:2-3, the faithful who are subjected to the persecution under Antiochus IV. In 11:35, it is the *maskilim* (מַשְׂכִּילִים) or wise, who would be purified, cleansed, and refined. But the persecution would affect all, not just the wise. The wicked, on their part, would continue to act wickedly. None of the wicked would understand; but the wise would understand. The wicked would nevertheless continue down the road to destruction. This may refer to the Hellenistic Jews, complicit with Antiochus, who do not understand the importance of the events outlined in the vision.

Continuing the explanation, the angelic mediator introduces another span of time, 1290 days. This period is measured from the time the regular burnt offering (תָּמִיד, *tamid*) is taken away and the abomination of desolation put in place (v. 11). When Antiochus IV desecrated the temple by taking away the daily burnt offerings (the *tamid*) and setting up an idolatrous shrine devoted to the Olympian Zeus at the altar of sacrifices in the temple courtyard (December 167 BCE), this period apparently began. Another period is then added, 1335 days, that evidently extends the 1290 by forty-five days (v. 12). Unfortunately, the terminus of these periods is not indicated, so interpretation is uncertain. Several approaches have been proposed.[24]

The first accepts that these time periods (1290, 1335) are related initially to the Antiochene oppression but also become predictive of earth's final days, the last great time of tribulation. Young thus finds the ultimate or secondary fulfillment in the "arch-enemy of the Lord known as the Antichrist." He reads the obscure line, "when the shattering of the power of the holy people has come to an end" (v. 7), as the time when the "Antichrist will

---

23. Crenshaw, *Story and Faith*, 364.
24. Linder, *Daniel*, 489-94, gives an inventory of the attempts to solve these numbers.

practically have destroyed God's people." That times are specified indicates that God restricts their duration. As Jesus indicated, "If those days had not been cut short, no one would be saved; but for the sake of the elect those days will be cut short" (Matt 24:22). The whole period of Antiochus's oppression, in Young's view, is typical of the reign of the antichrist in the last days of earth's history.[25]

Similarly, Whitcomb places these dates within the reign of the eschatological antichrist. The 1290 days adds another thirty to the 1260 days in verse 7. This represents the month following the Lord's cleansing of the reconstructed temple in Jerusalem. This would occur just past the middle of the seventieth week in Dan 9:27. The 1335 represents another extension, possibly to allow time for the judgment of the nations, to determine who is eligible to enter the Messiah's kingdom.[26]

For Wood, the extra forty-five days allows time for the setting up of the divine government at the beginning of the millennium.[27] These calculations, it seems to me, are based on pure speculation. In accordance with the dispensational perspective, the time periods are transferred to the modern era, when they are expected to be fulfilled. Daniel is read to predict time periods far in the distant future from the author's own day. Because these predictions were not fulfilled in Daniel's time is the most obvious reason for futurists to extend them into the distant future. Otherwise, they must come to terms with a failed prophecy, which in turn conflicts with their idea of an inerrant Bible.

A second more widely accepted view understands verses 11–12 as glosses, intended to extend the original period predicted for the restoration of the temple, 2300 evenings-mornings, or 1150 days during which the evening and morning *tamid* sacrifices would be absent from the temple liturgy (see comments on Dan 8:13–14).[28] They are initiated "from the time the regular burnt offering is taken away and the abomination of desolation put in place" (v. 11). The temple was desecrated by Antiochus Epiphanes on December 6, 167 BCE, and reconsecrated by Judas Maccabeus on December 14, 164, three years and eight days, or 1103 days later.[29] The Antiochene oppression of 167–164, in other words, lasted a little over three

---

25. Young, *Prophecy of Daniel*, 259–64. Walvoord also applies these periods to the "last period preceding the second coming of Christ which brings conclusion to the time of the end" (Walvoord, *Daniel*, 293). See Talbot, *Prophecies of Daniel*, 222–23.

26. Whitcomb, *Daniel*, 168; see also Gaebelein, *Daniel*, 206–8).

27. Wood, *Daniel*, 328. On the millennium, see Rev 20.

28. Jeffery, "Introduction and Exegesis," 548. This view goes back to Hermann Gunkel (1895) but is probably the original sense of these predictions.

29. See 1 Macc 4:41–59.

years.³⁰ The additional time periods (1290 and 1335) indicate that whatever was expected at the conclusion of these periods had not yet occurred. If the reconsecration of the temple was expected, the author or the editors who supplied these new time periods evidently lived to see that reconsecration. Since Antiochene desecration of the temple ended in 164,³¹ there would have been no need to extend the time after the restoration of the temple. So why add additional periods of time? Evidently, the author or editors did not perceive in the reconsecration of the temple—as important as the event was—the complete fulfillment of the community's hopes. Nevertheless, at the end of these periods, notes Newsom, "the entire eschatological scenario, with the decisive breaking of the Gentile kingdoms, the deliverance of the people, and the resurrection of the righteous and the wicked had not taken place."³² The prophecy had not been fulfilled.

While these computations do not play a significant role in the interpretation of the book, there remains the third option of understanding them as symbolic; they were not intended to provide any precise beginning and ending dates. This symbolic significance, what Shedl calls "mystical arithmetic,"³³ may have been obvious to the original audience but remains obscure to us. This resolution may not seem very satisfying, but at least is more realistic than trying to figure out how these dates fit into actual history.

The comment "happy are those who wait and arrive" at the 1335 days presumably indicates a date at which this period would have ended. The final words of the angel mediator assure Daniel that, should he endure in his mission (v. 13), he will rest in the grave or Sheol, and rise in the resurrection mentioned in verse 2, at the end of the days. Daniel's final destiny, in other words, is to be resurrected along with the righteous.

Thus ends the Hebrew/Aramaic text of Daniel, the book as found in the Palestinian (Hebrew) canon. In the LXX Greek tradition, there are three or four additions or supplements to the book. To these Additions we now turn.

---

30. See 7:23–27; 8:23–25; 11:31–36; 12:11.

31. Hartman and Di Lella, *Daniel*, 313–14. See Dan 7:23–27; 8:23–25; 11:31–36; 12:11.

32. Newsom, *Daniel*, 367.

33. Shedl, "Mystische Arithmetik," 101–5.

PART III

The Additions to Daniel

The Prayer of Azariah

Daniel 3:24-45

There is an "Archimedian" point outside the world which is the little chamber where a true suppliant prays in all sincerity, where he lifts the world off its hinges.

—SØREN KIERKEGAARD

Inserted between Dan 3:23-24 in the LXX translation of Daniel, at the strategic point in the narrative where the reader eagerly waits to know what is going to happen in the furnace, appear two liturgical poems: the Prayer of Azariah (vv. 24-45) and the Song of the Three Young Men (vv. 46-90).[1] These insertions considerably delay the action of the main narrative, but at the same time heighten the sense of the miraculous and, to a certain extent, enable the reader imaginatively to enter into the experience of the three youths amid the crackling flames. These constitute Dan 3:24-90 in the LXX, with an introductory narrative at verses 46-51, describing the appalling effects of the furnace. Here, for purposes of analysis, we will treat the prayer and the song separately.

According to the story in Dan 3, three Jewish youths were to be burned alive for failing to worship Nebuchadnezzar's huge golden idol set up on the open field. The executioners who fearlessly cast them into the furnace were

---

1. The Prayer of Azariah and the Song of the Three form chs. 8-9 in the Odes or appendix to Psalms in the LXX, where they are titled Prayer of Azariah and Hymn to Our Fathers, respectively. Some have suggested that the prose introduction (vv. 46-51) was original in the Aramaic text of Daniel, but has fallen out during its transmission, only to reappear in reconstructed form in the LXX. We have no textual evidence of this, however.

violently burned to death. But the three young men were not consumed, because God sent a heavenly being into the furnace to deliver them.

The Prayer of Azariah is formally a communal confession or national lament for Israel's sinfulness like the prayer in Dan 9:4-19.[2] Azariah is one of the three young men flung into the furnace for refusal to bow down to the king's golden image. It is his voice we hear in the prayer, according to the Theodotian text.

Why was the prayer inserted? The answer is lost in the mists of ancient history. That it is an insert is clear from the repetitious character of the prayer's introduction (Dan 3:24-25), the use of Hebrew rather Babylonian names, as is generally the case in Daniel for the three youths, and the inappropriateness of much of the content for its present context.[3]

The original language of the Prayer of Azariah was probably Hebrew, while that of the Song of the Three, either Hebrew or Aramaic.[4] A Semitic original suggests a Palestinian or perhaps a Babylonian provenance. Allusions in the Prayer of Azariah to "lawless and hateful rebels," may refer to the apostate Jews who adopted Hellenism, and to an "unjust king, the vilest in all the land" (Dan 3:32), are reminiscent of the critical period when the oppression of Antiochus IV (175-164 BCE) was in full force. Although it is uncertain, both Susanna and Bel and the Dragon—the other Additions—also may have come from Semitic originals.

Whatever their original language, daSilva thinks they were present in the Greek text of Daniel from its beginning.[5] Other scholars suppose they were added, perhaps at different times, after Daniel had reached its final Hebrew/Aramaic form.[6] There are "strong grounds for doubting whether the two main Additions formed part of the original [Hebrew] text," insists Oesterley. The Additions "are not only unnecessary, they are intrusive, and break the otherwise even flow of the story."[7] Some think the Additions, or at least the bulk of them, were present in the original Hebrew/Aramaic text of Daniel but deleted about the time when the text reached its final form.

---

2. See also similar prayers in Ezra 9:6-15; Neh 9:6-37; Bar 1:15-3:8.

3. Moore, *Daniel, Esther, and Jeremiah*, 60.

4. daSilva, *Introducing the Apocrypha*, 224-25.

5. "It is highly probable that the Additions to Daniel were present in the Greek versions from the beginning (and not inserted later into the Greek Daniel)" (daSilva, *Introducing the Apocrypha*, 224).

6. Moore, *Daniel, Esther, and Jeremiah*, 29, 24; Oesterley, *Introduction to Books of Apocrypha*, 275; Bennett, "Prayer of Azariah," 629.

7. Oesterley, *Introduction to Books of Apocrypha*, 275. Note Hartman and Di Lella: "These sections were not deleted from the MT; they never formed part of the edition represented by the MT" (Hartman and Di Lella, "Daniel," 408).

As regards the question of canonicity, there is no clear citation of the prayer or the song in rabbinic writings such as the Talmud[8] prior to the Middle Ages. Nor do NT writers quote from the Additions, unless the letter to the Hebrews alludes to the Song of the Three Young Men (Heb 11:33-34). Josephus, the Jewish historian of the first century CE, does not appear to have been aware of them.[9] The first indication of their scriptural use among the Church Fathers is found in Justin Martyr (d. 165). He is followed by Clement of Alexandria (c. 215), Tertullian (c. 160-220), Cyprian of Carthage (c. 205-258), and then several others.[10] Evidently, Julius Africanus (d. after 240) was the first Church Father to question their canonicity. Jerome (c. 340-420), who translated the Latin Vulgate, followed him. However, when one considers the citations from the Additions by many of the Church Fathers, it is evident most of the Church Fathers regarded them as integral parts of Daniel.[11]

Azariah is the Hebrew name of one of the three young men in Daniel. Azariah is the same as Abednego (Dan 1:7). The author has attributed this prayer to Azariah and placed it in the Greek text of Daniel. Neither the literary form nor its content, however, fits the context. It seems incredible, as purported, to think Azariah uttered this prayer while standing in the flames. "There is no hint that the suppliant is standing in a fiery furnace," insists daSilva, "nor would it be possible to pray such a prayer for deliverance in the furnace—either it would have been granted before the word was spoken, or no word would have been spoken at all."[12] Furthermore, the prayer contains a personal confession of sin (3:29-30), ill-suited for those who have just been cast into the furnace because of their faithful adherence to Hebrew law.[13]

The Jewish literature of the Second Temple period (the era following the Babylonian exile) contains several instances where martyrs, tottering on

---

8. The Talmud is the traditional collection of Jewish stories, customs, folklore, and legal argumentation. There are two versions: the Babylonian Talmud and the much shorter Jerusalem Talmud.

9. Josephus, *Ant.* 10:10.5.

10. Justyn Martyr, *Apologia* (*First Apology*) 1:46; Clement of Alexandria, *Eclogae propheticae* (*Extracts from the Prophets*) 1; Tertullian, *De Oratione* (*On Prayer*) 15; Daubney (*Three Additions to Daniel*, 76-80) lists citations through the sixth century, while Julius provides an even more exhaustive list ("Griechischen Danielzusätze").

11. The Roman Catholic and Orthodox traditions include Daniel (with the Additions), along with Tobit, Judith, Wisdom of Solomon, ben Sira (Ecclesiasticus or Sirach), etc., with some variation as to the number of works included, in what Protestants call the Apocrypha of the Old Testament. Because these books are regarded as canonical in Catholic and Orthodox traditions, they are more respectfully known as the deuterocanonical (secondary canon) books.

12. daSilva, *Introducing the Apocrypha*, 227.

13. Eissfeldt, *Old Testament*, 590.

the verge of death, express solidarity with sinful Israelites and offer themselves vicariously, as it were, for the entire community.[14] Daniel 3 is akin to such a martyr story. At the place where this Addition occurs (vv. 23-24), it is uncertain whether the three young men are going to be martyred. Whoever inserted the prayer thought it fitting to introduce at this point an eloquent petition on behalf of the entire Jewish community. Perhaps this editor saw the three young men standing in some way for the whole people of Israel. Whatever may have been his intent, in its present position, the prayer heightens the wonder of the deliverance from the fiery furnace.

The prayer may be divided into two parts. A contrast between God and the community is drawn in a confession in verses 26-38. The people's need to worship and comply with God's will, with a plea for divine aid on behalf of the community, forms the second part (vv. 38-45).[15] Expressed in poetical form in the prayer comes one of the great themes of the HB: God is on the side of God's people, delivering those who trust.

> 3 [24] And they were walking amid the flame, singing hymns to God and blessing the Lord. [25] Then, having stood, Ananias opened his mouth amid the fire and said:

This line provides a transition from the previous verse, "Then these three men, Shadrach, Meshach, and Abednego, fell bound into the midst of the furnace of burning fire" (Dan 3:23). Referring specifically to the three men in the furnace, "singing hymns . . . and blessing the Lord" provides a preface for the prayer and the hymn. There is a striking resemblance between this scene and Paul and Silas praying and singing hymns to God while in prison (Acts 16:25). According to the Theodotion text, Azariah is the one praying, while the LXX text has all three engaged in prayer ("Then Ananias, Azariah, and Mishael prayed").[16] Azariah is standing amid the fire. The threat to him and his two associates is genuine. The fiery heat is horribly real. We recall Azariah and his colleagues had resolutely insisted, "Our God is able to rescue us from this flame, O King. But if not, we will never bow down to your god" (3:18). Now the moment of truth had suddenly come.

---

14. Frizzell, "Azariah, Prayer of," 361. See 2 Macc 6–7, esp. 7:30-38.

15. There are at least two different modern systems of indicating the verses in the prayer. One follows the LXX and Theodotion versification; the other treats the prayer as independent and numbers the verses beginning with number one. Since the rayer and the Song of the Three have been included in Dan 3, this translation and commentary follows the LXX/Theodotion enumeration.

16. Interestingly, Azariah is not regarded in Daniel as the most important of the three (Moore, *Daniel, Esther, and Jeremiah*, 56).

A CONFESSION (3:26-37)

²⁶ "Blessed are you, Lord, the God of our fathers,
   and praiseworthy and glorified also is your name forever.
²⁷ For you are just in all you have done to us.
   And all your works are true and your ways right,
   and all your judgments are true.
²⁸ True judgments you have executed
   according to all that you have brought upon us
   and upon the holy city of our fathers—Jerusalem—
   because in true judgment you have carried out
   these things because of our sins.
²⁹ For we have sinned in all things and acted lawlessly to fall away from you,
   and in all things we have erred,
   and thus your commandments we have not obeyed.
³⁰ Nor have we carefully kept in mind,
   neither done as you commanded us,
   that it might be for our good.
³¹ And all that you have brought upon us,
   and all that you have done to us,
   in true justice you have acted.
³² You handed us over into the hands of our enemies,
   lawless and hateful rebels,
   and to an unjust king, the vilest in all the land.
³³ And now it is not for us to open our mouths,
   shame and disgrace have come upon your servants,
   even to those who worship you.
³⁴ Do not hand us over to a complete end because of your name,
   and do not smash into pieces your covenant.
³⁵ And do not withdraw your mercy from us,
   for the sake of Abraham, your beloved,
   and for the sake of Isaac, your servant,
   and Israel, your holy one,
³⁶ To whom you spoke,
   'Their seed will multiply as the stars of the heaven
   And as the sand upon the shore of the sea.'

> ³⁷ For, Lord, we have been reduced beside all the nations,
> and we are brought low in all the earth today
> because of our sins."

Azariah begins by affirming the justice of God and God's worthiness to receive praise (v. 26). Even in God's judgments upon Israel and Jerusalem, however severe they may have appeared, God has been true and right (vv. 27-28). He admits this because Israel has erred and been unfaithful to God's commandments. The prayer moves beyond individual confession and becomes a corporate confession of guilt characteristic of the prayers in Ezra 9:6-15, Bar 1:15—3:8, and Dan 9:4-19. By using the first person plural (we, our), Azariah identifies with Israel and thus intercedes for the entire people.

Because Israel has not done as God commanded (vv. 29-31), they have been turned over to their *enemies*, who are identified in the parallel line (v. 32) as *lawless and hateful rebels* and an *unjust king, the vilest in all the land*. The unjust king is probably a veiled reference to Antiochus IV, although in the circumstances of the exile, it would apply as well to Nebuchadnezzar, who has just consigned the three youths to the furnace. The lawless rebels, an oblique phrase probably referring to the Hellenistic Jews described in 1 Macc 1:11-15, 41-43, were allied with Antiochus IV. "In those days certain renegades came out from Israel and misled many . . . They joined with the Gentiles and sold themselves to do evil" (1 Macc 1:11, 15).

In their exilic plight, Azariah confesses Israel has become a shame and disgrace (v. 33). As a people defeated and driven from their homes, they would be shamed and ridiculed because of their devotion to an impotent God who lacked the ability to deliver them from their enemies. The confiscation of the temple vessels (Dan 1:1-2) and their desecration in Belshazzar's drunken festival (5:2-4) made this shame and reproach palpable. The prayer and singing of hymns are bold testimony that the conditions of exile—even the sentence of death in the flames—are not the ultimate reality Israel has to accept. "When you walk through fire you shall not be burned, and the flame shall not consume you. . . . Do not fear, for I am with you" (Isa 43:2b, 5a). The holy God is their refuge, even in the flames of exile.

Azariah pleads with God not to abandon the people, not to annul the covenant God has made (v. 34). Such abandonment would mean God had gone back on the promises to Abraham, Isaac, and Israel "your holy one" (v. 35). Long ago, God promised Abraham a progeny like the stars of the heaven, but instead Israel has now been brought low in the eyes of the nations because of their sin (vv. 36-37). Appeal to Israel's ancestral memory calls attention to God's past reliability as a premise for God's "saving presence in the future."[17] The prayer now moves from confession to a direct plea for God's intervention.

PLEA FOR DIVINE AID (3:38-45)

> [38] "And there is in this time no ruler, no prophet, no leader;
>   no burnt offering, no sacrifice, no oblation, no incense;
>   no place to bring first fruits before you and find mercy.
> [39] But with a contrite heart and humble spirit,
>   may we be accepted,
>   as with burnt offerings of rams and bulls,
>   and as with ten thousand fattened lambs,
> [40] thus may our sacrifice be before you today
>   and be complete before you,
>   because there is no shame to those who trust in you.
> [41] And now we follow with the whole heart,
>   and fear you and seek your face.
> [42] Do not put us to shame;
>   but deal with us according to your kindness
>   and according to the fullness of your mercy.
> [43] Deliver us in accordance with your wonderful deeds
>   and bring glory to your name, O Lord.
> [44] And let all be put to shame who show harm to your servants,
>   and let them be deprived of all power,
>   and let their strength be broken in pieces.
> [45] Let them know that you alone are Lord God,
>   and glorious over the whole world. "

Humiliated, shamed, Israel is now without ruler (ἄρχων, *archon*, prince, leader), prophet, (community) leader, burnt offering, sacrifice, oblation, or incense, or place wherein to offer first fruit sacrifices, necessary to find mercy (v. 38).[18] This is an obvious reference to exilic conditions, after the first temple had been destroyed. Absence of these leaders indicates exilic circumstances. Reference to the absence of a prophet would not have been true during the Babylonian exile, because Jeremiah and Ezekiel were then active. This applies more to the time of Antiochus IV, who profaned the temple and

---

17. Smith-Christopher, "Additions to Daniel," 161-62.
18. See Hos 3:4; 2 Chr 15:3.

suspended its sacred rites (see Dan 8:11-14), than to the exile. In Daniel's prayer, there is a similar concern for the disgraced temple. "Listen to the prayer of your servant and to his supplication—for your sake—and let your face shine upon your devastated sanctuary" (9:17). Here a great dilemma presents itself: what happens when the one place specifically designated for the temple rites is gone?[19] When the sacrificial ritual is suspended? When the priests grow silent?

Azariah's prayer transcends external temple ritual and appeals directly to the inner attitude of the devotee (v. 39). A contrite and humble spirit finds acceptance before God, "as with burnt offerings of rams and bulls, and as with ten thousand fattened lambs." In lieu of burnt offerings, in other words, the brokenhearted and crushed in spirit will be heard. The figure ten thousand is hyperbolic, indicating a countless number of sacrifices is offset by a humble, contrite spirit. We think of Micah's powerful word: "Shall I come before him with burnt offerings, with calves a year old?" Micah asks, "He has told you, O mortal, what is good; and what does the Lord require of you, but to do justice, and to love kindness, and to walk humbly with your God? (Mic 6:6-8). To fellowship humbly with God, demonstrating love and mercy to fellow human beings is more than all the sacrifices in the world.[20]

Those who thus trust in God will be complete (v. 40). This is a remarkable statement. The word complete in the Theodotion text is ἐκτελέω (ekteleo), which is often used of the completion of a building. Here it seems to refer to bringing to completion the spiritual disposition of the worshiper. The parallel line indicates it is those who trust in God who are without shame rather than those who depend on cultic rituals. The LXX text, in fact, uses ἐξιλάσκομαι (eksilaskomai, propitiate) instead of ἐκτελέω.[21] This is a cultic term. These remarkable statements have in view the temple cult (system of worship). But since we do not have the presumed Semitic text of the prayer, it is impossible to know what the LXX or Theodotion meant by this rendition. The passage is obscure, in any event, and may be textually corrupt.[22] The prayer echoes the sentiments about the temple ritual found frequently in the prophets. A sincere, heartfelt attitude, a trusting spirit, even without literal sacrifices, finds forgiveness of sin and puts an individual (and a community) into right standing before God.

---

19. See Deut 12:8-18.
20. See also Ps 51:16-17; 141:2; Isa 57:15; 66:2; Hos 6:6; Amos 5:21-24.
21. BDAG, 243, 276.
22. The Theodotion rendering "be complete before you" (ἐκτελέσαι ὄπισθέν σου, ektelesai opisthen sou) is odd, but probably means something like "follow with perfect obedience and fidelity" (See Bennett, "Prayer of Azariah," 628).

Azariah now shifts to a commitment to follow with the whole heart, while at the same time seeking the presence of God (v. 41). To seek the face of God refers to approaching God in worship at the temple or other designated site. Such a commitment involves grateful acceptance of divine mercy (v. 42), especially evident in God's θαυμάσιά (*thaumasia*, wonderful deeds). It is participation in God's longsuffering patience that removes the shame inherent in Israel's status as the oppressed (v. 43). Wonderful deeds probably refers to the decisive salvific acts of Yahweh, such as the liberation of Israel from Egypt. The same Greek word negatively designates the plagues against Pharaoh in the LXX of Exod 3:20. The plea for a wonderful deliverance renders this line pertinent to the three young men in the furnace.

In keeping with the individual and national laments found in the Psalms, which often urge judgment upon one's enemies (v. 44),[23] Azariah now asks that those who harm Israel be themselves humiliated and put to shame: may they suffer disgrace and be deprived of power, with their strength broken.

The result of these judgments, however, is not so much punitive, as it is that the oppressor nations may come to recognize the God of Israel alone as God (v. 45), whose glory is pervasive through the whole land. The adjective μόνος (*monos*, alone, singly existing) is probably a monotheistic affirmation. God alone is sovereign over all inhabited land; the various gods of the nations are not.

The prayer teaches one of the great lessons of the HB: God is at work in human lives, especially in those of the chosen people. The prose narrative accompanying it shows God is with people individually, delivering those who trust. The Song of the Three indicates God is the Lord of all, the Creator exalted above his creation. Such affirmations are a part of post-exilic Judaism in general and with the book of Daniel in particular.[24]

---

23. See Ps 109:26–29; 137:7–8.
24. Moore, *Daniel, Esther, and Jeremiah*, 51.

The Song of the Three Young Men

Daniel 3:46–90

Someone reading Dan 3:23, "the three men . . . fell down, bound, into the furnace of blazing fire," would not know what happened to the three young men. Were they suddenly engulfed by the superheated flames? Burned alive? Were they somehow still preserved miraculously alive? Only Nebuchadnezzar, the next verse indicates, really knew (v. 24). Such missing information creates a gap between these two verses. The delay and abrupt resumption of the narrative in verse 24, while it may have been an intentional narrative strategy, has caused many to wonder whether something has fallen out of the Aramaic text. The leading candidate for what may have fallen out is the prose narrative appearing in the LXX (3:46–51) between the Prayer of Azariah and the Song of the Three Young Men (3:46–51) or something very much like it. This prose narrative now constitutes both an introduction to the song and a transition from the prayer. It admirably fills in the hypothetical gap. The setting is still the blazing furnace.

THE PROSE NARRATIVE (3:46–51)

[46] The king's servants—who had cast them in—did not cease stoking the furnace with naphtha, pitch, flax, and brushwood. [47] And the flame spilled out above the furnace forty-nine cubits, [48] and spread out and burned those found near the furnace of the Chaldeans. [49] But the angel of the Lord came down into the furnace together with those around Azariah and shook the flame of fire out of the furnace [50] And he made the inside of the furnace like a moist wind whistling and the fire did not touch

them at all, nor cause pain or trouble them. ⁵¹Then the three as one voice sang praises, glorified, and blessed God in the furnace.

This gory, gruesome introduction precedes the song. In contrast to the prayer in the LXX, however, here all three men, instead of only one, join in testifying. The king's servants continue stoking the fire of the kiln with naphtha, pitch, flax, and brushwood until it flares upward more than seventy feet (forty-nine cubits), so intense it burned those found near the opening of the furnace (v. 46-48). The ghastly lines heighten the impact of the extraordinary deliverance.

Completely neutralizing the roaring flames, driving them out as though they had no effect on Azariah and his companions, the angel of the Lord made the inside of the furnace like a moist wind whistling (vv. 49-50). A first-century BCE Jewish text puts it this way: "The three companions in Babylon who had voluntarily surrendered their lives to the flames so as not to serve vain things, you rescued unharmed, even to a hair, moistening the fiery furnace with dew and turning the flame against all their enemies" (3 Macc 6:6). A δρόσος (*drosos*, dew), translated as moist wind, is said to pass through the furnace. Dew occurs in several passages, where it is metaphorically associated with God's grace.[1] The dew is not merely moisture in contrast to fire' it is analogically God's grace in reassuring the people.[2]

The figure described as an angel of the Lord in the Aramaic text of Dan 3:25 is likened here to the appearance of a god. Jewish tradition identifies this mysterious godlike figure or angel with Gabriel, who appears elsewhere in Daniel.[3] The astonishing effect of the angel's appearance results in the three remaining unharmed, leading them to break out in song (v. 51).

THE SONG (3:52-90)

The Song of the Three Young Men is really a hymn, consisting of two litanies and a doxology in Dan 3:52-56, an invitation for all creation to praise God (vv. 57-87), and a concluding benedictive (vv. 88-90). The first part of the song resembles Pss 96-97, where both the people and the creation are urged to praise God, while the second part is akin to Ps 148, where the angels, sun, moon, and waters sing praise. Its arrangement is comparable to Ps 136, wherein a half-line expression, sung by a choir or soloist, is followed by a

---

1. "I will be like the dew to Israel; he shall blossom like the lily; he shall strike root like the forests of Lebanon" (Hos 14:5; see also Micah 5:7; Zech 8:12; Isa 26:19).
2. Smith Christopher, "Additions to Daniel," 164; J. Collins, *Daniel* (Hermeneia), 204.
3. b. Pesah. 118a-b. See Dan 8:15; 9:21.

repetitive refrain, sung by the congregation. The author of the song has obviously drawn upon the Hebrew hymnic tradition. He has placed the song here perhaps because the Aramaic text of 3:23–30, despite the extraordinary rescue, omits any expression of gratitude to the Lord on the part of the three young men. The only voice heard in the Aramaic text after the young men are delivered from the furnace is Nebuchadnezzar extolling the God of the three (vv. 28–29).

The song lives on in Christian liturgy. In the rubric of the first prayer book of Edward VI (1549), the song was read during Lent as a response to the Old Testament lection at the morning prayer.

PRAISE TO THE LORD (3:52–56)

> [52] Blessed are you, Lord God of our ancestors,
>   and worthy of praise and highly exalted forever.
> And blessed is your holy, glorious name,
>   and praised and exalted forever.
> [53] Blessed are you in the temple of your holy glory,
>   and highly praised and glorified forever.
> [54] Blessed are you who peers into the underworld,
>   seated upon the cherubim,
>   and praiseworthy and highly exalted forever.
> [55] Blessed are you upon the throne of your kingdom,
>   and praised and highly exalted forever.
> [56] Blessed are you in the firmament of the heaven,
>   and lauded and glorified forever.

On a note of praise, the song begins, using the second person singular throughout. Emphasis goes to divine sovereignty displayed from the highest heaven all the way down to the underworld, the shadowy realm of the dead. Divine sovereignty is a major theme in Daniel, but here it is presented in largely spatial imagery. The sovereign God, as it were, occupies all the spaces in the cosmos from highest to lowest.

The cherubim (χερουβίμ, cheroubim) in verse 55 are represented in ancient art as hybrid creatures, usually lionlike, with wings. They attend the presence of God. The large temple sculptures of cherubim (Heb. plural of cherub) show cherubim on both sides of the king's throne like guardians, forming two sides of the throne itself. A thirteenth-century BCE bas-relief of King Ahiram of Byblos depicts Ahiram seated upon a throne beside a lionlike creature with the wings of the bird and the head of a woman.[4] Such imagery calls to mind the transcendent God of Israel sitting upon a throne like an oriental potentate, surrounded by angelic attendants.

CALL TO PRAISE (3:57-63)

> [57] Bless the Lord, all works of the Lord;
> sing praise and highly exalt him forever.
> [59] Bless the Lord, O heavens;
> sing praise and highly exalt him forever.
> [58] Bless the Lord, angels of the Lord;
> sing praise and highly exalt him forever.
> [60] Bless the Lord, all waters above the heaven;
> sing praise and highly exalt him forever.
> [61] Bless the Lord, all powers of the Lord;
> sing praise and highly exalt him forever.
> [62] Bless the Lord, sun and moon;
> sing praise and highly exalt him forever.
> [63] Bless the Lord, stars of heaven;
> sing praise and highly exalt him forever.

Now the song shifts to the second person plural imperative, summoning the community to join in the praise of God. The poem has an responsive structure, apparently designed for a liturgical antiphony. In an antiphonal structure, the choral leader calls or chants a stanza, then the audience responds with another, generally repetitious, refrain. This provides a repetitive format not unlike Ps 136, which antiphonally repeats the half line "for his steadfast love endures forever" about every other line. In the song, the antiphonal response is "sing praise and highly exalt him forever," repeated over and over.

The basis for such praise is the works of the Lord (v. 57), the created works of God. Each line mentions one of these, beginning with the heavens, where clouds drift randomly with the winds (v. 59). We come across some irregularities in the versification of the text in the printed LXX. Verse 59, for instance, comes before verse 58, and verses 71–72 are also out of order.[5]

Next praised are the angels; the waters above the earth, source of rain poured out in the Noachian flood (see Gen 7:11–12); the powers; the sun,

---

4. *ANEP*, fig. 458. See Gen 3:24; Ezek 1:4–28; 1 Kgs 6:23–25.
5. I have followed the order of verses in the Rahlffs edition of the Theodotion text.

moon, and stars, who were often objects of worship. Notice how the Wisdom of Solomon puts it:

> All people who were ignorant of God were foolish by nature;
> And they were unable from the good things that are seen to know the
>   one who exists,
> Nor did they recognize the artisan while paying heed to his works;
> But they supposed that either fire or wind or swift air,
>   or the circle of the stars, or turbulent water,
>   or the luminaries of heaven were the gods that rule the world.[6]

Here, however, these created entities are under the sovereignty of the Lord. God should thus be praised, highly exalted, or lifted above all creation.

The circumstances appearing in verses 64–73 have to do with meteorological conditions or weather, as we would put it. Winter and summer, rain, dew, and snow, are all celebrated as gifts of God.

> [64] Bless the Lord, all rain and dew;
>   sing praise and highly exalt him forever.
> [65] Bless the Lord all winds;
>   sing praise and highly exalt him forever.
> [66] Bless the Lord, fire and burning heat;
>   sing praise and highly exalt him forever.
> [67] Bless the Lord, frost and cold;
>   sing praise and highly exalt him forever.
> [68] Bless the Lord, dew and falling snow;
>   sing praise and highly exalt him forever.
> [71] Bless the Lord, nights and days;
>   sing praise and highly exalt him forever.
> [72] Bless the Lord, light and darkness;
>   sing praise and highly exalt him forever.
> [69] Bless the Lord, ice and cold;
>   sing praise and highly exalt him forever.
> [70] Bless the Lord, frost and snow;
>   sing praise and highly exalt him forever.
> [73] Bless the Lord, lightning and clouds;
>   sing praise and highly exalt him forever.

---

6. Wis 13:1–3; cf. Rom 1:24–32.

These atmospheric phenomena call to mind a comparison between Yahweh and the Canaanite deity Baal. Baal was the storm God, often depicted as the rider of clouds, who presided over the meteorological phenomena mentioned here. The lightning and clouds, with their shaded darkness, punctuated by sudden shafts of light, which ends the list, were thought particularly to be his domain.[7] Reference to fire and burning heat (v. 66), while it may be an atmospheric allusion, also calls to mind the fiery furnace where the three youths presumably stand as they sing these praises.

> 74 Let the earth bless the Lord;
>   let it sing praise and highly exalt him forever.
> 75 Bless the Lord, mountains and hills;
>   sing praise and highly exalt him forever.
> 76 Bless the Lord, all that grows upon the ground;
>   sing praise and highly exalt him forever.
> 78 Bless the Lord, seas and rivers;
>   sing praise and highly exalt him forever.
> 77 Bless the Lord, springs;
>   sing praise and highly exalt him forever.
> 79 Bless the Lord, sea monsters and all that move in the waters;
>   sing praise and highly exalt him forever.
> 80 Bless the Lord, all birds of the heaven;
>   sing praise and highly exalt him forever.
> 81 Bless the Lord, all wild animals and cattle;
>   sing praise and highly exalt him forever.

The song next focuses on the earth and the waters on it. Over these, too, God reigns. God's authority as Creator gives God dominion over all the gods represented in animal or human form, including the gold-plated idol set up by Nebuchadnezzar in this story. Among the creatures God has made are the sea monsters that move in the waters (v. 79). The Greek term is κῆτος (sea monster), the same word used in the NT for the aquatic creature that swallowed Jonah (Matt 12:40). Although the NRSV renders this word as whales, it no doubt included various large and unknown sea creatures. It calls to mind the Leviathan of Job. "On earth it has no equal, a creature without fear" (Job 41:33).

> 82 Bless the Lord, O mortals;
>   sing praise and highly exalt him forever.

---

7. Smith-Christopher, "Additions to Daniel," 168.

> [83] Bless the Lord, Israel;
>> sing praise and highly exalt him forever.
> [84] Bless the Lord, priests;
>> sing praise and highly exalt him forever.
> [85] Bless the Lord, servants of the Lord;
>> sing praise and highly exalt him forever.
> [86] Bless the Lord, spirits and souls of the righteous;
>> sing praise and highly exalt him forever.
> [87] Bless the Lord, holy and humble in heart;
>> sing praise and highly exalt him forever.

In addition to the people of earth, Israel, the priests in Israel, the servants of the Lord, and the holy and humble in heart are to break out in praise. These groups may refer to what Joel Weinburg calls the "Citizen-Temple-Community." This community lived in occupied Palestine under the Persians (and later the Greeks) and held authority over the temple and temple personnel, such as the priests.[8] The spirits and souls of the righteous sounds like a reference to the faithful who have died (v. 86), but probably refers instead to the living righteous rather than disembodied spirits.[9] They, too, are bidden to join the holy and humble in heart (v. 87) in the praise of God.

> [88] Bless the Lord, Hananiah, Azariah, and Mishael;
>> sing praise and highly exalt him forever,
>> because he has delivered us out of Hades,
>> and saved us out of the hand of death,
>> and rescued us out of the midst of the burning fiery furnace,
>> and rescued us out of the midst of fire.
> [89] Thank the Lord because he is good,
>> for his mercy is forever.
> [90] Bless the God of gods, all who worship;
>> sing praise and highly exalt him,
>> because his mercy is forever.

The concluding lines of the hymn call upon the three young men, using their Hebrew names, to exalt and praise God. God has delivered from Hades—the grave—from the power of death, and from the burning fiery furnace. Note the parallel repetition: Hades/death; fiery furnace/midst of

---

8. Weinberg, *Citizen Temple Community*, as cited in Smith-Christopher, "Additions to Daniel," 168.

9. Moore, *Daniel, Esther, and Jeremiah*, 73.

fire (v. 88). We are brought back to the literary setting of the song: three youths sentenced to die in the flames. The controversy in this chapter—the command to worship Nebuchadnezzar's golden idol—is resolved when the call goes out to all who worship (v. 90). Interestingly, the word for these worshipers is σεβόμενοι (*sebomenoi*), a religious term later applied to gentiles who had come to accept the one God of Judaism and attend the synagogue but did not become proselytes by undergoing circumcision, the so-called God-fearers (Acts 10:2; 17:17). There is no reason, however, to think it has here acquired this meaning. Here it addresses all—Jew and gentile—even those who worship Nebuchadnezzar's image. All are called to praise the God of gods. The Lord of the Hebrews is the God of gods. By providing an opportunity for the three young men to express their gratitude for God's rescue, these lines no doubt provide at least one reason why the entire song has been inserted into the Greek Danielic text.

The hymn closes with the mercy of the Lord, which is forever (v. 89). Mercy comes when an enemy threatens. Now it has been demonstrated in rescuing the three youths from certain death. While the song, like the prayer, is clearly an insertion into the story, it offers a theological perspective not apparent in the Aramaic text of Dan 3. God, the Lord of creation, has worked God's majestic power in delivering these three faithful servants. The implication of the song is that God, Creator and Lord, will indeed deliver all God's people from the machinations of evil.

Susanna

Daniel 13

Let justice be done though heaven should fall.
—LUCIUS CALPURNITUS PISO CAESONINUS (D. 43 BCE)

Susanna is one of the first courtroom dramas of world literature. Unlike the stories in Dan 1–6, it takes place in a small provincial Jewish court in the Babylonian diaspora, not in the high, rarified echelons of Babylonian government. The Theodotion text places the story before Dan 1, while the LXX and the Latin Vulgate puts it after Daniel as chapter 13. Acknowledging Daniel's age, Theodotion's order accordingly puts the story before anything in Dan 1–6 takes place. The stories in Dan 1, where Daniel is taken into Nebuchadnezzar's court, and Dan 2, where Daniel interprets the king's dream, are also stories of the youthful Daniel.

Susanna and Bel and the Dragon are classified as edifying fictional short stories, or haggadic folktales, probably added to Daniel to make the book more consistent with other novelistic literature of the period, such as Tobit, Judith, and Esther. They are part of a cycle of Daniel stories that circulated among the Jewish people in the last centuries before the Common Era.[1]

While the differences between the LXX and Theodotion in the other Additions to Daniel are minimal, with Susanna they are more significant. The Theodotion text contains numerous small additions not found in the LXX. A casual side-by-side reading of the LXX and the Theodotion versions of Susanna, even in an English translation, reveals significant differences

---

1. Wills, "Susanna," 1470.

in phrasing, word selection, and sentence structure. Most of these, clarifies Collins, "can be explained as redactional" or editorial.[2]

Let us take a few examples. At the outset, Theodotion tells us the elders "were ashamed to admit their lust" (v. 11). This observation is noticeably absent in the LXX. Again, in verse 39, the LXX has, "We approached and recognized her, but the young man covered himself and fled," whereas Theodotion reads, "While seeing them engaging in sexual intercourse, we were unable to restrain the man, because his strength was greater than ours, and having opened the doors, he ran away." Verse 51a of the LXX ("Daniel said to them") has been deleted by Theodotion. The ending of the story, which reads in the LXX "Let us also watch out for capable young sons, for youths will be pious, and there will be in them a spirit of knowledge and understanding for ever and ever," has been reworked in Theodotion: "And Daniel was honored greatly before the people from that day and onward" (v. 64).

Although the plot and the essential elements of the story remain unchanged, even these small differences raise textual questions. If the LXX represents the older text, as seems likely, was Theodotion a new edition, or a revision of the LXX? Was it an independent translation of the same source text (*Vorlage*) as used by the LXX?[3] If an independent translation of a different *Vorlage*, was it written in Aramaic? Hebrew? Unfortunately, the evidence bearing on these questions is so fragmentary, it precludes an answer.[4] My translation of the main text below is from Theodotion. Occasional reference will be made to the LXX translation.

Although the Theodotion text softens the contrast between young and old, Daniel appears as a gifted youth who counters the purported wisdom of the shrewd local village elders. Two wily elders are caught in sexual misconduct and harassment. By exposing their crime, a young Daniel turns the tables on the wise elders.[5] Unlike anything else in Daniel, this story raises the issue of women's rights and social place in ancient Israelite society.[6] In the Hebrew/Aramaic Daniel, few women are even mentioned. The queen mother, probably Adda-guppi, appears in Dan 5:10, while Berenice, daughter of Ptolemy II—daughter of the king of the south—is alluded to as a pawn

---

2. J. Collins, *Daniel*, 428. Collins provides a side-by-side English translation (420–25). While I translate the Theodotion text here, I have drawn the translations from the LXX below from Collins.

3. A source text is known technically as a *Vorlage* (lit., that which lies before).

4. Moore, *Daniel, Esther, and Jeremiah*, 78–80. Theodotion is usually dated c. 190 CE, but scholars now think there existed an earlier edition made between 50 BCE and 50 CE (Würthwein, *Text of the Old Testament*, 107).

5. Brown, *Character in Crisis*, 88.

6. Smith-Christopher, "Additions to Daniel," 175–76.

in an arranged, political marriage (Dan 11:6). Also, as a woman given in marriage, Cleopatra, daughter of Antiochus III, appears in 11:17. None of these women is referred to by name; all are relatively insignificant to the narrative. Susanna breaks with this pattern. On the one hand, as the wife of Joachim, a community leader, she enjoys great respect. On the other, she is shamed when her words and experience are silenced by the false accusations of the male elders, who enjoy greater privilege and authority in the community. They are believed; Susanna is denied and ignored.

The story may be divided into three dramatic movements (vv. 7–62), prefaced by an introduction (vv. 1–6) and concluded by an epilogue (vv. 63–64).

INTRODUCTION (13:1–6)

> ¹ There was a man dwelling in Babylon, and his name was Joakim. ² He had taken a wife whose name was Susanna, the daughter of Hilkiah, beautiful in appearance and one who feared the Lord. ³ Her parents were also righteous and taught their daughter according to the law of Moses. ⁴ Joakim was very wealthy and had a garden adjacent to his house; the Jews used to come to him because he was the most distinguished of them all.
>
> ⁵ Two elders from the people had been appointed judges in that year, concerning whom the Lord said, "Lawlessness came out of Babylon, from elders—judges—who were supposed to govern the people." ⁶ These men were continually at Joakim's house, and all who engaged in litigation used to appear before them.

Although the story is set in Babylon, it is difficult to imagine such a serene, luxurious setting among the Jews during the Babylonian exile (vv. 1, 5) The Murashu texts[7] as well as Jeremiah do indicate, however, that some Jewish exiles may have economically flourished. The wealthy, prominent Joakim may be an example. He has a beautiful wife named Susanna, the daughter of the equally outstanding Hilkiah. Beautiful in appearance (καλὴ σφόδρα, *kale sphodra*, exceedingly good appearance), one who feared God, she had been raised according to the law of Moses (v. 3). This calls attention to her circumspect moral character, which figures later in the story. Her beauty is

---

7. At Nippur, about sixty miles southeast of Babylon, were discovered hundreds of business records on clay tablets containing Jewish names like Benjamin, Gedaliah, and Hananiah. These documents of the Murashu family show that some Jews in Nippur were quite successful in business in the exilic period (see Hoerth, *Archaeology*, 387; Coogan, "Life in the Diaspora," 6–12). Cf. Jer 29:5–7.

linked with her morality in such a way Susanna is valued—or desired—for her beauty and moral character.

Two elders, elected by the people, and carrying out their traditional role in Jewish society, were serving as judges. They appeared at Joakim's house frequently because it was evidently the community venue for litigation (v. 6). Ezekiel, the Hebrew prophet among the Babylonian exiles, mentions the elders customarily gathering at his home to hear the word of the Lord (Ezek 14:1-5), much as the elders in Susanna assembled at Joakim's home for judicial proceedings. The author tips his hand regarding these two elders, vilifying them by claiming that "lawlessness came out of Babylon, from elders—judges—who were supposed to govern the people." No citation like this may be found in the HB. The closest is a vision of Zechariah in which wickedness is transported in an ephah (or basket) to Babylon.[8] Jeremiah's reference to two false prophets living in Babylon, Ahab and Zedekiah, is often regarded as the model for the two elders in this story. Ahab and Zedekiah, Jeremiah says, "perpetrated outrage in Israel and have committed adultery with their neighbors' wives," besides speaking lying words in the Lord's name (Jer 29:21-23). Like the two elders, they were to suffer death for their crimes.

THE SEXUAL HARASSMENT OF SUSANNA (13:7-27)

> [7] Now it happened after the people left, at midday Susanna entered and walked about in her husband's garden. [8] The two elders used to watch her entering each day and walking around, and they began to lust for her. [9] And they perverted their minds and turned their eyes away so as not to be aware of Heaven nor mindful of just decisions. [10] Both were deeply conflicted in conscience about her; but they did not inform each other of their distress [11] because they were ashamed to admit their lust, for they wanted to have sexual intercourse with her. [12] And so they eagerly watched each day to catch sight of her.
>
> [13] They said to one another, "Let's now go home, because it is the lunch hour." And upon leaving, they parted from one another. [14] Having turned back, they came to the same place, and upon questioning each other on the reason, they admitted their lust, and then mutually arranged a time when they would be able to find her alone.

---

8. Zech 5:5-11; cf. Jer 23:13-14; 29:20-23.

About noon, apparently after all the judicial proceedings of the day had concluded and the household was quiet, Susanna usually took a stroll in her husband's enclosed garden (v. 7). This was not a vegetable garden, but an enclosure with trees and other plants on the order of a royal Persian park, only smaller.[9] The two elders have observed her routine for several days, the desire for her intensifying all the while. They begin to lust for her (v. 8). The Greek term ἐπιθυμία (*epithumia*, strong desire, lust) has both negative and positive connotations. Here it is used for illicit sexual desire.

They suppress their conscience, however, turning away from heaven, a circumlocution for God (Dan 4:31–34), a common stylistic device in Second Temple Jewish writings. As they "perverted their minds and turned their eyes away" from God, in so doing they also turned away from their sworn moral duty to administer justice (v. 9). Just as they violated their own moral values, they became willing to violate others. Desire and obsession for Susanna deeply conflicted both men, although they were ashamed to admit their inner struggle (v. 10–11). Similarly, Amnon, David's son and heir apparent, "made himself ill because of his sister Tamar" (2 Sam 13:2). "No, my brother," Tamar cried out, "do not force me." Amnon refused to listen, so "being stronger than she, he forced her and lay with her" (2 Sam 13:2, 11–14). The two elders had similar intent (v. 12). They desperately wanted intercourse with the beautiful Susanna, Joakim's wife. With illicit desire smoldering within, daily they bided their time, longing for every glimpse of her.

At lunch one day, they part company. Each thinks privately to return by a different way to continue stalking Susanna. When they circle back by separate routes, they suddenly encounter each other. Grudgingly, they have to explain their mutual intentions (vv. 13–14). They then collude to find an opportune time to sexually confront Susanna.

> [5] Now it happened while they carefully watched for an opportune day, she entered just as before on the third day, alone with two of her maids, and wished to bathe in the garden, for it was hot. [16] There was no one there except the two elders, hidden and watching her. [17] She said to the maids, "Now bring me olive oil and ointment, and shut the doors of the garden so that I may bathe." [18] And they did as she said: they shut the doors of the garden and went out by the side doors to bring the things she had instructed, but they did not see the elders, for they were hiding.
> [19] Now as soon as the maids left, the two elders rose and accosted her. [20] They said, "Look, the doors of the garden have

---

9. J. Collins, *Daniel*, 429.

been shut and no one can see us. We desire you; therefore, consent and be with us. ²¹ But if you do not, we will testify against you that a young man was with you, and for this reason you sent the maids away from you." ²² Susanna groaned and said, "I am completely trapped! For if I do this, death is mine; if I do not, I cannot escape your hands. ²³ My decision is not to do this—to fall into your hands rather than sin before the Lord."

²⁴ And so Susanna cried out with a loud voice; the two elders also cried out loudly against her. ²⁵ Moving quickly, one of them opened the doors of the garden. ²⁶ When those in the house heard the clamor in the garden, they rushed in the side door to see what had happened to her. ²⁷ When the two elders told their story, the servants were very ashamed because never at any time had anything like this been said about Susanna.

Soon the opportunity comse. We should not miss the third day motif here. The Theodotion text reads τρίτης ἡμέρας (*trites hemeras*, third day), an expression generally used for the appointed time of an event. In the NT, it becomes formulaic for Jesus's resurrection.¹⁰ On a hot, sultry third day, Susanna enters the garden to bathe (v. 15). This appears to be an impromptu decision on the part of Susanna; she did not bathe in the garden every day. "The bathing scene not only excites the elders," admits Moore, "but it can also fire the imagination of some readers."¹¹ The whole scene makes us think of the story of David and Bathsheba. Walking around on his roof one evening, David saw a woman bathing, and she was "very beautiful" (2 Sam 11:2). Susanna sends her maids for olive oil and ointment but remains alone—and vulnerable—in the garden (v. 16–17). Whether the reference is to soaps, ointments, or cosmetics is not clear. These lotions were normally used after the bath.

Hiding in the shadows, the two elders rush Susanna (v. 18–19). "We are alone," they insist, "no one can see us. Agree to lie with us. If you don't, we'll tell people we came upon you and a young man making love, after you had dispatched your maids [v. 20]. Although we tried to apprehend him, he was too strong for us and fled the scene." Her word against theirs!—a familiar dilemma. "They now have the power of the male over the female," Smith-Christopher notes, "of an elder over a young person, and of judges within the community."¹²

---

10. Hosea 6:1–3; Matt 16:21; Mark 8:31; 1 Cor 15:4.

11. Moore, *Daniel, Esther, and Jeremiah*, 97. Verses 15–18 are missing from the LXX, which raises suspicion the bath scene may be an insertion into the story.

12. Smith-Christopher, "Additions to Daniel," 179. "It is worth pausing to reflect on the fact that false accusation is a threat *only* when there is an unequal distribution of

Susanna flatly refuses (vv. 23–24). In so many words, decisively she says, "No!" She realizes her dilemma. Should she submit, she would commit adultery, the penalty for which in the Jewish community was death (Deut 22:22–24). Should she resist, they would no doubt rape her. My decision, quickly calculating, she resolves, is not to do this. Instead, she would put her trust in God. Although the text does not explicitly tell, what happened was attempted rape, if not rape itself. The illicit charges the elders bring against her at trial assume intercourse had taken place—although at the hands of an anonymous youth—and she was therefore guilty of adultery (vv. 34–41).

She desperately cries out—her only defense in this critical situation—and they also react by shouting, probably so others within earshot could hear (v. 24). By crying out, Susanna fulfilled the letter of the law. When assaulted within a village or inhabited area, if a woman cried out against her assailant, she would be deemed innocent (Deut 22:23–27). One of the elders, however, hastily opens the gates of the garden, presumably to provide evidence that the young man who had allegedly been there had escaped (v. 39). The people outside the compound rush in to see what all the hubbub is about (v. 25–26). Caught almost red-handed, the two elders promptly offer their twisted account of Susanna's alleged treachery. The text is silent on whether Susanna reacts. Presumably, being a woman in this awkward situation, she does not. Like many rape victims today, she has to endure humiliation while fuming in silence. The two male judges, however, are immediately—without question—believed. Even the servants who knew her well draw back (v. 27), very ashamed, because Susanna had never been accused of such decadence.

THE INDICTMENT AND TRIAL OF SUSANNA (13:28–46)

> [28] Now it happened the next day when the people came to the house of her husband Joakim, the two elders arrived, full of the wicked plot against Susanna to put her to death. [29] They said in the presence of the people, "Send for Susanna, the daughter of Hilkiah, who is the wife of Joakim." They summoned her. [30] And she came, and her parents, and her children, and all her relatives.
> [31] Now Susanna was very elegant and beautiful in appearance. [32] The offenders ordered her to be uncovered, for she was veiled, so that they might be sated with her beauty. [33] But those with her—all who saw her—were weeping.

---

power" (italics in original).

³⁴ Then having stood up amid the people, the two elders placed hands on her head. ³⁵ But while weeping, she looked up to heaven, because her heart trusted in the Lord. ³⁶ The elders said, "While we were walking around in the garden alone, this woman entered with two maids, shut the doors of the garden, and dismissed the maids. ³⁷ And a young man, who was hiding, came to her and lay with her. ³⁸ However, we were in the corner of the garden, and seeing the lawlessness, we ran to them. ³⁹ While seeing them engaging in sexual intercourse, we were unable to restrain the man, because his strength was greater than ours, and having opened the doors, he ran away. ⁴⁰ But having taken hold of this woman, we asked who the young man was, ⁴¹ but she would not tell us. We testify to these things." The assembly believed them as elders and judges of the people and condemned her to die.

⁴² Then Susanna cried out with a loud voice and said, "O Eternal God, Knower of hidden things, who knows all things before they exist, ⁴³ you know that they have given false testimony against me, and behold, I am to die, having done nothing of which these men have wickedly accused me."

⁴⁴ The Lord heard her voice. ⁴⁵ And as she was being led away to perish, God stirred up the spirit of a young man named Daniel. ⁴⁶ And he cried out with a loud voice, "I am innocent of this woman's blood!"

Even though the LXX locates the trial in a synagogue, presumably in the same vicinity, the Theodotion text situates it at the home of Joakim and Susanna, adjacent to the scene of the alleged crime (v. 28). Here the people gather. The two elders come fully prepared to prosecute the case. Susanna is accompanied by her children, mother and father, and her relatives. Joakim is not mentioned as present, which makes the reader wonder if he also had become suspicious of her innocence (v. 30). The elders have her unveiled, a way of shaming her in public (v. 32). The LXX claims Susanna was stripped, exposing her breasts. This was evidently a process for shaming one accused of adultery.[13] According to the Mishnah (the rabbinical code of laws, now preserved in the Jewish Talmud), should a woman refuse to admit guilt, thus pleading not guilty, a priest was required to mess up her hair, rip and tear her clothes away, exposing her breasts. If the woman were physically attractive, as here, these actions were not literally to be taken.[14] Theodotion mentions her beauty as the reason why the elders wanted her unveiled,

---

13. Cf. Ezek 16:37–40; Hos 2:2–3, 10.
14. m. Sotah 1.5.

but it is more likely this procedure was designed to humiliate, much like having a prisoner come into a courtroom dressed in orange prison scrubs, feet shackled, hands cuffed. Susanna understandably is weeping (v. 33), anxiously anticipating the verdict soon to be rendered.

As the trial begins, the elders place their hands upon Susanna's head, evidently to bear witness against the accused (v. 34).[15] Earlier, they had laid hands on her intending to rape; now they do so to condemn. As they testify against her, they emotionally rape her all over again. With tears streaming down her face, Susanna looks toward heaven, indicating in her despair that she still trusts in God. Here the LXX adds her prayer: "O Lord, eternal God, who knows all things before they come into existence, you know that I did not do what these wicked men have so falsely accused me." Theodotion relocates the prayer to follow Susanna's conviction (vv. 42–43), where it more appropriately fits.

The testimony the elders offered is quite believable (v. 41) and includes all the major elements of the alleged incident. While they were strolling in the garden, they relate, they observed Susanna dispatch her attendants and shut the gates of the garden (v. 36). Then a young man, who had been hiding, emerged, and joined Susanna, at which point they engaged in sexual intercourse (συγγίνομαι, *sunginomai*, engage in sexual intercourse) in the presumed privacy of the garden (v. 37). But the elders were watching (v. 38). Springing out of hiding, they abruptly interrupted the coital embrace and tried to restrain the young lover, but he proved too strong for both and escaped, leaving the garden gates open behind him (v. 39). They pressed Susanna as to his identity (v. 40), but she would not tell (v. 42). Both elders swear to the accuracy of their recollection. Since they are elders and judges in Israel, they are presumed beyond suspicion. They are not subject to cross-examination.[16] After hearing their testimony, the assembly judges Susanna guilty and condemns her to death. As an innocent victim, Susanna cries out to God—her only hope—for vindication. "I am to die, having done nothing of which these men have wickedly accused me" (vv. 42–43). Her prayer, containing the line that God "knows all things before they exist," or before they happen, may be a subtle allusion to Daniel's visionary experiences.

Daniel, we now learn, happens to be present. His outcry—"I am innocent of this woman's blood!"—introduces him into the story. The delayed mention of Daniel has led some to suspect Daniel is a later insertion into the story. Whether this is true—there is no textual evidence—his assertion, like

---

15. See Lev 24:14.

16. "Only on the evidence of two or three witnesses shall a charge be sustained" (Deut 19:15).

Pilate at the trial of Jesus,[17] evidently signifies he is absolved of any culpability in the verdict against Susanna. He has spoken, the text tells us, because the Lord has stirred his spirit to act on behalf of a young woman unjustly accused (vv. 45–46). The Lord, in other words, had heard her prayer (v. 44). Although it is from a later time, the Jewish Mishnah relates the procedure of execution for one condemned:

> When the person to be stoned is led out, a herald must precede proclaiming these words: "This person, [name] son of [name], is on the way to being stoned for the crime of [specific offense], on the testimony of [name] and [name]; whosoever can show his innocence, let him approach and set forth his reasons." If none appeared, when they came within ten cubits of the place of stoning, the condemned was invited to confess, in deference to Joshua 7:19.[18]

DANIEL RESCUES SUSANNA (13:47–64)

[47] All the people turned to him and said, "What is this word that you have spoken?" [48] As he stood in their midst, he said, "Are Israelites thus fools, having not examined or clearly acknowledged, have you condemned a daughter of Israel? [49] Return to the tribunal, because these men have given false testimony against her."

[50] So all the people returned with haste, and the elders said to him, "Come, sit in our midst and inform us, because God has given you the gift of honor." [51] Daniel said to them, "Separate them far from each other and I will examine them."

[52] When they were separated one from the other, he called one of them and said to him, "Having grown old of evil days, now your sins have come home—what you did previously—[53] rendering unjust judgments, on one hand, and condemning the innocent, and on the other, acquitting the guilty, when the Lord said, 'The innocent and the just you shall not put to death.' [54] Now then, if you saw this woman, under what tree did you see them consorting with each other?" He said, "Under a mastic tree." [55] Then Daniel said, "Correct! You have lied against your

---

17. "He [Pilate] took some water and washed his hands before the crowd, saying, 'I am innocent of this man's blood; see to it yourselves'" (Matt 27:24).

18. m. Sanh. 6:1–2. Having been found guilty of appropriating sacred spoils of war, Achan is required to confess: "My son, give glory to the Lord God of Israel and make confession to him . . . tell . . . what you have done; do not hide it" (Josh 7:19).

own head, for already the angel of God, having received a sentence from God, will split you down the middle."

⁵⁶ And having removed him, he ordered to bring the other, and he said to him, "Seed of Canaan and not Judah, beauty has deceived you and lust perverted your heart. ⁵⁷ Thus you have acted toward the daughters of Israel, and being afraid, they have consorted with you, but a daughter of Judah would not put up with your lawlessness. ⁵⁸ Now then, tell me, under what tree did you catch them consorting with each other?" He said, "Under an evergreen oak." ⁵⁹ Daniel said to him, "Correct! You have lied, and against your own head, for the angel of God is waiting, having the sword to split you down the middle; thus, he may destroy you (both)."

Daniel calls attention to the glaring injustice. Susanna has not been fairly examined. Her testimony has not been heard (v. 48), a requirement under Jewish law.[19] The people, recognizing Daniel's honorable reputation—a gift of honor—quickly reassemble (v. 50). Does Daniel possess some exculpatory evidence, aside from the fact Susanna's testimony had not be heard, or does he just intuitively sense something was wrong with both the accusation and the verdict? We are not told. He nonetheless instructs the court to separate the two elders from each other to prevent any collusion (v. 51) and allow him to cross-examine them.

Daniel examines the first elder. After rebuking him for his past rendering of sinful, unjust judgments (vv. 52–53),[20] he turns to ask him, "Under what tree did you see them consorting with each other?" (v. 54). The word, ὁμιλέω (homileo, be in company with or consort with) can refer to sexual intercourse,[21] which is probably the sense here. Daniel's question leaves little doubt that the accusation the elders have made concerns adultery or, at least, sexual abuse. "Under a mastic tree," the elder responds. This species of tree is evidently the σχῖνος (schinos), probably the *Pistacia Lentiscus*, which produces a sweet-smelling gum. σχῖνος rhymes with σχίζω (schizo), the penalty for false testimony in verse 55: an angel of God "will split [σχίζω] you down the middle." Daniel accuses the elder of lying and denounces him.

Having summoned the second elder, Daniel accuses him of sexual lust on account of Susanna's beauty. But Susanna managed to thwart his perverted desire. "A daughter of Judah would not put up with your lawlessness" (v. 57), while presumably a daughter of Israel ironically would. This remark may offer a hint of the rancor many Judean exiles felt toward the Northern

---

19. See m. Avot 1:9.
20. See Isa 5:23; 29:21; Jer 7:6; 19:4; 22:3, 17; Prov 24:24.
21. *LSJ* 1222.

Kingdom, Israel, which had been taken into exile in the late eighth century BCE, a century and a half before Judah also went into exile. Focusing on the elder, Daniel asks, "Under what tree did you catch them consorting with each other?" The elder curtly replies, "Under an evergreen oak" (v. 58). The πρῖνος (*prinos*) is probably the ilex or scarlet oak (*Querus coccifera*), but as is apparent, this identity differs from the testimony of the first elder. The name of this tree, πρῖνος, rhymes with πρίζω (*prizo*) which is used in the penalty exacted for false testimony: "split [πρίζω] you down the middle." πρίζω means saw (in two) or cut in two (with a saw). This penalty seems horrific but may simply be a metaphor for capital punishment (v. 59), like our "they will crush you."

This answer obviously contradicts the first elder. Daniel has ensnared them in conflicting testimony (v. 61). They stand condemned. The penalty for such false accusation was that the accuser would suffer the same fate as the falsely accused. In terms of retribution, this would mean the death penalty. Daniel alludes to this in his comment "You have lied against your own head" (v. 55). "You shall do to the false witness," says Deuteronomy, "just as the false witness had meant to do to the other" (Deut 19:19).

> 60 Then all the assembly raised a great cry and blessed the God who delivers those who hope in him. 61 They rose up against the two elders, because Daniel had convicted them out of their own mouth for having borne false testimony, and they did to them according to the same manner they had sought to do evil against the neighbor, 62 to act in accordance with the law of Moses and to put them to death. Thus, the blood of innocence was spared on that day.
> 63 Hilkiah and his wife praised God regarding their daughter Susanna, together with Joakim, her husband, and all her relatives, because there was not found in her a shameful deed. 64 And Daniel was honored greatly before the people from that day and onward.

With this verdict, the people raise a great cry and bless the God who delivers those who hope in him (v. 60). Their reaction links this story with others in Dan 1–6, especially chapters 3 and 6, which end with doxologies.[22] Here is the role reversal we see elsewhere in Daniel; the guilty receive condemnation; the innocent, vindication.

Shame and embarrassment are now lifted from the house of Joakim. Joakim, Susanna, and all the relatives rejoice in God (v. 63). A deadly weight has been lifted. Justice has come for the powerless. Significantly, the story

---

22. J. Collins, *Daniel* (Hermeneia), 434.

closes with an accolade to Daniel. He was honored greatly before the people from that day and onward (v. 64). Since he is a young man in this story, the Theodotion text, as we have noted, places this narrative before Dan 1. Two additional stories about Daniel now follow in Dan 14.

Bel

Daniel 14:1-22

Thus shall you say to them: "The gods who did not make the heavens and the earth, these shall perish from the earth and from under the heavens."

—JEREMIAH

Bel and the Dragon features two stories about the futility of idol worship. The first (Dan 14:1-22) tests the boastful claim that an idol named Bel is indeed a living deity. Evidence for this, the Persian King Cyrus insists, lies in the idol's nightly consumption of an enormous amount of food, "twelve bushels of fine wheat and forty sheep and six measures of wine" (v. 3). The second story—the Dragon—follows in vv. 23-42. The name Bel is from the Akkadian *belu* (he who rules), a title for the god of Babylon otherwise known as Marduk. From ancient times, the Babylonians regarded Marduk as the deity who created heaven and earth out of the body of the vanquished goddess Tiamat.[1]

The legendary story of Bel tells of Daniel's challenge to Cyrus that he be allowed to demonstrate Bel is not a living god, but merely an idol of clay, wrapped in bronze, inert, capable of nothing. This story is an idol parody,

---

1. Moore, *Daniel, Esther, and Jeremiah*, 133. The famous Akkadian text Enuma Elish relates in gory detail that Marduk "with his unsparing mace . . . crushed her skull. When the arteries of her blood he had severed, the North Wind bore (it) to places undisclosed . . . He split her like a shellfish into two parts: half of her he set up and ceiled it as sky . . . he squared Apsu's quarter . . . which he made as the Firmament" (translated by E. A. Speiser [*ANET*, 67b]).

which complements other idol parodies in the HB.[2] By making fun of idolatry, a parody exposes the foolishness, especially the worship of a handmade object fashioned by human craftsmanship. Concern about idolatry was especially important during and after the Babylonian exile. The story highlights the folly of confusing divine qualities with a handcrafted image. The narrative also speaks to the providential protection of the faithful and the clever boldness of Daniel.

Although they cannot be dated precisely, these two stories may have originated in the Babylonian (or Persian) diaspora among the Jewish exiles. Some scholars, such as daSilva, are inclined instead to a Palestinian provenance.[3] They were translated from Hebrew or Aramaic, probably in Alexandria (c. 100 BCE), where the LXX originated. If in Egypt, they may have served to criticize the Jewish people who had been tempted by Egyptian idolatrous practices.[4] As with Susanna, there are some differences, although not as great, between the LXX and Theodotion versions of the stories. These will be noted in the commentary.

As previously noted, what is even less clear is how Bel and the Dragon came to be included in Daniel. Generally, scholars assume the story was first introduced into the book by the Old Greek (LXX) translator of Daniel (c. 100 BCE).[5] In the Hebrew/Aramaic Daniel, tales are set in the reigns of Nebuchadnezzar (chs. 1–4), Belshazzar (ch. 5), and Darius (ch. 6). Furthermore, there are visions set in the times of Belshazzar (Dan 7:1; 8:1), Darius (9:1), and even Cyrus (10:1). The introduction in Theodotion sets Bel, at least, in the early reign of Cyrus. The king in the Dragon is left unidentified.

Bel and the Dragon was apparently widely accepted by the early church as an essential part of the book of Daniel.[6] Present in the LXX and the daughter translations (translations made from the LXX), this meant Bel and the Dragon continued to nurture the church for generations.[7] Irenaeus (c. 130–200 CE) quotes Dan 14:4–5, 25, where reference is made to the Lord as the living God. This is offered as support for Jesus's comment, "He is God not of the dead, but of the living" (Matt 22:32). Clement of Alexandria (c.

---

2. See Ps 115:4-8; 135:15-18; Isa 40:18-20; 44:9-20; 46:1-7; Jer 10:3-9; Hab 2:18-19; Wis 13:1-15:17; Letter of Jeremiah. Most idol parodies, including Bel and the Dragon, equate the god with an image. The idol was merely a representation of the god, however, not identical with the deity whom it symbolized.

3. daSilva, *Introducing the Apocrypha*, 240.

4. Oesterley, *Introduction to Books of Apocrypha*, 291–93; Wis 11:15–16; 15:18–19.

5. J. Collins, *Daniel* (Hermeneia), 412.

6. For an exhaustive list of citations from the Church Fathers, see Julius, "Griechischen Danielzusätze."

7. daSilva, *Introducing the Apocrypha*, 243.

150–215) curiously refers to Bel and the Dragon (Dan 14:33) as evidence for the historicity of the prophet Habakkuk. Habakkuk was still alive, according to Bel and the Dragon, in the late sixth century BCE.[8] In Tertullian's (c. 160–220) *De idololatria* (18), Bel and the Dragon are also taken to indicate that Christians may occasionally wear garments associated with idol worship, just as Daniel in the story wore purple, even though this color was also worn by the priests of Bel.

In this commentary, I have separated the two stories for purposes of analysis, even though they are joined in the same text in both the LXX and Theodotion. While the author of Bel and the Dragon remains anonymous, in the LXX, the story is preceded by an ascription: "From the prophet Habakkuk, son of Jesus, from the tribe of Levi." In the Theodotion text, as presented in the fifth-century CE Codex Alexandrinus, it is preceded by the phrase "vision twelve." This editorial note evidently designates Bel and the Dragon as the twelfth and last in the series of visions making up an expanded edition of Daniel (including the Additions).

The story of Bel falls into the following sections: introduction, with Daniel at the Persian court (14:1–2); the worship of Bel (vv. 3–7); and the wager about Bel (vv. 8–22).

DANIEL AT THE PERSIAN COURT (14:1–2)

> [1] King Astyages was laid to rest with his ancestors, and Cyrus the Persian took over his kingdom. [2] Daniel was a companion of the king and the most honored above all his friends.

These lines indicate a historical problem. That Cyrus the Persian took over the kingdom from the Median king Astyages (c. 585–550 BCE) (v. 1), blurs the reality that Cyrus had forcefully seized the kingdom from his grandfather Astyages in 550, rather than through a conventional, peaceful succession, as intimated here.[9] Daniel is represented as an intimate acquaintance of Cyrus, indeed, the most honored of all the king's familiars (v. 2). The LXX text identifies Daniel as a priest, the son of Abal, while at the same time declaring him a companion of the king, one who held a favored position at the royal court. Reckoning Daniel as a priest and the son of Abal has led

---

8. This is somewhat prescient on the part of Clement. Modern scholars tend to date the book of Habakkuk near the end of the seventh century BCE (Eissfeldt, *Old Testament*, 417–20).

9. Herodotus, *Hist.* 1.130; Grabbe, *Judaism from Cyrus to Hadrian*, 122; J. Cook, *Persians*, 39–40.

many to question whether the Daniel in this story was originally identified with Daniel the prophet.[10]

THE WORSHIP OF BEL (14:3-7)

> [3] The Babylonians had an idol by the name of Bel, and each day they provided for him twelve bushels of fine wheat and forty sheep and six measures of wine. [4] The king revered it and came each day to worship. But Daniel prayed to his God. [5] And the king said to him, "Why do you not worship Bel?" He replied, "Because I do not revere handmade idols, but the living God, who created heaven and earth and has dominion over all flesh."
>
> [6] The king said to him, "Does not Bel seem to you to be a living god? Do you not see how much he eats and drinks each day?" [7] Laughing, Daniel said, "Do not be deceived, O king, for this thing on the inside is surely clay, but bronze on the outside; it has never eaten or drunk anything."

The name Bel is equivalent to the Akkadian *belu* (he who rules or lord), the linguistic equivalent of the Ugaritic *b'l* (Hebrew: *Baal*), as well as a title for Marduk, the supreme god of Babylon. The writer fails to distinguish between the god and the god's image. In Mesopotamian belief, an image was the receptacle or contact point between the god and the image. The deity was present in the image when "it showed certain specific features and paraphernalia and was cared for in the appropriate manner,"[11] as by supplying food offerings such as indicated here (v. 3). Babylonian sacrifices, like this, were known to be extravagant: twelve bushels of fine wheat, forty sheep, and six measures of wine. Six measures of wine would be about fifty gallons.

Although it appears strange to hear of the Persian Cyrus worshiping a Babylonian deity, according to the Cyrus Cylinder, Cyrus did give deference to Marduk—for political purposes—as the national deity of Babylon (v. 4). It is impossible to read his motives for doing so. He was known to respect religions other than his own. Marduk was "the great lord, a protector of his people ... [who] beheld with pleasure his [Cyrus's] good deeds and his upright mind (and therefore) ordered him to march against his city Babylon." As Cyrus advanced militarily against Babylon, he felt Marduk was "going at his side like a real friend."[12]

10. Moore, *Daniel, Esther, and Jeremiah*, 132–33.

11. Oppenheim, *Ancient Mesopotamia*, 184.

12. "Cyrus Cylinder," translated by A. Leo Oppenheim (*ANET*, 315b). In contrast, notice how the prompting of Cyrus to issue a decree granting the Jews to return to

Daniel's commitment to his God—Yahweh—provokes Cyrus to ask, "Why do you not worship Bel?" (v. 5). Daniel replies by distinguishing between gods or images made by hand and the living God, who created and has dominion over all. In verse 5, the LXX has Daniel refuse the king's request with this affirmation: "I serve none except the Lord, who created the heaven and the earth, and who is sovereign over all flesh." The Theodotion text has Daniel say, "I do not revere handmade idols, but the living God." The confusion between the idol image and the god it represents (Marduk) in this text is typical in most, if not all, of the idol parodies in the HB. More sophisticated worshipers, even in antiquity, no doubt realized the deity represented by the physical image was not identical with the god. An idol parody, of course, is a caricature, a cartoonish description of idol worship.

Cyrus responds by pointing to the huge amounts of food offerings Bel consumes in a single night as proof of Bel's living potency (v. 6). Ironically, the necessity of eating is a sign of mortality, not of deity. As the story turns out, Bel could not eat and so was not a living god; the snake in the following story eats too much and so dies.[13] Once more, food is at the heart of a story about Daniel. In Dan 1, the conflict revolves around what Daniel and his colleagues eat; here, it is the food Bel allegedly eats.

Daniel derisively laughs (γελάω, *gelao*, laugh, sneer at) and boldly lampoons the idol, made of clay covered in bronze sheathing, as something inert that simply cannot eat or drink (v. 7). Daniel's laughter is understood as derision and scorn.[14] In this situation, his laughter proves dangerous, because the king had absolute power of life and death over his subjects, even those previously considered political allies.

THE WAGER ABOUT BEL (14:8–22)

> [8] Having become angry, the king called his priests and said to them, "If you do not tell me who is eating these provisions, you shall die! But if you can prove that Bel is eating them, Daniel shall die, because he has blasphemed Bel." [9] Daniel said to the king, "Let it be according to your word." [10] There were seventy priests of Bel, besides women and children. So, the king went with Daniel into the house of Bel. [11] The priests of Bel said, "See,

---

Jerusalem following the exile is attributed in the HB to Yahweh. "Yahweh stirred up the spirit of King Cyrus of Persia" (Ezra 1:1, AT).

13. Moore, *Daniel, Esther, and Jeremiah*, 135.

14. Laughter in the HB is usually an act of mockery (Smith-Christopher, "Additions to Daniel," 188). See Gen 17:17; 18:12–13; 21:6; Ps 52:6–7; Job 8:21; 17:6.

we are going outside; you, O king, set out the food and prepare the wine, then shut the door and seal it with your ring. Having come early in the morning, see if you do not find all the food eaten by Bel. We will die—or Daniel, who is lying about us." ¹² They were unconcerned, because they had built a hidden entrance under the table, and through it entered continuously and consumed it. ¹³ And when they had gone out, the king also put out the food for Bel. ¹⁴ Daniel ordered his servants and they brought ashes and spread them throughout the entire temple in the presence of the king. ¹⁵ The priests came at night according to their custom—along with their women and children—and they ate and drank everything.

Although the king is angry with Daniel, he directs his anger instead toward the priests of Bel (v. 8). As in Dan 3, the king's anger warns a serious challenge is about to be set out. His ire may imply he thinks his naïveté has obviously fooled him.[15] "Tell me who eats these food offerings," he taunts the priests. "Otherwise, you will die!" On the other hand, should the priests prove Bel eats them, Daniel will be guilty of blasphemy and must die. The priests of Bel in the LXX of verse 8 quickly assure the king, "It is Bel himself who eats these things," before Daniel agrees to the king's challenge. Daniel concurs with these conditions (v. 9). The contest—wager—is therefore joined. Like Elijah, Daniel is now pitted alone against a body of priests.[16]

Having thrown down the gauntlet, Daniel and the king go to the temple of Bel (v. 10). After leaving the king to set out the usual quantity of food, the priests explain, they would exit the temple, then close the door. It would then be sealed with the royal seal against unauthorized entrance (v. 11). When the king returns in the morning, they explain, he will find Bel has eaten all the food so carefully laid out (v. 12). At this point, the Theodotion text inserts a parenthetical comment not found in the LXX: "They had built a hidden entrance under the table, and through it entered continuously and consumed it" (v. 13). Before leaving the temple, however, while the king observes, Daniel has servants spread ashes throughout the entire temple (v. 14). When the priests come for the food, Daniel surmises, they would leave footprints everywhere in the fine gray ashes. That night, just as Daniel had inferred, the priests and their families enter and eat and drink everything (v. 15).

¹⁶ Early in the morning the king arose, and Daniel with him. ¹⁷ The king said, "Are the seals intact?" Daniel replied, "They are

---

15. J. Collins, *Daniel* (Hermeneia), 413.
16. See 1 Kgs 18:20–40.

intact, O king." ¹⁸ As soon as the doors were opened, the king looked at the table, and cried out with a loud voice, "You are great, O Bel, and there is not any deceit in you!"

¹⁹ Daniel laughed and held the king back from entering, then said, "Look at the floor, and notice whose footprints these are." ²⁰ And the king said, "I see the footprints of men, women, and children."

²¹ Enraged, the king then arrested the priests, the women, and their children. They showed him the hidden doors through which they used to enter and freely consume the things on the table. ²² The king put them to death and handed Bel over to Daniel, and he destroyed him and his temple.

Early the next morning, Daniel and the king check the royal seals to verify they are unbroken and the temple secure (v. 17). Upon entering, the king notices the empty table on which the food had been placed (v. 18). At first glance, this seemed to demonstrate Bel's reality. He exclaims, "You are great, O Bel, and there is not any deceit in you!"

In the LXX, Daniel laughs exceedingly, greatly (σφόδρα, *sphodra*), thus intensifying the mockery, then turns to restrain the king. "Look at the floor," he directs, "and notice whose footprints these are" (v. 19). Across the floor, particularly in front of the table, are footprints of men, women, and children (v. 20). The priests have been caught in the act. The smoking gun! The LXX (v. 21) heightens the drama by including a brief scene where the king and Daniel surprise the priests at their home, only to discover there the missing food intended for Bel.

Enraged at discovering this deceptive plot, the king arrests the priests and their families (v. 22). He uncovers their scam: they have fashioned a hidden door under the table through which they enter to retrieve the food offering, making it appear Bel has eaten it. The furious king has them summarily executed, but turns over the idol Bel to Daniel, who destroys it and the temple where it was seated. In the LXX, the king personally destroys the idol of Bel, but in Theodotion, Daniel destroys both Bel and his temple.

The Greek historian Herodotus says it was Xerxes I (486–465 BCE), rather than Cyrus, who plundered and probably destroyed Bel's image in the temple of Esagila in Babylon. Its eighteen-foot statue of Marduk he melted down into eight hundred pounds of gold bullion.[17] This event may provide the background for this story.

In Bel, Daniel comes across as a kind of detective like Sherlock Holmes. Recognized as a faithful worshiper of the living God, he demonstrates the

---

17. Herodotus, *Hist.* 1.183. See also Delcor, *Livre de Daniel*, 289.

keen insight and wisdom for which he had become famous. As in Dan 5, he is capable of unraveling riddles such as strange writing on the walls and of figuring out how a clay and metal object consumes such huge quantities of food.

Since the Jews at the time of Antiochus IV lived in a world filled with the gods of other nations, concentrated, as it were, in the idol of Zeus imposed upon them at the sacred temple in Jerusalem, such criticisms as Bel and the Dragon became essential fare for the faithful. Such stories urged them to hold onto their awareness of the unseen, imageless God, Yahweh, Creator of heaven and earth, and Ruler of all upon it.[18]

---

18. daSilva, *Introducing the Apocrypha*, 241.

The Dragon

Daniel 14:23–42

Give us a God—a living God,
One to wake the sleeping soul,
One to cleanse the tainted blood
Whose pulses in our bosoms roll.

—C. G. Rosenberg, The Winged Horn

This remarkable story is about a dragon (δράκων, *drakon*), a large reptilian serpent or snake, that the Babylonians were worshiping. Since we have no evidence that such snake worship was practiced in Babylon, the story may point instead to an Egyptian environment, where serpent worship was practiced.[1] Like the accompanying tale about Bel, the story of the Dragon mocks idol worship. Unless referring to the traditional title of this story ("The Dragon"), I will use the words snake, serpent, or reptile to refer to the creature at issue here.

If the story's purpose is to ridicule pagan snake worship, who was its audience? Gentiles living in Babylon—or elsewhere? Jews in the eastern or western diaspora? Jews in Palestine? Since idolatry was a temptation especially for the large Jewish population in Egypt during the Hellenistic period, Egypt is the most likely location of the audience. Others point to Babylon or even Palestine.[2] The text was probably written c. 100 BCE.

---

1. Hoenig, "Bel and the Dragon," 376–77.
2. See Moore, *Daniel, Esther, and Jeremiah*, 127–28.

What is the origin of this bizarre tale? The prototype, according to Hermann Gunkel, is the mythic slaying of the Mesopotamian goddess, Tiamat, by Marduk, and the creation of heaven and earth from her corpse. The serpent that Daniel slays seems to echo this Tiamat myth.[3] But there are other similar myths. In the HB, for instance, Yahweh crushes the heads of Leviathan (Ps 74:14), who elsewhere is described as the "fleeing serpent . . . the twisting serpent . . . the dragon that is in the sea" (Isa 27:1). The Yahweh speeches in Job describe the Leviathan: "Its sneezes flash forth light . . . out of its mouth comes smoke . . . and a flame comes out of its mouth" (Job 41:18-21). All these mythic snakes and dragons may be related, imaginatively carved out of the same stock of ancient Near Eastern imagery. In Christian folklore, we also note the story of St. Michael or St. George slaying the dragon.[4] The tale in Daniel likely has its source in these ancient Near Eastern dragon myths.[5]

This story is obviously related to Dan 6, where Daniel is also thrown into the lions' pit on account of his faith. While Dan 6 caricatures the king's gullibility, this story mocks the foolish worship of a reptile. Another curious feature is the strange involvement of the prophet Habakkuk during Daniel's confinement in the lions' pit.

The story falls into two main parts: the destruction of the snake (vv. 23-27) and Daniel in the lions' pit (vv. 28-42).

THE DESTRUCTION OF THE SNAKE (14:23-27)

> [23] There was a great serpent, and the Babylonians revered it. [24] The king said to Daniel, "Can you not admit this is a living god and worship it?" [25] Daniel said, "The Lord, my God, I worship, for he is the living God. But you, O king, give me authority and I will kill the snake without sword or staff." [26] And the king said, "I grant it to you."
>
> [27] And Daniel took pitch, fat, and hair, and boiled them together and made patties and placed them in the serpent's mouth. Having eaten, the serpent burst open. Then Daniel said, "Behold, your object of worship!"

---

3. Gunkel, *Schöpfung und Chaos*, 320.
4. Pfeiffer, *History of New Testament*, 456.
5. It is more likely such mythic dramas were the primary inspiration for this story than a midrashic reading of Jer 51:34, 44 ("I will punish Bel in Babylon, and make him disgorge what he has swallowed," v. 44), as some scholars propose. See Day, *God's Conflicts*.

The tale opens with the worship of a serpent as a viable, living god. The large serpent the Babylonians worship is designated by the Greek term δράκων. *Drakon* is the obvious source of our English word dragon (v. 23). δράκων can be rendered either dragon or serpent/snake,[6] the preference here being snake or serpent. In the supposed Hebrew (or Aramaic) original of the story, δράκων may have translated the Hebrew תַּנִּין (*tannin*, serpent) or its Aramaic equivalent. In some contexts of the HB, תַּנִּין is used for the Leviathan, the mythic sea monster slain by Yahweh at the creation.[7]

The king urges Daniel to worship the serpent. The king's challenge, "can you not admit this is a living god" and so worship it (v. 24), is a clear allusion to the story of Bel which precedes it (vv. 1–22), the difference being the snake is alive and not some handcrafted bronze-coated clay image. Daniel's response is the same. He worships the "Lord, my God . . . for he is the living God" (v. 25). Even though the text uses standard Greek terms for the deity, a Jewish reader would not miss in this declaration a reference to Yahweh, the God of Israel. Daniel's affirmation is essentially monotheistic, precluding any reverence for the snake. The snake is part of the divine creation, he realizes, not the transcendent Creator and Lord of all.

Since the debate centers around who is superior, the snake or Daniel's God, the king grants Daniel's request to kill the snake without sword or staff, without the usual weapons of warfare (v. 26). This is a fantastic claim, beyond belief. No show of force here; instead, cunning and wit serve as the instruments. The king evidently believes the snake—as a deity—is impervious to whatever scheme Daniel may have in mind, so does not hesitate to put the snake at risk.

Daniel's hideous concoction, a boiled mixture of pitch, fat, and hair, does not appear lethal in itself (v. 27). From the mixture, however, he makes cakelike patties or rolls the mixture into balls,[8] perhaps like dumplings, and feeds them to the snake. In the Tiamat myth, Marduk causes the force of wind to split open Tiamat, but here the ingestion of the patties causes the snake to swell and burst open. How this concoction may have worked has led to plenty of speculation. In the Genesis Rabbah, from the thirteenth century CE, we read, "He [Daniel] took straw, and hid nails in the midst thereof; then he cast it before it, and the nails pierced its intestines." Another

---

6. *LSJ* 448. From the large amount of food the snake consumes, it must have been some type of python or boa constrictor.

7. See Isa 27:1; Ps 74:12–14; 104:26; 148:7; Job 9:13; 26:12; 41:1–34; Amos 9:3.

8. The Greek word used here, μάζα, *maza*, can be translated barley cake, lump, mass, or ball, hence the NJB translates, "Daniel . . . took some pitch, some fat and some hair and boiled them up together, rolled the mixture into balls and fed them to the dragon." See *LSJ* 1072.

Jewish text, known as the Chronicles of Jerahmeel, indicates, "Daniel went and took pitch and fat and flax and hair, and rolled them into one lump, and he made unto himself iron hatchets, and rolled all that round and round the hatchets, and he threw it into the dragon's mouth." Curiosity about Daniel's strategy has naturally provoked a whole series of imaginative explanations.[9] When the snake dies in obvious agony, Daniel taunts the king with tangible proof that the object of worship—the snake—is not a deity. It is mortal and vulnerable like any other creature. Due to Daniel's clever tactic, it has perished in an untimely, humiliating death.

DANIEL IN THE LION PIT (14:28–43)

> [28] And as soon as the Babylonians heard, they became very angry and turned against the king and said, "The king has become a Jew; he has destroyed Bel, killed the serpent, and slaughtered the priests." [29] Having come to the king, they said, "Hand Daniel over to us. If not, we will kill you and your household." [30] The king saw that they were agitating greatly against him; having felt compelled, he handed Daniel over.
>
> [31] They threw him into the lions' pit, and he was there six days. [32] There were seven lions in the pit, and they used to give them daily two carcasses and two sheep. But on this occasion, nothing was given to them so that they would devour Daniel.

Outraged by these events, the citizenry turns on Daniel (v. 28) and threatens the king with violence should he fail to hand Daniel over to the vigilante mob (v. 29). Verse 29 is curiously missing in the LXX. The translation of verse 29 here is from Theodotion: "We will kill you and your household!" The king's aiding and abetting Daniel in the slaying of the snake is to the crowd clear indication the king has converted to the Jewish religion; he "has become a Jew." The word Jew or Jewish (Ιουδαῖος, *Ioudaios*), by being placed first in the clause (v. 28), is emphasized in both Theodotion and the LXX. The text, however, is not claiming the king converted to Judaism, only that the crowd accuses him of doing so. During the Achaemenid and Hellenistic periods, indeed even earlier, royalty lived in constant fear of internal revolt and rebellion on the part of their subjects.[10] Faced with the prospect of such uprisings, the king feels he has no choice but to hand Daniel over (v. 30).

---

9. For a review of these explanations, see Zimmermann, "Bel and the Dragon," 438–40.

10. Smith-Christopher, "Additions to Daniel," 193.

Daniel is summarily thrown into the lions' pit (v. 31). We are immediately reminded of the story in Dan 6, where Daniel is thrown into the lions' pit. Are the two stories doublets (parallel accounts) of the same event? Although there are definite similarities, when the plot and minor details in the two stories are considered, the connection between the two is minor.[11] It does seem strange, however, that in the same book Daniel would have twice experienced identical punishment—with identical results.

In preparation for the execution (v. 32), the lions have been denied their usual daily fare, two carcasses and two sheep. Since the lions had gone hungry beforehand, they would likely quickly devour Daniel.

Daniel's fate thus seems inevitable. To verse 32, the LXX adds "that he not receive a burial"—the ultimate insult—as a part of Daniel's punishment.

> [33] The prophet Habakkuk was in Judea, and he had boiled a stew and crumbled bread into a bowl and was going into the field to take it to the reapers. [34] The angel of the Lord said to Habakkuk, "Take the meal which you have to Babylon to Daniel in the lions' den." [35] Habakkuk said, "Sir, Babylon I have never seen, and the den I do not know." [36] The angel of the Lord took hold of the crown of his head and carried him by the hair of his head; with the speed of the wind he put him in Babylon over the den.
> [37] Habakkuk cried, "Daniel, Daniel, take the meal that God has sent you!" [38] Daniel said, "You have indeed remembered me, O God, and not abandoned those who love you." [39] Then the angel of God immediately returned Habakkuk to his own place.

Unlike the preceding story of Bel, here there is swift divine intervention. While the prophet Habakkuk is preparing a stew with dumplings to take to the reapers in the field, an angel of the Lord says to him, "Take the meal which you have to Babylon to Daniel in the lions' pit" (v. 34). When Habakkuk complains he has never even seen Babylon, much less the lions' pit in question, the angel abruptly seizes him by the hair of his head and whisks him by the speed of the wind and sets him down directly over the den (v. 36). Ezekiel in a vision was similarly transported by the hair of his head from Babylon to Jerusalem (Ezek 8:1–4). In a chariot of fire, Elijah was transported to heaven (2 Kgs 2:9–12). Mircea

---

11. Moore, *Daniel, Esther, and Jeremiah*, 148.

Eliade reports similar ecstatic travel among shamans and holy men in various cultures.[12]

When Habakkuk calls to Daniel in the pit, Daniel gives glory to God. Seemingly ignoring Habakkuk, he exclaims, "You... O God, [have] not abandoned those who love you" (v. 38).[13] The food signals that God has intervened in Daniel's behalf, as did preservation from the claws and teeth of the ravenous lions. Both are implicitly acknowledged in this affirmation. We should not overlook the line concluding this scene. His mission accomplished, the angel whisks Habakkuk back to Judea (v. 39). The author gives no hint why Habakkuk was selected for this venture. Habakkuk, who would have been an older contemporary of the sixth-century Daniel, was active in Judah in the last years of the seventh century. Perhaps Habakkuk's strong condemnation of idolatry (Hab 2:18-19) may have recommended this prophet to the writer.[14]

> [40] On the seventh day the king went to mourn Daniel, and so arrived at the den and looked in, and behold, Daniel was sitting there! [41] And having shouted with a loud voice, he exclaimed, "You are great, O Lord, God of Daniel, and there is no other except you!" [42] He pulled Daniel out. But those responsible for his destruction he cast into the den, and they were immediately devoured before him.

Now comes the finale. Assuming he was about to mourn Daniel, devoured by lions, with only bloody fragments of his body lying around on the floor of the pit, the king arrives, looks in, and finds Daniel sitting there alive and unharmed, not a scratch on him (v. 40). The king shouts aloud, extolling Daniel's God, "You are great, O Lord, God of Daniel, and there is no other except you!" (v. 41). This is not an indication of conversion, but an acknowledgment of the predominance of Daniel's God over the snake—or any other god the king may have had in mind. This ending is like other endings in Dan 3:26-29; 4:34-37; and 6:25-27, where each king also recognizes the God of Daniel.

In a cruel irony, but in accordance with the *lex talionis* (eye for eye, tooth for tooth, hand for hand, foot for foot [Exod 21:24]), the king executes those responsible for Daniel's aborted execution by meting out to them the

---

12. Eliade, *Shamanism*, 125-27, 403-11.

13. The word ἐγκαταλείπω, used here in the aorist second person singular form, can mean abandon. The stronger rendition is called for because Daniel has been in the pit a week, apparently abandoned by God.

14. Smith-Christopher, "Additions to Daniel," 193-94.

same punishment (v. 42). Cast into the lions' pit, they are immediately devoured by the hungry lions.

Considering the literary arrangement of the Greek versions of Daniel, the book gives the last word not to the apocalyptic visions, but to two stories aimed at discrediting the deities of Judah's captors. Bel and the Dragon wholly discredits the gods venerated by the Babylonians and the Persians under Cyrus II, the nations who conquered Judea or who now are sovereign. Judea is still in exile and must contend with the deities of captor nations. Whoever arranged the sequence of stories and visions in the Greek edition of Daniel evidently wanted to end the expanded scroll with these two stories of how Israel's God prevailed over the deities of the Babylonians and Persians. Although the same theme of vindication occurs prominently in the apocalyptic visions, in this literary sequence, there is no glorious eschatological vindication of Israel through a resurrection to life, but only daily existence amid the difficult realities of life far from home in an alien, idolatrous gentile world.[15] Yet both stories witness to the truth put into the mouth of the king: "You are great, O Lord, God of Daniel, and there is no other except you!" (v. 41).

These lines from the king offer an epitome of the book of Daniel. It is as though the editor who placed the Additions in the book astutely knew these lines would serve admirably as a conclusion to the whole. God's eternal purpose, despite all difficulties, would eventually prevail over all evil and evil machinations. God's faithful people, constantly under the dreadful maw of hostile powers, would eventually prevail. Truth, righteousness, and justice would triumph. God the Lord would prevail. After evil has had its sway for a time, God would guide the broken slivers of human civilization into the eternal kingdom. This is the enduring message of Daniel. Its inspiring tales of faithfulness under duress and deliverance from mortal trouble strengthen the resolve of the faithful to live authentically and generously in a world created and finally to be redeemed by God Almighty.

---

15. daSilva, *Introducing the Apocrypha*, 242–43.

Bibliography

Abegg, Martin, Jr., et al., eds. *The Dead Sea Scrolls Bible: The Oldest Known Bible Translated for the First Time into English.* San Francisco: Harper/SanFrancisco, 1999.
Aland, Barbara and Kurt Aland, eds. *Novum Testamentum Graece.* 27th ed. Stuttgart, Germ.: Deutsche Bibelgesellschaft, 1979.
Albright, W. F. "The Date and Personality of the Chronicler." *JBL* 40 (1921) 104–24.
Abusch, Tzvi. "Marduk." In *DDD* 543–49.
Alt, Albrecht. "Zur Menetekel Inschrift." *VT* 4 (1954) 303–5.
American Psychiatric Association. *Diagnostic and Statistical Manual of Mental Disorders.* 5th ed. Arlington, VA: APA, 2013.
Anderson, R. A. *Signs and Wonders: A Commentary on the Book of Daniel.* Grand Rapids: Eerdmans, 1984.
Andreasen, Niels-Erik A. "The Role of the Queen Mother in Israelite Society." *CBQ* 45 (1983) 179–94.
Archer, Gleason L., Jr. "Daniel." In *The Expositor's Bible Commentary*, edited by Frank Gaebelein, 7:3–157. Grand Rapids: Zondervan, 1985.
———. *A Survey of Old Testament Introduction.* Rev. ed. Chicago: Moody, 1974.
Avalos, Hector. "Nebuchadnezzar's Affliction: New Mesopotamian Parallels for Daniel 4." *JBL* 133 (2014) 497–507.
Baillie, John. *The Sense of the Presence of God.* London: Oxford University Press, 1962.
Baldwin, Joyce G. *Daniel: An Introduction and Commentary.* TOTC. Downers Grove, IL: InterVarsity, 1978.
———. "Is There Pseudonymity in the Old Testament?" *Them* 4 (1978–1979) 6–12.
Barr, James. "Jewish Apocalyptic in Recent Scholarly Study." *BJRL* 58 (1975) 9–25.
———. "Daniel." In *Peake's Commentary on the Bible*, edited by Matthew Black and H. H. Rowley, 591–602. London: Thomas Nelson, 1962.
Barton, G. A. "The Composition of the Book of Daniel." *JBL* 17 (1898) 62–86.
Baumgartner, Walter. "Das Aramäische im Buche Daniel." *ZAW* 45 (1927) 81–133.
Beale, G. K. *The Book of Revelation.* Grand Rapids: Eerdmans, 1999.
Beaulieu, P. A. *The Reign of Nabonidus, King of Babylon, 556–539 B.C.* New Haven, CT: Yale University Press, 1989.

Beckwith, Roger. *The Old Testament Canon of the New Testament Church*. Grand Rapids: Eerdmans, 1985.
Beel. M. A. *Das Danielbuch*. Leiden, Neth.: J. Ginsberg, 1935.
Bennett, W. H. "The Prayer of Azariah and the Song of the Three Children." In *APOT* 1:625-37.
Bentzen, Aage. *Daniel*. HAT 19. Tübingen, Germ.: Mohr, 1952.
———. *Introduction to the Old Testament*. 2nd ed. 2 vols. Copenhagen: G. E. C. Gad, 1952.
Berkouwer, G. K. *The Return of Christ*. Studies in Dogmatics. Grand Rapids: Eerdmans, 1972.
Bertholdt, Leonard. *Daniel, aus dem Hebräisch-Aramäischen neu übersetzt und erklärt, mit einer vollständigen Einleitung und einiger histor. und exeget. Exkursen*. Erlangen, Germ.: N.p., 1806-1808.
Berossus. *The Babyloniaca of Berossus*. Edited and translated by Stanley M. Burstein. 2nd ed. Sources from the Ancient Near East. Malibu, CA: Undena, 1978.
Bevan, Edwyn R. *The House of Seleucus*. 2 vols. London: Edward Arnold, 1902.
Bickermann, Elias J. "The Edict of Cyrus in Ezra 1." *JBL* 65 (1946) 247-75.
———. *Four Strange Books of the Bible: Jonah, Daniel, Koheleth, Esther*. New York: Schocken, 1968.
———. *Der Gott der Makkabaer: Untersuchungen über Sinn and Ursprung der makkabäischen Erhebung*. Berlin: Schocken, 1937.
Blom, J. D. "When Doctors Cry Wolf: A Systematic Review of the Literature on Clinical Lycanthropy." *History of Psychiatry* 25, no. 1 (2014) 87-102.
Boice, J. M. *Daniel: An Expositional Commentary*. Grand Rapids: Zondervan, 1989.
Borg, Marcus. *The God We Never Knew*. San Francisco: HarperSanFrancisco, 1997.
Boring, M. Eugene. "Numbers, Numbering." In *NIDB* 4:298-99.
———. "The Revelation of St. John." In *NISB* 2211-2239.
Borowski, Oded. "Goat, Goatherd." In *NIDB* 2:585.
Boutflower, C. *In and Around the Book of Daniel*. London: SPCK, 1923. Reprint, Grand Rapids: Kregel, 1977.
Brown, William P. *Character in Crisis: A Fresh Approach to the Wisdom Literature of the Old Testament*. Grand Rapids: Eerdmans, 1996.
———. *A Handbook to Old Testament Exegesis*. Louisville: Westminster John Knox, 2017.
Bruce, F. F. *The Canon of Scripture*. Downers Grove, IL: InterVarsity, 1988.
Brugmann, H. "Die Interkalation in den Sieben Jahrwochen des Sonnenkalenders." *RevQ* 10 (1979-1981) 67-81.
Buchanan, George W. "Eschatology and the 'End of Days.'" *JNES* 20, no. 3 (1961) 188-93.
Burkholder, Byron. "Literary Patterns and God's Sovereignty in Daniel 4." *Direction* 16 (1987) 45-54.
Burkitt, F. Crawford. *Jewish and Christian Apocalypses*. London: Milford, 1914.
Burridge, Kenelm. *New Heaven, New Earth: A Study of Millenarian Activities*. Oxford, UK: Blackwell, 1969.
Calquot, A. "Sur les quatre Bêtes de Daniel VII." *Semitica* 5 (1955) 5-13.
Carey, Greg. *Ultimate Things: An Introduction to Jewish and Christian Apocalyptic Literature*. St. Louis: Chalice, 2005.
Cargill, Robert. "Strata: Gods on Parade." *BAR* 46, no. 3 (2020) 16.

Carroll, John T., et al. *The Return of Jesus in Early Christianity.* Peabody, MA: Hendrickson, 2000.

Carver, Daniel. "The Use of the Perfect in Daniel 7:27." *JBL* 136 (2019) 325–44.

Casey, Maurice. "Porphyry and the Origin of the Book of Daniel." *JTS*, n.s., 27, no. 1 (1976) 15–33.

———. *Son of Man: The Interpretation and Influence of Daniel 7.* London: SPCK, 1979.

Charles, R. H. *A Critical and Exegetical Commentary on the Book of Daniel.* Oxford, UK: Clarendon, 1929.

Childs, Brevard S. *Introduction to the Old Testament as Scripture.* Philadelphia: Fortress, 1979.

Chilton, David. *Paradise Restored: An Eschatology of Dominion.* Tyler, TX: Reconstruction, 1985.

Clement of Alexandria. *Eclogae propheticae (Extracts from the Prophets).* In *ANF* 2:163–629.

Clermont-Ganneau, C. "Mané, Thécel, Pharès, et le Festin de Balthasar." *JA* 8 (1886) 44–45.

Clifford, Richard. "History and Myth in Daniel 10–12." *BASOR* 220 (1975) 23–26.

Cline, Eric H. *Jerusalem Besieged: From Ancient Canaan to Modern Israel.* Ann Arbor, MI: University of Michigan Press, 2004.

Clouse, Robert G., ed. *The Meaning of the Millennium: Four Views.* Downers Grove, IL: InterVarsity, 1977.

Cogan, Mordecai. "Into Exile: From the Assyrian Conquest of Israel to the Fall of Babylon." In *The Oxford History of the Biblical World*, edited by Michael Coogan, 321–65. New York: Oxford, 1998.

Collins, Adela Yarbro. "Numerical Symbolism in Jewish and Early Christian Apocalyptic Literature." *ANRW* 21/2 (1984) 1224–49.

———. "Son of Man." In *NIDB* 5:342–43.

Collins, Anthony. *The Scheme of Literal Prophecy Considered; in a View of the Controversy, Occasioned by a Late Book, A Discourse of the Grounds and Reasons of the Christian Religion.* London: N.p., 1727.

Collins, John J. "Apocalypse: The Morphology of a Genre." *Semeia* 14. Missoula, MT: Scholars, 1979.

———. *The Apocalyptic Imagination: An Introduction to the Jewish Matrix of Christianity.* 2nd ed. New York: Crossroad, 1998.

———. *The Apocalyptic Vision of the Book of Daniel.* HSM 16. Missoula, MT: Scholars, 1977.

———. "The Court-Tales in Daniel and the Development of Apocalyptic." *JBL* 94 (1975) 218–34.

———. "Daniel." In *DDD* 219–20.

———. *Daniel: A Commentary on the Book of Daniel.* Hermeneia. Minneapolis: Fortress, 1993.

———. "Daniel, Book of." In *ABD* 2:29–37.

———. *Daniel, with an Introduction to Apocalyptic Literature.* FOTL 22. Grand Rapids: Eerdmans, 1984.

———, ed. *The Encyclopedia of Apocalypticism.* 3 vols. New York: Continuum, 1998.

———. *Introduction to the Hebrew Bible and the Deutero-Canonical Books.* 2nd ed. Minneapolis: Fortress, 2014.

———. "Old Testament Apocalypticism and Eschatology." In *NJBC* 298–304.

Collins, John J., and Adela Yarbro Collins. "Apocalypses and Apocalypticism." In *ABD* 1:279–92.
Collins, John J., et al., eds. *The Book of Daniel: Composition and Reception*. 2 vols. FOTL. VTSup 83.2. Leiden: Brill, 2001.
Coogan, Michael D. "Life in the Diaspora: Jews at Nippur in the Fifth Century BC." *BA* 37 (1974) 6–12.
Cook, Edward M. "In the Plain of the Wall (Dan 3:1)." *JBL* 108 (1989) 115–16.
Cook, J. M. *The Persians*. Rev. ed. London: Folio Society, 1999.
Cook, Stephen. *The Apocalyptic Literature*. Nashville: Abingdon, 2019.
Coppens, J. "Le livre de Daniel et ses problèms." *ETL* 56 (1980) 1–9.
Cornfeld, Gaalyahu, ed. *Daniel to Paul*. New York: Macmillan, 1962.
Cornfeld, Gaalyahu, and David N. Freedman. *Archaeology of the Bible: Book by Book*. New York: Harper & Row, 1976.
Costa, Uriel da (Gabriel Acosta). *Sobre a mortalidade da alma*. N.p.: Amsterdam, 1624.
Cousland, J. R. C. "Michael." In *NIDB* 4:77–78.
Craven, Toni. "Daniel and Its Additions." In *The Women's Bible Commentary*, edited by Carol A. Newsom and Sharon H. Ringe, 191–94. Louisville: Westminster/John Knox, 1992.
Crenshaw, James L. *Story and Faith: A Guide to the Old Testament*. New York: Macmillan, 1986.
Cross, Frank M. *The Ancient Library of Qumran and Modern Biblical Studies*. Rev. ed. New York: Doubleday, 1961. Reprint, Grand Rapids: Baker, 1980.
———. *Canaanite Myth and Hebrew Epic: Essays in the History of the Religion of Israel*. Cambridge, MA: Harvard University Press, 1973.
———. "Fragments of the Prayer of Nabonidus." *IEJ* 34 (1984) 260–64.
———. "New Directions in the Study of Apocalyptic." *JTC* 6 (1969) 157–65.
Cross, J. A. J. *Notes on the Defense of the Book of Daniel*. Dublin: M'Gee, 1878.
Da Riva, Rocio. "Dangling Assyriology." *BAR* 45, no. 6 (2019) 25–32.
Darmester, James, trans. *The Zend-Avesta*. Sacred Books of the East 4. 2nd ed. Oxford, UK: Clarendon, 1895.
daSilva, David A. *Introducing the Apocrypha: Message, Context, and Significance*. Grand Rapids: Baker Academic, 2002.
Daubney, William H. *The Three Additions to Daniel*. Cambridge, UK: Deighton Bell, 1906.
Daugherty, R. P. *Nabonidus and Belshazzar*. New Haven, CT: Yale University Press, 1929.
Davidson, Richard. "The Sanctuary Doctrine." *Adventist Review* 197, no. 9 (2020) 20–21.
Davies, P. R. *Daniel*. Sheffield, UK: JSOT, 1985.
———. "Eschatology in the Book of Daniel." *JSOT* 17 (1980) 33–53.
Davies, Witton T. "Bel and the Dragon." In *APOT* 2:652–64.
Day, John. *God's Conflicts with the Dragon and the Sea: Echoes of a Canaanite Myth in the Old Testament*. Cambridge, UK: Cambridge University Press, 1984.
Delcor, Mathias. *Le livre de Daniel*. SB. Paris: Gabalda, 1971.
Dexinger, Ferdinand. *Das Buch Daniel und seine Probleme*. SBS 36. Stuttgart: Katholisches Bibelwerk, 1969.

Dingermann, Friedrich. "Die Botshaft von Vergehen dieser Welt und von den Geheimnissen der Endzeit. Beginnende Apokalyptik im Alten Testament." In *Wort und Botschaft*, edited by J. Schreiner, 329–42. Würzburg: Echter, 1967.

Diodorus Siculus. *The Bibliotheca historica*. Edited by F. M. Salter and H. L. R. Edwards. Translated by John Shelton. 2 vols. Early English Text Society 233, 239. London: Oxford University Press, 1956.

Dion, P.-E. "Medical Personnel in the Ancient Near East: *asu* and *āšipu* in Aramaic Garb." *Aram Society for Syro-Mesopotamian Studies* 1 (1989) 213–16.

DiTommaso, Lorenzo. *The Book of Daniel and the Apocryphal Daniel Literature*. Leiden, Neth.: Brill, 2005.

Dommerschausen, Werner. *Nabonid im Buche Daniel*. Mainz, Germ.: Grünewald, 1964.

Douglas, Mary. *Purity and Danger*. London: Routledge and Kegan Paul, 1966.

Doukhan, Jacques. "The Seventy Weeks of Daniel 9: An Exegetical Study." *AUSS* 17 (1979) 1–22.

Doverspike, William F. "Boanthropy, Lycanthropy, and Zoanthropy: Bipolar Disorder, Delusional Disorder, or Schizophrenia?" Unpublished manuscript. 2019.

Driver, G. R. "Sacred Numbers and Round Figures." In *Promise and Fulfillment: Essays presented to Professor S. H. Hooke in Celebration of his Ninetieth Birthday*, edited by F. F. Bruce, 62–90. Edinburgh: T & T Clark, 1963.

Driver, S. R. "The Aramaic of the Book of Daniel." *JBL* 45 (1926) 110–19.

———. *The Book of Daniel*. CBC. Cambridge, UK: Cambridge University Press, 1922.

———. *An Introduction to the Literature of the Old Testament*. International Theological Library. Rev. ed., 1913; Reprint, New York: Charles Scribner's Sons, 1950.

Efird, J. M. *Daniel and Revelation*. Valley Forge, PA: Judson, 1978.

Eggler, Jürg. *Influences and Traditions Underlying the Vision of Daniel 7:2–14: The Research from the End of the Nineteenth Century to the Present*. OBO 177. Göttingen: Vandenhoeck & Ruprecht, 2000.

Eissfeldt, Otto. *The Old Testament: An Introduction*. Translated by P. R. Ackroyd. New York: Harper and Row, 1965.

Eitan, I. "Some Philological Observations in Daniel." *HUCA* 14 (1939) 13–22.

Eliade, Mircea. *Shamanism: Archaic Techniques of Ecstasy*. Bolingen 76. Princeton, NJ: Princeton University Press, 1972.

Emerson, Ralph Waldo. *Ralph Waldo Emerson: Selected Essays, Lectures and Poems*. Edited by R. Richardson. New York: Bantam Books, 1990.

Emerton, John A. "The Origin of the Son of Man Imagery." *JTS* 9 (1958) 225–42.

Emery, D. L. *Daniel: Who Wrote the Book?* Ilfracombe, UK: Stockwell, 1978.

Engel, H. *Die Susanna-Erzählung*. OBO 61. Freiburg, 1985.

Ephrem the Syrian. "In Danielem." *Sancti patris nostri Ephraem Syri Opera omnia*, edited by J. A. Assermani, 2:16. Rome: N.p., 1727.

Erickson, Millard J. *Contemporary Options in Eschatology: A Study of the Millennium*. Grand Rapids: Baker, 1977.

Farley, Norman. "'The Sanctuary Doctrine': Asset or Liability." http://www.rethinkingadventism.com/support.files/cottrell_1844.pdf.

Ferch, A. J. "The Book of Daniel and the 'Maccabean Thesis.'" *AUSS* 21 (1983) 129–41.

Fewell, Dana Nolan. *Circle of Sovereignty: A Story of Stories in Daniel 1–6*. BLS 20. Sheffield, UK: Almond, 1988.

Fiorenza, Elizabeth Schüssler. "Transforming the Legacy of *The Woman's Bible*." In *A Feminist Introduction*, edited by Elizabeth Schüssler Fiorenza and Shelly Matthews, 1–23. Vol. 1 of *Searching the Scriptures*. New York: Crossroad, 1993.
Fitzmyer, J. A. *A Wandering Aramean: Collected Aramaic Essays*. SBLMS 25. Missoula, MT: Scholars, 1979.
Flew, Anthony. "Miracles." In *The Encyclopedia of Philosophy*, edited by Paul Edwards, 5:346–53. New York: Macmillan, 1967.
Flint, P. W. "The Daniel Tradition at Qumran." In *Eschatology, Messianism, and the Dead Sea Scrolls*, edited by C. A. Evans and P. W. Flint, 41–60. Grand Rapids: Eerdmans, 1997.
Flusser, David. "Apocalypse." In *EncJud* 2:256–58.
———. "The Four Empires in the Fourth Sybil and in the Book of Daniel." *IOS* 1 (1972) 148–75.
Fohrer, Georg. *Introduction to the Old Testament*. Translated by D. E. Green. Nashville: Abingdon, 1968.
Ford, Desmond. *Daniel*. Nashville: Southern Publishing Association, 1978.
Fox, D. E. "Ben Sira on OT Canon Again: The Date of Daniel." *WTJ* 49 (1987) 335–50.
Francisco, C. T. "The Seventy Weeks of Daniel." *RevExp* 37 (1960) 126.
Freedman, David N. "The Babylonian Chronicle." In *Ancient Israelite History and Religion*, edited by John R. Huddlestun, 31–42. Vol. 1 of *Divine Commitment and Human Obligation*. Grand Rapids: Eerdmans, 1997.
———. "On Method in Biblical Studies: The Old Testament." In *Ancient Israelite History and Religion*, edited by John R. Huddlestun, 152–67. Vol. 1 of *Divine Commitment and Human Obligation*. Grand Rapids: Eerdmans, 1997.
———. "The Prayer of Nabonidus." *BASOR* 145 (1957) 31–32.
Frizzell, Lawrence. "Azariah, Prayer of." In *NIDB* 1:361.
Froom, Leroy Edwin. *The Prophetic Faith of our Fathers*. 4 vols. Washington, DC: Review and Herald, 1946–1955.
Frost, S. B. "Daniel." In *IDB* 1:761–68.
———. "Mene, Mene, Tekel, and Parsin." In *IDB* 3:348–49.
———. *Old Testament Apocalyptic: Its Origins and Growth*. London: Epworth, 1952.
Fuller, Robert C. *Naming the Antichrist: The History of an American Obsession*. New York: Oxford, 1995.
Gadd, C. J. "The Harran Inscriptions of Nabonidus." *Anatolian Studies* 8 (1958) 35–92.
Gaebelein, Arno C. *Daniel: A Key to the Visions and Prophecies of the Book of Daniel*. New York: Our Hope, 1911. Reprint, Grand Rapids: Kregel, 1955.
Gammie, John G. "The Classification, Stages of Growth, and Changing Intentions in the Book of Daniel." *JBL* 95 (1976) 191–204.
———. *Daniel*. Knox Preaching Guides. Atlanta: John Knox, 1983.
———. "On the Intention and Sources of Daniel I–VI." *VT* 31 (1981) 282–92.
———. "Spatial and Ethical Dualism in Jewish Wisdom and Apocalyptic Literature." *JBL* 93 (1974) 356–85.
Garfinkel, Yosef. "The Face of Yahweh?" *BAR* 46, no. 4 (2020) 30–33.
General Conference of Seventh-Day Adventists. *Seventh-Day Adventists Believe*. 2nd ed. Boise, ID: Pacific, 2005.
Gerstenberger, J. *Das Buch Daniel*. HSAT 8, no. 2. Bonn, Germ.: Hanstein, 1928.
Gese, H. "Die Bedeutung der Krise unter Antiochus IV. Epiphanes für die Apokalyptik des Danielbuches." *ZTK* 80 (1983) 373–88.

Ginsberg, Harold L. "The Composition of the Book of Daniel." *VT* 4 (1954) 264–75.
———. "Daniel, Book of." In *EncJud* 5:419–25.
———. "The Oldest Interpretation of the Suffering Servant." *VT* 3 (1953) 400–404.
———. *Studies in Daniel*. New York: Jewish Theological Seminary, 1948.
Gladson, Jerry A. *The Five Exotic Scrolls of the Hebrew Bible: The Prominence, Literary Structure, and Liturgical Significance of the Megilloth*. Lewiston, NY: Mellen, 2009.
Goldingay, John E. *Daniel*. WBC 30. Nashville: Thomas Nelson, 1996.
Good, E. M. "Apocalyptic as Comedy: The Book of Daniel." *Semeia* 32 (1984) 41–70.
Gordon, Cyrus, and Gary A. Rendsburg. *The Bible and the Ancient Near East*. 4th ed. New York: W. W. Norton, 1997.
Gorman, Michael. *Elements of Biblical Exegesis*. Rev. ed. Grand Rapids: Baker Academic, 2009.
Gowan, Donald E. *Bridge between the Testaments: A Reappraisal of Judaism from the Exile to the Birth of Christianity*. PTMS 14. Pittsburgh: Pickwick, 1976.
Grabbe, L. L. "Antiochians." In *NIDB* 1:181.
———. "Fundamentalism and Scholarship: The Case of Daniel." In *Scripture: Meaning and Method: Essays presented to Anthony Tyrrell Hanson for his Seventieth Birthday*, edited by Barry P. Thompson, 133–52. Atlanta: Society of Biblical Literature, 1990.
———. *Judaism from Cyrus to Hadrian*. Vol. 1 of *The Persian and Greek Periods*. Minneapolis: Fortress, 1992.
Grayson, Albert K. *Assyrian and Babylonian Chronicles*. TCS 5. Locust Valley, NY: J. J. Augustin, 1975.
Greenspahn, Frederick. "Aramaic." In *Beyond Babel: A Handbook for Biblical and Related Languages*, edited by John Kaltner and Steven L. McKenzie, 93–108. Society of Biblical Literature Resources for Biblical Study 42. Atlanta: Society of Biblical Literature, 2002.
Greenspoon, Leonard J. "Between Alexandria and Antioch: Jews and Judaism in the Hellenistic Period." In *The Oxford History of the Biblical World*, edited by Michael D. Coogan, 421–65. New York: Oxford, 1998.
Grillo, Jennie. "'From a Far Country': Daniel in Isaiah's Babylon." *JBL* 136, no. 2 (2017) 363–80.
Gruenthaner, M. J. "The Last King of Babylon." *CBQ* 11 (1949) 406–27.
Gruenwald, Ithamar. *Apocalyptic and Merkavah Mysticism*. Leiden, Neth.: Brill, 1980.
Gunkel, Hermann. "Fundamental Problems of Hebrew Literary History." In *What Remains of the Old Testament*, translated by A. K. Dallas, 57–68. New York: Macmillan, 1928.
———. *Schöpfung und Chaos in Urzeit und Endzeit: Eine religionsgeschichtliche Untersuchung über Gen 1 und Ap Joh 12*. With contributions by Heinrich Zimmern. Göttingen: Vandenhoeck & Ruprecht, 1895.
Gurney, R. J. M. *God in Control: An Exposition of the Prophecies of Daniel*. Worthington, UK: Walter, 1980.
Gzella, Holger. "Introduction." In *TDOT* 16: xxxv–xlvii.
Haag, Ernst. *Die Errettung Daniels aus der Löwengrube Untersuchungen zum Ursprung der biblischen Danieltradition*. SBS 110. Stuttgart: Katholisches Bibelwerk, 1983.
Hackett, Jo Ann. "Hebrew (Biblical and Epigraphic)." In *Beyond Babel: A Handbook for Biblical Hebrew and Related Languages*, edited by John Kaltner and Steven L. McKenzie, 139–56. Society of Biblical Literature Sources for Biblical Study 42. Atlanta: Society of Biblical Literature, 2002.

Hallo, W. W., ed. *The Context of Scripture*. 3 vols. Leiden, Neth.: Brill, 1997–2002.
Hammer, Raymond. *The Book of Daniel*. CBC. Cambridge, UK: University Press, 1976.
Hanson, Paul D. "Apocalypse, Genre." In *IDBSup* 27–28.
———. "Apocalypticism." In *IDBSup* 28–34.
———. "Apocalyptic Literature." In *The Hebrew Bible and Its Modern Interpreters*, edited by Douglas A. Knight and Gene M. Tucker, 465–88. Chico, CA: Scholars Press, 1985.
———. *The Dawn of Apocalypticism: The Historical and Sociological Roots of Jewish Apocalyptic*. Philadelphia: Fortress, 1989.
———. *Old Testament Apocalyptic*. Nashville: Abingdon, 1987.
———. "Old Testament Apocalyptic Reexamined." In *Visionaries and their Apocalypses*, edited by Paul Hanson, 37–60. IRT 2. Philadelphia: Fortress, 1983.
———. *The People Called: The Growth of Community in the Bible*. San Francisco: Harper & Row, 2001.
Harrison, Roland K. *Introduction to the Old Testament*. Grand Rapids: Eerdmans, 1969.
———. *Old Testament Times*. Grand Rapids: Eerdmans, 1970.
Hartman, Louis, and Alexander Di Lella. *The Book of Daniel*. AB 23. Garden City, NY: Doubleday, 1978.
———. "Daniel." In *NJBC* 406–20.
Hasel, Gerhard F. "The Book of Daniel." *AUSS* 19 (1981) 37–49, 211–25.
———. "The Four World Empires of Daniel 2 against Its Near Eastern Environment." *JSOT* 12 (1979) 17–30.
———. "The Seventy Weeks of Daniel 9:24–27." *Ministry* (May 1976) 1D–21D.
Haskell, Stephen N. *The Story of Daniel the Prophet*. Berrien Springs, MI: Advocate, 1903.
Hayes, Christopher. "Chirps from the Dust: The Affliction of Nebuchadnezzar in Dan 4:30 in its Ancient Near Eastern Context." *JBL* 126 (2007) 305–25.
Heaton, E. W. *Daniel*. London: SCM, 1956.
———. *Everyday Life in Old Testament Times*. New York: Charles Scribner's Sons, 1956.
Hellholm, D. *Apocalypticism in the Mediterranean World and the Near East*. Wiesbaden, Germ.: Franz Steiner, 1985.
Hengel, Martin. *Judaism and Hellenism: Studies in their Encounter in Palestine during the early Hellenistic Period*. Translated by John Bowden. Philadelphia: Fortress, 1981.
Hengstenberg, E. W. *Christology of the Old Testament and a Commentary on the Messianic Predictions*. 2nd ed. Translated by Theodore Meyer. Edinburgh: T & T Clark, 1856–1858. Reprint, Grand Rapids: Kregel, 1970.
Henze, Matthias. "Daniel." In *NISB* 1231–52.
———. *The Madness of King Nebuchadnezzar: The Ancient Near Eastern Origins and Early History of Interpretation of Daniel 4*. JSJSup 61. Leiden, Neth.: Brill, 1999.
Herodotus. *History*. Translated by William Beloe. Philadelphia: Edward Earle, 1814.
Hesiod. *Opera et dies (The Works and Days; Theogony; The Shield of Heracles)*. Translated by Richmond Lattimore. Ann Arbor, MI: University of Michigan Press, 1959.
Hick, John. *An Interpretation of Religion: Human Responses to the Transcendent*. London: Macmillan, 1989.
Hoenig, S. B. "Bel and the Dragon." In *IDB* 1:376–77.
Hoerth, Alfred J. *Archaeology and the Old Testament*. Grand Rapids: Baker, 1998.

Hoffecker, W. A. "Darby, John Nelson." In the *Evangelical Dictionary of Theology*, edited by W. A. Elwell, 292–93. Grand Rapids: Baker, 1984.
Hommel, F. "Die Abfassungszeit des Buches Daniel und der Wahnsinn Nabonids." *Theologie Litteraturblatt* 23 (1902) 145–50.
Horn, Siegfried, and Lynn H. Wood. *The Chronology of Ezra 7*. Washington, DC: Review and Herald, 1953.
House, Paul R. *Old Testament Theology*. Downers Grove, IL: InterVarsity, 1998.
Howie, C. G. *The Book of Ezekiel, the Book of Daniel*. Richmond, VA: Knox, 1961.
Humphreys, W. L. "A Life-Style for the Diaspora: A Study of the Tales of Esther and Daniel." *JBL* 92 (1973) 211–23.
Ice, Thomas. "The Seventy Weeks of Daniel." In *The End Times Controversy*, edited by Tim LaHaye and Thomas Ice, 307–53. Eugene, OR: Harvest House, 2003.
James, William. *The Varieties of Religious Experience*. Toronto: Random House, 1902.
Jastrow, Marcus, ed. *A Dictionary of the Targumim, the Talmud Babli, and Yerushalmi, and the Midrashic Literature*. 2 vols. New York: Traditional, 1943.
Jeffrey, Arthur. "Introduction and Exegesis of the Book of Daniel." In *IB* 6:339–549.
Jerome (Eusebius Sophronius Hieronymous). *Jerome's Commentary on Daniel*. Translated by Gleason L. Archer Jr. Grand Rapids: Baker, 1958.
———. *The Principal Works of St. Jerome*. Translated by W. H. Fremantle. *NPNF*. Grand Rapids: Eerdmans, 1983.
Johns, Alger F. *A Short Grammar of Biblical Aramaic*. Andrews University Monographs 1. Rev. ed. Berrien Springs, MI: Andrews University Press, 1972.
Jones, B. W. "The Prayer in Daniel 9." *VT* 18 (1968) 488–93.
Josephus, Flavius. *Josephus: Complete Works*. Translated by William Whiston. Grand Rapids: Kregel, 1960.
Julius, Caspar. "Die Griechischen Danielzusätze und ihre kanonische Geltung." BibS(F) 6 (1903) 1–183.
Jung, Carl. *The Symbolic Life: Miscellaneous Writings*. Translated by G. Adler and R. Hull. Princeton, NJ: Princeton University Press, 1977.
Junker, Hubert. *Untersuchungen über literarische und exegetische Probleme des Buches Daniel*. Bonn, Germ.: Hanstein, 1932.
Justin Martyr. *The First Apology, the Second Apology, Dialogue with Trypho, Exhortation to the Greeks, Discourse to the Greeks, the Monarchy, or Rule of God*. Fathers of the Church. Washington, DC: Catholic University of America Press, 1965.
Kaddari, Ramat Gan M. Z. "אכל (I, II)." In *TDOT* 16:27–28.
Kaiser, Walter C., Jr. *A History of Israel: From the Bronze Age through the Jewish Wars*. Nashville: Broadman & Holman, 1993.
Käsemann, Ernst. "Die Anfänge christlicher Theologie." *ZTK* 57 (1960) 160–85.
Keel, Othmar. *The Symbolism of the Biblical World: Ancient Near Eastern Iconography and the Book of Psalms*. Translated by Timothy J. Hallett. New York: Seabury, 1978.
Keel, Othmar, and Urs Staub. *Hellenismus und Judentum: Vier Studien zu Daniel 7 und zur Religionsnot unter Antiochus IV*. OBO 178. Göttingen, Germ.: Vandenhoeck & Ruprecht, 2000.
Keil, C. F. *Ezekiel, Daniel*. In *Commentary on the Old Testament*, edited by C. F. Keil and F. Delitzsch, translated by M. G. Easton, 9:399–402. Edinburgh, 1891. Reprint, Grand Rapids: Eerdmans, 1983.
Kepler, T. S. *Dreams of the Future: Daniel and Revelation*. Nashville: Abingdon, 1963.

Kessler, Werner. *Zwischen Gott und Weltmacht: Der Prophet Daniel.* Stuttgart, Germ.: Calwer, 1950.
Kitchen, Kenneth A. *Ancient Orient and Old Testament.* Chicago: Inter-Varsity, 1966.
———. *Notes on Some Problems in the Book of Daniel.* London: Tyndale, 1965.
———. *On the Reliability of the Old Testament.* Grand Rapids: Eerdmans, 2003.
Klausner, Joseph. *The Messianic Idea in Israel: From Its Beginning to the Completion of the Mishna.* Translated by W. F. Stinespring. New York: Macmillan, 1955.
Klein, William W., et al. *Introduction to Biblical Interpretation.* Rev. ed. Nashville: Thomas Nelson, 2004.
Klieforth, T. *Das Buch Daniel.* Schwerin: Sandmeyer, 1868.
Knight, George A. F. "The Book of Daniel." In *The Interpreter's One-Volume Commentary on the Bible,* edited by Charles M. Laymon, 436–50. Nashville: Abingdon, 1971.
Koch, Klaus. *Das Buch Daniel.* BKAT 22. Neukirchen-Vluyn, Germ.: Neukirchner, 1986.
———. "Is Daniel Also among the Prophets?" *Int* 39 (1985): 117–30.
———. *The Rediscovery of Apocalyptic.* SBT/2, 22. Napierville, 1972.
———. "Vom profetischen zum apokalyptischen Visionsbericht." In *Apocalypticism in the Mediterranean World and the Near East,* edited by D. Hellholm, 413–46. Tübingen, Germ.: Mohr, 1983.
Kraeling, E. G. "The Handwriting on the Wall." *JBL* 63 (1944) 11–18.
Kraft, Charles F., et al., eds. *The Illustrated Family Encyclopedia of the Living Bible.* 14 vols. Chicago: San Francisco Productions, 1967.
Kuhl, Curt. *Die drei Männer im Feuer.* Giessen, Germ.: A. Töpelmann, 1930.
Küng, Hans. *Theology for the Third Millennium: An Ecumenical View.* Translated by Peter Heinegg. New York: Doubleday, 1987.
Lacocque, André. *The Book of Daniel.* Translated by D. Pellauer. Atlanta: John Knox, 1979.
Ladd, George E. "Why Not Prophetic Apocalyptic?" *JBL* 76 (1957) 192–200.
LaHaye, Tim, and Thomas Ice, eds. *The End Times Controversy: The Second Coming under Attack.* Eugene, OR: Harvest House, 2003.
Lambert, W. G. *The Background of Jewish Apocalyptic.* London: University of London, 1978.
Lang, G. H. *The Histories and Prophecies of Daniel.* London: Oliphants, 1942.
Lasine, Stuart. "Solomon, Daniel, and the Detective Story: The Social Functions of a Literary Genre." *HAR* 11 (1987) 247–66.
Lebram, J. C. H. *Das Buch Daniel.* Zurich, Switz.: Theologische, 1984.
Lefèvre, André. "The Deuterocanonical Books." In the *Introduction to the Old Testament,* edited by A. Robert and A. Feuillet, translated by P. W. Skehan et al., 505–53. New York: Desclee, 1968.
Lenglet, A. "La Structure Littéraire de Daniel 2–7." *Bib* 53 (1972) 169–90.
Leupold, H. C. *Exposition of Daniel.* 2nd ed. Grand Rapids: Wartburg, 1969.
Levenson, Jon D. *Resurrection and the Restoration of Israel.* New Haven, CT: Yale University Press, 2006.
Linder, J. *Commentarius in Librum Daniel.* Cursus Scripturae Sacrae 23. Paris: P. Lethielleux, 1939.
Longman, Tremper, III. *How to Read Daniel.* Downers Grove, IL: IVP Academic, 2020.
———. *Literary Approaches to Biblical Interpretation.* Foundations of Contemporary Interpretation 3. Grand Rapids: Zondervan, 1987.
Longman, Tremper, III, and Raymond Dillard. *An Introduction to the Old Testament.* 2nd ed. Grand Rapids: Zondervan, 2006.

Löwinger, S. "Nebuchadnezzar's Dream in the Book of Daniel." In *Ignace Goldziher Memorial Volume*, edited by S. Löwinger and J. Somogyi, 1:336–52. Budapest: Globus, 1948.
Lucas, Ernest C. "Daniel, Book of." In *DTIB* 156–59.
MacKenzie, R. A. F. "The Meaning of the Susanna Story." *CJT* 3 (1957) 211–18.
Maier, G. *Der Prophet Daniel*. Wuppertal, Germ.: Brockhaus, 1982.
Manasee, J. de. *Daniel*. Paris: Cerf, 1958.
Marti, K. *Das Buch Daniel*. Tübingen, Germ.: Mohr, 1901.
Matthews, Victor H., and Don C. Benjamin. *Old Testament Parallels: Laws and Stories from the Ancient Near East*. 3rd ed. New York: Paulist, 2006.
McDonnell, E. W. "Apocalyptic Movements." In *NCE* 1:547-48.
McDowell, J. *Daniel in the Critics' Den*. San Barnardino, CA: Here's Life, 1979.
McNamara, M. "Nabonidus and the Book of Daniel." *ITQ* 37 (1970) 131–49.
McNamara, M., and Alexander Di Lella. "Daniel, Book of." In *NCE* 4:509-13.
Meadowcroft, Tim J. *Aramaic Daniel and Greek Daniel: A Literary Comparison*. JSOTSup 198. Sheffield, UK: Sheffield Academic, 1995.
———. *Like the Stars Forever: Narrative and Theology in the Book of Daniel*. Hebrew Bible Monographs. Sheffield, UK: Sheffield Phoenix, 2020.
Meier, John P. *A Marginal Jew: Rethinking the Historical Jesus*. ABRL 3 vols. New York: Doubleday, 1991.
Mertens, A. *Das Buch Daniel im Lichte der Texte vom Toten Meer*. SBM 12. Stuttgart, Germ.: Echter, 1971.
Milik, J. T. "Prière de Nabonid et autre ecrits d'un cycle de Daniel: Fragments arameens de Qumran 4." *RB* 63 (1956) 407–17.
Millar, William R. *Isaiah 24-27 and the Origin of Apocalyptic*. HSM 11. Missoula, MT: Scholars, 1976.
Miller, J. Maxwell, and John H. Hayes. *A History of Ancient Israel and Judah*. Philadelphia: Westminster, 1986.
Miller, Stephen R. *Daniel*. NAC 18. Nashville: Broadman & Holman, 1994.
Moltmann, Jürgen. *Theology of Hope*. Translated by James W. Keitch. London: SCM, 1964.
Montgomery, James A. *A Critical and Exegetical Commentary on the Book of Daniel*. ICC 22. Edinburgh: T & T Clark, 1927.
Moore, Carey A. *Daniel, Esther, and Jeremiah: The Additions*. AB 44. Garden City, NY: Doubleday, 1977.
Moynahan, Brian. *The Faith: A History of Christianity*. New York: Doubleday, 2002.
Mullen, E. Theodore Jr. *The Assembly of the Gods: The Divine Council in Canaanite and Early Hebrew Literature*. HSM 24. Chico, CA: Scholars, 1980.
Müller, Hans-Peter. "Die weisheitliche Lehrerzählung im Alten Testament und seiner Umwelt." *WO* 9 (1977) 77–98.
Murdock, William R. "History and Revelation in Jewish Apocalypticism." *Interpretation* 21 (1967) 167–87.
Murphy, Frederick J. "Introduction to Apocalyptic Literature." In *NIB* 7:1–16.
Myers, Jacob M. *First and Second Esdras*. AB 42. Garden City, NY: Doubleday, 1974.
Newsom, Carol A. *Daniel: A Commentary*. With contributions by Brennan W. Breed. OTL. Louisville: Westminster John Knox, 2014.
———. "Daniel and Additions to Daniel." In *The Oxford Encyclopedia of the Books of the Bible*, edited by Michael D. Coogan, 1:159–73. New York: Oxford University Press, 2011.

Newton, Isaac. *Observations upon Prophecies of Daniel and the Apocalypse of St. John* [1733]. In *Sir Isaac Newton's Daniel and the Apocalypse*, edited by William Whitlaw, page range unavailable. London: Murray, 1922.

Nichol, Francis D., ed. *Seventh-Day Adventist Bible Commentary*. 7 vols. Washington, DC: Review and Herald, 1953–1955.

Nicholson, E. W. "Apocalyptic." In *Tradition and Interpretation: Essays by Members of the Society for Old Testament Study*, edited by G. W. Anderson, 189–213. Oxford, UK: Clarendon, 1979.

Nickelsburg, George W. E. *Resurrection, Immortality, and Eternal Life in Intertestamental Judaism*. HTS 26. Cambridge: Harvard University Press, 1972.

Niditch, Susan. *The Symbolic Vision in Biblical Tradition*. HSM 30. Chico, CA, 1983.

Niskanen, Paul. "Daniel's Portrait of Antiochus IV: Echoes of a Persian King." *CBQ* 66, no. 3 (2004) 378–86.

Oesterley, W. O. E. *An Introduction to the Books of the Apocrypha*. London: Society for Promoting Christian Knowledge, 1935.

Olmo Lete, Gregorio del, and Joaquin Sanmartin. *A Dictionary of the Ugaritic Language in the Alphabetic Tradition*. Handbook of Oriental Studies. Translated by Wilfred G. E. Watson. 2 vols. Rev. ed. Atlanta: Society of Biblical Literature, 2004.

Oppenheim, A. Leo. *Ancient Mesopotamia: Portrait of a Dead Civilization*. Chicago: University of Chicago Press, 1964.

———. "Dreams." *TAPS* 46 (1956) 179–373.

Owens, J. J. "Daniel." In *The Broadman Bible Commentary*, edited by C. J. Allen et al., 6:373–460. Nashville: Broadman, 1971.

Parker, S. B., ed. *Ugaritic Narrative Poetry*. SBLWAW. Atlanta: Scholars Press, 1997.

Pate, C. Marvin. *Interpreting Revelation and Other Apocalyptic Literature: An Exegetical Handbook*. Grand Rapids: Kregel Academic, 2016.

Payne, J. Barton. *Encyclopedia of Biblical Prophecy: The Complete Guide to Scriptural Predictions and Their Fulfillment*. New York: Harper & Row, 1973.

Pentecost, J. Dwight. *Things to Come*. Grand Rapids: Zondervan, 1958.

Pfeiffer, R. H. *History of New Testament Times with an Introduction to the Apocrypha*. New York: Harper & Brothers, 1949.

———. *Introduction to the Old Testament*. New York: Harper & Brothers, 1948.

Plöger, Otto. *Das Buch Daniel*. KAT 18. Gütersloh: Gerd Mohn, 1965.

———. *Theocracy and Eschatology*. Translated by S. Rudman. Richmond, VA: John Knox, 1968.

Polaski, Donald C. "*Mene, Mene, Tekel, Parsin*: Writing and Resistance in Daniel 5 and 6." *JBL* 123, no. 4 (2004) 649–69.

Polybius. *The Histories*. Translated by W. R. Paton. LCL 128, 137–38, 159–61. Cambridge, MA: Harvard University Press, 1922.

Porphyry (Malchus). In PL 25:572.

Porteous, Norman W. *Daniel*. OTL. Philadelphia: Westminster, 1965.

Prince, J. D. *A Critical Commentary on the Book of Daniel*. New York: Lemcke & Buechner, 1899.

Pusey, Edward H. *Daniel the Prophet*. Oxford, UK: Parker, 1865.

Rahlfs, Alfred, ed. *Septuaginta*. 2 vols. 7th ed. Stuttgart, Germ.: Württembergische Bibelanstalt, 1935.

Reid, S. B. "The Sociological Setting of the Historical Apocalypses of 1 Enoch and the Book of Daniel." PhD diss., Emory University, 1981.

Riesenfeld, Harald. *Jésus transfiguré: l'arriére-plan récit évangélique de la transfiguration de Notre-Seigneur.* ASNU 16. Copenhagen: E. Munksgaard, 1947.

Riessler, Paul. *Das Buch Daniel erklärt.* Kurzgefasster wissensschaftlicher Kommentar zu den Heiligen Schriften des Alten Testaments 3. Vienna: Mayer, 1902.

Rillera, Andrew Remington. "A Call to Resistance: The Exhortative Function of Daniel 7." *JBL* 138, no. 4 (2019) 757–776.

Rist, Martin. "Apocalypticism." In *IDB* 1:157–61.

Robinson, H. Wheeler. *Corporate Personality in Ancient Israel.* Rev. ed. Philadelphia: Fortress, 1980.

Rosenthal, Franz. *A Grammar of Biblical Aramaic.* PLO, n.s., 5. Wiesbaden, Germ.: Otto Harrasowitz, 1968.

Rossing, Barbara. *The Rapture Exposed: The Message of Hope in the Book of Revelation.* Boulder, CO: Westview, 2004.

Rost, Leonhard. *Judaism Outside the Hebrew Canon: An Introduction to the Documents.* Translated by D. E. Green. Nashville: Abingdon, 1976.

Rowland, Christopher. "Apocalyptic." In *DTIB* 51–53.

———. "Apocalypticism." In *NIDB* 1:190–95.

———. *The Open Heaven: A Study of Apocalyptic in Judaism and Christianity.* New York: Crossroad, 1982.

Rowley, H. H. *The Aramaic of the Old Testament.* London: Oxford, 1929.

———. *Darius the Mede and the Four World Empires in the Book of Daniel: A Historical Study of Contemporary Theories.* Cardiff: University of Wales Press, 1959.

———. *The Relevance of Apocalyptic: A Study of Jewish and Christian Apocalyptic from Daniel to Revelation.* London: Lutherworth, 1944.

Rubinkiewicz, R. "The Apocalypse of Abraham." In *OTP* 2:681–705.

Rudolph, W., and K. Elliger, eds. *Biblia Hebraica Stuttgartensia.* Stuttgart, Germ.: Deutsche Bibelgesellschaft, 1967–1977.

Russell, D. S. *Daniel.* Daily Study Bible. Philadelphia: Westminster, 1981.

———. *Divine Disclosure: An Introduction to Jewish Apocalyptic.* Minneapolis: Fortress, 1992.

———. *The Method and Message of Jewish Apocalyptic.* OTL. Philadelphia: Westminster, 1964.

Ryken, Leland, and Tremper Longman III, eds. *A Complete Literary Guide to the Bible.* Grand Rapids: Zondervan, 1993.

Ryrie, Charles C. *Dispensationalism Today.* Chicago: Moody, 1965.

Sacchi, Paolo. *Jewish Apocalyptic and its History.* Translated by William J. Short. JSPSup 20. Sheffield, UK: Sheffield Academic, 1990.

Saggs, H. W. F. *The Babylonians: A Survey of the Ancient Civilisation of the Tigris-Euphrates Valley.* 2nd ed. London: Folio Society, 1988.

Sandy, D. B., and R. L. Giese, ed. *Cracking Old Testament Codes: A Guide to Interpreting Literary Genres of the Old Testament.* Nashville: Broadman & Holman, 1995.

Schäfer, Peter. "The Hellenistic and Maccabean Periods." In *Israelite and Judaean History,* edited by J. H. Hayes and J. M. Miller, 93–111. OTL. Philadelphia: Westminster, 1977.

Schedl, C. *Geschichte des Alten Testaments.* 5 vols. Innsbruck, Aus.: Tyrolia, 1964.

Schmidt, Johann M. *Die jüdische Apokalyptik: Die Geschichte ihrer Erforschung von den Anfangen bis zu den Textfunden von Qumran.* Neukirchen-Vluyn, Germ.: Neukirchener, 1969.

Schmidt, Nathaniel. "Daniel and Androcles." *JAOS* 46 (1926) 1–7.
Schmidt, Werner H. *Old Testament Introduction*. 2nd ed. Translated by Matthew J. O'Connell. Louisville: Westminster John Knox, 1995.
Schmithals, W. *The Apocalyptic Movement: Introduction and Interpretation*. Translated by J. Steely. Nashville: Abingdon, 1975.
Schürer, Emil. *A History of the Jewish People in the Time of Jesus*. Edited by N. Glatzberg. Translated by J. Macpherson et al. 5 vols. Edinburgh: T & T Clark, 1924.
Schwantes, S. J. "'*Erebbōqer* of Dan 8:14 Re-Examined." *AUSS* 16 (1978) 375–85.
Scofield, C. I., et al., eds. *New Scofield Reference Bible: King James Version*. Rev. ed. London: Oxford University Press, 1967.
Shea, William H. "Dan 9:24–27." Paper presented at the Biblical Research Institute Committee, Berrien Springs, MI, May 13, 1981.
Shedl, C. "Mystische Arithmetik oder geschichtliche Zahlen (Dan. 8, 14; 12, 11–13)." *BZ* 8 (1964) 101–105.
Sims, James H. "Daniel." In *A Complete Literary Guide to the Bible*, edited by Leland Ryken and Tremper Longman III, 324–36. Grand Rapids: Zondervan, 1993.
Slotki, Judah. *Daniel, Ezra, Nehemiah*. Soncino Books of the Bible. Edited by A. Cohen. London: Soncino, 1951.
Smith, Abraham. "Second Thessalonians." In *NIB* 11:741–72.
Smith, Uriah. *The Prophecies of Daniel and the Revelation*. Rev. ed. Nashville: Southern Publishing Association, 1944.
Smith-Christopher, Daniel L. "The Additions to Daniel." In *NIB* 7:153–94.
———. "The Book of Daniel." In *NIB* 7:17–152.
Soggin, J. Alberto. *A History of Ancient Israel*. Translated by John Bowden. Philadelphia: Westminster, 1984.
———. *Introduction to the Old Testament*. Translated by John Bowden. 3rd ed. OTL. Louisville, KY: Westminster/John Knox, 1989.
Soulen, Richard N., and R. Kendall Soulen. *Handbook of Biblical Criticism*. 3rd ed. Louisville: Westminster John Knox, 2001.
Sparks, Kenton L. *Ancient Texts for the Study of the Hebrew Bible: A Guide to the Background Literature*. Peabody, MA: Hendrickson, 2005.
Steinmann, Jean. *Daniel*. Paris: Editions du Cerf, 1950.
Steussy, M. J. *Garden in Babylon: Narrative and Faith in the Greek Legends of Daniel*. SBLDS 141. Atlanta: Scholars, 1993.
Stevenson, Kenneth, and Michael Glerup, eds. *Ezekiel, Daniel*. Ancient Christian Commentary on Scripture, OT 13. Downers Grove, IL: IVP Academic, 2008.
Stone, Michael E. "Apocalyptic Literature." In *Jewish Writings of the Second Temple Period*, edited by M. E. Stone, 383–441. Philadelphia: Fortress, 1984.
———. "The Book of Enoch and Judaism in the Third Century." *CBQ* 40 (1978) 479–92.
Stuhlmueller, C. "Apocalyptic." In the *NCE* 1:545–47.
Swain, Joseph Ward. "The Theory of the Four Monarchies: Opposition History under the Roman Empire." *CP* 35 (1940) 1–21.
Sweet, Ronald F. G. "The Sage in Akkadian Literature." In *The Sage in Israel and the Ancient Near East*, edited by John G. Gammie and Leo G. Perdue, 45–65. Winona Lake, IN: Eisenbrauns, 1990.
Swinburne, Richard. *The Concept of Miracle*. London: Macmillan, 1970.
Talbot, Louis T. *The Prophecies of Daniel in the Light of Past, Present and Future Events*. Wheaton, IL: Van Kampen, 1940.

Talmon, Shemaryahu. "Daniel." In *The Literary Guide to the Bible*, ed. Robert Alter and Frank Kermode, 343–56. Cambridge, MA: Harvard University Press, 1987.
Tate, W. Randolph. *Biblical Interpretation: An Integrated Approach*. 3rd ed. Peabody, MA: Hendrickson, 2008.
Tertullian. *Opera (Works)*. Corpus Christianovus, Series Latina 1–2. Turnholti, Belg.: Typographi Brepols, 1953–1954.
Thompson, H. O. *The Book of Daniel: An Annotated Bibliography*. Books of the Bible; Vol. 1 of *Garland Reference Library of the Humanities 1310*. New York: Garland, 1993.
Tov, Emanuel. *Textual Criticism of the Hebrew Bible*. 3rd ed. Minneapolis: Fortress, 2012.
Towner, W. S. *Daniel*. IBC. Atlanta: John Knox, 1984.
———. "Daniel." In *HBC* 623–34.
———. "Daniel, Book of." In *NIDB* 2: 15–23.
———. "The Latter Prophets Major: Daniel." In the *Hebrew Bible: History of Interpretation*, edited by J. H. Hayes, 239–48. Nashville: Abingdon, 2004.
Tracy, David. "Theological Method." In *Christian Theology: An Introduction to Its Traditions and Tasks*, edited by Peter C. Hodgson and Robert A King, 35–60. Rev. ed. Minneapolis: Fortress, 1994.
Trever, J. C. "The Book of Daniel and the Origin of the Qumran Community." *BA* 48 (1985) 89–102.
Tucker, Gene M. "The Book of Isaiah 1–39." In *NIB* 6:27–305.
———. *Form Criticism of the Old Testament*. GBS: Old Testament. Philadelphia: Fortress, 1971.
van der Toorn, Karel. "In the Lion's Den: The Babylonian Background of a Biblical Motif." *CBQ* 60 (1998) 626–40.
Van der Woude, A. S., ed. *The Book of Daniel in the Light of New Findings*. BETL 106. Leuven, Belg.: Leuven University Press, 1993.
VanderKam, James. *Enoch and the Growth of an Apocalyptic Tradition*. CBQMS 16. Washington, DC: Catholic Biblical Association of America, 1984.
VanGemeren, Willem A. "Daniel." In the *Evangelical Commentary on the Bible*, edited by Walter A. Elwell, 589–601. Baker Reference Library 3. Grand Rapids: Baker, 1989.
Vawter, Bruce. "Apocalyptic: Its Relation to Prophecy." *CBQ* 22 (1960) 33–46.
Veldkamp, H. *Dreams and Dictators: On the Book of Daniel*. Translated by T. Plantinga. St. Catharines, Ontario: Paideia, 1973.
Vermes, Geza. *The Complete Dead Sea Scrolls in English*. New York: Penguin, 1997.
Vielhauer, Philipp. "Apocalyptic." In *NTApoc* 2:581–600.
von Rad, Gerhard. *Old Testament Theology*. Translated by D. M. G. Stalker. 2 vols. New York: Harper & Row, 1962–1965.
———. *Wisdom in Israel*. Translated by James D. Martin. Nashville: Abingdon, 1972.
Vriezen, Th. C. *An Outline of Old Testament Theology*. 2nd ed. Newton, MA: Charles T. Branford, 1970.
Wallace, R. S. *The Lord Is King: The Message of Daniel*. Downers Grove, IL: InterVarsity, 1979.
Waltke, Bruce K. and Charles Yu. *An Old Testament Theology: An Exegetical, Canonical, and Thematic Approach*. Grand Rapids: Zondervan, 2007.
Waltke, Bruce K., and Murray O'Connor. *An Introduction to Biblical Hebrew Syntax*. Winona Lake, IN: Eisenbrauns, 1990.

Walvoord, John F. *Daniel: The Key to Prophetic Revelation; A Commentary.* Chicago: Moody, 1971.
Wambacq, B. N. "Les prières de Baruch (1,15–2,19) et de Daniel (9,3–19)." *Bib* 40 (1959) 463–96.
Weinfeld, Moshe. "'Rider of the Clouds' and 'Gatherer of the Clouds.'" *JNES* 5 (1973) 421–26.
Weiser, Artur. *The Old Testament: Its Formation and Development.* Translated by Dorothea M. Barton. New York: Association, 1961.
Whitcomb, John C. *Daniel.* Chicago: Moody, 1985.
———. *Darius the Mede: The Historical Chronology of Daniel.* Phillipsburg, NJ: Presbyterian and Reformed, 1959.
Widengren, George. *The King and the Tree of Life in Ancient Near Eastern Religion: King and Saviour IV.* UUA 4. Uppsala, Swed.: Lundequistska, 1951.
Willis, Amy C. Merrill. *Dissonance and the Drama of Divine Sovereignty in the Book of Daniel.* New York: T & T Clark International, 2010.
Wills, Lawrence. *The Jew in the Court of the Foreign King: Ancient Jewish Court Legends.* HDR 26. Minneapolis: Fortress, 1990.
———. "Susanna." In *HarperCollins Study Bible,* edited by H. W. Attridge. Rev. ed. New York: HarperCollins, 2006.
Wilson, Joseph D. *Did Daniel Write Daniel? The Genuineness and Authenticity of the Book of Daniel.* New York: Charles C. Cook, 1906.
Wilson, Robert R. *Prophecy and Society in Ancient Israel.* Philadelphia: Fortress, 1980.
Wiseman, D. J. *Chronicles of Chaldean Kings (626–536 BC) in the British Museum.* London: British Museum, 1956.
———. "Some Historical Problems in the Book of Daniel." In *Notes on Some Problems in the Book of Daniel,* edited by D. J. Wiseman et al., 9–18. London: Tyndale, 1965.
Wolters, Albert. "Untying the King's Knots: Physiology and Wordplay in Daniel 5." *JBL* 110 (1991) 117–22.
Wood, Leon. *A Commentary on Daniel.* Grand Rapids: Zondervan, 1973.
Wright, Charles H. H. *Daniel and His Critics: Being a Critical and Grammatical Commentary.* London: Williams and Norgate, 1906.
Wright, G. Ernest. *Biblical Archaeology.* Rev. ed. Philadelphia: Westminster, 1962.
Würthwein, Ernst. *The Text of the Old Testament: An Introduction to the* Biblia Hebraica. Revised and expanded by A. A. Fischer. Translated by E. F. Rhodes. 3rd ed. Grand Rapids: Eerdmans, 2014.
Wyatt, Nicolas. "The Titles of the Ugaritic Storm-God." *UF* 24 (1992) 403–25.
Young, Edward J. "Daniel." In *The New Bible Commentary: Revised,* edited by D. Guthrie et al., 688–702. Grand Rapids: Eerdmans, 1970.
———. *An Introduction to the Old Testament.* Rev. ed. Grand Rapids: Eerdmans, 1964.
———. *The Prophecy of Daniel: A Commentary.* Grand Rapids: Eerdmans, 1949.
Zimmerman, Frank. "The Aramaic Origin of Daniel 8–12." *JBL* 57 (1938) 255–72.
———. "Bel and the Dragon." *VT* 8 (1958) 438–40.
———. "The Story of Susanna and Its Original Language." *JQR* 48 (1957/58) 237–41.

www.ingramcontent.com/pod-product-compliance
Lightning Source LLC
Chambersburg PA
CBHW050617300426
44112CB00012B/1541